# ART, LAW, POWER

ART, LAW, POWER

# Art, Law, Power

Perspectives on Legality and Resistance
in Contemporary Aesthetics

Lucy Finchett-Maddock
Eleftheria Lekakis

COUNTERPRESS
OXFORD

First published 2020
Counterpress, Oxford
http://counterpress.org.uk



ISBN: 978-1-910761-07-6 (paperback)

Typeset in 10.5 on 12.5 pt Sabon

Cover image by Amy Frances Wishart Corcoran

Global print and distribution by Ingram

# Foreword

A thought that, in thinking, does better than think, since it finds itself to be already responsibility for the other, whose mortality—and consequently whose life—regards me.

— Emmanuel Levinas, *Alterity and Transcendence*, 36

Doing 'better than thinking' about art, law, and power is a thought offered in the following pages. I will preface that exploration by thinking-with the idea of transgression.

Resistance and liberation enacted through activism occur, are stretched across, formed by, and confronted with art, law, and power; moments in which these intersections happen can be made through transgressions, some of them loud and public and some momentary and subjective. Transgressions force the articulation of power relations by forcing power to express itself, and being able to grasp power means being able to, possibly, remake it. Being able to see, touch, read, smell, and feel the nature of a power is a being-able that can be created through transgression in artistic practices or the law. This wonderful collection connects and critiques exactly these moments in which art, law, and power intersect and in intersecting are articulated and become available to contest.

Thinking transgression is one way to understand what this collection presents, because it shifts the ground from sheer opposition to sinuous interplays in which power is made, as Foucault once said, as a relation. If there is no need for queer activists, for example, to be told of power as a relation, then it is worth remembering what this means, because remaking genders in prisons or creating a sexuality that expresses itself and can be expressed at a formal tribunal, will ensure both the most obvious of controls as well as the relations in which micro-powers are woven can be seen, touched and felt. Such interventions are fluid, working without an either/or boundary, a for/against, to articulate and to make it possible to alter boundaries.

These intersections may at times seem like they come up against an absolutism of the law, sometimes we might be tempted to think of the law as clearly written regulation, backed by police, courts, and prisons to enforce such regulation, and that the clarity of the law as regulation is what art and transgression come up against; the law as the Law. Yet finding the law, whether through representative transgression in art or bodily transgression in shifting gender genres or collective transgression in protests, means finding the articulation of forms of power, which are wider and more complex than the route the law takes from the statute books to the prison. Moreover, the law itself may be an agent of transgression.

Consider the famous transgression of copyleft. It both inverts and affirms existing property laws which say that if you own something then it is yours to decide what to do with. If you then decide that what you own, which in the case of software is potentially infinitely copyable, has to be made available to everyone and that no one can have it exclusively, then what is legally distributed and what is legally exclusive are shifted, their boundaries remade in a creative transgression. The law may express, even instantiate, repressive and dominant powers but it may also be turned.

Boundaries may show themselves as absolute. Every border crossing should remind us of this, a moment of helplessness before the armed guards. Yet the border is also not the physical place but the actions taken on it expressing laws and powers, which may be extended to making each street into a hostile place, its own border. Art may also migrate to the everyday moments of the street, the murals of Belfast and Glasgow or the golden ages of graffiti offering ways art has been unboundaried by institutions. However, we should also be wary of transgression as it is not an answer in-itself but a way of articulating and expressing a form of power, and so may have other uses than remaking powers.

Transgression may be called for from within art institutions, so studied and familiar with transgressions that they welcome and integrate them, raising the question of whether here transgression has lost its ability to articulate and make an opening to remaking; the possibility that some recursions know how to utilize transgression within themselves offering the image of a transgression within a process that reaffirms the institutional authority of the gallery, library, or museum. The actions of culture jammers and subvertisers similarly may be reintegrated and presented back to the world as the symbols they aimed to subvert. Lost in the empire of signs, transgression has to be careful it does not lose its meaning—the ability to make power available for remaking through articulation.

Yet even the ability of some institutions to enjoy transgressions as further enhancing their own power, alters that transgressions gain meaning when they can force power to articulate itself and make itself available to be contested and remade (even if remade as a gallery wants). In what name should we contest powers and look for a remaking? In all the names of those subjected to power relations that extract benefits, often obscenely large benefits, to few from many: money, land, visibility, control of bodies, ability to make symbols, ability to define truth. All the names of the others that can be found in the stories told in the following pages.

And we need these stories and this thinking! These analyses, these critiques and these inspirations on the intersections of art, law, and power. In a world where spreading information that can be available to all in its full value is controlled with prison; in a world that dithers on or denies that climate disasters are linked; in a world where trans may be treated as a fashion rather than a necessary right; in a world where fascism has made itself legitimate again: in this complex world, in which all four horsemen of power have been opposed with activism, art and transgression, in this world of ours reading these pages will offer hope, complexity and ethics that may define a better world; thought that does better than thinking.

Tim Jordan
Professor of Digital Cultures
University of Sussex

# Acknowledgements

We would like to thank our colleagues who reviewed chapters for this volume; Omar Al-Ghazzi, Alan Bradshaw, Victoria Brookes, Andreas Chatzidakis, Red Chidgey, Thom Giddens, Andres Guadamuz, Simon Lindgren, Dan Mercea, Paula Serafini, Emma Patchett, Lauren van Haaften-Schick.

Lucy Finchett-Maddock would like to thank all those who have collaborated and converged in the Art/Law Network who have made the critical, practical, and intellectual space for thought on art, law, and power to happen.

Eleftheria Lekakis would like to recognize the work of the transnational collective Subvertisers International as a trigger for questioning connections between art, law, and power.

# Contents

## 11. Regulating the Image of the City: Art, Law, and Power in the Built Environment of Delhi


Swastee Ranjan



## 12. Performative Agoras: The Use and Misuse of Public Space


Daniel Hignell-Tully



## 13. Twitter as a Space of Resistance to Brexit: Stories of Belonging and the Concept of Affective Citizenship in #1DayWithoutUs


Photini Vrikki

14. **Everyday Resistances: Walking and Talking the Hostile Environment** ...................................................281

LIZZY WILLMINGTON

# Contributors


*Editors*

**Lucy Finchett-Maddock** is Senior Lecturer in Law and Art at Sussex Law School. Lucy's work predominantly focuses on the intersection of property within law and resistance, interrogating the spatio-temporality and aesthetics of formal and informal laws, property (squatting and housing), commons, and protest. She is author of monograph *Protest, Property and the Commons: Performances of Law and Resistance* (Routledge, 2016). Her work also looks to broader questions around the intersection of art and law, resistance, legal and illegal understandings of art, property, aesthetics and politics. She is currently developing an 'Art/Law Network' (in collaboration with Sussex's Art and Law Research Cluster), where artists, activists, lawyers, practitioners, and other such agitators can share their work and ideas, create art projects on law; law projects on art; collaborate on methodological and pedagogical approaches to law, through art; art, through law—and anything else in between.

**Eleftheria Lekakis** is Senior Lecturer in Media and Communications at the University of Sussex. Her research interests stem from the intersection of politics, economy and culture, and include topics related to consumer politics and anti-consumerism, as well as digital media, nationalism, and alternative media. Her teaching crosses over such issues including media, development and humanitarianism, as well as global communication and the politics of promotional culture. Her long-titled monograph, *Coffee Activism and the Politics of Fair Trade and Ethical Consumption*, explores the politics of consumption, cause communication, and civic engagement through the case of the fair trade movement and market. Eleftheria is the curator and editor of GreekDocs (digital archive of independent documentaries about the crisis in Greece) and Re.Framing Activism (digital platform showcasing research, critique, and resources on media activism).

*Authors*

**Micheál O'Connell's** doctoral project, entitled 'Art as "Artificial Stupidity"' (2017) discussed strategies—often carried out under the moniker MOCKSIM—of interaction with everyday functional processes, including misuse, lampooning and tinkering with technological systems. His writing and activities draw upon a background that includes an unusual mix of experience with engineering and computational systems, performance-oriented artistic practice, and periods of committed political activism. O'Connell is a member of ABC Artists' Books Cooperative (international), The London Group or artists, APEC Artists' Studios (Brighton, UK) and The Cybernetics Society (UK). Currently he teaches at University of Sussex in areas of photography, technology, art and activist media practice, and, in the past, taught digital media theory and practice, art and design, and art history. He lives in Brighton, UK with his two daughters, and has exhibited work and presented in Britain, Ireland, France, and Spain.

**Jeremy Pilcher** is a law lecturer at Birkbeck School of Law, University of London. His academic work on the intersection of art and law builds on his early career in the law and academic qualifications in cultural studies, art law, and art history. After first being employed in New Zealand as a Crown prosecutor, Jeremy worked in commercial litigation. He subsequently moved to England, where he qualified as a solicitor and worked in both the public and private sectors as a fraud investigator.

**Isidro Jiménez Gómez** holds a PhD in Audiovisual Communication and Advertising. He is Associate Professor at Complutense University of Madrid and consultant professor at The Open University of Catalonia (UOC). He has been cofounder of the group ConsumeHastaMorir in 2002 and of the alternative media El Salmón Contracorriente in 2014. This project has being integrated into El Salto, a magazine and information website. He also has participated as a researcher in projects such as 'Global Change Spain 2020/50' (*Cambio Global España*) of *CCEIM*, and 'Psychosocial and communicative aspects of sustainable mobility' of the Association of Psychological and Social Studies, and *ADECS*. His main line of research in recent years has been environmental communication and climate change.

**Mariola Olcina Alvarado** holds a degree in Journalism (Complutense

University of Madrid) and a Master in Education 2.0 (UNED). Over the last she ten years has worked in the field of social communication and environmental journalism, writing and researching on topics related to climate change, ecofeminism, and solidarity economy for media such as El Ecologista, El Salmón Contracorriente, El Salto, the blog 'Última Llamada' in Eldiario.es, the journal Papeles de relaciones ecosociales and global change, and the magazine 'Soberanía Alimentaria, Biodiversity and Cultures'. She has directed several short documentaries and animation films and is a member of Cine Sin Autor, a film experimentation project. In addition, as a co-founder of the social communication company MenosMedia, she advises the audiovisual communication of various entities of the Third Sector. She also is co-author of the *Communication Manual for Organized Citizenship* (Libros en Acción, 2017).

**Sean Mulcahy** is a joint-PhD candidate in the Centre for Theatre and Performance, Monash University, and the Warwick Law School, University of Warwick. Having graduated from Monash University with a Bachelor of Performing Arts and Bachelor of Laws, Sean has worked in research and law reform across the public service, unions and non-government organizations. His research interests include the relations between law and performance in common law court proceedings. Currently working on a doctoral thesis on law as performance, Sean is also developing a performance-led research piece on legal testimony through video-link.

**Virginia Villaplana Ruiz**'s artistic practice expands into critical theory, editorial work, curatorship and teaching, with a focus on the political. She is Professor of Media Studies at the University of Murcia, as well as of Cultural Studies at Colef Social Sciences at the Autonomous University of Baja California, Tijuana, and researcher of the Institute of Communication at Autonomous University of Barcelona. Villaplana is the author of the books *Softfiction: Políticas visuales de la emocionalidad y el deseo*, *El instante de la memoria* and co-editor of *Cárcel de amor: Relatos culturales sobre la violencia de género*. She is a member of the Research Network Project 'Unearthing Pre-HIV/ AIDS Queer Sexual Cultures' at the European Science Foundation. Additionally, she has written a number of articles and book chapters about communication and digital memory communities. Her current research projects include feminist and queer politics in Europe and Latin America: transnational violence, social movements, resistance and social change in digital media. She is also co-editor of the journal 'Art and Politics of Identity.'

**María Ángeles Alcántara Sánchez (Gelen Jeleton)** is a visual artist with a PhD in Fine Arts from the University of Murcia (2016) based on her project 'Una Archiva del DIY: una fanzinoteca feminista-queer' (An Archive of DIY: A Feminist-Queer Zine Library). In 2014, she began to work with 'Spiral Women: Juridical System, Gender Perspectives and Pedagogies in Resistance' ('*Mujeres en Espiral: sistema de justicia, perspectivas de género y pedagogías en resistencia*') making zines in the Women's Prison in Santa Martha Acatitla in Mexico City.

**Marisa Belausteguigoitia** has a PhD in Ethnic Studies with an emphasis on women, race, and sexuality from the University of California at Berkeley (2000). She is a Professor at the School of Humanities at the Universidad Nacional Autónoma de México (UNAM), and director of the project 'Spiral Women: Juridical System, Gender Perspectives and Pedagogies in Resistance' ('*Mujeres en Espiral: sistema de justicia, perspectivas de género y pedagogías en resistencia*').

**Tania Gisel Tovar Cervantes** has a Bachelor in Pedagogy from the Universidad Nacional Autónoma de México (UNAM); her project focuses on work done with Leelatu zines.

**Radwa Othman Sharaf** holds a Master's degree in Media Practice for Development and Social Change from Sussex University and a Bachelor's degree in Political Science from Cairo University. Radwa published her first academic multimedia essay in 2015 about graffiti art as a means of documentation and activism in the African Conflict and Peacebuilding Review (ACPR) published by Indiana University. Radwa's research focuses on communication, politics and media activism. From 2015 to 2017, she worked as a researcher and was the Deputy Managing Editor of Ida2at.com. From 2012 to 2013, she was an intern at the Arabic Network for Human Rights Information and the House of Wisdom Foundation for Strategic Studies.

**Fidèle A. Vlavo** is a digital media scholar whose research interests combine digital activism, technology studies, gender theory and digital media arts. She has written about cybercultures, electronic civil disobedience, cyberterrorism, digital performance, and piracy. Her most recent work examines digital piracy and hacking as creative practices.

She is the author of *Performing Digital Activism: New Aesthetics and Discourses of Resistance* (Routledge 2018), a book that retraces the practice of digital action since the late 1990s and proposes a creative and performative interpretation of digital resistance. She is currently Assistant Professor at the Department of Communication of Universidad Iberoamericana in Mexico City.

**Alexander Araya López** is a Marie Curie Fellow (2018–20) at the Department of Linguistics and Cultural Comparative Studies of Ca' Foscari, University of Venice (Italy). He received his doctoral degree in sociology from the Freie Universität Berlin (Germany) in 2014, with a dissertation focusing on the narratives about graffiti and pichação/ pixo practices published by local newspapers in both Costa Rica and Brazil. He is currently working on the ambivalence of tourism as a global industry, studying the emergence of social movements targeting the negative outcomes of tourism in Venice, Amsterdam, and Barcelona from the theoretical perspective of the 'right to the city.'

**Marta Iljadica** is Lecturer in Intellectual Property at the University of Glasgow. She is the author of *Copyright Beyond Law: Regulating Creativity in the Graffiti Subculture* (Hart, 2016) on copyright protection for graffiti and the copyright-like social norms adopted by graffiti writers. She has also written about copyright and moral rights for graffiti writers and street artists, freedom of panorama and the 'right to the city', and the intersection between intellectual property and land law.

**Swastee Ranjan** is a Doctoral Candidate at the School of Law, Politics and Sociology at the University of Sussex. Her thesis explores the relationship between law and objects by drawing attention to the role of affect and aesthetics in the material environment of the city. Swastee completed her M.Phil. from the Centre for the Study of Law and Government (CSLG) at Jawaharlal Nehru University (JNU) at New Delhi. She is currently an advisory member of Art/Law Network and has previously been a student anchor for Law and Social Sciences Research Network (LASSnet) in New Delhi.

**Daniel Alexander Hignell-Tully** is a researcher and multi-disciplinary artist whose work explores notions of community, political action, ethics, and creativity. He received his PhD from the University of Sussex in 2017, completing a research project that sought to score everyday creativity. Frequently collaborating with researchers and practitioners both within the arts and beyond, he has worked alongside theologians, ecologists, statisticians, and acousticians, and spearheaded site-specific projects across Europe. He writes frequently about experimental music, and as a composer, he has released work internationally under the moniker 'Distant Animals.'

**Photini Vrikki** is Lecturer in Digital Media and Culture at King's College London. Her research and teaching focus on the links between social and digital inequalities; power and data; and algorithmic cultural developments. By combining multi-disciplinary approaches with concepts and theories drawn from sociology, political economy and cultural theory, her work explores how digital media can be used to both reinforce and challenge racism, inequality and oppression; and the questions of power, agency and ideology within the digital, cultural and creative economies. Photini holds a PhD in Digital Culture and Society from King's College London.

**Lizzy Willmington** is a PhD candidate at Cardiff Law School, sitting within the Cardiff Law and Global Justice Research Centre. She joined Cardiff Law School in 2017 after completing her MA in International and Comparative Legal Studies at SOAS and her BA in Art History at Leeds University. Her research interests are in critical race theory, feminist theory, colonial histories, and grassroots creative resistances. Her PhD project explores these interest through the Hostile Environment; the immigration policy in the UK. Lizzy is part of the three year *Who Are We? Project with Counterpoints Arts* at the Tate Exchange. She is an advisory board member of the Art Law Network and involved in grassroots activism that centres the voices of those who are the subjects of law, rather than the makers or enforcers of laws.

# Introduction

*Lucy Finchett-Maddock and Eleftheria Lekakis*

Walls have historically been constructed as symbols and objects delimiting nations and peoples, us and them, legally, physically, and in our imaginations. On the cover image, a protester is scaling down the Israeli West Bank barrier. While recognizing we cannot do justice to the Israel-Palestine conflict in passing mention, we chose to refer to the wall that separates them in the cover image in order to visually address the complex intersections between art, law, and power. Power is vested, granted, or taken by those who build walls to control people and their passage, as well as the environments that they inhabit. Law can refer to the rules and rulers who create boundaries between and within people, as well as acceptable and unacceptable forms of aesthetics. 'Art' can be institutionalized or (of the) public, amateur or professional, progressive or regressive—it can also be transgressive of these real or fictitious categories and divisions.

Walls are ephemeral or permanent structures that don visible or invisible messages of acceptance or rejection. They come into being through movements of legal process, the most spectacular through power hoarding of executive orders; those most notorious and dangerous as enforced boundaries of immigration controls, detention encampments, prisons, and the ordering of protest. Walls may be removed as mutually legislated demarcations of peace, such as the iconic call of the Berlin wall, its absence as opening and healing from segregation and war. Perhaps these material constructions are no more symbolic of order as they are the very matter of property through and on which artists, activists, and citizens make their mark. From the concrete walls erected by Egyptian military forces in downtown Cairo to block the demonstrators, to the mosaic wall full of colourful post-it notes constructed by protesters during Occupy Central in Hong Kong, walls are a good starting point for an exploration of art, law, and power.

Walls, as we will see in this book, involve space, performance, and legality playing out in different forms, whether it be street artists daubing city surfaces, women in prison making their own media to raise their voice and earn an income, or a culture jammer hacking the voting system. Property appears and reappears as a form and process of landed 'walling' where what is seen as resistance, community building, legislating, or controlling, vacillates in a legal artifice of wall-making that this collection seeks to cross-examine, to use a fitting term of court process. The walls are very thin indeed between the halls of art, law, and power. It is this juxtapositioning and delimiting of art, law, and power that this volume seeks to evidence.

The intersection of law, politics, and aesthetics is no newcomer to scholarly endeavour. It is an old but re-emerging field of research across a number of disciplines, striating theory and practice. The coupling of politics and aesthetics has been a thematic within critical thinking for many years, famously postulated by the Frankfurt School.[1] Aesthetics and law have been discussed at length in critical legal thinking, from law and literature studies to legal semiotics.[2] Approaches have spoken to traditional understandings of legal aesthetics (or how law is represented aesthetically).[3] Criminologist Alison Young has investigated the role of law and affect in the production of illicit art.[4] Nevertheless, as of yet there is little work that has brought together contemporary theories of activism, aesthetics, and law together as a scholarly endeavour.

The political nature of art and its strategic use in resistance movements has been discussed within the fields of art, communication, and sociology from the Situationist International to the anti-globalization movement and the Arab Spring.[5] Significant has been T.V. Reed's analysis of culture and social movements in the USA in terms of the cultural texts that they produce, as well as their own existence as subcultures.[6] More recently, scholarship has explored the political aesthetics of uprisings since the Arab Spring in a broader transnational context through the study of uses of poetry, song, graffiti, posters, and performance.[7] A focus on performance has also been enabled by works exploring embodiment, labour, and the instrumentalization of art beyond its own sake.[8] Yet, an explicit collection of accounts where the law is contested, appropriated, or enforced within negotiations of art and power is largely missing from that scholarship. The chapters that follow seek to contribute by intersecting understandings of law, legitimacy, and legal form with the political aesthetics of activism.

Within the employment of art in processes of social and environmental justice, the work of culture jammers or 'subvertisers,'[9] graffiti writers or street artists all over the world, there is an excellent opportunity to explore the imbrication of art, law, protest, and property. The appearance of graffiti and street art in urban spaces brought the impact of law to the fore, where the tragedy of the commons and the privatization of public space in the form of enclosed property is performed through the daubing of the street—and the punitive responses of the law.[10] As Halsey and Young point out, the spraying of paint on the street is not an unreasonable concern of the functioning of the state,[11] and now arguably the market as 'art-washing.' It works for the neoliberal order we have not yet escaped from, to commodify the art forms as licenced street art and graffiti that can become tools for gentrification as forms of advertising, not least their value as moveable property in the global art market. This brings property/commodity full circle in the mainstreaming of culture jamming. There is a critical urgency to us wanting to bring together this collection on art, law, and power through a global political context, an interdisciplinary theoretical lexicon, as well as questions raised in the academic scholarship regarding the relationship between art, politics, and law.

The pieces to follow have been commissioned as a much-needed reflection on the role of law within contemporary art practices and resistance movements. The present collection is the only one of its kind specifically dedicated to thought on this unique intersection of art, law, and power. There is a crucial need to respond to a global political contingency in transformation where rights and responsibilities are enabled or disabled, sometimes on the basis of identity politics (sexual orientation, gender identity, class, race), sometimes on the basis of material politics (property), and an inevitable (or underlying) intersection of the material and the performative. We are inspired by works that liquidate and sometimes escape the institutional frameworks of knowledge dissemination.[12] There are several reasons as to why this is a timely and significant endeavour.

First, at the broader political context we have witnessed the concentration of political and economic power in the hands of transnational elites, while income inequality and poverty have significantly increased. The role of art within everyday or institutional public or private settings can significantly reinforce or challenge such injustices. Forms of protest and creative resistance have increasingly been suppressed or criminalized. A notable example is the *Ley Orgánica de protección de la seguridad ciudadana* (aka ley mordaza or gag law) which was implemented by the Spanish government in 2015 and which curbed the rights of freedom to expression and assembly, resulting in fines and imprisonment of activists and journalists. At the time of writing, the state of Brunei is introducing new laws that make homosexuality punishable by stoning to death, threatening the rights and lives of its LGBTQ citizens. Furthermore, as public space becomes increasingly privatized, with regimes to keep the urban environment cleansed and free of anti-social behaviour, the governance of private property through law resounds clearly through the criminalization of art on the street. No more tragic is 18-year-old Felipe Becerra shot dead by the police as he painted in Bogota in 2015. Such specific legal or political events, alongside broader shifts in the landscape of global politics, signify the necessity of holding power accountable to law through art or understanding art, artists, and citizens as connected to and in dialogue with specific legal-political contexts.

Secondly, at the level of theory, this edited volume contributes to an understanding of the relationship between art as aesthetics and law as politics, bridging sociology and communications scholarship with critical legal studies. As stated by Deleuze, 'The act of resistance has two faces. It is human and it is also the act of art.'[13] It seems as though there may be one more face to consider—that of law; or is all art, law, resistance the same, and what it is to be human in sum? There has been much academic debate across disciplines concerning the relationship between words and images. There have been arguments about the rising significance of the latter in what W.J.T. Mitchell and others have discussed as the 'pictorial turn.'[14] Updates to these arguments regarded the expansion of the relationship between words and images through Gottfried Boehm's 'iconic turn.'[15] In any case, the visual and its role within social and legal processes has been put centre stage.[16] More recently, the significance of centring citizens' practices related to the media has been highlighted with regards to everyday life.[17] This together with moments of civic activation and political mobilization has heralded the emergence of the 'performative turn.'[18] Theories of affect and performativity in the politics of resistance have thus signified a broadening area of interest in the spatio-temporal dimensions of law, aesthetics, and resistance.[19] The volume at hand contributes to scholarship that points to the deliberate use of art and creative practices within resistance, while at the same time pointing to a conscious paradigm shift within art to become participatory, or as Bishop would term, as a turn to the social.[20] Our work moves more towards recent art historical narratives of 'socially engaged art,'[21] accounting for a shift towards political art and the use of creative tactics within social movements. At the same time, it moves towards sociological, cultural studies, and communication approaches to culture and power, highlighting and accounting for shifts towards performance, participation, and pedagogy.

Finally, the relationship between art and law can be observed across several settings, from questions of agency to questions of media and space in the relation to protest, property, and power. A number of the pieces within our collection relate to a collective aesthetics of resistance, new ways of responding to the legal spaces and boundaries of neoliberal capitalism through street art, graffiti, and subvertising. Yet, we also observe cases where the production of art is not always for democratic aims. In the negotiations between art, law, and power, power can operate in a dialectical way, between oppressor and contender, between democratic aims and non-democratic aims. Alternately, power can also be transferred in physical spaces, walls, and bodies, where the effect and affect of law is to resist and create art. This volume recognizes that and offers contextual depth in articulations of art within revolutionary times. By doing so, it contributes to a growing body of literature on politically driven art and creative practices aiming to highlight the importance of the legal context and its negotiations within those practices.

As its editors, we have curated the present volume to speak to the gaps identified in the scholarship mentioned above. Our perspectives, as scholars of social sciences and humanities, and specifically working on critical legal theory, cultural studies, and communication, frame our approach to this volume. We invited contributions from artists, activists, and academics to question the intersection between art, law, and power in their own work. Discussions from the role of the judge in determining aesthetic value, to the law of art, to the role of creativity in rehabilitative pedagogies, sit alongside pieces that question the structures of property and power in determining legal and illegal expression and the punishments in turn, and how this can be countered through subverting and reclaiming spaces in aesthetic resistance. The cases analyzed come from Brazil, Egypt, India, Sweden, Spain, UK, Mexico, Australia, and USA. While this book does not aim to produce a 'global' framework for working through issues around art, law and power, it offers a variety of perspectives from countries with different legal systems and at different stages of 'modernity,' thus producing a nuanced framework regarding the negotiations of legality and artistic production. Common social justice questions regarding discrimination and oppression frame concerns across borders.

We are pleased to present this broad range of chapters, which allows for a consideration of both the structures and processes within the production of art and law as well as the representational and strategic approaches to the uses of art and law. Certain themes allow the pieces to be read in conversation with one another; the location of power and perceptions of law, resistance through art or law, street art and the politics of public art, rules and regulation of public space and the clashing of interests and subjectivities within public and private space. The collection comes at a poignant juncture in contemporary power and politics, seeking to contribute a call to renegotiate and cross old boundaries between the disciplines and practices of art and law, in the hope of demonstrating the agential nature of the aesthetic, the legal and the political as a locus for change.

The book begins with contributions that directly discuss the nature of legitimacy in law and legitimacy in art, and the connections between these apparently distinct forms of authority. Micheál O'Connell opens with an engagement on what he describes as 'laws of the art system,' adapted from McKee's notion of the 'art system' and complimenting Becker's networked art worlds.[22] The piece observes the obedience artists hold towards their own practices, as he describes, being a 'law unto themselves.' This, he further asserts, is paradoxically no obligation to follow any juridical movement at all. Here he questions art and artists' structures of legitimacy in relation to the role of politics within aesthetics, with a specific concern for deliberately socially engaged art. How can we come to understand what role law plays in the ordering of the aesthetic? And are we talking state law or a form of artists' law, as O'Connell states—or are they one and same thing?

Jeremy Pilcher's contribution challenges understandings of democracy, protest, legality, and artistic form with reference to 'Voteauction,' a website/piece of art that (purported to) allow individuals to buy and sell their votes in the United States' Presidential election of 2000, which was declared a piece of 'corporate art' by its creators, Ubermorgen. Pilcher discusses the site as an iteration of the subversive, the creative, and the legal through the lens of a Derridean haunting and performativity. He questions whether Voteauction can simultaneously be a prank, while also creating a space for legal and democratic alteration, the presence of the site as that which questions the futurority of the presidential election, and the legitimacy of the 'legal' democratic voting process overall. A journey into the legal, illegal, art, and protest, this culture jam of the US constitution brings us full circle to questions of legitimacy and authority in today's administration; the piece highlighting ways in which the intersection of art, law, and activism can bring forth political alteration whether legitimately or otherwise.

A contribution by members of the Spanish activist group ConsumeHastaMorir follows Isidro Jiménez Gómez and Mariola Olcina Alvarado reflecting upon seventeen years of subvertising practice. In response to the question of their artistic practice in relation to law and power, they highlight the negotiation of legal strategies of subvertising activists in their articulation of anti-consumerism, demonstrating further dichotomies of legality and illegality, as well as how these dialectics are formed, and how they can be broken down. In particular, they draw insights from their unexpected encounters with intellectual property law and their creative responses to the law's confinements when working with advertising content. Their practice endorses a definition of subvertising as the unsolicited reaction to the visual pollution of advertising where 'removing, replacing, and defacing advertising is an act of civil disobedience that is both legally and morally defensible.'[23]

Sean Mulcahy's exploration of evidence of sex in court during a claim for refugee status unravels the tensions between live performance and recording as evidence, inside and outside the courtroom. Mulcahy narrates the case of a gay couple offering to perform a live 'act of homosexual intercourse' to prove their sexuality to a Refugee Review Tribunal, whereby the delineation between the experience of live performance is outlawed as proof. Mulcahy cleverly demonstrates the aesthetic ordering of the law with its heightened intensity in the court, the role of performance in law, and the construction of intersecting legally gendered and racialized space.

Virginia Villaplana Ruiz's text in conversation with transgender people in jail is written in the form of a dialogue as part of the author's media art project in prison (*Diaries of Intermittent Dreams*). This is produced as an embodied text with the artist, activist, academic facilitating a dialogue through her methodological approach of mediabiography. Ruiz's practice centres the subjectivities of transgender people in a Spanish prison and calls for the need to generate narratives that break with stereotypes about incarceration. Where the law has withdrawn the freedom of peoples, art (oral and written dialogues) can operate as a tool to express oppression and resistance within the lived experience of incarceration.

Following on, another exploration of gender within artistic practices in the space of prison is that by artist, activist, and academic Gelen Jeleton (María Ángeles Alcántara Sánchez). She and her contributors explore the potential of art for pedagogical practice in prisons through the genre of a collaborative fanzine. They analyse the fanzines produced through the 'Women in Spiral' project within a Mexican prison and reflect on the role of the medium of the zine in terms of freedom of expression in a space of limited freedom as well as the practices it enables and the forms of space appropriation it makes possible.

Radwa Othman explores different art forms and their performative and aesthetic ordering in the Egyptian Revolution of 2011. Her chapter questions the use of art by authoritarian regimes for legitimation and public control. Othman highlights the government of General Al-Sisi's controlled cultural production and orchestrated campaign of pro-coup artworks and thus engagement in aesthetic ordering. Art can be a means of control, as it can be a means of freedom. Her chapter discusses different melodramatic revolutionary artworks in contrast to pro-coup melodramatic artworks, while questioning the effect of aesthetics on moralizing political tensions and rationalizing authoritarianism.

Fidèle A. Vlavo's chapter questions the criminalization of a digital file-sharing platform and the kind of digital resistance, which The Pirate Bay poses. Following Foucault, she engages in a textual reading of the Swedish court proceedings where the three founders and the businessman who facilitated technical support to the site were convicted. Vlavo argues that the file-sharing platform is an ephemeral but also effective space producing resistance that can expose the limits of law. Furthermore, she makes a broader claim about the historical significance of The Pirate Bay by arguing that 'digital piracy is not merely a means for illicit media consumption; it is a politics that aims to counter the capitalistic control of digital media.'

Street art as a subcultural practice is the focus of a number of the contributions, in its urban roadside aesthetic as well as highly mediated and domesticated within the private spaces of galleries and coffee shops. Street art remains controversial both in its urban setting and in the gallery. Alexander Araya López examines the representation and criminalization of pichação/ pixação (pixo) in Brazil, a street art practice that uses black ink to create calligraphy in urban settings. As Araya López describes it, it is a 'cultural practice of public writing combined with a radical politics of recognition .... an adapted form of 'tagging' with a Brazilian socio-political twist.' Through a discourse analysis of representations of pixo in *Folha de São Paulo*, the author discusses the ways in which this transgressive practice shifts debates about artistic and critical praxes, while it also highlights the punitive practices employed by the state to control pixo. Pixadores insert themselves in the visual environment of the city to resist stigmatization and exclusion and thus to engage in a radical politics of recognition. Araya López's chapter explores how news reports about street art in Brazil frame the legality of art and analyses the consequences of these practices for street artists targeting art institutions.

Marta Iljadica unpacks the real property and intellectual property intersections of street art and graffiti, lamenting the commercialization of these illicit art forms and seeking solutions to cooptation through legal form as well as right to the city arguments for counter-regulation. Her chapter opens up accounts of graffiti and street art resisting law, to not just copyright but extending to legal space within which the art is created, questioning the meeting points of real and intellectual property. Iljadica poignantly highlights the role of commercialization in street art and graffiti, evidencing law and property as not just ordering the way the art is represented on the street, but also its transfer to the art market; and the effect this has on those who make the works, in turn. She discusses how this market co-optation brings us back to the way law can be used to protect and the art works for the communities in which they and their creators are found, such as through heritage laws, whose right it is to destroy work (the moral right of integrity), and the role that legal (and illegal) ownership plays in this.

Swastee Ranjan brings to us the materiality of law, with an insightful and astute questioning of the surface and affect in relation to law and the city. Ranjan relays the role of affect and legitimacy in the art on city walls of New Delhi, and how buildings, their bye-laws, and legitimate public art fix aesthetic juridical registers as a result. Ranjan speaks of the material environment of commissioned art projects as sites by which aesthetic meaning and judgement is construed. She takes two cases in Delhi and delimits the role of law in aesthetic decision making through its affectual ordering and contact with urban surfaces in the specific instance of the city.

Dann Hignell-Tully brings to life the Ancient Greek agora, as a legally (dis)ordered spaced, into the contemporary setting of Public Spaces Protection Orders (PSPOs) within UK law. PSPOs are spaces within which both resistance and law can abound. Hignell-Tully draws upon Plato, Simondon, and Michel de Certeau to bring us a collective performance of public space that is unbounded by categories of being, such as the cleaner, the farmer, the city worker, where agents exist beyond and transcend these roles. A utopic and positive vision of what shared space can mean, this piece questions the bounded and exclusionary nature of PSPOs in the name of the majority, bringing forth an agoric performance of the Other, a call to responsibility and sharing that seeks law not to coerce but to facilitate the everydayness of multiplicities.

Photini Vrikki takes the case of the #1daywithoutus to discuss the fluid dynamics in contemporary citizenship. Juxtaposing legal citizenship with affective citizenship as performed on Twitter, she sketches out the centrality of affect in contemporary politics and the importance that needs to be placed on the stories of belonging that emerge as a response to the mobilization of affect by the state for purposes of intimidation or delineation of an in-out group which either adheres to British national identity, culture, and values or doesn't. Through her chapter, we are able to see the dynamics between the institutional mobilization of affect and the mobilization of affect by citizens through everyday uses of social media as resistance in the post-Brexit referendum. Vrikki's chapter defends an expansion of the static legal concept of citizenship through an analysis of how social media can be performances of 'fluid citizenship' through stories of belonging in the #1daywithoutus hashtag protest against Brexit.

Lizzy Willmington's piece closes the collection with a poignant and timely discussion of collaboration, participation and spectacle, from an art historical sense as well as that of the legal. She interrogates the role of participatory art as a critical space of opening, a creative place for countering and questioning juridical strategies around immigration and the internalization of border controls. Willmington's own personal curatorial experience as part of the 'Who are we? Project' Hostile Environment Tour, illustrates the role of the spectator within participatory art, while at the same time demonstrating the use of participation as a technology of control and exclusion, through the networked borders of the Immigration Act 2016 and the Hostile Environment policy.

The spatial, temporal and affective liminalities of art, law, and power are illustrated most poignantly in some diverse pieces on legitimate versus illegitimate art in the postcolonial city by Ranjan, the privatization and regulation of public spaces by Hignell-Tully, and the aesthetics of border politics by Willmington. Hignell-Tully analyses the legal regulation of space in the form of Public Space Protection Orders (PSPOs) and how these can be countered in forms of collective legal re-interpretation. Willmington discusses the privatization of border controls and oppositional creative tactics of resistance through story-telling and counter-narratives of immigration's racialized and illegalized bodies. Ranjan accounts for the way law creates affect through its objects and surfaces and the resultant legal space created.

What does all this say about the connections between art, law and power? Arguably that, in recent years, citizens, activists, and artists have become progenitors of change, by engaging with global politics—and realizing that there is little that change can bring without the legislative and juridical performances needed to implement it—in order to alter the political landscape. Justice and injustice are clearly catechisms that are troubling not just jurists, judges, and politicians (or you would hope), but also artists seeking to be the filter for those who are experiencing justice and injustice in all its myriad and phantasmic forms, relayed back to us through our online networks or our corporal engagement. A key force has been the transformation of social life through new forms of media and communication, the sharing of skills, artistic works, memes, and protest actions across the digital landscape, where new events, people, and facts are judged in the 'court of online,' and the local reporter no longer exists to report the 'facts' in a post-truth era. It is important to question the dynamic exchanges between art, law, media, practices, and power and the answers are provided in this volume by scholars of the critical social sciences and humanities.

Laws can be walls, keeping people safe and protected. They can authoritatively or inadvertently leave people out, draw markers between those citizens who are 'legal' and those who are not. This is a particularly powerful narrative in times of migration due to political, economic, or environmental causes. If laws cannot keep us safe, if laws cannot recognize us, if laws do not offer the possibility of expression and transformation, then laws lead to an abuse of power and hence an abuse of people. What we witness through the interventions in this volume are the negotiations of law and power in and through art, as well as the locations of power within negotiations of law and art.

What role does law play within art or aesthetics? Where does aesthetic judgement lie? How do artists and/or activists engage with the location of power within and beyond law, and how are activists using art and law to protest? To what extent do negotiations of law provide new spaces for action? What role does property play in delineating orders of acceptable and unacceptable art? The contributions to this collection have been selected to provide commentary on these key provocations on art, law, power, and beyond. We invite you to explore this volume for answers to these questions.

## Notes

1.    Theodor Adorno et al. *Aesthetics and Politics* (London: Verso, 1977)

2.    Peter Gabel, 'Reification in Legal Reasoning,' in vol. 3 of *Research in Law and Sociology*, ed. Stephen Spitzer (Greenwich: JAI Press, 1980), 25–51; Roberta Kelveson, *The Law as a System of Signs* (New York: Plenum Press, 1988).

3.    Costas Douzinas and Lynda Nead, *Law and the Image: The Authority of Art and the Aesthetics of Law* (Chicago: University of Chicago Press, 1999) and the expansive legal aesthetics of Peter Goodrich, *Legal Discourse: Studies in Linguistics, Rhetoric and Legal Analysis* (London: Macmillan, 1987), speaks directly to the role of imagery and representation in law. Gearey further muses on poetry, and literary form in relation to law, see Adam Gearey, *Law and Aesthetics* (Portland Oregon: Hart Publishing, 2001); as well as the work of Desmond Manderson and music and literary form in relation to law (Desmond Manderson, *Songs without Music: Aesthetic Dimensions of Law and Justice* [Berkeley: University of California Press, 2000]). Socio-legal thinkers Linda Mulcahy (Linda Mulcahy, 'The Eyes of the Law: A Visual Turn in Socio-Legal Studies?', *Journal of Social and Legal Studies* 44 [2017], 111–28; Linda Mulcahy and Tatiana Flessas, 'Limiting Law: Art in the Street and Street in the Art,' *Law, Culture and the Humanities* [2016], 1–23), Les Moran (Les Moran, 'Every Picture Speaks a Thousand Words: Visualising Judicial Authority in the Press,' in Priska Gisler, Sara Steinert Borella, and Caroline Wiedmer, eds., *Intersections of Law and Culture* [Basingstoke: Palgrave, 2012]) and Amanda Perry-Kessaris (Amanda Perry-Kessaris, 'The Pop-up Museum of Legal Objects Project: An Experiment in Socio-Legal Design,' *Northern Ireland Legal Quarterly* 68/3 [2017], 225–45.) have further discussed the role of the visual, the image, and the object within legal discourses. In 2019, there has been an edited collection commissioned by Desmond Manderson, *Law and the Visual: Representations, Technologies, Critique* (Toronto: University of Toronto Press). Furthermore, there have been a number of collections on art and law (Peter Goodrich, *Legal Emblems and the Art of Law: Obiter Depicter as the Vision of Governance* [Cambridge: Cambridge University Press, 2013]; Peter Goodrich, *Legal Emblems and the Art of Law: Obiter Depicter as the Vision of Governance* (Cambridge: Cambridge University Press, 2013); Oren Ben-Dor, ed., *Law and Art: Justice, Ethics and Aesthetics* [London: Routledge, 2011]).

4.    Alison Young's work on street art, graffiti, and the performative nature of law and aesthetics is important, but has had a specifically criminological focus so far, not always relaying the role of law within illicit art (Alision Young, 'Aesthetic Vertigo and a Jurisprudence of Disgust,' *Law and Critique*, 11 [2000], 241–65; Alison Young, *Judging the Image* [London: Routledge, 2005]; Alison Young, *Street Art, Public City: Law, Crime and the Urban Imagination* [London: Routledge, 2013]). Marta Iljadica, who we are very pleased to have included in the book, specifically works on the nature of copyright relating

to the work of street artists and graffiti writers (Marta Iljadica, 'Graffiti and the Moral Right of Integrity,' *Intellectual Property Quarterly* [2015], 1-23).

5.  Stephen Duncombe, *Dream: Re-imagining progressive politics in an age of fantasy* (New York and London: The New Press, 2007); Stevphen Shukaitis, *The Composition of Movements to Come: Aesthetics and Cultural Labor after the Avant-Garde* (London and New York: Rowman and Littlefield, 2016).

6.  T.V. Reed's (2005, 2019) works include examples from the African American civil rights movement and the black power movement, the Chicano/a movement and brown power, the Native American red power movement, the AIDS Coalition to Unleash Power, and, in the more recent edition, Occupy Wall Street and Black Lives Matter.

7.  Pnina Werbner, Martin Webb, and Kathryn Spellman-Poots, eds., *The Political Aesthetics of Global Protest: The Arab Spring and Beyond* (Edinburgh: Edinburgh University Press, 2014).

8.  Paula Serafini. *Performance Action: The Politics of Art Activism* (London: Routledge, 2018); Paula Serafini, Jessica Holtaway and Alberto Cossu, eds., *artWORK: Art, Labour and Activism* (London and New York: Rowman and Littlefield, 2018).

9.  The term 'subvertisers' is used here instead of 'subvertizers' due to the transnational movement Subvertisers International. For more information on such activist media practices, see: Marilyn DeLaure and Moritz Fink, *Culture Jamming: Activism and the Art of Cultural Resistance* (New York: NYU Press, 2017); Eleftheria J. Lekakis 'Culture jamming and Brandalism for the Environment: The Logic of Appropriation,' *Popular Communication* 15/4 (2017), 311–27.

10.  Carolina Olarte-Olarte and Illan Rua Wall, 'The occupation of public space in Bogotá: internal displacement and the city,' *Social & Legal Studies* 21/2 (2012), 321–339; Rosalyn Deutsche, *Evictions, Art and Spatial Politics* (Cambridge: MIT Press, 1996); Lucy Finchett-Maddock, *Protest, Property and the Commons: Performances of Law and Resistance* (London: Routledge, 2016).

11.  Mark Halsey and Alison, Young 'Our Desires are Ungovernable' *Theoretical Criminology*, 10/3 (2006), 276–77.

12.  We highlight the work done by Free Universities (Lambros Fatsis, 'The Practice of Public Sociology: Common Practice or Wishful Thinking?' *The Sociological Review*, 29 March 2017, accessed 1 June 2019, https://www. thesociologicalreview.com/the-practice-of-public-sociology-common-practice-or-wishful-thinking/). Specifically regarding art and power, the expansion of academia beyond its institutional teaching practices and scholarly works is evident in the work of The (New York-based) Center for Artistic Activism, a research and training institute focused on advising, educating, and researching artistic activism and disseminating its resources through different pedagogical channels and practices.

13.     Gilles Deleuze, 'What is the Creative Act?' in *Two Regimes of Madness*, ed. David Lapoujade, trans. Ames Hodges and Mike Taormina (Cambridge: MIT Press, 2007), 312–24.

14.     W.J.T. Mitchell, *Picture Theory: Essays on Verbal and Visual Representation* (Chicago: University of Chicago Press, 1995).

15.     Dominik Bartmanski, 'The Word/Image Dualism Revisited: Towards an Iconic Conception of Visual Culture ,' *Journal of Sociology* 50/2 (2012),164–81.

16.     Jacques Rancière, *The Future of the Image* (London: Verso, 2007); Nicholas Mirzoeff, *How to See the World* (London: Verso, 2015); Linda Mulcahy, 'The Eyes of the Law: A Visual Turn in Socio-Legal Studies?', *Journal of Social and Legal Studies* 44 (2017), 111–28.

17.     Nick Couldry, *Media, Society, World: Social Theory and Digital Media Practice* (Cambridge: Polity, 2012).

18.     Laura Iannelli and Pierluigi Musaró, *Performative Citizenship: Public Art, Urban Design, and Political Participation* (Milano: Mimesis International, 2017); Fidèle A. Vlavo, *Performing Digital Activism: New Aesthetics and Discourses of Resistance* (London: Routledge, 2017); Serafini, *Performance Action: The Politics of Art* Activism; The turn to 'performative democracy' is also recognized and echoed in the artworld; Peter Weibel, ed., *global aCtIVISm: Art and Conflict in the 21st century* (Karlsruhe: ZKL Center for Art and Media, 2014).

19.     Lucy Finchett-Maddock, *Protest, Property and the Commons: Performances of Law and Resistance* (London: Routledge, 2016).

20.     Claire Bishop, 'The Social Turn: Collaboration and its Discontents,' *Artforum* 44/6 (2006), 178–83. At the same time as the protest tactics are changing, so too does contemporary art; art historian Nicolas Bourriand's 'Relational Aesthetics' (Nicolas Bourriand, *Relational Aesthetics*, trans. Simon and Pleasance and Fronza Woods [Les presse du réel, 2002]) relaying the deliberately political nature of art. Art historian Yates McKee (Yates McKee, *Strike Art: Contemporary Art and the Post-Occupy Condition* (New York: Verso, 2016) spoke of the role of in these movements, and most predominantly, the Occupy movement, where the encamped protests are perceived as a form of art through its performative and subversive gestures of alternative ways of being in the face of the 1%. Scholette, Charnley, and Lippard (Gregory Scholette, Kim Charnley, and Lucy Lippard, *Delerium and Resistance: Activist Art and the Crisis of Capitalism* [New York: Pluto Press, 2017]) critique this to the point that we now have art/life completion, one with which Rancière would have been proud, but this at the detriment of anything really being 'new,' inspiring, or the understanding of the limits of phenomena that may not be art forms, where the 'artification' of areas of life just mean that they become new commons that can be extracted by capital alongside the further value-added nature of the artist's role.

21.     For example, we highlight the works of Yates McKee, *Strike Art:*

*Contemporary Art and the Post-Occupy Condition* (New York: Verso, 2016); Gregory Scholette, *Dark Matter: Art and Politics in the Age of Enterprise Culture* (New York: Pluto Press, 2010); Scholette et al. *Delerium and Resistance*; Nato Thompson, *Seeing Power: Art and Activism in the 21st Century* (New York: Melville House, 2016); Alana Jelenik, *This is Not Art: Activism and Other Not-Art* (London: Tauris, 2013).

22.    Yates McKee, *Strike Art: Contemporary Art and the Post-Occupy Condition* (New York: Verso, 2016); Howard S. Becker, *Art Worlds* (Berkeley: University of California Press, 1983).

23.    Hogre, *Subvertising: The Piracy of Outdoors Advertising* (London: Dog Section Press, 2017).

# 1

## Artists are Only 'a Law unto Themselves'

*Micheál O'Connell*

It is evident that the law is not as rigid as some presume. Legal specialists are trained to understand the importance of flexibility and not only of the need for certainty, in its application.[1] A few possible explanations can be given for why artists, investigative journalists, and others appear entitled to bend the law and frequently test its limitations. This is not the case everywhere, nor at all times, but some degree of it is a characteristic of liberal democracies, wealthier economies, and occasionally even more classically authoritarian regimes. From a wholly logical perspective the state of affairs is odd: laws by definition should be strict. Yet, we all know that there is a difference between the law as it is written and its actual enforcement. Take the 20 mph speed limit which is now common in urban parts of Britain:[2] 'Figures released by the Department for Transport show that 81 percent of cars recorded at nine sites across the country in 2016 broke the limit, with a handful—15 per cent—travelling at more than 30 mph.'[3] Clearly the rule is not being imposed. Reasons of efficiency, lack of resource, or the unreasonableness of the limit, may be cited but undoubtedly ideological forces are a key factor. Competing sets of codes and vying moralities are at play. Concerning the matter of artistic activity, a greater degree of freedom with respect to ethical conventions, and at times even the law, seems to be acknowledged. This chapter looks at how that is so, suggests what the origins are for certain artistic autonomies, and lists reasons why those in power would be willing to accept or even support such law-bending. A controversial postulation put forward, given the turn towards activism and the times we inhabit, is that privileges are granted precisely because artists do not pose a threat to the status quo. Connected with this, we reflect on the argument that didactic art is poor art, whilst, ironically, likely to be ineffective in its practical goals and attempt to change minds. The latter insinuation brings into question any conscious attempt at the instrumental employment of art, as panacea for societal ills say (a top-down position) or in order to prompt social change (the activist position). Having considered these issues, counterpoints are made in the second half of the chapter, relating to how artists can address the socio-political landscape. Examples are given of materials which are simultaneously politically committed and judged positively within art contexts. One chapter in a book is inadequate to discuss the multifarious interconnections between artistic practice and political imperatives. Enough is done here to demonstrate that the conflation of the two is conceivable, whilst remaining sceptical and defensive of the distinctions.

On the face of it, the addressing of taboo subjects, and carrying out of inflammatory actions, by those who call themselves artists is regularly accepted. The degree of tolerance for the pursuit of alternative lifestyles or transgressive conduct by essentially aristocratic groupings— take Byron and his circle, or a century later the Bloomsbury Set—was extended to others with the advent of popular culture during the twentieth century. Artists have been shocking, not only in the nature of their wonted breaks with preceding artistic convention but in their general behaviours. The misdemeanours were not always tolerated of course: 'There is no such thing as a moral or an immoral book,' proclaimed Oscar Wilde but in real life he faced persecution.[4] Egon Schiele was imprisoned in 1912, following a court case during which the presiding judge burnt one of the artist's offending erotic drawings. Such cases of boldness punished, however, also provide evidence of the expectation of greater leniency in the first place. The sense of entitlement exists because the tag artist often does offer real protection when ethical, moral, and sometimes even legal codes are violated. In more recent times, when members of performance art and activist group, Pussy Riot, were jailed in 2012, the international outcry which followed must have improved their predicament.[5] At least the band were embraced by a global community of sorts, within the worlds or art and popular culture, on their release. A disturbing incident, which nevertheless provides further indication of the presumption that greater ethical leeway is extended to artists, was paramilitary Michael Stone's claiming his intrusion, with explosives, into Northern Ireland's Stormont parliament in 2006 was 'performance art.'[6] Unsurprisingly Stone eventually failed in his attempt to convince the court.[7] On the other hand Pyotr Pavlensky who is famous for his many provocative public performance actions in Russia, including nailing his scrotum to the cobblestones on Red Square in 2013 and setting fire to the entrance of a Federal Security Service building in 2015, escaped being incarcerated.[8] It was unclear whether his actions were devoid of artistic merit.[9] Further confirmations of the latitude extended when the 'art' word is used are not difficult to find. The references to risk in Arts Council England's advice for grants applicants, are couched in terms that are ambiguous enough for it not to be clear whether what is meant, are aesthetic considerations only: 'Risk is important in many artistic activities. By taking artistic risks, artists often find ways to break new ground, reach new audiences or increase the range of work they do.'[10]

Of course not all artists are attempting to provoke or incite radical change, but we might wonder what the nature of the additional freedoms being discussed is, and how they came about. Is there something essential for a society in the, mostly tacit, acceptance of nonstandard conduct by a minority? The suggestion of a class basis for such privileges alone cannot explain everything. Even within privileged or celebrity circles, order has to be maintained and the excusing of moral or legal violations is not always guaranteed, as some of the examples already given indicate. Still, motives can be listed for why sections of those who exercise control might support conduct which, at first sight, is critical and challenging of that very authority. For instance, the semiotics of such permission-granting is evidence of a liberal environment, and it may be important to give that impression. During the Cold War era, 'soft power' was wielded, which even included surreptitious support for avantgarde art by the CIA, in order to promote the idea that the United States was a freer place than the USSR.[11] To view the advocating of artistic freedoms as a one-dimensional effort by those in power to exert control is too simplistic though. It seems obvious to state that any presiding class will have genuine cultural interests, and a need for artefacts as confirmation of its significance and prowess. In addition, art may serve some useful prognostic role, against the backdrop of existing orthodoxies as indicated in the next paragraph (which is different to it being critical on a systemic level).

The trajectory over time, in terms of artists' interactions with, and influence on, the law is worth noting. As well as actions, behaviours and lifestyles, the tangible works produced or presented as art become sources of disagreement. A famous case, against United States customs, was won by Constantin Brancusi about whether, in 1926, his *Bird in Space* could be imported as art object. Customs 'officials had classified it as a utilitarian object (under "Kitchen Utensils and Hospital Supplies") and levied against it 40% of the work's value.'[12] A few centuries earlier, lobbying for the introduction of a means of preventing piracy in Britain, had resulted in the Engraving Copyright Act, often called 'Hogarth's

Law.'[13] By the twentieth century, however, from Marcel Duchamp's famous gesture in exhibiting a 'readymade' onwards, artists were doing the opposite: challenging notions of authorship, appropriating, performing, and working with concepts instead of creating physical commodifiable items.[14] In light of these developments, Seth Siegelaub and Robert Projansky's legal document, drawn up in 1971 and used by notables such as Jackie Winsor and Hans Haacke—which was designed to protect contemporary artists' rights precisely in the spirit of Hogarth's Law—arguably amounted to a conservative adaptation to capitalism.[15] Whilst the often discussed 'art market' really does not impact on the activities of most artists, most of the time—Dave Beech reminds us that 'the vast majority of artworks do not enter the market at all'—artefacts complicate relations in a society built around commodity production in which definition and clarity, in the interests of trade, are crucial.[16] Art controversies prefigured the situation today when, contradictorily, openness, a culture of sharing, and appropriation is advocated, especially in the realm of software development, but proprietorial imperatives remain an inescapable chief concern. Speculatively, this perceived predictive capacity and, in effect, querying of received wisdom, but not to the extent of wanting to 'overthrow the system,' allows art to curry favour within the hegemony.

Despite the sometimes seditious connotations of art, then, and the risks associated with encouraging the creative impulse, power is interested in holding these practices close. And, there is a history of this. The artist as trickster has often been put forward.[17] This idea in turn is evocative of the jester of old. In medieval times, the court fool, sometimes actually licensed, was able to speak truth to power in ways that others could not.[18] Following a battle lost to the English, Phillippe VI's jester comforted him with the exclamation that the English sailors 'don't even have the guts to jump into the water like our brave French.'[19] Mikhail Bakhtin makes points about medieval carnival which, if seen as connected with the sanctioning of creative practices today, undermine common preconceptions about instrumental usages of art. It is important to recognize that the authorizing of carnival and similar was not only a means of allowing the repressed multitude an opportunity to vent off; in other words, it was not purely about social control. Evidence of this is The Paris School of Theology, in 1444, defending the long-standing *Feast of Fools* which involved, as described by Bakhtin, 'grotesque degradation of various church rituals ... gluttony and drunken orgies on the altar table, indecent gestures and disrobing,' by pointing out that, 'foolishness and folly ... are ...

man's second nature.'"[20] The poets and 'fili' of ancient Ireland deserve a mention. They were 'feared and respected,' 'enjoyed high prestige' and were understood as the ones who 'held open connections with the power of nature.'[21] Moral and legal latitudes were extended partly, but not solely, for cynical strategic reasons then. Mystique was attached to the character and behaviours of the lower orders, and a certain value was attributed to the practices of individuals such as clowns, poets, and artists.

Nowadays the notion of 'creativity' itself is valued and creativity is strongly associated with art. There is a genuine interest in the harnessing of creative potential because it is also equated with entrepreneurialism, industrial inventiveness, and allied business objectives. Claire Bishop elucidates frankly on the subject:

> New Labour built upon the Conservative government's openly instrumental approach to cultural policy: a 2001 Green Paper opens with the words 'Everyone is creative,' presenting the government's mission as one that aims to 'free the creative potential of individuals.' This aim of unleashing creativity, however, was not designed to foster greater social happiness, the realisation of authentic human potential, or the imagination of utopian alternatives but to produce, in the words of sociologist Angela McRobbie, 'a future generation of socially diverse creative workers who are brimming with ideas and whose skills need not only be channelled into the fields of art and culture but will also be good for business.'[22]

A deduction one could make then, is that the relatively relaxed attitude towards creative practices, which infringe on either written codes or moral standards, is due to them presenting no essential threat to power. This is a brazen assertion to make, especially now, when contemporary art's ties with political dissent are supposed, and the institutions reflect that development: 'Turner Prize 2018 rewards art activists tackling crime, rights and race' declared a BBC news item.[23] The shortlist included Forensic Architecture whose work we will return to.[24] Could it be though that artists, rather than being 'a law unto themselves' in the typical usage of the phrase, operate in a way that is more in tune with the original biblical meaning? This refers to groupings already inherently possessing an understanding of the appropriate moral values, which is construed to a recommendation that no law needs to be imposed upon them.[25] The most common manner in which art transgresses has already been mentioned. For artists, it is often only the laws of the 'art system,' if we care for such a term, which are being broken.[26] In fact, the main implicit rule for art, since the Romantic period, has been to break with previous orthodoxy. This is not to reduce the process to a simple formulation because breaking convention itself can become a convention. Secondly, even the most extreme disruptions are likely to be knowingly reflexive on other movements. Artists react in complex and original ways, given the inevitable instrumentalist tendency and what Situationists referred to as 'recuperation,' namely capitalism's appropriation and commodification of what was radical yesterday.[27] René Magritte wore a suit so that 'he looked like a small town banker'[28] and appropriation poet Kenneth Goldsmith encourages *Uncreative Writing*.[29] Henri Matisse's, in effect, extolling a bourgeois lifestyle and Tracey Emin's newfound political conservativism are partly results of this impulse no doubt. There may be a link, then, with the disregard for speeding violations mentioned in the first paragraph, in that artistic gestures are associated often not with universal concepts of freedom, but libertarian, individualistic, and somewhat elitist ones.

What about art that purports to be aligned with progressive social change? Here too weighty critical positions are easy to locate. Even the avant-garde, according to the hugely influential Clement Greenberg, 'was provided by an elite among the ruling class of that society from which it assumed itself to be cut off, but to which it has always remained attached by an umbilical cord of gold.'[30] In an important essay Theodore Adorno wrote that political commitment—he was referring critically to the trajectories being taken by Jean-Paul Sartre and Bertolt Brecht at that time—'often means bleating what everyone is already saying or at least secretly wants to hear. The notion of a "message" in art, even when politically radical, already contains an accommodation to the world.'[31] In the book already cited, Claire Bishop interrogates the 'social turn' in art in the 1990s and 2000s with reference to historical periods of relevance and case studies from around the globe.[32] She looks at various scenes, of both the bottom-up and government-driven variety. Even in the opening pages, she describes an insidious plan to commandeer art for encouragement of 'social participation [which] is viewed positively because it creates submissive citizens who respect authority and accept the 'risk' and responsibility of looking after themselves in the face of diminished public services.'[33]

Yates McKee's *Strike Art* also gives intermittent airplay to Bishop's ideas, her drawing on philosopher Jacques Rancière, to confront *Relational Aesthetics* and provide 'a rigorous tonic for those who would posit art as an agent of naive consensus, harmony, or identification.'[34] The book's standpoint, though, is that Occupy Wall Street and the broader Occupy movement, from 2011, owed everything to the overlap between kinds of artistic practice and political activism. It is clear that, for McKee, what counts now is the:

> entire world of artistic practice emerging throughout the 2000s not from the institutions of the mainstream contemporary art system but rather from the autonomous cultural and political ferment of the alterglobalization movement marked in the Global North by the Battle of Seattle in 1999.[35]

This narrative would eventually include the Wall Street occupation and, in turn, other movements. The book is invaluable in its chronological documenting, and it provides insights into all of the tendencies and forces at work during Occupy, along with eloquent framings and interpretations. Space is given to other critical voices with, for example, two references to Slavoj Žižek's remark at Zuccotti Park: 'Carnivals come cheap. Don't fall in love with yourselves!'[36] Bishop's thesis is cautiously contested at first by pointing out that she 'seldom addressed art embedded in social movements that would involve actually confronting the police as forces of state violence, as opposed to isolated artistic gestures.'[37] In the paragraph cited above, referring to the difference between two notions of political art, existing within and outside of institutions, McKee adds that he does not want to 'privilege one mode of working over another.'[38] In endeavouring to 'cover all bases' in this way and cram in references to practitioners, groups, theoreticians, and political texts, argumentative clarity at times feels lost. Would it not be dangerously complacent, for example, to accept all modes of working if some were known to be politically ineffectual? Is it the case that any kind of activism will do? In the conclusion art is described as 'a force of imagination and action, anger and joy, resistance and community, witnessing and dreaming, discomfort and healing.'[39] On a surface level, this sentence is an agreeable and all-encompassing one. Just because the associations between art practice and imagination, dreaming, passion, expression, healing and so on, have become clichés, does not make them untrue. Is McKee asking too much of art though? What's more, in having such high expectations, are art activists of this ilk not inadvertently mimicking that archetypally bourgeois lauding of 'the arts'? In a 2002 book David Beech and John Roberts had questioned that 'tendency to treat art as inestimably worthy, noble, or even as being among the greatest preoccupations of humanity, rather than a series of ruminations or troublespots.'[40] Downgrading art's status was considered by some more revolutionary than presuming its benevolence.

McKee is well aware of the history of the avant-garde which included anti-art, but for him avant-gardism now equals 'the reinvention of art as direct action.'[41] Anti-art was, and is, not merely nihilistic as he intimates though: one knock-on effect in fact is to make space for proper attention to be paid to the political dimension. The thought that 'Occupy itself could be considered an artwork,' as McKee put it at the book launch, is beset with political dangers, and these were touched upon by him with a reference to the ideas of Walter Benjamin.[42] There is a difference between treating politics as art and expecting art to become political, McKee points out.[43] Additional questions arise however, some of which begin to sound ridiculous given the imperatives of a political struggle. If Occupy Wall Street is an art work, then how is its artistic quality to be judged? This is not to undermine the significance of Occupy on a political level, but to question the remit of the book. The excessive citing of art in connection with every facet of Occupy smacks of desperation.[44] For sure *Strike Art* was written a number of years after the event and naturally the history will be mined in interesting ways as time goes on. Noam Chomsky and David Graeber, who published on the subject during the period of the revolt itself, needed to be mindful of the propagandistic impact of their words. Understandably, they focused primarily on its contribution to the progressive causes they espouse. For Chomsky Occupy was 'the first major public response to thirty years of class war,' representing a reawakening which changed the civic conversation.[45] Graeber characterized it as *The Democracy Project*.[46] In another book of primary source materials, compiled by Sarah Ruth van Gelder, '10 Ways the Occupy Movement Changes Everything' were listed.[47] Now that a decade has passed, and Donald Trump is in the Whitehouse, Occupy's political shortcomings warrant inspection too though. Not that the participants inability to take things to a conclusion can be blamed for the apparent swing to the right in US politics. Occupy would have been unlikely to achieve its purported aim of overthrowing global capitalism at that stage, but maybe the partakers did not fully heed Žižek's warning. And, is it possible that Occupy's failings had something to do precisely with the stress on inventiveness, celebrated by McKee and others, rather than leveraging existing bodies of political knowledge, and re-visiting theoretical and practical frameworks? At points a general strike was called for, but it seems that more could have been done from the beginning to link with the broader workforce and what, in the United States, still amounts to an embryonic labour movement. Naomi Klein had not been frightened to counsel the protestors in a speech delivered in 2011:

It is a fact of the information age that too many movements spring up like beautiful flowers but quickly die off... Being horizontal and deeply democratic is wonderful. But these principles are compatible with the hard work of building structures and institutions that are sturdy enough to weather the storms ahead.[48]

Returning to this chapter's themes, namely art's political ramifications and the nature of subversive and politically motivated art. Since the global financial crisis in 2008 and its aftermath, the frequency with which art addresses, but often also dabbles with (and might be said to be decorated with) political meaning has increased. In addition, as with Occupy, wholly politically motivated practices have occasionally been characterized as art. The stance adopted in this chapter is to be sceptical about these developments, but not cynical. The paragraphs which follow attempt to tease out ways in which art, whether intentionally didactic or not, can indeed be considered political or somehow aligned with emancipatory causes.

In the same essay on commitment, referred to already, Adorno gave the twist: 'Kafka's prose and Beckett's plays, or the truly monstrous novel *The Unnamable*, have an effect by comparison with which officially committed works look like pantomimes.'[49] Conceivably this leaves room for political agency in literary or artistic work, but to be arrived at by contrary means. The implication is that, paradoxically, the more intentionally didactic an author or creator is, the less potent the result is likely to be. The distinction between the realms of art and politics can be defended, but surely one has to admit to a scope for intersection, dependant on how these two terms are defined. Beckett himself had been active against the Gestapo in France during World War II, and had taken great personal risks.[50] Those experiences were not, on a surface level, to find their way into his writing. Having said that, surely it was inevitable that his work would somehow be influenced, if abstrusely, by the events of the early 1940s, and the bleak realisation of what human beings were capable of. Recent books testify to Beckett's 'political imagination' and the many 'causes that framed his writing.'[51] Harold Pinter, who was vociferous against war and politically active his whole life, devoted his Nobel Prize speech to impassionedly clarifying the difference between being a playwright and his role as citizen but undoubtedly one realm fed the other.[52] The political import of art which is, at the same time, reckoned exceptional by other standards cannot simply be disregarded: its meanings unfold less straightforwardly.

Dan Fox, a former Turner Prize juror, writes that 'the art system is fascinated by its own politics and worries about contemporary art's traction on society' inferring that is a key reason why topical questions are addressed.[53] He goes on to declare that 'the truth is most 'political' art is commentary and reflection, and the degree to which it impacts those who see it is either impossible to assess, or has unpredictable consequences.'[54] His point appears cynical but is revealing too. Curiously related to Fox's statement is John Roberts' argument (expanding on thinking by Ariella Azoulay and others)[55] about photography's agency, using Dorothea Lange's well-known *Migrant Mother* as case study. He refers to the diachronic possibilities and different

> actant positions (of photographer, photographed, spectator present and futural) as fundamentally nonequivalent to the particularist claims of the material interests and discourses in which they are embedded: that is, none of the material interests and discourse positions inscribed in the production and reception of the Migrant Mother photograph—the producer (photo history and art history), the editor (popular journalism), the historian (social history), or the subject (first person reminiscence)—speaks for the truth of the photography. Each of these actant positions may participate individually in shaping the truth-discourse of the photograph, but in the final analysis, they cannot control, in their own interests and image, the ends (emancipatory, counterintuitive, or reactionary) to which the image will be put.[56]

Furthermore, he says that 'this emergent emancipatory content will be dependent on the social and historical conditions of its future reception.'[57] Photography cannot be a special case in this regard. If the practical bearing of a work is beyond the control of any one influencing group, then it follows that, at times, artefacts must be able to produce political effects.

So, despite Adorno and Bishop's concerns about committed art and suspicions about socially engaged art respectively, there exists the possibility for work which is celebrated on aesthetic grounds to be impacting in terms of social change too. Adorno and Bishop's arguments can be read as critical reflection or warning rather than rule. If not, politically charged works such as Goya's infamous *The Disasters of War* series, Turner's *The Slave Ship*, Picasso's *Guernica*, Barbara Kruger's *We don't Need Another Hero,* and *Martha Rosler Reads 'Vogue'* would have to be dismissed as meritless. To avert one's gaze would be more dramatically specious. What's more, at certain points in history, the imperative is surely for artist's to play a more overtly active role, as Beckett and others did. In such situations particular cultural pursuits become either inappropriate or must reinvent themselves in ways which align with urgent demands. Thinker, literary critic, Russian revolutionary, and on occasion, victim of that movement, Viktor Shklovsky, made assertions about what a new art could be. Art should make objects 'unfamiliar,' referring in turn to Tolstoy's technique of 'defamiliarization,' and it should make forms difficult.[58] John Heartfield's 1920s and 1930s daring anti-fascist collages, as well as being completely defendable politically, are now discussed formally and in terms of aesthetics. One graphic design book refers to the 'beautiful example' of his 1934 editorial illustration *As in the Middle Ages ... so in the Third Reich*, in a chapter dealing with gestalt principles and formal considerations such as shape, size, colour, proximity, and angle.[59]

Returning to Roberts' scheme, his notion of 'actants,' and taking it in a contrary direction: something which was created with no political intention in mind might well be adopted and interpreted in ways which are beyond an artist's control: 'You can't cause anything by art,' claimed Martin Kippenberger.[60] One poster, *The Anti-Apartheid Drinking Congress,* he described as his 'first and only political act.'[61] Conversely, others see his work as 'social critique,' 'as critical and politicised.'[62]

The already mentioned Forensic Architecture's work is phenomenal in its meticulous rigour, communicative clarity, in its choice of subject matter and sheer bravery in exposing acts of violence and subsequent cover-ups by state forces and sometimes involving ominous far-right groups and gangsters. Their outcomes have a bearing on actual legal challenges and human rights cases.[63] The 'investigations seek to provide new kinds of evidence for international prosecution teams, political organizations, NGOs and international institutions such as the UN.'[64] To ask whether this is art or not seems, at first, crass. They don't categorize themselves as such but the Turner Prize panel of judges clearly did.[65] Certainly, it is not only a question of them being thorough and data-obsessed in the stereotypical manner of engineers or lawyers say. Their reappropriating a corporate look is ironic and imaginal thinking as a route to understanding clearly plays a huge role in the investigations too. Their use of scale to amplify the significance of timelines is just one of many elegant innovations. 'Space reserved for being serious is hard to come by in a modern society,' wrote Susan Sontag in her final book.[66] She went on to problematize different means by which depictions of emotionally or ideologically loaded subject matter, and specifically war photography, can be appreciated: 'A narrative seems likely to be more effective than an image. Partly it is a question of the length of time one is obliged to look, to feel.'[67] Forensic Architecture's work, by its nature, and in how it was curated at The ICA in London early in 2018, and to a lesser extent, later in that year for the Turner Prize at Tate Britain, encouraged precisely those possibilities for thoughtful, slower, narrative-oriented appreciation.[68] Phineas Harper warned of the risk of 'the arts world co-opting their work as grisly' or 'insensitive entertainment' and Mania Oikonomou alerted to the danger of 'riding the fashionable train of compassion for those in trouble' but it seems unlikely that Forensic Architecture fits these categories.[69] The aestheticization of data and imagery dealing with important traumatic incidents has not emerged as the kind of contentious issue it could be. This is possibly because their work is rightly scientific, cartographic, having more in common with Florence Nightingale's coxcombs than that typical of spectacularizing journalistic channels. Forensic Architecture's work has the very practical added effect of undermining contemporary received wisdom about the nature of surveillance. From the notorious case of Rodney King in the 1990s onwards it has become clear that the proliferation of recording technologies works in both directions: cameras and other readily available equipment are also tools to utilize when confronting injustice.[70] That is not the whole story of course. In the Rodney King example, despite the footage of him being beaten, 'three of the four officers were acquitted,' but such material can feed resistance campaigns.[71] The rationale for naming Forensic Architecture's ICA show *Counter Investigations* and their use of the term *Counter Forensics*, was directly related to the prospects for progressive uses of data, incidental footage, ubiquitous technology, surveillance and sousveillance, crowdsourcing, activist photography, re-enactments, computer modelling, and so on. Their work is a return to the idea of artist as honest observer, which is especially relevant in the era of 'fake news' and 'post-truth.'

There are risks for Forensic Architecture of course including that of recuperation, already defined. Being branded artists perhaps compounds the problem. The work could become formulaic or be diluted by others doing similarly but less scrupulously: the quality is crucial here. Adam Branson informs us that while much of Forensic Architecture's 'work centres on parts of the world with dubious human rights records, [they are] increasingly concerned about the situation in countries long thought to be bastions of liberal democracy.'[72] Despite the obstinate nature of their investigations, Forensic Architecture's activities are, so far, condoned and even approved of in establishment circles in Britain. It will be interesting to see whether that support continues when they start directing their exposures at targets closer to 'home' such as Grenfell Tower.[73] They are protected to some degree by their situating in Goldsmiths University with its interdisciplinary culture. Forensic Architecture's freedom to conduct their activities as they do, owes something also to being associated with a realm, namely 'the art world,' which includes many ostensibly unpolitical kinds of practices.

Vigilance would be advisable for political activists who, as well as embracing art because the cultural sphere offers some protection as we have said, see it as a vital channel for social change. In fact, it can be argued that the usually imagined scheme operates in reverse: perhaps it is art which is parasitic on other systems.[74] Amusingly this logic would also apply to situations in which corporate, bureaucratic, and governmental entities harbour designs on cultural activity. Rather than art being envisaged as somehow pathetic and dependant, it may operate as a court jester of sorts, shrewdly manipulating power in its own interest, in order to survive.

To summarize and conclude: through a contemplation of why it is that controversial activity by artists is often accepted, arguments were made which challenge the perception that art is somehow fundamentally politically subversive. It was stressed that power often endorses what appear to be provocative practices for reasons which can be, but are not always, schemingly strategic. Then the significance of consciously politically motivated art was considered. The implications that such output is likely to be inferior and problematic in an aesthetic sense, and ironically also less impacting politically—with reference to writing by Theodore Adorno and Claire Bishop—were probed into. Yates McKee's characterization of Occupy in art terms was looked at. Next, however, converse points were made about the potential for didactic or campaigning work to be at once judged impressive in art contexts and for there to be no contradiction in their combining. John Roberts' ideas, as applied to an iconic historical photograph, were called upon in an attempt to appreciate the different forces at play when it comes to determining the meaning and impact of artefacts. John Heartfield's collages were referred to and Forensic Architecture's projects were discussed in more detail. The number of legal controversies referred to in this chapter alone is symptom of the complex and tense relationship between art and politics. To add to the complexity, the suggestion was put that, feasibly, it is art which uses politics for its own ends and not the other way around. It would seem apt to remain cautious, then, and give the last word to Bishop who has questioned the new trend for socially engaged art. She makes essential general points about the counterintuitive forces at work writing that 'artistic practice has an element of critical negation and an ability to sustain contradiction that cannot be reconciled with quantifiable imperatives.'[75] She warns too that 'ethical reasoning' can fail 'to accommodate the aesthetic or to understand it as an autonomous realm of experience' and calls for 'a reassertion of art's inventive forms of negation as valuable in their own right.'[76]


## Notes

1.  John Bell, 'Certainty and Flexibility in Law,' in *The New Oxford Companion to Law* (Oxford: Oxford University Press, 2008).

2.  The rolling out of new speed limits may seem an obscure example to raise but the phenomenon is of interest as part of my own interventionist practice (Micheál O'Connell 'MICHEÁL O'CONNELL / MOCKSIM,' 2016, accessed 1 June 2019, http://www.mocksim.org/works/Speeding.htm).

3.  Henry Bodkin, 'Most Drivers Ignore 20 mph Speed Limits, Official Figures Show,' *The Telegraph*, accessed 15 June 2019, https://www.telegraph.co.uk/news/2017/07/03/drivers-ignore-20mph-speed-limits-official-figures-show.

4.  Oscar Wilde and John M. L. Drew, *The Picture of Dorian Gray* (Ware: Wordsworth Editions, 1992), ll. 30–1/3212.

5.  Miriam Elder, 'Pussy Riot Sentenced to Two Years in Prison Colony over Anti-Putin Protest,' *The Guardian*, accessed 13 March 2018, https://www.theguardian.com/music/2012/aug/17/pussy-riot-sentenced-prison-putin.

6.  Bernadette Buckley, 'The Workshop of Filthy Creation: Or Do Not Be Alarmed, This Is Only a Test,' *Review of International Studies* 35/4 (2009), 835–36.

7.  Michael Holden, 'Michael Stone Jailed for Stormont Assault,' *Reuters*, 8 December 2008, accessed 1 June 2019, https://uk.reuters.com/article/uk-britain-stone-idUKTRE4B74ER20081208.

8.  Walker, Shaun. 'Petr Pavlensky: Why I Nailed My Scrotum to Red Square,' *The Guardian*, 5 February 2014, accessed 9 April 2019, http://www.theguardian.com/artanddesign/2014/feb/05/petr-pavlensky-nailed-scrotum-red-square; Elise Morton, 'Russian Performance Artist Pyotr Pavlensky Released and Fined | News,' The Calvert Journal, 8 June 2016, accessed 9 April 2019, https://calvertjournal.com/news/show/6165/russian-performance-artist-pyotr-pavlensky-released-and-fined.

9.  This contrasts with the severe treatment of Pussy Riot. A person would be forgiven for suspecting gender bias.

10.  'Grant for the Arts—Help Notes: Understanding the Assessment Criteria and Overview,' *Arts Council England*, accessed 1 June 2018, https://forms.artscouncil.org.uk/officeforms/How-to-apply-help-notes-page-9.html.

11.  Frances Stonor Saunders, *Who Paid the Piper?: The CIA and the*

*Cultural Cold War* (London: Granta, 2000).

12.    Ronald D. Spencer and Tamara Mann, 'The Brouhaha: When the Bird Became Art and Art Became Anything,' *Spencer's Art Law Journal* 2/2 (November 2011), accessed 9 April, 2019, http://www.artnet.com/magazineus/news/spencer/spencers-art-law-journal-12-9-11.asp.

13.    Ronan Deazley, 'Commentary on the Engravers' Act (1735),' Primary Sources on Copyright (1450-1900), 2008, accessed 9 April 2019, http://www.copyrighthistory.org/cam/tools/request/showRecord?id=commentary_uk_1735.

14.    Sophie Howarth and Jennifer Mundi, 'Marcel Duchamp, "Fountain" 1917, Replica 1964,' *Tate*, August 2015, Accessed 9 April, 2019, http://www.tate.org.uk/art/artworks/duchamp-fountain-t07573.

15.    Seth Siegelaub and Robert Projansky 'The Artist's Reserved Rights Transfer And Sale Agreement' Accessed 1 July 2019, http://primaryinformation.org/files/english.pdf.

16.    Dave Beech, *Art and Value: Art's Economic Exceptionalism in Classical, Neoclassical and Marxist Economics* (Chicago: Haymarket Books, 2016), 303.

17.    Lewis Hyde, *Trickster Makes This World : How Disruptive Imagination Creates Culture* (Edinburgh: Canongate, 2008); John Roberts, 'Trickster,' *Oxford Art Journal* 22/1 (1999), 83–101; David Garcia, 'As If: The Media Artist as Trickster—Interview with the Curators,' *New Tactical Research* (blog), 7 March 2017, accessed 9 April 2019, http://new-tactical-research.co.uk/blog/1746/.

18.    This origin of the terms 'poetic license' and 'artistic license' which have different, but related, meanings today, may stem from this literal licencing historically.

19.    Beatrice K Otto, *Fools Are Everywhere: The Court Jester Around the World* (Chicago, London: University of Chicago Press, 2001), 113.

20.    Mikhail Mikhailovich Bakhtin, *Rabelais and His World*, trans. Hélène Iswolsky, 1st Midland book ed. (Bloomington, IN: Indiana University Press, 1984), 74–75.

21.    Robert Anthony Welch, *The Cold of May Day Monday: An Approach to Irish Literary History*,(Oxford: Oxford University Press, 2014), 28.

22.    Claire Bishop, *Artificial Hells: Participatory Art and the Politics of Spectatorship* (London: Verso, 2012), 15.

23.    'Art Activists on Turner Prize Shortlist,' *BBC News*, 26 April 2018, accessed 9 April 2019, http://www.bbc.co.uk/news/entertainment-arts-43905016.

24.    *Forensic Architecture*, accessed 7 May 2018, https://www.forensic-architecture.org/.

25.    'International Theological Commission: "In Search of a Universal Ethic: A New Look at the Natural Law",' *The Holy See*, accessed 15 May 2018, http://www.vatican.va/roman_curia/congregations/cfaith/cti_documents/rc_con_cfaith_doc_20090520_legge-naturale_en.html.

26.    Sociologist and systems theorist Niklas Luhmann provided the most notable text in this regard: Niklas Luhmann, *Art as a Social System*, trans. Eva M. Knodt (Stanford, CA: Stanford University Press, 2000).

27.    Robert Chasse, Bruce Elwell, Jonathon Horelick, and Tony Verlaan, 'Faces of Recuperation,' *The American Section of the Situationist International*, June 1969, accessed 9 April 2019, https://www.cddc.vt.edu/sionline/si/faces.html.

28.    René Magritte, *René Magritte: Selected Writings*, eds. Kathleen Rooney and Eric Plattner, trans. Jo Levy (Minneapolis: University of Minnesota Press, 2016), xi.

29.    Kenneth Goldsmith, *Uncreative Writing : Managing Language in the Digital Age* (New York: Columbia University Press), 2011; 'Kenneth Goldsmith,' *Electronic Poetry Center* (University of Pennsylvania), 2000, accessed 9 April 2019, http://writing.upenn.edu/epc/authors/goldsmith/.

30.    Clement Greenberg, *Art and Culture: Critical Essays*. Beacon Press edition (Boston: Beacon Press, 1992), 8.

31.    Theodor W. Adorno, 'Commitment,' in *Aesthetics and Politics*, ed. Fredric Jameson (London: Verso, 2007), 193.

32.    Bishop, *Artificial Hells*.

33.    Bishop, *Artificial Hells*, 15.

34.    Yates McKee, *Strike Art: Contemporary Art and the Post-Occupy Condition* (London: Verso, 2016), 291/5793; 1326/5793; Bourriaud, Nicolas. *Relational Aesthetics* (Dijon, France: Les Presse Du Reel, 1998); Bishop, Claire. 'Antagonism and Relational Aesthetics,' 110 (October 2004), 51–79.

35.    McKee, *Strike Art*, 293/5793.

36.    McKee, 1904/5793; 3775/5793.

37.    McKee, 293/5793.

38.    McKee, 293/5793.

39.    McKee, 3860/5793.

40.    Dave Beech and John Roberts, *The Philistine Controversy* (London: Verso, 2002), 14.

41.    McKee, 120/5793.

42.    Jay, Martin. '"The Aesthetic Ideology" as Ideology; Or, What Does It Mean to Aestheticize Politics?' *Cultural Critique* 21 (1992), 41–61, accessed 9 April 2019, https://doi.org/10.2307/1354116.

43.    McKee, *Strike Art*.

44.    There are 500 incidences of the word 'art' and its derivatives in *Strike Art*.

45.    Noam Chomsky, *Occupy*, Kindle edition (Westfield, New Jersey: Zuccotti Park Press, 2013), 35/1073.

46.    David Graeber, *The Democracy Project: A History, a Crisis, a Movement*, Kindle edition (London: Allen Lane, 2013).

47.    Sarah Van Gelder, ed., *This Changes Everything: Occupy Wall Street and the 99% Movement* (San Francisco: Berrett-Koehler Publishers, 2011), 17.

48.   Van Gelder, *This Changes Everything*, 40–41.

49.   Adorno, 'Commitment,' 191.

50.   James Knowlson, 'Samuel Beckett's Biographer Reveals Secrets of the Writer's Time as a French Resistance Spy,' *Independent*, 23 July 2014, accessed 1 July 2019, https://www.independent.co.uk/arts-entertainment/books/features/samuel-becketts-biographer-reveals-secrets-of-the-writers-time-as-a-french-resistance-spy-9638893.html.

51.   Emilie Morin, *Beckett's Political Imagination* (New York: Cambridge University Press, 2017); James McNaughton, *Samuel Beckett and the Politics of Aftermath* (Oxford: Oxford University Press, 2018).

52.   'Nobel Lecture: Harold Pinter,' *The Nobel Prize*, 2005, accessed 1 July 2019, https://www.nobelprize.org/prizes/literature/2005/pinter/lecture/.

53.   Dan Fox, 'Yes the Turner Prize 2018 Is Political, and We Shouldn't Be Surprised,' *Frieze*, 27 April 2018, accessed 9 April 3019, https://frieze.com/article/yes-turner-prize-2018-political-and-we-shouldnt-be-surprised.

54.   Fox, 'Yes the Turner Prize 2018 Is Political.'

55.   Ariella Azoulay, *The Civil Contract of Photography* (New York : Cambridge, Mass: Zone Books, MIT, 2012).

56.   Roberts, John, *Photography and Its Violations*, Kindle Edition (New York: Columbia University Press, 2014), 243/6041.

57.   Roberts, 250/6041.

58.   Viktor Shklovsky, 'Art as Technique,' in *Modern Criticism and Theory: A Reader*, ed. David Lodge, trans. Lee T. Lemon and Marion J. Reis (London: Longmans, 1988),16–30.

59.   Amy E. Arntson, *Graphic Design Basics*, 6th ed. (Boston, Mass.: CENGAGE Learning Custom Publishing, 2010), 74–6.

60.   Martin Kippenberger, Norman M. Klein, and Peter Noever, *Martin Kippenberger : The Last Stop West* (Ostfildern-Ruit, Germany: Cantz Verlag, 1999), 76.

61.   Lucy Watling, 'Martin Kippenberger: The Anti-Apartheid Drinking Congress with Kippenberger 1986,' *Tate*, accessed 1 June 2018, http://www.tate.org.uk/art/artworks/kippenberger-the-anti-apartheid-drinking-congress-with-kippenberger-p79104; Ann Goldstein and Lisa Gabrielle Mark, eds., *Martin Kippenberger: The Problem Perspective* (Los Angeles : Cambridge, Mass: The MIT Press, 2008), 350.

62.   Jutta Koether, 'A Cacophony for a Formidable Iconoclast,' *Tate Etc.*, Spring 2006, accessed 9 April 2019, http://www.tate.org.uk/context-comment/articles/cacophony-formidable-iconoclast, 36.

63.   'Battir Wins Case Against the Wall,' *Forensic Architecture*, 4 March 2015, accessed 9 April 2019, https://www.forensic-architecture.org/battir-wins-case-wall/.

64.   'Investigations,' *Forensic Architecture*, accessed 1 June 2019. https://www.forensic-architecture.org.

65.   Javier Pes, '"We Don't Consider Ourselves to Be Artists": Forensic

Architecture Reacts to Their Surprise Turner Prize Nod,' artnet News, 26 April 2018. Access 9 April, 219, https://news.artnet.com/exhibitions/turner-prize-nomination-forensic-architecture-1273889.

66.    Susan Sontag, *Regarding the Pain of Others* (London: Hamish Hamilton, 2003), 110.

67.    Sontag, *Regarding the Pain of Others,* 110.

68.    'Counter Investigations: Forensic Architecture,' *Institute of Contemporary Arts,* accessed 12 May 2018, https://www.ica.art/whats-on/season/counter-investigations-forensic-architecture.

69.    Phineas Harper, 'Forensic Architecture Winning the Turner Prize Would Risk Turning Sensitive Investigative Work into Insensitive Entertainment,' *Dezeen,* 4 May 2018, accessed 9 April, 2019, https://www.dezeen.com/2018/05/04/forensic-architecture-turner-prize-warning-phineas-harper/; Mania Oikonomou, '… activism @ Forensic Architecture @ ICA,' Architecture As…, 2 May 2018, accessed 9 April 2019, https://architectureas.wordpress.com/2018/05/02/activism-forensic-architecture-ica/.

70.    Douglas O. Linder, '"The Trials of Los Angeles Police Officers" in Connection with the Beating of Rodney King,' Famous Trials, 2019, accessed 9 April, 2019, http://www.famous-trials.com/lapd/584-home.

71.    'ICA | Counter Forensics,' Accessed 15 June 2019, https://www.ica.art/counter-forensics.

72.    Edwin Heathcote, 'Forensic Architecture — from Rubble and Ruins to Justice,' *Financial Times,* 6 March 2018, accessed 9 April 2019, https://www.ft.com/content/218bd9c0-212b-11e8-a895-1ba1f72c2c11.

73.    'The Grenfell Tower Fire,' *Forensic Architecture,* accessed 12 May 2018. https://www.forensic-architecture.org/case/grenfell-tower-fire/.

74.    O'Connell, Micheál. 'Art as "Artificial Stupidity",' Doctorate, University of Sussex, 2017. http://sro.sussex.ac.uk/67604/, 175–77.

75.    Bishop, *Artificial Hells,* 16.

76.    Bishop, *Artificial Hells,* 284.

# 2

# Voteauction: A Cautionary Tale

*Jeremy Pilcher*

The question is,' said Humpty Dumpty, 'which is to be master — that's all.'[1]

## Introduction

In the lead up to the 2000 presidential election ('Election') in the United States it seemed that voters were being offered the opportunity to buy and sell their votes through 'Voteauction,' which was an online site with the slogan, '[b]ringing democracy and capitalism closer together.'[2] As reported in the media at the time, responses to Voteauction varied between treating it as a prank which critiqued electoral practices, or a site to buy and sell votes.[3] In the context of this uncertainty, legal actions were commenced in order to bring the site to an end. However, it was argued that the work raised freedom of speech issues and should be protected under the First Amendment of the US Constitution.[4] Eventually the proceedings brought against Voteauction led to a declaration by those operating it that it was 'corporate legal art.'[5] In the context of such a declaration the work might appear to exemplify the oppositional nature of the relationship between the art and law by which the two spheres are typically characterized.[6] Yet, to do so would be to neglect the way in which responses to Voteauction oscillated. In the lead up to the Election, the location of the work on the internet disrupted the ability to contextualize it securely as an artistic joke. The networked real-time digital nature of Voteauction made it conceivable that the site would be used to trade votes both domestically and internationally.[7] Nevertheless, the technological aspect of Voteauction will not be my focus in this chapter.[8] Instead, I will engage with the significance of how, prior to its declaration as art, the work invited people to respond to it as either exclusively an opportunity to trade votes, or alternatively as a prank, but potentially also initially as a prank and then subsequently as an auction site. Approached in terms of this fluctuation the work opened the prospect of it bringing about a transfiguration of democracy in the United States.

The work's oscillation was undecidable in the sense that term is employed by Derrida, who states it 'is always a determinate oscillation between possibilities (for example, of meaning, but also of acts). These possibilities are themselves highly determined in strictly defined situations (for example, discursive—syntactical or rhetorical—but also political, ethical, etc.). They are pragmatically determined.'[9] In the context of the lead up to the Election, the choice opened by the ambiguity of *Voteauction* invited reflection on electoral practices, which of course included the possibility of buying and selling votes. Given the significance of elections for nation states, when understood in terms of the performative, the work had the potential to undermine democracy in the United States. As Hillis Miller has discussed, there are a variety of different meanings for the term 'performativity.'[10] In extremely brief terms, J.L. Austin coined the term 'performative' to account for the way it is possible to do something by saying something.[11] However, in this piece I deploy Derrida's theory, which understands performatives as being able to bring about 'an absolute rupture between the present and the past.'[12] Approached in this way, even if Voteauction was intended to be a prank by those running it, the work opened the prospect of democratic elections being undermined. In the process, its oscillation between interpretations invited those who encountered it to engage with the laws, values, and norms that frame democracy in the United States. Voteauction, in its current existence as art, is the transfigured call for a decision and the remainder of an encounter with the way in which the law structures experiences of the everyday.[13]

**The Legal Proceedings**

On 24 October 2000 CNN's 'Burden of Proof' programme was introduced by the co-host Roger Cossack as follows: 'In just two weeks, the citizens of the United States will elect their next commander-in-chief. But could that decision be rerouted over the Internet? A Website engineered halfway around the world is offering to literally buy your vote.'[14] Voteauction was taken seriously enough for '[s]everal US States (Missouri, Wisconsin, Chicago, Arizona, Nevada, California, Massachusetts, New York) [to issue] temporary restraining orders or injunctions for alleged illegal vote trading.'[15] In proceedings issued in

Cook County, Illinois, for example, Voteauction was alleged to be a site on which business, in the form of vote selling in the Election was being carried out contrary to state and federal laws.[16] In the CNN broadcast, Cossack described how, although the site had been shut down over the weekend as a result of the legal action, it was operating again but under a slightly different name. In the Illinois proceedings the plaintiffs, who included the Board of Election Commissioners of the City of Chicago, alleged that James Baumgartner created the site, which appeared on the Internet 'in or about August 2000.'[17] Baumgartner, a student in New York, apparently sold the rights to Voteauction when threatened with legal action. [18] By the time of the CNN broadcast the site was allegedly being operated by Hans Bernhard, who was described as 'an Austrian businessman.'[19]

In order to explain how it was possible to operate a business trading in votes, the proceedings provided a general description of the electoral system.[20] Under the Electoral College system in the United States, presidential electors would first be elected. They would then meet and vote for the nation's President and Vice President. After which, 'candidates for President and Vice President of the United States receiving the most electoral votes cast by electors in the various States would be declared elected.' The pleadings went on to describe how the availability of absentee ballots could be used to circumvent the prohibition against buying and selling votes [21] 'Wired' reported Baumgartner describing how a voter could register on-line with Voteauction and complete an absentee ballot.[22] He explained that an auction enabled by the site would then determine the voter's selection from the presidential candidates.[23] Voteauction would allow bidders to 'submit bids for a block of votes consisting of all the votes offered for sale in any particular state'[24] and 'when the time comes, whoever wins the auction decides who this group is going to vote for.'[25]

There was a lack of clarity over whether a successful bidder using Voteauction would be able to verify that purchased votes would be cast as specified. Initially Baumgartner seems to have planned that he would verify absentee votes were being used in accordance with the outcome of an auction.[26] However, once the site was being operated from Austria, the problem with that possibility was the practical issue of the delay associated with absentee votes being sent from, and then back to, the United States. [27] By the time of the Illinois proceedings, verification was apparently the responsibility of the winning bidder.[28] It seems the matter had not been resolved by mid October 2000 as Bernhard commented that it remained a problem although apparently he expected it to be resolved.[29] It has been suggested that this practical issue might, in practice, make concerns over the potential subversion of the electoral process by Voteauction redundant.[30] But, irrespective of whether the work ever managed to resolve the problem of verification, there were those who considered the measures taken to close down the site unnecessarily repressive.[31] Voteauction, variously described as a satire, parody, or being in jest, was argued to express a view critical of a decision by the Supreme Court refusing to accept limits on campaign spending as being unconstitutional.[32] In short, the site might be protected under the First Amendment because it was a twist on the critical evaluation of the permissibility of electoral practices, which range 'from the giving of large campaign contributions to legislative logrolling,' by comparing them to vote buying.[33]

The anxiety generated by Voteauction seems to have been exacerbated by the inconsistencies in the accounts from both Baumgartner and Bernhard about their motivations for the site. Initially Baumgartner said 'The clearest language is, we're selling votes.'[34] However, when faced with the prospect of legal action he is reported to have stressed that 'his site holds a mirror up to a largely corrupt electoral system.'[35] Bernhard framed the site in terms of a market for votes and commented that: 'The question of if it's a hoax, I can answer with a clear no,' before adding, '[i]t's very obvious, because we're not running projects like that to make hoaxes. We're running businesses.'[36] Yet, in the CNN programme, when Cossack had suggested to Bernhard 'perhaps, you weren't serious with this web site, that what you were trying to do was parody the American voting system and, perhaps the way it's financed. Was that your intent?' Bernhard was more evasive and replied, 'yes and no.'[37] The chair of the Voting Integrity Project, Deborah Phillips, who didn't believe the work was a satire, was quoted in 'Wired' as saying that, '[i]f it's true it's just been a hoax, then the only way they can prove that is to open their site to FBI technologists.'[38] In the same article Dan Stewart, a lawyer representing Baumgartner, said: 'That's exactly what we did. The FBI conducted an investigation.'[39] Yet, whatever the nature of that inquiry and its results, it seems the outcome was not made public.

The secret of whether Voteauction would have enabled people to buy and sell votes in the Election apparently remained unknown as it was forced to close down as the result of an Internet domain name denial of service.[40] On 6 November 2000, immediately prior to the election, a press release was issued stating 'our legal department is sure that all cases will be dropped after evidence can be revealed. Vote-auction does not sell or buy votes, vote-auction does not even solicit [sic] the buying or selling of votes.'[41] After listing the ongoing lawsuits and inquiries at the time, the press release went on to state: 'We finally have to consider this as corporate legal art! Our art department is considering an offer to do an exhibition in the SF MOMA, with exclusive legal documents.'[42] Voteauction has since been extensively exhibited as art at a variety of museums and won an Award of Distinction from Prix Arts Electronica 20005. These exhibitions have displayed '[V]ote-auction CNN tape, Voteauction-Seals and original legal Documents.'[43] As has been proposed, these documents should be regarded as 'an integral part of the project itself.' [44] Equally, however, Voteauction has been described as a 'genuine exchange system.'[45] My argument is that these documents are the precipitate of the project as it existed prior to the time it ceased to actively function online as an invitation to trade votes. As recognized art, the work is the remainder of the call for a decision rather than representing a preceding 'real' situation.[46] In the event that people who wished to auction votes were able to connect through the site, there is an important distinction to be drawn between the work as it operated prior to the Election and the closure of that situation following the domain name denial of service. As a point of exchange, Voteauction was a potential risk to democracy in the United States irrespective of the intentions of those operating the project.

## A Prank or a Vote Auction?

In a press release on 7 November 2000, Voteauction observed, '[i]f you think it is hard to know for sure if our site was a game or a business, well, then that's a good lesson you have learned. Try any website and try to check out if they are for "real".'[47] Yet, approached in terms of Derrida's account of the performative, a unilateral declaration by those responsible for the work could not, by itself, resolve this issue and determine that it would be responded to as art. The reason for this is central to the significance of the fluctuation by Voteauction between being a site at which votes might be auctioned or a 'real' prank. My argument begins with a discussion of 'readymade' art and one work in particular, 'Fountain.'[48] The artist, Marcel Duchamp, under the pseudonym Richard Mutt, submitted the work in 1917 for an art exhibition by the Society of Independent Artists in America.[49] It was a men's urinal turned on its side and placed on a plinth. As with Voteauction, at the time of its initial appearance, it seems unclear how Duchamp intended people would respond to it. A contemporary commentator, Louise Norton, is quoted as saying that there where those who 'anxiously ask, "Is he [Duchamp] serious or is he joking?" Perhaps he is both! Is it not possible?'[50] In any event, Fountain did not appear in the exhibition and it, as was the case with a number of earlier readymades, slipped 'back into the world of the everyday where they were used and discarded.'[51]

Benjamin Buchloh has identified how, after Duchamp, art could be understood in terms of 'a new aesthetic of the speech act ("this is a work of art if I say so").'[52] Yet, as Derrida has argued, an author's intentions are relevant but not determinative of the meaning and effect of such performative language.[53] Indeed, as Buchloh goes on to discuss, the work of the artist Robert Morris in the period from 1961–3, 'already pointed toward an understanding of Duchamp that transcended the limited definition of the readymade.'[54] Instead of a work of art being approached as the product of the artist's declaration, Morris presented it as 'the ultimate subject of a legal definition and the result of institutional validation.'[55] But, if an artist's declaration is not finally determinative of whether something is taken as art, then nor is its institutional recognition (or rejection). Although Fountain was not accepted into the Society of Independent Artists' exhibition it is now widely considered to be one of the most influential works of the twentieth century.[56] It may be understood as a work 'whose force of rupture produces the institution, the law itself, which is to say also the meaning that appears to, that ought to, or that appears to have to guarantee it in return.'[57] In other words, Fountain had a transformative effect on the art world irrespective of Duchamp's intent and despite the initial institutional response to it. Whilst Voteauction opened the prospect of being responded to as an artistic hoax, I am not suggesting that it had a transformative impact on the art world comparable to Fountain. Instead, I propose that its oscillation between being treated as either a prank or as enabling the creation of a vote market opened the possibility it would be used as an opportunity to disrupt the established electoral system. Approached from that perspective, the work threatened to transfigure democracy in the United States. Unsurprisingly, the response of the law was to regard the work as illegally facilitating the sale and purchase of votes.

It might be thought that a decision by the law as to the status of Voteauction, backed by its 'super performative' force, would bring any uncertainty around the work to an end.[58] However, approached through Derrida's account of the performative, 'the ostensibly greater force can also be the lesser' and so the project may still have had the potential to undermine the legal system.[59] This is because the law's on-going power, which is founded on a 'performative and interpretative violence,' is crucially 'not something that simply affects the origin of the law: it is not simply an exterior force which determines law, but rather a force internal to law.'[60] The law has no performative effect without being iterable.[61] Legal systems are enfolded by iterability as, 'every referent, all reality has the structure of a differential trace, and that one cannot refer to this "real" except in an interpretative experience. The latter neither yields meaning nor assumes it except in a movement of differential referring. That's all.'[62] This differential structure of reality, which Derrida calls *différance*, means that the repetition of some thing or event as itself 'ensures that the full presence of singularity thus repeated comports in itself the reference to something else, thus rendering the full presence that it nevertheless announces. This is why iteration is not simply repetition.'[63] The point is that in order for the law (of the United States) to have an ongoing legitimacy, 'the violence of the foundation must be repeatable, or rather iterable.' [64] But, simultaneously and inextricably, this brings with it the possibility of a breach in the legal system, which cannot be perpetuated without iterability.

Voteauction opened the prospect of a rupture in the electoral system before its domain name denial of service and declaration as art. Ulrich Mücke points out 'elections are very important for the idea of the nation state' because they are 'about defining the most basic foundation of the nation state. Elections define, for example, the borders of a nation state.'[65] Approached in performative terms, the creation and perpetuation of the United States and its legal system must be iterable.[66] But, crucially, this same feature means that there is no fixed, unchanging, 'pure identity.'[67] Understood in this way, in order for that nation to perpetuate—or iterate—itself in its current democratic form it must continue to hold elections as provided for by its electoral system. Iterability simultaneously and unavoidably means a democratic system is susceptible to change. The potential for Voteauction to have undermined democracy in the United States was inextricably bound up with the scope for a system that was more democratic to have been implemented. In general terms, the ambiguity of the work invited voters to engage both with the prospect of the perpetuation of democracy as well as its subversion. More specifically, if citizens had decided to take the project seriously it could have been used to undermine the existing democratic system; but understood as a parody or joke the work could have been protected by the First Amendment under the very system it might undermine.[68]

Voteauction had a parasitic relationship to the legal framework of the United States. It had no meaningful existence without that country's electoral laws and yet, by potentially facilitating the creation of a market for votes, it posed a threat to the democracy that had enacted the laws by which that nation was also protected.[69] To understand the work as inviting a negative comparison between vote buying and legal campaign financing strategies employed in the United States was one way of approaching this dynamic.[70] However, to the extent the work did so, it unsettled the persuasive force of this very method for deciding what amounts to an acceptable electoral strategy. The point may be illustrated by an exchange during the CNN broadcast. Van Susteren asked Bill Wood, Chief Counsel, Secretary of State of California, how Voteauction differed from a scenario in which, 'you give your $1,000 campaign contribution on November sixth and November eighth you show up at your Congressman's office and say: "Remember me? I'm a big contributor. I would like to talk to you about some project? How is that different?"'[71] Wood responded, 'Well, it's absolutely different because it's fundamentally different.'[72] This tautologous response exemplifies the difficulties there may be in framing precisely what electoral strategies should be (il)legal and why. The problem in trying to determine the validity of an electoral practice by looking at how similar it is to vote-buying is that, as exemplified by Wood's response, it, 'fails to provide an explicit standard for assessing the relevant similarities between core and non-core vote buying.'[73] In this respect, *Voteauction* made it more difficult for those who encountered the work to unquestioningly fall back on the inheritance of an electoral system in which vote selling is illegal.[74]

When analyzing whether a particular electoral tactic is acceptable by comparison to buying votes the difficulties are particularly acute in relation to campaign promises.[75] There is, as mentioned earlier, case law authority in the United States to the effect that limits on political donations amount to an impermissible curb on freedom of political speech under the First Amendment. However, as Hasen has identified, the answer to the question of whether any given vote buying practice (e.g. logrolling; payment for turnout) should be legal may be unclear or even negative, depending on which criterion is used to analyse matters.[76] In the context of this piece there is only the scope to observe that Hasen identifies that there are some campaign promises and contributions that might be regarded as 'virtually indistinguishable from core vote buying.'[77] It was recognized in the media that some voters might have understood Voteauction either exclusively as a prank or, in the alternative, as a marketplace for votes. However, it does not seem unimaginable that some voters may have regarded buying and selling votes with repugnance but still have decided to use the site to buy and sell votes.[78] In other words, voters might have understood the project as being intended to provoke a critical stance but then, for a range of potential reasons, could have seized upon it as a means to use the Election as an opportunity to act against the electoral system.[79] Indeed, when presented with Voteauction, the fact it appeared to be a hoax may have incited some voters to decide not to act in accordance with the legal and the social norms and values which currently guard democracy in the United States. The performative outcome of such individually taken decisions might then have had (even if unintentionally) a collective effect that resulted in a transfiguration of the political foundation of the USA. Of course, after the point at which *Voteauction* was no longer actively operating online no such disruption would have been possible.

## The Aporia of the Demos

The potential implications of voters seeing the project as creating a vote market may be explored through an exchange during the CNN 'Burden of Proof' programme. Van Susteren asked Bernhard, 'What is the purpose of your website, then? What does it—does it broker votes? What's the purpose?' Bernhard replied, 'we have free speech here and we don't see why this weakness of democracy. Why can't we attach capitalistic principles to this kind of voting industry which is currently going on?'[80] In response it might be observed that the freedom of the people to do whatever they want in a democracy is 'unthinkable without equality, since the plurality of people only can constitute themselves as an entity if everyone is equally free.'[81] In modern democracies the prohibition against buying and selling votes is one example of a range of restrictions on freedom that are widely accepted in order to promote equality (of voting power). It is generally accepted that vote markets would compromise democracy because of wealth inequalities. Importantly, 'Derrida does not deny that the two principles [freedom and equality] are contradictory, but he emphasizes that the contradiction is irresolvable and constitutive of democracy.'[82] Approached in such terms, it's necessary to appreciate that in a democracy 'the people (*demos*) have the power (*kratos*) to govern themselves,' and it may only protect itself (i.e. democratic equality) from the threat that this freedom implies by attacking itself.[83] In short, democracy is autoimmune. Paradoxically, it follows from this that restrictions on freedom are productive of democracy: 'Freedom is compromised by equality, and the equality is compromised by freedom, but without such compromise there can be no democracy.'[84] Framed in this way the critical impact of Voteauction extended beyond, 'revealing and questioning underlying assumptions at the interface of business and society.'[85] The questions generated by the work in relation to democracy in the United States became: what freedoms; what equalities?

Approached in terms of autoimmunity, there is no 'right measure' in a democracy between freedom and equality.[86] Voteauction opened the prospect that voters would make a decision about how to use their vote from the perspective that '[t]here is no absolute paradigm, ... no idea of democracy.' [87] From such a standpoint, a pragmatic response to the asymmetries of power brought about by legal election tactics might be that it should, or perhaps could only, be opposed by auctioning votes. In the event the work had been understood and protected by the law in terms of freedom of expression, the prospect of this risk would have been constitutionally protected. As such, Voteauction potentially posed a threat to the sovereignty of the USA. During 'Burden of Proof' Bernhard said, 'we'll find legal ways in order to bring this market to the American people, but also to other people in the whole world.'[88] Given that the project was situated online it opened the prospect of a global market in presidential votes, which would have undermined the borders that unify and confine the plurality of the USA. It is necessary for a sovereign nation state to have boundaries because 'the power of the people can only constitute itself by drawing a border that defines who does and does not belong to "the people."'[89] The closure brought by the borders of a nation state is required by the *demos* to ensure effective rule. The laws of any given nation state that are enacted to ensure this, and so bring about its perpetuation, will always necessarily involve some form of violent exclusion. Yet, this simultaneously destroys the very multiplicity that underpins the formation of democracy.

Understood in terms of autoimmunity, Voteauction gestured towards the way in which 'the inherited concept of democracy is the only one that welcomes the possibility of being contested, of contesting itself, of criticizing and indefinitely improving itself' but at the same time this promise is always already riven by the prospect of its corruption. The work invited those who encountered it to reflect on how democracy can never be fully present whilst also simultaneously and unavoidably it 'risks and must always risk being perverted into a threat.'[90] It 'remains impossible because of the aporia of the demos.'[91] The demos is comprised of people, who are to be understood simultaneously as citizens equal 'before the law, the social bond of being together' but also in terms of the 'incalculable singularity of anyone, before any "subject," the possible undoing of the social bond by a secret to be respected, beyond all citizenship, beyond every "state," indeed every "people".' [92] This aporia is irreducible and without it there would be no prospect of democracy improving itself, but equally an acknowledgement is necessitated that it may also be entirely subverted. In the context of the role elections have for the perpetuation of nation states, my argument is that the Voteauction may ultimately be understood to have been an invitation to voters to decide whether, in the 'course of human events,' it had become 'necessary for one people to dissolve the political bands which have connected them with one another.'[93] From this perspective the work invited established norms and laws regarding the compromises inherent in the electoral system of the United States to be interrogated and, potentially, re-affirmed or undermined. This call for a decision regarding the nature of the existence of the United States as a democracy ceased with the end of its undecidable oscillation. At that point the site was declared as corporate legal art and subsequently received various artistic awards.[94]

## Conclusion

In parasitizing the electoral system, Voteauction fluctuated between being responded to by voters as a prank, and as a site from which to trade votes. This alternation is reflected in the observation that 'the project is not "political" in the sense that normally applies to political art or activism. [V]ote Auction does not condemn, protest against something. All it does is give rise to a very ambiguous, dynamic situation, and sustain its position consistently right to the end.'[95] Framed in terms of a 'determinate oscillation between possibilities' that was enabled by its online location in the lead up to the Election the project did not overtly prescribe or advocate a specific politics.[96] But, as Derrida has argued, 'situations characterized by undecidability demand a decision.'[97] Approached in these terms, Voteauction participated in what Richard Beardsworth has called the 'political as the instance of judgment.'[98] In this regard, even if the work had initially been responded to as a hoax, it might subsequently have been taken as an opportunity to participate in a market for votes. As illustrated by the legal proceedings, there were those who elected to treat the work seriously as having the potential to undermine the existence of the United States as a sovereign nation state rather than as a parody or prank protected under the Constitution.

Whilst the work invited voters to think about the contingency of the electoral system, that does not mean it proposed the dissolution of democracy in the United States.[99] Nevertheless, a failure to close down Voteauction would have left the possibility open that citizens would have responded to it as an opportunity to buy and sell votes. This implied the prospect of the nation's democratic electoral system being undermined. Approached in these terms, the project invited reflection on the way in which a democracy may, in enabling and protecting the democratic freedoms of its citizens, bring about the possibility of both its improvement but also its own subversion and destruction.

The legal proceedings had the effect of preempting the possibility of citizens deciding to use the site to engage with the electoral system in the United States by selling their votes. Whilst protective of the country's democratic framework, the law's stance may be criticized as having been incompatible with the freedom of expression of its voters. The call for a decision opened by *Voteauction* drew attention to the way in which the promise of democracy is inseparably fractured by the prospect it may be subverted. Approached in terms of autoimmunity, the problem exemplified by the work may seem intractable given there are no absolute parameters for a democratic relationship between freedom and power. However, as Hasen argues, illegal core vote buying may be distinguished from other legal strategies by 'delineating how targeted and enforceable the campaign promise must be before it crosses the line into illegal vote buying.'[100] Voteauction could have been responded to as a platform from which to trade votes. However, this would have had the effect of more tightly constraining the future of the United States to a 'past embodied and reproduced in the present' than was the case with the existing contentious (but legal) electoral practices.[101] Such a decision would have preferred a strategy that more narrowly constrained the future, and been even more inconsistent with keeping open the promise of democracy, than other tactics that were being used in the Election. Voteauction, which now exists as art, marks the site of an oscillation that opened the opportunity for people to examine their established (legal) norms and values. The project is what now remains of an exploitation of the fissure in democracy, which called for a decision as to whether democracy as it exists in the United States would be affirmed and so perpetuated. Voteauction invited voters to reflect on how the law frames such an inheritance and the way, and extent to which, the United States as a nation state was, and is, open to the undecidability of the future.[102]

## Notes

1.      Lewis Carroll, *Alice's Adventures in Wonderland and Through the Looking-Glass* (London: Penguin Classics, 1998), 186.

2.      The work exists as art online at *[V]ote-auction*, http://vote-auction. net/, accessed 13 February 2019. The name has appeared in various forms and it will be referred to throughout this piece as *Voteauction*. The Election took place on Tuesday, 7 November 2000.

3.      *Voteauction* is also referred to as a 'satire' or 'parody.' Christine Harold, 'Pranking Rhetoric: "Culture Jamming" as Media Activism,' *Critical Studies in Media Communication* 21/3 (2004), 194, contrasts pranksters with parodists and my use of 'prank' is inspired by her affiliation of the term with comedians who 'diagnose a specific situation, and try something to see what responses they can provoke.' This is evoked by the description of the work as a 'jest' by Doug Kellner, a representative on the New York City Board of Elections, 'Voteauction Bids the Dust,' *Wired,* 22 August 2000, accessed 15 November 2018, https://www.wired.com/2000/08/voteauction-bids-the-dust/, or as a 'hoax,' by Deborah Phillips, chair of the Voting Integrity Project, 'Selling votes or peddling lies?' *Wired,* 30 October 2000, accessed 15 November 2018, https://www.wired.com/2000/10/selling-votes-or-peddling-lies/.

4.      U.S. Const. amend. I. Stuart Biegel, a participant in CNN's 'Burden of Proof' programme, observed for example that, whilst selling votes is not legal, 'in reality, this could just be a form of satire or street theatre, and if so, arguably protected under the First Amendment.' The rush transcript of 'Bidding for Ballots: Democracy on the Block' of the CNN programme 'Burden of Proof' ('Transcript'), *Ubermorgen*, accessed 8 May 2018, http://ubermorgen. com/vote_auction_cnn_transcript.txt.

5.      'Press Release,' *Voteauction*, 6 November 2000, accessed 9 May 2018, www.vote-auction.net/ARCHIVE/02_PRESS/00_PRESS_ RELEASES/06_11_2000/va_press_release_061100.doc.

6.      Costas Douzinas, 'Whistler v. Ruskin: Law's Fear of Images,' *Art History*, 19/3 (1996), 353–69; Costas Douzinas and Lynda Nead, 'Introduction' in *Law and the Image*, eds. Douzinas and Nead, (Chicago, Chicago University Press, 1999); Daniel McClean, ed., *The Trials of Art* (London, Ridinghouse, 2007).

7.      Corey Sparks makes the point that the involvement of international interests in the domestic politics of the United States is not a hypothetical issue. In Corey R. Sparks, 'Foreigners United: Foreign Influence in American Elections After Citizens United v. Federal Election Commission,' *Cleveland State Law Review* 62/245 (2014), 246 he refers to *Supreme Court in Citizens United v Federal Election Commission* 588 U.S. 310 (2010) and observes, it 'has resulted in the ability of foreign entities to circumvent a Congressional ban that prohibits any foreign national from contributing, donating, or spending funds in connection with ... election in the United States,' 247.

8.    There is not the scope to discuss the issues around the impact of digital technologies on societies in terms of writers such as Lev Manovich, *The Language of New Media* (Cambridge, Mass. and London: MIT Press, 2001); Marshall McLuhan, *Understanding Media: The Extensions of Man* (New York: McGraw-Hill, 1964); and Harold Innis, *The Bias of Communication* (Toronto: University of Toronto Press, 1951). In terms of its status as so-called 'new media art' it raises issues regarding the relationship between art and systems that may be approached through Jack Burnham in *Beyond Modern Sculpture: The Effects of Science and Technology on the Sculpture of this Century* (New York, George Braziller, 1968); *Great Western Salt Works: Essays on the Meaning of Post-Formalist Art* (New York: George Braziller, 1973).

9.    Jacques Derrida, *Limited Inc* (Evanston, Illinois: Northwestern University Press, 1988), 148.

10.    J. Hillis Miller, 'Performativity as Performance / Performativity as Speech Act: Derrida's Special Theory of Performativity,' *South Atlantic Quarterly* 106/2 (Spring, 2007), 220.

11.    J.L. Austin, *How to Do Things with Words*, eds. J.O Urmson and Marin Sbisà, 2nd ed. (Oxford: Oxford University Press, 1980), cited by Miller in 'Performativity as Performance,' 226.

12.    Miller, 'Performativity as Performance,' 219, 231. Derrida, *Limited Inc.*

13.    My use of 'transfigured' is inspired by Arthur Danto, *The Transfiguration of the Commonplace: A Philosophy of Art* (Cambridge, Mass. & London: Harvard University Press, 1981).

14.    Transcript. An online video of the programme is available, accessed 8 May 2018, https://vimeo.com/19218313.

15.    *Voteauction,* http://vote-auction.net/.

16.    Documents relating to the proceedings issued in the Circuit Court of Cook County by the Board of Election Commissioners of the City of Chicago are available from the *Voteauction* site, accessed 8 May 2018, http://vote-auction.net/VOTEAUCTION/2000_LEGAL_DOCUMENTS/CHICAGO_ILLINOIS/207.70.85.119/> .

17.    Complaint for Declaratory Judgment, Injunction and Other Relief ('Complaint'), paragraph 24, accessed 15 May 2018, http://vote-auction.net/VOTEAUCTION/2000_LEGAL_DOCUMENTS/CHICAGO_ILLINOIS/207.70.85.119/complaint.htm.

18.    'Brief Statement of Relevant Facts' in the 'Memorandum of Law in Support of Emergency Motion for Temporary Restraining Order or Preliminary Injunction' ('Memorandum'), 8 May 2018, http://vote-auction.net/VOTEAUCTION/2000_LEGAL_DOCUMENTS/CHICAGO_ILLINOIS/207.70.85.119/memorandumoflaw.htm. Also Ronna Abramson, 'Want to Sell Your Vote? Not so Fast' *Slate*, 14 October 2000, accessed 8 May 2018, http://www.slate.com/articles/news_and_politics/net_election/2000/10/want_to_sell_your_vote_not_so_fast.html.

19.    The proceedings do not refer to Ubermorgen.com, which is an artist duo of Lizvlx and Hans Bernhard that acquired *Voteauction* from Baumgartner; see Domenico Quaranta, 'Ubermorgen.com. The Future is Now' in *Ubermorgen.com*, ed. Domenico Quaranta (Brescia, fpeditions, 2009), 67. *Wired* reported that Baumgartner had disclosed the sale had been 'brokered by the corporate satire collective RTMark,' 'Selling Votes Or Peddling Lies?' Information on Ubermorgen.com and RTMark is readily available online, for example: 'RT Mark,' *Media Art Net*, accessed 15 May 2018, http://www.medienkunstnetz.de/works/tmark/.

20.    Jamin B. Raskin, *Overruling Democracy: The Supreme Court vs. The American People* (New York & London: Routledge, 2004).

21.    Complaint, paragraph 20. It was said that officials in Chicago were particularly sensitive about the issued given that there had been complaints of absentee ballot tampering in elections of aldermen in 1995 which had 'prompted the elections board to survey 5 percent of absentee votes to ensure there [was] no fraud,' Abramson, 'Want To Sell Your Vote? Not So Fast.'

22.    'Close Vote? You Can Bid On It,' *Wired*, 17 August 2000, accessed 15 November 2018, https://www.wired.com/2000/08/close-vote-you-can-bid-on-it/.

23.    'Close Vote? You Can Bid On It,' *Wired*.

24.    Complaint, paragraph 28.

25.    'Close Vote? You Can Bid On It,' *Wired*.

26.    Baumgartner would 'tell those people you should vote for this person. Then they fill in the form, and then they send it to me. And I just verify that they're voting for the correct person.' 'Close Vote? You Can Bid On It,' *Wired*.

27.    Bernhard elaborated that 'They may have send in their absentee ballots for verification, they may have the voters take photographs inside the voting booth, or they go to the honor system that is the system that many vote-purchasing endeavours have used in the past.'

28.    Complaint. Paragraph 31. Also 'Austrian Takes Bids on US Votes,' *Wired*, 6 September 2000, accessed 15 November 2018, https://www.wired.com/2000/09/austrian-takes-bids-on-u-s-votes/.

29.    Abramson, 'Want To Sell Your Vote? Not So Fast.'

30.    Anthony Sanders, 'In Defence of Vote Buying: How "Nader Traders" Can Defeat Rent Seeking' *Hamline Journal of Public Law & Policy* 26 /43 (2004), 43–72, 55.

31.    Transcript, *Ubermorgen*, for example, comments by Stuart Biegel.

32.    *Buckley v Valeo*, 424 U.S. 1, 48–9 (1976) and Raskin, *Overruling Democracy*, 139. In 'Close Vote? You Can Bid on It,' Raskin said the site might be able to test the 'Supreme Court's 1976 "money equals speech" ruling.'

33.    U.S. Const. amend. I, and see Richard L. Hasen, 'Vote Buying' *California Law Review* 88/5 (2000), 1326 who describes one way of analysing whether a practice, 'should be illegal, legal but discouraged, or encouraged?' is by asking 'how similar the given practice is to core vote buying.' If it 'is similar

enough to core vote buying, it should be illegal.' The practice of logrolling involves one legislator effectively 'buying' another legislator's vote on one piece of legislation in exchange for her vote on a different piece of legislation, 1338. In 'Voteauction.net: Protected Political Speech or Treason' *J. High Tech. L.* 5/357 (2005), 361, Murray observes that '[w]hile the Supreme Court decided in *Buckley* that campaign spending limits were unconstitutional, years later, in *Brown v Hartlage*, they differentiated between campaign spending and actual vote purchasing and held states could enact laws proscribing the purchase and sale of votes.'

34.   'Close Vote? You Can Bid On It,' *Wired.*

35.   'Voteauction Bids the Dust,' *Wired.*

36.   'Selling Votes Or Peddling Lies?', *Wired.*

37.   Transcript, *Ubermorgen.*

38.   'Selling votes or peddling lies?', *Wired.* The Voting Integrity Project apparently followed the *Voteauction* story from its early days in August 2000. Phillips remarks included the observation that, 'Satire doesn't usually involve the exchange of money, nor does it usually cross international boundaries or involve international security threats.'

39.   'Selling votes or peddling lies?', *Wired.*

40.   Murray, 'Voteauction.net,' 368: 'Vote-auction's Internet domain name administrators buckled under the legal pressure from the governmental authorities, and on October 21, 2000, DomainBank.com forced Vote-auction to close.'

41.   Press release, *Voteauction*, 6 November 2000, accessed 9 May 2018, www.vote-auction.net/ARCHIVE/02_PRESS/00_PRESS_RELEASES/06_11_2000/va_press_release_061100.doc.

42.   SF MOMA stands for San Francisco Museum of Modern Art.

43.   *Voteauction.*

44.   Quaranta, *Ubermorgen.com*, 6. In this regard, a contrast may be drawn between the artwork as it now exists and its operation prior to the Election as 'tactical media,' which involves understanding it as a dynamic system rather than as a 'static object,' and 'emphasizes viewer experience and engagement,' Rita Raley, *Tactical Media* (Minneapolis and London, University of Minnesota Press, 2009), 12. The possibility of such direct connections is a matter discrete from the issue of verification. Also compare the vote-swapping sites that were created during the Election, which are discussed in, for example, Jamin B. Raskin, *Overruling Democracy* (London & New York, Routledge, 2004).

45.   Alessandro Ludovico, ed., *Ubermorgen.com: Media Hacking vs. Conceptual Art* (Basel: Christoph Merian Verlag, 2009), 66.

46.   Richard Beardsworth, *Derrida & the Political* (London & New York, Routledge, 1996), 12.

47.   Press release, *Voteauction*, 7 November 2000, accessed 15 November 2018, www.voteauction.net/ARCHIVE/02_PRESS/00.../07.../

press_release_071100.pdf.

48.   The term 'readymade,' is defined, for example, by Tate Modern on its website as having been 'first used by French artist Marcel Duchamp to describe the works of art he made from manufactured objects. It has since often been applied more generally to artworks by other artists made in this way.' 'Art term: readymade,' *Tate*, accessed 2 February 2019, https://www.tate.org.uk/art/art-terms/r/readymade.

49.   Louise Norton, *The Blind Man*, No. 2, May 1917,6, accessed 15 November 2018, https://monoskop.org/images/6/6f/The_Blind_Man_2_May_1917.pdf.

50.   Norton, *The Blind Man*, 5.

51.   Martha Buskirk, *The Contingent Object of Contemporary Art* (Cambridge, Mass., The MIT Press, 2003), 68.

52.   Benjamin H.D. Buchloh, 'Conceptual Art 1962–1969: From the Aesthetic of Administration to the Critique of Institutions,' *October 55* (1990), 116.

53.   As a result of the breaching and dividing of the self-presence of intentions, iterability 'leaves us no choice but to mean (to say) something that is (already, always, also) other than what we mean (to say),' Jacques Derrida, *Limited Inc.* (Evanston, Northwestern University Press, 1988), 62. But this does not prevent 'a relative stability of the dominant interpretation (including the "self"-interpretation) of the text being commented upon,'143.

54.   Buchloh, 'Conceptual Art 1962–1969,' 116.

55.   Buchloh, 'Conceptual Art 1962–1969,' 117.

56.   The literature on Duchamp, readymades, and *Fountain* is extensive. One readily accessible account of the work is, 'Marcel Duchamp: Fountain,' *Tate*, accessed 2 February 2019, https://www.tate.org.uk/art/artworks/duchamp-fountain-t07573.

57.   Jacques Derrida, *Spectres of Marx* (New York & London: Routledge, 1994), 31.

58.   Julie Stone Peters, 'Legal Performance Good and Bad,' *Law, Culture and the Humanities* 4 (2008), 179–200, 185. Jacques Derrida, *Limited Inc.*, 149–50: 'Once there is the exercise of force in the determination and imposition of meaning, and first of all in the stabilizing determination of a context, it is inevitable there be some form of repression.'

59.   Derrida, *Limited Inc.*, 149. Of course, in this respect democracy is not only protected by the law but also by 'wider processes, tendencies, and dynamics,' such as the wider social condemnation of vote buying. Susan Marks, 'False Contingency,' *Current Legal Problems* 62/1 (2009), 17. I have discussed how installation art may invite awareness of the false necessity of norms and the way in which both legal and artistic frameworks may constrain challenges to established values in 'State Britain and the Art of (Im)proper Democratic Protest,' *Law, Culture and Humanities*, Pre-published January 1, 2016. DOI: 10.1177/1743872115625433.

60.   Margaret Davies, 'Derrida and Law: Legitimate Fictions,' in *Jacques Derrida and the Humanities: A Critical Reader*, ed. Tom Cohen (Cambridge, Cambridge University Press, 2001), 226.

61.   J Hillis Miller, 'Performativity as Performance / Performativity as Speech Act,' 229.

62.   Derrida, *Limited Inc.,*148.

63.   Derrida, *Limited Inc.,*129.

64.   Davies, 'Derrida and Law: Legitimate Fictions,' 226.

65.   Ulrich Mücke, 'Section Comment: Elections and Euro-American Modernity' in *Constitutional Cultures: On the Concept and Representation of Constitutions in the Atlantic World*, eds., Silke Hensel et al. (Newcastle upon Tyne, Cambridge Scholars Publishing, 2012), 453. And in the same volume, regarding inclusion and exclusion due to elections, also see Hedwig Richter, 'Discipline and Elections: Registration of Voters in the USA,' 427–28.

66.   '[T]he founding act of an institution – the act as archive as well as the act as performance—*must maintain within itself the signature*,' Jacques Derrida, 'Declaration of Independence,' in *Negotiations: Interventions and Interviews 1971-2001*, ed. Elizabeth Rottenberg (Stanford, Stanford University Press, 2002), 48. 'In order to function, that is, to be readable, a signature must have a repeatable, iterable, imitable form; it must be able to be detached from the present and singular intention of its production.' Derrida, *Limited Inc.*, 20.

67.   Derrida, *Limited Inc.,*76.

68.   In short, the oscillation of *Voteauction* directed attention to the undecidable relation 'between the general and the singular,' which translates the iterability of the law, see Beardsworth, *Derrida & the Political,* 25.

69.   Hasen describes how although 'explicit vote buying in political elections,' which he terms 'core vote buying,' is widely considered to be unacceptable there is disagreement on 'the underlying rationales for its prohibition;' Hasen, 'Vote Buying,' 1326.

70.   Hasen, 'Vote Buying,' 1325–6.

71.   Transcript, *Ubermorgen.*

72.   Transcript, *Ubermorgen.*

73.   Hasen, 'Vote Buying,' 1326.

74.   In this respect, *Voteauction* tended to unsettle, 'the realm of sedimented practices;' Chantal Mouffe, 'Artistic Activism and Agonistic Spaces,' *Art and Research* 1/2 (Summer, 2007), 1-5, 2. accessed 17 February 2019, http://www.artandresearch.org.uk/v1n2/mouffe.html Although, as Hasen notes, 'Despite current law, vote buying has a long, if ignoble, history in the United States;' Hassen, 'Vote Buying,' 1327.

75.   Hasen, 'Vote Buying,' 1359–64.

76.   Hasen, 'Vote Buying,' 1368–71.

77.   Hasen, 'Vote Buying,' 1359. He describes the decision in *Brown v Hartlage*, which dealt with the situation in which 'a candidate for county commissioner promised to return to the public treasury part of his salary if

elected' as being without 'much analytic clarity,' 1360.

78.   In doing so it puts into issue responsibility for the continuation of a democratic nation state. As regards responsibility, see Rosalyn Diprose, 'Derrida and the Extraordinary Responsibility of Inheriting the Future-to-come' 16 /3 (2006), Social Semiotics, 441.

79.   In broad terms the same sort of perspective may account for the online sites that facilitated vote-swapping in a variety of different forms. See *Porter v Bowen* 496 F. 3d 1009 (9th Cir. 2007) for a decision holding that there was a violation of First Amendment rights when William (Bill) Jones, who was at the time California Secretary of State, threatened a vote-swapping site with criminal prosecution.

80.   Transcript, *Ubermorgen*.

81.   Martin Hägglund, *Radical Atheism: Derrida and the Time of Life* (Stanford, Stanford University Press, 2008), 172.

82.   Hägglund, *Radical Atheism*, 173.

83.   Hägglund, *Radical Atheism*, 172.

84.   Hägglund, *Radical Atheism*, 173.

85.   Constance Kampf, 'Art Interrupting Business, Business Interrupting Art' in *Cyberactivism on the Participatory Web,* ed. Martha McCaughey (Abingdon & New York, Routledge, 2014), 163.

86.   Hägglund, *Radical Atheism*, 174.

87.   Jacques Derrida, *Rogues* (Stanford, Stanford University Press, 2003/2005), 37,62.

88.   Transcript, *Ubermorgen*.

89.   Hägglund, *Radical Atheism,*175.

90.   Jacques Derrida, 'Autoimmunity: Real and Symbolic Suicides—A Dialogue with Jacques Derrida,' in *Philosophy in a Time of Terror: Dialogues with Jurgen Habermas and Jacques Derrida,* ed. Giovanna Borradori (Chicago and London: University of Chicago Press, 2003), 120.

91.   Derrida, 'Autoimmunity,' 120.

92.   Derrida, 'Autoimmunity,' 120.

93.   Jacques Derrida, 'Declarations of Independence,' 51 where he quotes from the *incipit* of the Declaration of Independence (US 1776).

94.   Approached in terms of the performative after Derrida, there was no guarantee the work would be responded to as art even after the declaration by Ubermorgen.com.

95.   Domenico Quaranta, *Ubermorgen.com* (Brescia: fpeditions, 2009), 6.

96.   Derrida, *Limited Inc.*, 148.

97.   Sokoloff, 'Between Justice and Legality: Derrida on Decision.' *Political Research Quarterly*. 58/2 (June, 2005), 345.

98.   Beardsworth, *Derrida & the Political*, 40. *Voteauction* invited people to attend to the way that 'Every form of art has a political dimension' because it either perpetuates or critiques the 'reproduction of the given common sense.' Chantal Mouffe et al., 'Every Form of Art Has a Political Dimension,' *Grey*

*Room*, 2 (Winter, 2001), 100.

99.   Sokoloff, 'Between Justice and Legality,' 343.

100.  Hasen, 'Vote Buying,' 1363–4.

101.  Diprose, 'Derrida and the Extraordinary Responsibility,' 438, citing Nietzsche, *On the genealogy of morals and ecce homo*, trans. W. Kaufmann and R.J. Hollingdale (New York: Random House, 1967). As mentioned earlier, the vote-swapping (or vote-pairing) referred to earlier may be understood as a response to entrenched political interests invested in existing boundaries of the individual states and the established electoral system.

102.  Approached in terms of Beardsworth, *Derrida & the Political*, 20–4, *Voteauction* might be said to open the possibility of a less violent decision but contrast this with Hägglund, *Radical Atheism*, 170-1 who argues this is 'untenable, since all judgments must endure the experience of a violent economy.'

# 3

# ConsumeHastaMorir: Seventeen Years of Experimenting with the Legal Side of Subvertising

*Isidro Jiménez Gómez and Mariola Olcina Alvarado*

In May 2002, as activists from Ecologistas en Acción, the Spanish grassroots confederation of environmental groups, we congregated to discuss consumer society and its ways of communicating to and seducing citizens. We were a group of ten young people who wanted to do something exciting and maybe different. We discovered how organized groups in the USA, Canada, and France use advertising as communication in different ways, especially through modifying it in order to criticize consumer society. This type of communication, and our practice since that time, is known as culture jamming and subvertising (in English), antipub (licitaire) (in French) or contrapublicidad (in Spanish).

Advertising is the most powerful tool to communicate antisocial values. It is based on a monologue where nobody can answer. Subvertising seems to us to be the perfect way to start responding and to start a necessary dialogue. First, we needed our own space to communicate, so we created a website to upload our subvertisements (hereafter also referred to as subverts), all of which were intuitive and 'handmade.' Each one of those works was the result of our own learning process about consumer society, overconsumption, overproduction, as well as a fun and creative way to brainstorm collectively for the first time.

Seventeen years later, our records contain over 500 subverts, some books, a sixty-minute documentary, which has been viewed by over half a million viewers,[1] as well as approximately 250 poster exhibitions around Spain. During these years, we have learned much. Part of this learning was in unexpected areas, such as Intellectual Property (IP) Law. Now we know, for example, the difference between modifying the logo of a known brand as an artist and doing the same as a social group.

Knowing the laws that regulate the activities we do seems essential, especially when you are doing something as undefined and legally questionable as subvertising. What follows is our reflection on our subvertising practice over seventeen years in relation to its legal aspects.

## Subvertising and IP Law

In 1994, there was an alternative summit in Madrid called 50 años bastan (50 years are enough) in protest against the official summit by World Bank (WB) and the International Monetary Fund (IMF) that was taking place in the city. That event was a precursor to the anti-globalization movement that managed to endanger the World Trade Organization (WTO) Summit in Seattle in 1999. As the anti-globalization movement took shape and the most avant-garde institutional art approached it.[2] Nowadays, the influence of this movement is clearly visible in many museums and artistic institutions.

In fact, back in the 1990s, the Barcelona Museum of Contemporary Art (MACBA) called the artistic group La Fiambrera Obrera to organize some workshops with the presence of the British group Reclaim the streets and the international independent news network Indymedia.[3] All of them were social groups that mixed art with anti-globalization messages, and had achieved enough media coverage in those years. But what was supposed to be another artistic event coalesced with the social response to the summit in Barcelona and led to an unusual experiment: counterculture became, for a few months, counter-politics, and the MACBA became a media centre and artistic laboratory of the anti-globalization movement. This was a period of historical significance between the avant-garde world of the counterculture and the heterogeneous social platforms of the time. Driven by progressive political ideologies, artists were willing to collaborate with social movements and associations who were increasingly aware that access to the media was a key factor in their struggle.

ConsumeHastaMorir is the inheritor of that happy but unstable connection between risk and the need to report on the problems of consumer capitalism, which is based on infinite resources and the unlimited growth of demand. In addition, after all these years of subvertising, we realized that it is a link between the anti-consumerist movement and communication for social change. Since the 1980s, the link between counterculture and social activism has been forging an identity of its own, but not only as a critic of consumer society and its forms of expression. The Billboard Liberation Front (BLF), Reclaim the

Streets, Adbusters, The Yes Men, Casseurs de Pub, Yomango, Projecto Squatters, ConsumeHastaMorir, and other groups around the world have come together in the critique of the ideological role of advertising and, at the same time, they maintain a commitment to linguistic experimentation and expressive provocation. We wanted to openly challenge the monologue of commercial billboards, the advertising of supermarkets or the mass media. We wanted to reconquer its language across cities, on television, in spots, as pop art did years ago.[4]

However, the social imaginary, that space where different perspectives of reality converge in a polemic way, has rules that favour the most powerful people around the world. And this is not just a matter of economic power. We believe that IP laws, animated in their origin by the Renaissance ideal of creation and the romantic ideal of the artist-creator, have ended up benefiting the institution of advertising communication. 'Like the Church, the Monarchy and the Communist Party in other times and places, the corporation is today's dominant institution,' explained the authors of the documentary The Corporation,[5] an enlightening portrait of how companies have been able to take advantage of the laws originally created to protect the citizenry. According to the documentary, the modern citizen delegates power to the corporation-person, capable of defending their rights as creator while their legal responsibility is blurred in the corporation when the situation requires it. As Naomi Klein explained in her well-known work No Logo, the power of the corporation is made clear through legal actions undertaken by companies as soon as someone uses, even as a social protest, their logo.[6] The letters sent by the legal services of the company is perhaps the first step in the process of intimidation.

## The Intimidating Burofax

In April 2007, we received a 'burofax' from a law firm.[7] Their client, a private aesthetic and cosmetic surgery clinic network (Corporación Dermoestética S.A.), were asking us to withdraw a 'comment made by an unknown author' on our website. Corporación Dermoestética was one of those companies that mushroomed before the financial crisis, which started in 2008. The company is a good example of the bubble in Spain because it started trading in the stock market in 2005, that is, in the years of the economic boom, and deflated as soon as the crisis arrived.[8] When the corporation entered the Spanish stock market in July 2005, its president made a speech surrounded by fifty models dressed as nurses.[9] The act, described as sexist by the consumer association

FACUA and the Spanish Nursing General Council, symbolizes quite well the arrogance of a company whose advertising was denounced on several occasions.[10]

When Corporación Dermoestética became bankrupt in 2015, it collectively dismissed its entire workforce. But first, they sent hundreds of burofaxes like the one we received. El País, a national newspaper, in an article entitled 'A Finale without Beauty for the Scalpel Queen,' recognized that the entity 'had to silence, by judicial order, a website where former patients told cases of alleged medical malpractice.'[11] The company started a tireless campaign that lasted for years against any opinion published online that could annoy them. In our burofax, we were required not to publish any comment or critique 'that in any way undermines the image of the entity.'

One of the very first decisions we made as ConsumeHastaMorir in order to design subvertising posters was to avoid naming directly companies, not because of the legal repercussions, but because we wanted to denounce their practices, which are common to many large companies. It does not make sense to talk about one and not the other, as we were able to judge who is doing it right and who is not. In order to be able to speak on a more abstract level, we decided to make up brand names that sounded like other well-known brands. However, we kept receiving letters and faxes from companies because of the articles published critical of their reputation[12].

In March 2009, the sporting goods retailer Decathlon sent us a letter with the following heading: 'Use Infringement of DECATHLON Intellectual Property Rights.' The interesting thing was that they did not even focus their claim on any subvert made by us. Instead, they were accusing us of violating a law solely by posting a link on our website, and not by making a subvert against them. We did have subverts against that company, but in the letter they sent us, they did not talk about the subvert, but the link to the other website. But, according to them, we were 'infringing several DECATHLON trademarks' by posting on our website a video and a link to 'Decathlon Explota,'[13] a campaign created by workers who demanded the fulfilment of their labour rights. Are links also prohibited on the Internet?

In addition, Lacoste, through their law firm, sent us a burofax to let us know that we were using their logo fraudulently in a free store project. This was a space called 'Sincoste' (Spanish pun which translates to 'for free') in a social centre in Madrid, and the modified Lacoste logo (with the jaws of the famous crocodile tied) appeared on the news of several local television networks.

But a more interesting story was the attempt of a photo stock company to charge us for the use of some images. We had used some of their pictures to create several subverts, but they asked us for a large amount of money in exchange for using a current photo of the Eiffel Tower! Any tourist in Paris could have made the photo they claimed and they could never prove that the photo was theirs. Then, we realized the company's tactic and we did not pay any money. Not a cent. In the end, we changed some posters and we promised them we would not use any of their images anymore. We were definitely into the free culture movement and we had to learn to create our own material, and that is how we entered the pro-commons movement through Creative Commons copyright and, in addition, we learned to create and share our own photographs and other resources.

The basis of our subverts is the obvious alteration of the logos to highlight the social activism behind these critical materials. This strategy has ended up being a certain protective shield because companies think twice before denouncing these subverts in these frameworks. These years of experience have shown us that it is the companies themselves that have learned to weigh up whether it is worth their while to denounce subvertising. Their obsession with avoiding scandals leads them to not pursue subvertising actions except when they reach a level of notoriety dangerous to their public image. However, intimidation through IP law seems to have a stabilizing effect on the control of the social imaginary. Precisely what is at stake is this space, traditionally discursive, becoming a monologue.

## The Internet Monologue

The Internet is that place where you can find all kinds of photos on any topic. In a matter of minutes, and with a simple search, we can access a lot of material that apparently, but only apparently, is at our disposal. But it is not like that, and probably the first photograph we would find would belong to a large company that sells photographs as a hook for their business. This is especially interesting because the Internet continues to be understood as that promise land of freedom and dialogue. Maybe that is why it is interesting to understand its monologue.

In the mid-1990s, a minority group of 16 million people (0.4% of the world's population)[14] navigated (following the successful metaphor of cyberspace as a huge ocean full of information islands) between simple text documents using a program called Netscape. The relaxed interactivity of the Web forums or the interactions of the Geocities community has become massive and immediate with Messenger, Skype, Gmail, and especially social networks. The result is a culture of use that permeates all virtual activities. Music or video downloads give way to direct and instant playback via Spotify or Megaupload. The limited characters of Twitter make tireless and chaotic teletypes between the informative and the anecdotal. Perhaps the first clear sign that Web 2.0 was a cultural change is deduced from the success of the blogosphere. Blogs, those websites that collect the personal contributions of the navigator as a daily log of their experience, provide information space to a good part of the cybernetic population. From navigator to island owner. From receiver to emitter.

However, the 2.0 paradigm has not resided in the appropriation of the informative islands, but rather in the collective production of the cybernetic ocean. The 2.0 navigator intervenes in the places where s/he passes, contributing, ordering, or valuing the contents. And Wikis where visitors operate on collective documents is a good example of this. Wikipedia, a large encyclopaedia developed and maintained by thousands of volunteers, not only represents the success of a shared production system, but also a paradigm that is proposed as an alternative management in the increasingly decisive role of the big content companies. The Forum's manifesto for access to culture and knowledge reads:

> The information society and the new digital context has been a revolution in the creation of knowledge and culture, and, above all, in how they are accessed. Citizens, artists, and consumers have ceased to be passive and isolated subjects in the face of the content production and distribution industry. Now, each person collaborates, participates, and decides more directly and democratically.[15]

However, Web 2.0 is moving towards a kind of participation that does not get rid of large companies and even fragments an important part of their collective cyberspace. Facebook originates from a platform where Harvard university students shared information through their personal profiles. In other words, a digital social network is a network within another network. The Internet is a network of computers that allows people connected from different parts of the territory to share services such as e-mail, Web pages, or search engines. And a digital social network is based precisely on establishing more complex and powerful services among a group of Internet users, generating some kind of semi-closed network.

This semi-closed environment has its origin in the virtual communities established around thematic Web forums, mailing lists, and the messenger phenomenon and it is another dimension in the 2.0 paradigm: the digital social network starts from the affective bonds of the analogue or 'real' world to build a collective cyberspace with group identity. Precisely, the success of Facebook was not to connect strangers, but to reconnect people already linked emotionally through family, work, leisure, or territorial ties in the digital environment. Interactions within the network based on texts, videos, photos, or recommended links are, in this environment, producers of group identity, and they are definitely complex social relationships where the non-digital relationship still has an essential weight.

With social networks, classic navigation based on hyperlinks is replaced by in-depth navigation within spaces bounded by scattered microcommunities (family, group of friends, co-workers, etc.). Facebook or Tuenti are integrated Web services platforms where powerful databases manage information not only about the user, but also about the interactions between users. An example is the network of images tagged from Facebook: when a user uploads a photo of their friends and points out on each of them who that Facebook user is, it contributes to the generation of a network of links around those people in such a way that these or other users can navigate between the photographs of different users. However, Facebook is not compatible with Tuenti, Twitter, or other social networks in the sense that content from one social network cannot be moved from another, but must be recreated; so it is the user who does this, not the network. They are not complementary, each one fights for its share of captive navigation. But the links, the interactions, are the reasons the Internet exists. When an important part of the cyberpopulation shifts its interactions from the hyperlink network to a privative depth space, social networks become a problem for the collective network based on standards.

Since its inception, the Internet has been able to expand thanks to a concept as simple as it is difficult to achieve: standards. The protocols and languages used on the Internet are created or supervised by different associations, such as the World Wide Web Consortium (W3C), with the aim of making the Internet more interoperable, accessible, and usable. However, the most powerful companies in the network, such as Microsoft, Google, Facebook, AOL, Amazon, or Macintosh have also provided successful elements among users and become standard. For example, most of the videos displayed today on the Internet are in Flash format, created by another large software multinational, Adobe.

This company is also the creator of the PDF format, the standard in pre-printed documents. The history of the Internet is full of these ad hoc standards and reminds us of the difficulty of maintaining the network of networks as an open and consensual space.

In fact, the commons culture and the open collective production that encouraged the first Internet development was housed in the computer world. In the mid-twentieth century, almost all computer programs were developed by academics and researchers, so they were not seen as a product. The operating systems were maintained by user communities and their distribution included the source code so that users could correct errors or add other functionalities. Due to the progressive commercialization of the Internet in the last decade, all this has been reduced to the tireless movement for free software and common culture.

## The 2.0 Commercial Network

Today, the Internet is still an ocean prone to blogs and other islands of collective production, but it is above all, a large commercial space. As in the rest of the communication spaces, advertising has been landing on it to become the most profitable cyber message. In order to get closer to that 'tired' consumer who 'rejects' advertising, advertisers and advertising agencies have launched less aggressive strategies based on proximity to generate affective ties that provide added value. And precisely, the new communication channels seemed to be the most propitious spaces for this: 'Brands are accustomed to talk shouting,'[16] says a specialist Internet publicist, denouncing that new media requires a new advertising culture.

> They have learned to talk like that, and they do not know how to do it any other way, so when they come to the Internet they buy a banner and shout at it. But in the new advertising communication environment a new type of communication must be considered, based on the exchange, in dialogue, in intimacy, in the long-term relationship. Nobody likes to be shouted at in an intimate conversation.[17]

Thus, customer loyalty is not based on offering economic benefits or occasional gifts, but on reinforcing the emotional bond through identification with the values of the brand: 'It is not only the capacity to attract in an irremediable look towards one or several aspects of reality, it is also the valuable ability to generate an experience that captures the spirit and conquers the will,' says an ad by the advertising agency

Starcom MediaVest to explain its activity.[18]

In just a few years, Information and Communication Technologies (ICTs) have modified the communications panorama and, of course, the very stage in which advertising is developed:

> Mass communication has ceased to be the monopoly of the few (media, agencies, companies), becoming an opportunity open to an audience, which has evolved from the traditional consideration of audience (usually associated with the passive reception of content) to active user (with the ability to interact with information and the means by which it is consumed in many different ways, as well as to establish networks for the exchange of information with other users and even to become an issuer thereof).[19]

The agency Burson-Marsteller dares to speak of 'communication anarchy': 'Social media has made the control of the corporate message pass from the organization to consumers and other stakeholders, so that doing nothing it is no longer the safest option.'[20]

In the anarchy of the Internet, not everyone has the same ability to spread and communicate, and large companies are the first to act. Public managers themselves, aware of this new scenario, reflect on their profession and announce the challenges that await them: 'We no longer address journalists only as information amplifiers from our companies or clients. We have to reach another group of very different and segmented influencers (bloggers, active users, etc.). This forces us to know the network perfectly, who the main actors are, what issues interest them, and how they want to receive our information.'[21]

For years, Microsoft, through its advertising firm, Microsoft Advertising, has offered advertisers specialized tools for 'behavioural targeting.' The segmentation of Microsoft users according to their tastes and social characteristics: 'Messenger is much more than a communication system, it is a mean to share information, photos, files, videos, games. ... Hence, as an advertising platform, it is a true success story for all advertisers who have opted for Messenger and those ones who try, repeat,'[22] explains Marisa Manzano, commercial manager of Microsoft advertising. According to her, digital media has led the change of the communicative model with the consumer: 'Advertising has ceased to be intrusive, fulfilling the need to be interactive with the users, who are now the owners of their time and what content they want to receive.'[23]

Websites, online games, chat applications, video platforms, and of course social networks. The latter are the newest space, which now attracts experimental advertising campaigns and displays the full economic potential of the 2.0 paradigm. It was summed up by the Commercial Director of Facebook in Spain, Irene Cano, when talking about 'the era of social purchasing,' through her company: 'people go to their friends to ask for advice before buying something. A viral effect with which a brand could not but dream before.'[24] By shifting the activity of the network to private spaces, social networks fragment the network of standards in search of profitable information from customers and marketing experiences of great value to companies. The dream of 2.0 Web, creative pawn of collective intelligence, can end in another new nightmare of neoliberal capitalism.

But, as with everything, there are also alternatives. The 15M movement in Spain, for example, used N-1, an alternative social network, to manage internal communication. Yet, Facebook and Twitter continue to be essential to spread the revolution. Despite the fact that the movement has had (and still has) a close relationship with commercial social networks, it is aware of the paradox. There are many people on Facebook or Twitter, and the characteristic of 15M is its desire to be citizens. Nevertheless, it is not the digital space that corresponds to them: 'we have to be on the street, but also in the digital square, and commercial networks are not the digital public square,' propagated an activist in one of the communication meetings of 15M.

### The Law That Protects the Consumerist Monologue

In the 1970s, a wide range of washing machines, vacuum cleaners, dryers, and toasters nourished the media imaginary and the idea of comfort became the centre of manufacturing activity. Still, mass consumption became homogeneous. For Pierre Bourdieu, many seemingly ostentatious expenditures were actually obligated elements of a certain train of life,[25] and the purchase of standardized products for the American family was necessary in order to not be left out of the consumer middle class.

After the Second World War, it seemed that the new collection of consumer objects had a linguistic dimension and the vertiginous rhythm of product renewal and its calculated obsolescence saturated the communication of commercial allusions.[26] The supply of goods with universalized aspirations that the modern factory had made possible, needed an ever-increasing consumption of these objects, representations of a comfortable life under the ideal of progress. Precisely because of this, the protestant austerity of the beginning of the century or the forced austerity of the post-war period were suitable scenarios for the growth of a great middle class, but not for its maintenance. The 1960s and 70s were the necessary turnaround. Instead of promising access to the middle class, consumption promised an exit through a door full of mirrors: the consumer of the 1970s seeks, above all, differentiation. Advertising, which had begun to delimit the different targets with 'scientific' eagerness, now spreads slogans such as "Because I'm worth it" or 'Innovate, do not imitate.'

To this end, nothing better than a new model of retail establishment, the large area or the hypermarket, supposed materialization of the 'free purchase.' These spaces were presented as guarantors of the great variety on offer that the new consumer needs, making the consumer believe that he is an independent individual with any criteria when choosing the products for sale. As full-page ad from El Mundo said:

> You are in the sports shop. You do not know whether to buy a golf club or a tennis racket. Who do you consult with? Nobody. You take the two options and ready. There's no doubt you are going through the best stage of your life. That's why we offer you maximum safety standards in the complete Renault Laguna range.[27]

Shopping centres, a sweetened commercial alternative of an increasingly dangerous city, represent the most advanced set of sales techniques. These techniques systematically achieve a 20% higher amount in sales.[28] These standardized places, indistinguishable from each other, focus precisely on the different targets and take advantage of their profile in each case. They become an aseptic space for a consumption system that no longer revolves around people's homes but in mobility, a much more favourable scenario for that individual who no longer buys, but goes shopping, who no longer asks, but chooses, and who no longer has needs, but seeks satisfaction.

This kind of consumer, who, as the neoliberals insist, happens to be the most mature and rational consumer, seems, however, more lost than ever in an environment of information overload and commercial dependence: 'Before, if you wandered around a store without buying, they almost threw you out. Now it is about precisely that, you look. It doesn't matter if you buy. The consumer doesn't need anything; the consumer seeks the desire, the illusion, the irresistible impulse to buy and it come at any time,' explains the psychologist Javier Garcés. And he provides some data: 70% of purchasing decisions are made within the establishment in question, and 80% of those who enter a shopping center end up buying something.[29]

Well, the mass consumption imaginary, full of essential objects collections to enter the elitist group of the 3,000 million consumers worldwide,[30] is complemented in recent decades by a repetitive bunch of messages, one of which highlights our deficiencies (compared to the available collection of models for any area of life) as always being remedied through the purchase of available goods and services.

Here, the role of advertising is key. As an ideological channel consistent with the described consumption model, it certainly stops offering useful information about the product to take advantage of the communicative possibilities of audio-visual language and focus on the commercial benefits of sentimental transmission. As the president of an advertising agency said:

> There are few products that are sold leaving emotion aside. There are few differences between products; the difference lies in the link with the brand and in consumer confidence. That link is created over years after building an emotional bond that makes you choose one brand and not another.[31]

Advertiser companies, after years of increasing the value of their brands in the intangible market, now aspire to a more ambitious step together with the consumer: to generate experiences. A marketing specialist explains:

> The brand, beyond providing a specific product or service, connects with their interests, motivations, and lifestyle and, in the end, with all those aspects related to symbolic consumption (those factors with added emotional value, which cause, finally, the consumer to consume the brand beyond its own tangible characteristics).'[32]

While paradoxically consumption becomes a factory of experiences where companies are integrated into the lives of consumers, those same companies create all the legal resources to make true dialogue impossible. Naomi Klein speaks of companies' desire for complete cultural integration while embarking on a petty legal crusade.[33]

## Subvertising: A True Dialogue

While the subvertising movement took shape, other heterogeneous movements also arose in response to this model of overproduction and overconsumption: associations and NGOs in defence of consumer rights, the movement for organic agriculture and food sovereignty, as well as fair trade networks and alternative consumption. These all emerged from other social movements but focused their struggle around a new social subject, namely the 'prosumer,' the type of person willing to occupy an active role in consumption thus destabilizing the duality between production and consumption.

This new era of the prosumer requires a true dialogical framework. Intellectual property laws have ended up functioning as a tool that makes true dialogue impossible in that space we call the social imaginary. As we found out, the law ends up discouraging any type of criticism of those companies that have gradually registered the use of brands, symbols, and even colours to later claim that their natural image must always be clean and positive.

Only a few months after ConsumeHastaMorir was born, we began to host subvertising workshops and social communication tutorials, and to provide teaching materials. We are convinced that subvertising offers an educational approach to the language of consumption: a language of the things that surround us. Just by extracting an advertisement from its usual context (30 seconds of studied narrative through symbols, images, and slogans), we can detect the different commercial strategies and the values that support the neoliberal, normalizing, and legitimating ideology of this socioeconomic system. An increasingly important part of consumption language is the right of large companies to the non-criticizable image.

Critical analysis is a tool that enables us to approach issues as diverse as those addressed by advertising itself: gender relations, power roles, stereotypes of social success, exclusion and marginalization, environmental sustainability, and so on. But it is also a method to deepen the advertisers' contradictions who promise to solve our problems in each ad.

The difficulty of questioning consumption as a solution to the main economic and social problems clearly benefits those large companies that, in the face of the question: 'What do we do?', propose precisely commercialism whereby consumption is protected closely by law. 'Consuming our products avoids damaging the environment and, therefore, the advancement of climate change,' say the energy companies, the food industry, or the automotive industry in their ads.

Today, far from finding ourselves in the face of the most historically prepared consumer, we are short of tools that allow us to sift the overwhelming stimulus and information density of advertisement. Speeches, slogans, and proclamations have grown dramatically, but we still suffer from a vocabulary, as Baudrillard used to say, that allows us to move in an endless chain of consumer objects programmed to stop working. And above all, we are still imprisoned in the logic of 'progress' as infinite consumption or the inexhaustibility of raw materials, at the expense of the exploitation of a large part of humanity and after verifying that our happiness depends on other things.

In this scenario, an essential exercise in critical and responsible consumption is to break the monologue of consumerism and to challenge its slogans by well-directed questions such as: 'In what conditions has that product been made?' or 'What are benefits from its consumption?' After all, to what extent must we consume until we die?


## Notes

1.    This documentary has been accessible on the Internet since 2005. It was broadcast by TeleSur, and following that it was on its website for many years. It has been on several websites for direct download, but those pages no longer exist. It has been on channels like Vimeo, but it is no longer available through there.

2.    For example, el Centre de Cultura Contemporània de Barcelona (CCCB). Rius, Joaquim (2006) 'El MACBA i el CCCB. De la regeneració cultural a la governança cultural,' in Dossier La gestió de la cultura, una nova disciplina? [dossier en línia], ed. Glòria Munilla, 8 Digithum 2006, accessed 2 February 2019, http://www.uoc.edu/digithum/8/dt/cat/rius.pdf.

3.    *La Fiambrera Obrera* started in the 1980s in Valencia, and its members later moved to Madrid and Barcelona. One of its key figures is Jordi Claramont. For more information on this group see Lourdes de la Cruz, 'Contrapublicitat: apropiacionisme crític en l'era digital,' *Universitat Oberta de Catalunya*, accessed 2 February 2019, http://openaccess.uoc.edu/webapps/o2/handle/10609/43681).

4.    An example of pop art challenging consumer society and an example of subvertising challenging consumer society would be the collage by John McHale and Richard Hamilton 'Just what is it that makes today's homes so different, so appealing?'.

5.    *The Corporation*. A film directed and produced by Mark Achbar, Jennifer Abbott, and Joel Bakan (Big Picture Media Corporation, 2004).

6.    Naomi Klein, *No Logo* (Barcelona: Paidós, 1999).

7.    The burofax is a service that allows you to urgently send documents that may require proof before third parties, so it is a 'legal' fax.

8.    'Corporación Dermoestética deja de cotizar en Bolsa ocho años después,' (Dermoestética Corporation stops trading after eight years) *El Mundo*, 11 June 2013, accessed 2 February 2019, https://www.elmundo.es/elmundo/2013/06/11/economia/1370944538.html.

9.    'FACUA denuncia a Corporación Dermoestética por utilizar a modelos disfrazadas de enfermeras en la presentación de su salida a bolsa'

(FACUA denounces Corporación Dermoestética for using disguised models of nurses in the presentation of their IPO), *Facua*, 18 July 2005, accessed 2 February 2019, https://www.facua.org/es/noticia.php?Id=749.

10.   'Corporación Dermoestética deberá devolver el dinero de una operación por publicidad engañosa' (Dermoestética Corporation must return the money from an operation for deceptive advertising) *Europa Press*, 23 May 2005, accessed 2 February 2019, https://www.europapress.es/economia/noticia-corporacion-dermoestetica-debera-devolver-dinero-operacion-publicidad-enganosa-20050523145202.html; 'Condenan a Corporación Dermoestética a devolver el dinero a una paciente que no vio cumplidas sus expectativas' (Corporación Dermoestética is condemned to return the money to a patient who did not meet their expectations) 24 May 2005, accessed 2 February 2019, http://www.consumer.es/web/es/salud/2005/05/24/142194.php. Also, in 2001, the Spanish Women's Institute has denounced that Corporación Dermoestética advertises with negative stereotypes of women, accessed 2 February 2019, http://www.inmujer.gob.es/observatorios/observImg/informes/docs/informe-2001.pdf.

11.   Guillermo Hildebrandt, 'Final sin belleza de la reina del bisturí,' (A finale without beauty for the scalpel queen) *El País*, 4 January 2015, accessed 12 May 2017, https://elpais.com/economia/2015/01/03/actualidad/1420305057_693298.html.

12.   ConsumeHastaMorir published a series of articles on this. There is a report on sexist advertising that talks about Corporación Dermoestética adverts: Adriana Treto, 'Publicidad machista: Análisis de publicidad y taller de creación contrapublicitaria,' *Academia. edu*, accessed 12 May 2017, https://www.academia.edu/18409208/Publicidad_machista_y_contrapublicidad_Consume_Hasta_Morir.

13.   *Decathlon Explota*, accessed 12 May 2017, http://decathlonexplota. blogspot.com .

14.   *Internet World Statistics*, accessed 12 November 2017, http://www. internetworldstats.com.

15.   *Free Culture Forum*, accessed 7 August 2017, http://fcforum.net/es

16.   Daniel Solana, creative director of Double You, interviewed in 'El nuevo marketing 2.0,' *Revista Interactiva Digital*, 79 (2007) pp. 22-23.

17.   Solana interview.

18.   From our archive.

19.   Ludi García García, 'Los nuevos modelos de comunicación,' DirCom (2009) pp. 79-80.

20.   Burson-Marsteller Evidence-Based Communications Group, 'The Global Social Media Check-up,' *Influencia*, 2010, accessed 7 August 2017, http://www.influencia.net/data/document/barson.pdf.

21.   García García, 'Los nuevos modelos de comunicación.'

22.   Marisa Manzano, interviewed in Revista Interactiva Digital, 109 (2010) pp. 54-55.

23.    Manzano, 'Interactiva.'

24.    'Facebook podría alcanzar una valoración de 100.000 millones de dólares' (Facebook could reach a valuation of 100,000 million dollars), *Expansión*, 13 June 2011, accessed 2 May 2017, http://www.expansion.com/2011/06/13/empresas/digitech/1307984348.html.

25.    Pierre Bourdieu, *La distinction* (París: Les Editions de Minuit, 1979)

26.    Luis Enrique Alonso Benito, *La era del consumo* (Madrid: Siglo XXI, 2006).

27.    *El Mundo*, 30 March 2007, from our records.

28.    Javier Garcés interview in *Gran Superficie*, a documentary film directed by María González, Pedro Ramiro, and Isidro Jiménez (2005).

29.    Luz Sánchez-Mellado, 'Quiero esto y lo quiero ya,' *El País*, 11.

30.    Homi Kharas, 'The Unprecedented Expansion of the Global Middle Class: an update,' *Brookings*, accessed 2 May 2017, https://www.brookings.edu/wp-content/uploads/2017/02/global_20170228_global-middle-class.pdf.

31.    Ecologistas en accion, 'Qué sociedad de consumo, qué publicidad,' accessed 2 May 2017, https://www.ecologistasenaccion.org/?p=11183.

32.    Ecologistas en accion, 'Qué sociedad de consumo, qué publicidad.'

33.    Naomi Klein, *No Logo*.

# 4

# Performing Sexuality on the Legal Stage

*Sean Mulcahy*

**Introduction**

In 2007, a couple wrote to the then Refugee Review Tribunal of Australia offering to perform a live 'act of homosexual intercourse' to prove their sexuality.[1] The Tribunal declined. Some time later, a Tribunal Member sat down in their office in a glass building in Sydney to watch a compact disc of a different couple having sex. The Tribunal was reluctant at first, as was the couple,[2] but the then Federal Magistrates Court concluded that 'it was necessary that the Tribunal consider the evidence before it.'[3]

Both performances were for the purposes of demonstrating the applicants' sexuality in order to sustain claims for refugee status on the basis of homophobic persecution in their home country. With many thousands of refugee claims being based on sexual orientation, issues of the factual assessment of applicants' sexuality are prominent, with many decision-makers unlikely to believe applicants' claims.[4] Whilst there is extensive scholarship on the doctrinal development of refugee claims on the basis of sexuality, and contributions examining the narratives of such claims[5] and the emotions behind their adjudication,[6] this chapter examines the performance of sexuality in refugee claims in an Australian tribunal, utilizing the above two instances as case studies.

Examining these legal claims from a performance perspective raises a number of questions: Would the live performance be more real than that on the compact disc? Is the reason why the Tribunal declined to view a live performance because it would be too close, too real to bear? When a performance is taped and replayed, does the screen intercede to create a comfortable distance for its audience? All of these questions reflect an attempt to come to terms with the advent of video and screens in the modern courtroom.[7] In his incisive work, *Liveness: Performance in a Mediatized Culture*, performance studies scholar Philip Auslander poses some critical questions about the relationship between live and mediatized legal performance: 'what kind of presence live performance possesses, how that presence differs from mediatized representations, and just what presence and the temporal and spatial simultaneity ... contribute to the legal process.'[8]

Auslander was writing at the turn of this century, a time at which he could declare that 'the courtroom has proved ... resistant to the incursion of mediatisation.'[9] With the rise in courtroom technology,[10] I return to Auslander to ask not why the courtroom has proved resistant to mediatized performance but to question the implications of its embrace of video, particularly on queer refugee claimants. My work is part of a broader turn within legal studies towards theatre and performance studies. Despite calls at the turn of this century for law to be reconceptualized as a performing art,[11] law and performance is still an emerging field of scholarship. The 'performative turn' has been apparent in social sciences and humanities since midway through the last century as 'performance theorists recognize the ubiquity of cultural performances, and encourage the analysis of performances in many diverse fields and disciplines.'[12] As Julie Peters explains 'law's history is marked by an oscillation between the antinomies of theatricality and antitheatricality, in a relationship of attraction-revulsion—a kind of *fort-da*.'[13] Rejecting the parenthetical divide between performance and law, I try to give space for the two disciplines—legal and performance studies—to speak to each other and, in doing so, offer a new insight into legal performance and, in this instance, the performance of sexuality in the legal arena. 'Legal performance' is a term I borrow from Peters and Nicole Rogers to describe the idea of court proceedings as performance.[14] As Peters describes it, configuring law as performance is 'an alternative way of studying the law, more attentive to the material, affective and aesthetic textures of legal process.'[15]

I explore these two legal performances for refugee claims in their material sense: how they are framed and how the legal audience engages with these performances—or could engage with the performances—in an embodied way, through sight and also touch. The particular focus is on the difference between live and digital performances of sexuality. The chapter concludes with a reflection on the records of these performances, the material remnants left behind in the legal archive.

## Background

I will begin by providing a background to the two matters introduced in the introduction: *NAOX* and *SZQYU*. The reason that these matters are abbreviated is due to provisions that prevent the publishing of the names of applicants for protection visas.[16]

On 11 July 2007, in a letter to the Tribunal, a Bangladeshi couple claiming asylum on the basis of their sexuality wrote that, 'should you require it (although such a step would cause us significant embarrassment), we are prepared to have an adult witness view us engaged in an act of homosexual intercourse and then attest before you to that fact.'[17]

It is unclear exactly how the Tribunal responded to this offer. The decision record is not available because 'a direction was made by the presiding member not to publish the decision record.'[18] However, glimpses can be gained from the judgments on appeal. The judgments on appeal indicate that, following the applicants' offer to engage in an act of homosexual intercourse in the presence of a witness, the Tribunal put a question to the applicant as to their use of lubricant during sexual intercourse, which the applicant did not wish to answer. It then stated:

> Because the applicant had indicated, by making the offer of performing a homosexual act, that he was not shy, the Tribunal expected that he should be able to answer this otherwise basic question ... The Tribunal finds that this question is one which practising male homosexuals in a relationship together for over a decade, and who perform homosexual intercourse, would have no problem in answering. It is a question which goes to the heart of the question whether the applicants are in a homosexual relationship ... The Tribunal, with respect, has difficulty understanding how viewing an act of homosexual intercourse, where a lubricant may or may not be used, is less offensive to the applicants than answering a question as to whether a lubricant is used. Because of the refusal to answer the Tribunal's question, and the lack of a cogent response, the Tribunal finds that the first applicant is not a truthful or credible witness.[19]

As foreshadowed, the matter was appealed to the Federal Magistrates Court, which dismissed the appeal.[20] The matter was then appealed to the Federal Court, which handed down its judgment, asserting that 'the decision of the ... Tribunal was not made in good faith, and was unreasonable ... The Tribunal was guilty of bias, in the sense that it was predisposed to making its ultimate finding that the appellants were not in a homosexual relationship.'[21]

On 4 August 2011, another Bangladeshi couple claiming asylum on the basis of their sexuality handed a compact disc containing photographs of them having sex together to a Tribunal Member.[22] When the applicants' lawyers found out, they called the Tribunal and 'requested the Tribunal not to view "the CD".'[23] The CD was returned to applicant. The matter was subsequently appealed to the then Federal Magistrates Court, which handed down its judgment, asserting that the Tribunal's failure to consider the evidence of what was on the disc amounted to a jurisdictional error.[24]

The matter was then remitted to the Tribunal who reported that, 'following the second hearing, [redacted] provided a "memory stick" containing the sexually explicit photos of the applicant and [redacted].'[25] The Tribunal viewed the photographs and handed down its decision in the following terms:

> The Tribunal has considered the photographs submitted by the applicant and accepts that he has had intercourse with [redacted] on one occasion ... The Tribunal finds the fact that he engaged in sex with [redacted] on this occasion does not establish that he is gay, and is not satisfied that the sexual activity depicted in the photos was engaged in otherwise that for the sole purpose of strengthening the applicant's claim to be a refugee.[26]

> In the Tribunal's view the sexual activity depicted in the photographs submitted by the applicant following the second hearing do not establish that he is gay or that he is in a homosexual relationship.[27]

Both cases are fundamentally concerned with viewing an act of homosexual intercourse. In *SZQYU*, the Tribunal viewed photographs of sexual intercourse; in *NAOX*, the Tribunal did not view a live performance of sexual intercourse but instead questioned the applicants about their sexual practices to construct an image of the performance in their mind's eye. The Tribunal rejected the offer to view a live performance and accepted, on appeal, the offer to view a digital performance of sex.

### Live and Digital Performance; Performance-Led Research

As Auslander's work suggests, there is a lively debate on liveness within performance studies.[28] Fellow performance studies scholar Peggy Phelan argues that once a performance is recorded it is no longer a performance, as a performance is only a performance in the spatio-temporal moment at which it is performed.[29] Thus the sex, which is the subject matter of both cases, is a performance in the space and time at which it occurred, but once recorded and transferred to the compact disc or memory stick, it is no longer a performance. Against Phelan's thesis, Auslander argues that the screening of a televisual image is a performance.[30] An actor—in this case, the Tribunal Member—performs the technology, inserting the memory stick into their computer, opening up the files thereon and looking at the images. The images are not a 'petrified remnant' but rather an element of the performance. Yet there are differences between what would be termed 'live performance' and 'digital performance.' In live performance, bodies are together in shared space; in digital performance, bodies are together but mediated through a screen, which radically reshapes the actor's presence. Technologies of justice, and in particular virtual appearance, are reshaping not only presence but the entire legal performance.[31]

I determined to explore the questions raised by digitalization in the context of legal performance through performance-led research. It is fair to say that there is a general resistance to creative practice-led research in the law school, a methodology that is more typical in the visual or performing arts. For theatre and arts practitioners, innovative approaches are necessary to overcome this. In this regard, I was greatly influenced by Carolyn McKay, a legal scholar and artist who describes her practice as 'a habituation to materially thinking.'[32] Her work and practice radically reconceptualizes the software of justice and the technologies of audiovisual link as material objects, and focuses on their tactility or materialness. The hands interacting with a tablet computer, for example, are a material interaction joining hand, eye and mind together. McKay sees this kind of sensorial engagement as a way of creating new knowledge about the technologies of justice; moreover, a form of embodied experiential knowledge. This knowledge making also necessitates a reflexive practice, wherein the creative practitioner critically reflects on and analyses their work. McKay regards the analytical and creative as different forms along a range of cognition.[33]

Inspired by McKay, in August 2018, I created an installation that explored digital legal testimony, *Exploring*. Three screens were set up across a gallery-like space with an actor (myself) delivering testimony on a pre-recorded loop looking in three different directions: directly at camera, above camera, and to the side. The camera focused on three different angles: the testifier's head and shoulders, hands, and feet. Participants were invited to interact with the screens—walk around them, touch them and smell them—and then asked how they experienced the testimony and how the testimony made them feel in an embodied sense. What emerged were stimulating insights into the acoustic, visual, and other sensory dimensions of video and screens in court. What follows hereon is a response to the two legal performances of sexuality under study, one on screen and one never fulfilled, informed by my performance-led research practice.

## Frames

In digital performance, the audience's relationship with the performer or image on screens is mediated through the camera.[34] Elizabeth Bell writes that 'the presence of the video camera and its operator shows an untroubled faith in the *reproduction* of eventhood,'[35] implying that the camera and its operator are simply a neutral vehicle through which the performance event is transmitted. However, in *SZQYU*, the mediation of the performance through the photographic lens and its unknown operator radically shifts the reception of the performance.

A critical element of the visual is framing. The sex is 'framed as an event by ... cameras and then reframed for consuming audiences' through its transmission to a memory stick.[36] The framing lens of the camera through which it is filmed and the framing borders of the screen through which it is displayed create a boundary between what is seen and not seen.[37] The frame operates as a parenthetical device that exposes its inner scene to scrutiny,[38] but blocks what is out of frame from perception. The audience can only imagine what is happening outside the frame of vision or once the camera is turned off or the actor exits its field of vision. The audience is implicitly invited to question what is within and beyond the frame, and to come to a conclusion about whether what is being seen are indicia of a homosexual relationship. In this sense, the frames of the camera lens and screen are 'frames that fluctuate between play and belief':[39] Is what is being seen a real homosexual relationship or a performance for the camera? Costas Douzinas argues that:

> The criminal trial has always been a framing device. It isolates a particular defendant and a series of facts and homes in on them ... Trials are camera-like framing devices: they circumscribe and underline; they include as legally relevant and exclude as incidental, contingent, external; they turn facts into events, random happenings into causal sequences, people into heroes and villains. Trials frame and separate ... Trials were cameras and screens well before any technological innovations were introduced into their operations. They mirror, identify, (mis)recognise. Cameras and screens are the *mise en scene* of the trial: they stage and enframe it.[40]

Here Douzinas is putting forward the notion of law and the legal performance as a framing device, which is enhanced by the use of cameras and screens in court. If the legal performance is a framing device, how tight the frame is and what can be let in are dictated by those that direct the performance. A wide frame can bring more in; a close frame can focus down. The frame is not always true—as Douzinas says, it can misrecognize—and sometimes it creates not a new image but mirrors the audience's own face back at them through the reflection on a glass screen. Through this reflection, the Tribunal Member is imbricated in the performance

## Bodies

In this moment of reflection, the audience's body is superimposed over the actors' bodies on screen. There is a deep significance to the act of bodies gathering in space 'in each other's physical presence.'[41] Performance and law scholar Kate Leader questions 'what is at stake in the live presence of bodies together in the same space,'[42] and concludes that, 'the most obvious difference between the use of [televisual] testimony and evidence testing in a traditional trial is the absence of a witness's body from the courtroom. It is my contention that this 'absence' of the body has focused legal attention on the value of "presence".'[43] In her study of court architecture, Linda Mulcahy claims that physical presence endows an interaction with more meaning,[44] pointing to other events that are conducted through face-to-face interaction: parliamentary debates, weddings, funerals, etc. In these moments bodies gather together in shared space and through this physical proximity comes a physical connection.

Digital transmissions 'undermine the value of physical proximity.'[45] When a person is physically present, it 'makes it easier to evaluate the nuances of body language and demeanour.'[46] The distance that intercedes in the transmission of images makes it more difficult to pick up on these physical cues. On the contrary, however, it may be easier to pause, zoom in and more closely examine images on a screen. Through hand-held audiovisual devices, a viewer can now hold a person closer than social convention would normally allow, allowing the viewer to see them up-close and from different angles. The point, however, is that the audience is seeing an image not the actual body of the actor, and that there is something significant about bodily proximity in shared space.

Despite the advances in televisual spaces, 'there continue[s] to be something special about physical proximity'[47] that is unmet in mediatized interactions. As anyone who has lived away from their partner for an extended period of time can tell you—your author most unfortunately included—there is something lost in the digital interactions that you share with another—the haptic potentiality, the face-to-face interaction, the eye contact. As law and film scholar Richard Sherwin says, 'what the rational mind knows of the exterior world is based upon the effects of physical impacts on the perceptual apparatus.'[48] The absence of touch, smell and even taste in a video may affect viewers' perceptions of it.

In *SZQYU*, the actors' bodies are framed by images on a screen; in *NAOX*, the actors offer their bodies up for live viewing, unframed, with the audience in the same shared space as the actors in a moment of what Auslander terms 'temporal and spatial simultaneity.' This moment is resisted by the Tribunal.

## Touches

In thinking through the resistance of the Tribunal to a live performance of homosexual intercourse, I think about how this resistance is felt in an embodied sense; that is to say, how live versus mediatized performance affects the body and how the body responds to a performance—what may be termed its kinaesthetic response. In her work on performance composition, theatre-maker Anne Bogart describes kinaesthetic response as a 'spontaneous reaction to motion which occurs outside you.'[49] It is an impulsive, unmediated response to stimulation, a spontaneous bodily reaction responding to the energy generated by bodies in space.

To refine this idea somewhat, it could be argued that the atmosphere of performance is felt in terms of the haptic potentiality between actor and audience,[50] that is, the potential of touch between the two. The actor and audience being in the same space and time such that there is a potential of touch between the two, even if unfulfilled, lends a powerful potency to the performance. Conversely, when video is introduced, there is no possibility of touching the actor, thus it reduces the audience's relation to them. It feels something like the scene in Baz Luhrmann's *Romeo + Juliet* where the two lovers meet for the first time, but are separated by a glass fish-tank, distorting their view of one another and inhibiting their touch. There might be a very visceral visual reaction, but the connection would not sustain without the touch that follows.[51] As Mulcahy describes, 'the screen ... places a barrier of glass between ... participants that does not exist in the traditional trial.'[52]

In *SZQYU*, the screen inhibits the potentiality of touch. The Tribunal Member cannot reach out and touch the actors on screen. There is no potential for contact between the bodies because of the distance in time and space between them and the digital medium of performance. The screen thus operates as a barrier between audience and actors that would not be present were the actors performing live before an audience (as proposed in *NAOX*). In live performance, there is a meeting between actors and audience, whereas in digital performance there is not that moment of togetherness. The barrier of the screen creates a degree of separation between the actor and audience. Such barriers are increasingly common in legal performance, such as the glass screens in front of a defendant being held on remand. The barrier may lead to the dispassionate manner in which the Tribunal in *SZQYU* describes the sex act. There is very little sense, in the judgment, of any connection between the audience and actors.

There is also no depth but rather a flatness of images on screen.[53] The flat shape of the screen means the light has to travel farther to reach the edges, creating a pincushion effect whereby the image appears to be bowed towards the centre. This is in part why curved television screens have become more popular as they avoid this distortion and create a more immersive and deeper field of view for the viewer sitting directly facing the screen. The shape of the screens and the manner in which they control the light that illuminates or reflects off them can thus affect the audience's experience of the image.

Conversely, it could be argued that the encounter between audience and screen is an embodied interaction,[54] that video reaches out from the screen to the bodies of the audience, and that the audience can imagine what is happening on the screen felt within their bodies.[55] To imagine the images of sexual intercourse reaching out of the screen into the body of the Tribunal Member so that they can feel it within their own body is quite challenging. However, the intention of most pornographic images is to stimulate the viewer into autoeroticism and, potentially, to feel and act out the images on the screen on one's own self.[56] Bell posits a 'material consubstantiality of both male audience members and male performers,'[57] whereby the audience becomes so entwined with the performer that he imagines taking on his role. Was the Tribunal Member aroused when they watched these images? The decision record does not record their visceral response or reaction to the images. Indeed, there is remarkably scant attention to the physical dimensions of the sex in the Tribunal's judgment—the bodies, the sweat, the mouths, etc. It could be because this is uncomfortable to write about or because the Tribunal lacks the vocabulary to deal with inter-male sex. It could also be because the screen intercedes to create a comfortable spatiotemporal distance between viewer and the actors.

In my own work, participants stated that they would not have touched the screens if not invited to do so. This very much depended on the device. As the mode of delivery was via laptops, the desire to touch was not strong; this may have changed were it screened on a hand-held smart-phone or, conversely, on a mega-screen that endeared a more embodied response in the audience. The size of screens could affect the tactility of the performance. Thinking through legal performance tactilely is challenging given the prominence placed on the acoustic and visual senses. Whilst prohibitions on noise in the court are explicit through signage and the gavel, prohibitions on touching are more tacit. The architectural arrangement of space prevents most from touching the screens or, indeed, any live actor. However, the Tribunal Member viewing images on a screen in chambers is not so restricted.

In *NAOX*, the applicant offers the Tribunal Member or another adult witness the opportunity to 'view us,' but not explicitly to touch; thus seemingly instantiating a barrier similar to the glass wall of a screen. The audience was thus invited to read the performers' bodies as evidence of their sexuality, but at a distance. The audience is not invited, at least not explicitly in the letter, to participate in the 'act of homosexual intercourse' themselves. Yet there is little if no consideration given to how inserting the body of the audience into proximate relation with the bodies of the actors would affect their performance and how it may disrupt the usual script of intercourse. Even if not touching the actors, the audience is, by virtue of their presence as a body in the same space, a participant in the performance. As a static participant, the audience's gaze affects the bodies of the performers. On the inverse, through their participation, it would be more challenging for the audience to divorce their visceral reactions of arousal, disgust, shame, and so on from the act of impartial adjudication of the performers' sexuality.

## Eyes

The way in which an audience interacts with the visual in legal performance can be described as looking or gazing. There are various gazes within the courtroom in contrast to the singular focus of a camera.[58] The camera angle creates a particular perspective.[59] It could be argued that the camera used in *SZQYU* to photograph the legal subjects in sexual intercourse is the 'eye of the law.'[60] The camera replaces the eyes of the legal audience with a fixed frame from which to interpret matters. On the subject itself, it asserts a legal vision, framing action in a particular way. People tend to be cautious when they are aware they are being filmed for legal reasons—security, testimony, interrogation, etc. The lens exerts a pressure on those within its eye,[61] reminding them of their duty to comply with the law. In *SZQYU*, the actors are performing for a legal outcome, acceptance of their refugee claim. There is a certain degree of caution in this performance whereby the performers have to ensure that their performance of homosexuality is sufficiently credible to convince their Tribunal of their status as such. The lens is a reminder of their precarious status as a couple trying to prove their sexuality in order to remain in the country and avoid harm in their home country. The actor looks into the camera in place of a live audience, creating an unnatural social interaction between the audience and the actor, making the actor uncertain of where the fix their eyes.[62]

The introduction of these images into the Tribunal proceedings leads to eye witnessing mediated through screens.[63] Direct eye contact is crucial to communication;[64] it can often be used to test for truth or authenticity. In my performance-led research, I have found that when audiences look at images of an actor on screens, there is a focus on the face as a powerful centre of meaning capable of deconstruction because of its expressive qualities, particularly the eyes. Whilst it is referred to as eye contact, there is no physical contact, but a contact through looking—with two people looking into each other's eyes at the same time. The contact in this sense is not strictly haptic but a reciprocal communication. Nevertheless, there is a haptic potential within eye contact, the sense that by reaching out, one can touch. An audience can sometimes have a strong emotional reaction to an image on screen and touch the screen as a way of connecting with the image knowing they cannot actually feel it.[65] The physical distance remains, fracturing the haptic potentiality. To me, this suggests that eye contact brings a longing for touch that is unfulfilled through digital mediums. However, the audience when looking at images on a screen can touch or otherwise interact with the image however they so choose without the discomfort and judgment that comes with being looked back at. There is a level of discomforting voyeurism to this act—that is, the audience gaining sexual pleasure from watching the actors—which is heightened given that the actors are engaging in sexual intercourse.

In *NAOX*, an opportunity to view the actors in sexual intercourse was declined and live testimony preferred. In *SZQYU*, the Tribunal eventually viewed the images, but there is remarkably little attention given in their judgment to the photographs, their composition or the like. It is unlikely that the photographs would have provided the opportunity for the Tribunal Member/audience to look the actors in the eye and have that moment of contact and, through contact, connection with the actors. The judgment says nothing about how the Tribunal looked at these images, whether they printed them off and held them to look at them closer, whether they touched the screen as they looked, or anything about their embodied reaction to the images. All that comes from the judgment is that 'the Tribunal has considered the photographs.'[66] Similarly, there is little in the judgment about how the actors looked. In digital performance, the perspective of the camera subordinates the perspective of the actors within the screen by demanding that the actors look into it, creating a 'kind of obviousness, truth and reality.'[67] There is a documentary status to these images. Yet there is nothing in the judgment to indicate the actors' gaze.

From eyes to touches to bodies to frames, this chapter has thus far explored how sexuality is—or is not—performed on the legal stage of the Tribunal in an embodied way. One consistent theme emerging from the judgments under study is that there is very little attention given to the embodied performance of sexuality, despite both judgments being contingent on the veracity of the applicants' claim to be homosexual. In this final section of the chapter, I turn to the images of homosexual intercourse in *SZQYU* and attempt to engage with their own materiality.

## Records: The Petrified Remnants

In mid 2018, I submitted a freedom of information request to find out what happened to the images of homosexual intercourse in *SZQYU*. In a notice of decision, a Freedom Of Information Officer at the now Administrative Appeals Tribunal advised that 'the sexual images referred to in the decisions were located on a "memory stick" on the physical file for Case A' which 'contains 49 image files (JPEG).'[68] These 49 images still sit on a memory stick in the case file.

In her incisive study of the cultural afterlife of evidence, Katherine Biber argues that 'evidentiary objects often live before the trial, and sometimes continue to live afterwards.'[69] In this case, the images have now become 'information' capable of being published and accessed. Their afterlife is as data held in a file contained on a *memory* stick located in a physical file placed somewhere in the Tribunal's building. The images were, at one stage of their life, relevant evidence—and vital evidence at that. These images were an argument for the sexuality of the applicants. The memory stick on which they are located is not simply an object, but a discursive tool, yet its afterlife is limited by its hidden confinement in the archive. I have not seen, touched, smelt, tasted, or listened to the memory stick, its files, and the images therein. Its materiality is lost on me as a scholar. Nor do I know how the memory stick is placed in the archive and thus its material relation to the objects that surround it beyond it beyond its location 'on the physical file.' Without the ability to touch the memory stick, I am limited by my lack of sensorial engagement with the object itself but, through the discovery of the memory stick on the physical file, can try to understand its material relation to law and performance. As Biber concludes:

> Law's work is evident in the volume of papers it leaves in its wake, in its afterlife ... By understanding papers, files and folders as legal instruments, probative of the incremental accretion of ideas, decisions and strategies, we assume a new perspective on how law is made, enforced and preserved. And we are left with a trove of material which, in law's afterlife, provides us with clues, souvenirs and memorials to law's work.[70]

The images are evidence *for* the law—instruments in legal decision-making—and evidence *of* the law—mementos of the moment of decision, for legal decision-making is always reliant on evidence. Beyond the moment of decision, they constitute the afterlife of law as they sit preserved in the Tribunal's archive or trove.

In the notice of decision, I was refused access to the memory stick on the grounds that 'the individuals who own the information would have a reasonable expectation that their right to personal privacy would be respected and that their sensitive personal information would not be disseminated to third parties.'[71] To access these images would, to me, seem wrong. As Biber writes in relation to watching covert surveillance footage taken by police officers in a men's lavatory to secure convictions for sodomy, 'watching it outside and after the law seemed like a breach of some boundary.'[72] The law offers a comfortable boundary for the witnessing of evidence. Partly, this boundary is instantiated through the use of language.

The offer in *NAOX* challenged this boundary. Instead of witnessing images of a performance of sexual intercourse, the Tribunal was offered to be party to a live performance of sexual intercourse. The Tribunal declined and instead used the format of questions to educe information about the applicants' performance of sexual intercourse, including questions as to the applicant's use of lubricant. The Tribunal used language to recreate past acts of intercourse, focusing on the timing and intimate details of the act. These words can but paint a picture that would otherwise be clear in the witnessing of the act. On appeal it was never considered or concluded that the failure to witness the act of sexual intercourse was a jurisdictional error, as it was in regards to the images in *SZQYU*.

I was astonished that the Tribunal had kept the images, particularly given that they were returned to the applicant following the first Tribunal's decision. The notice of decision claims that the applicant's 'own the information.' The question of ownership and the propriety that ownership entails plagued this proceeding. Because of the assumption of ownership, the applicants' lawyers could request that the Tribunal not view the images. Yet, despite this assumption of ownership, the Court ruled on appeal that the Tribunal must view the images against the applicants' consent, and the memory stick containing the image files is still held by the Tribunal. It would seem from the notice of decision that the Tribunal is asserting ownership over the memory stick, but that the applicants still hold a proprietary interest in the images in the files thereon. The Tribunal holding this evidence in its archive and not releasing it could be seen as maintaining responsibility over the evidence and, in turn, a responsibility back to the applicants who tendered this evidence—a responsibility that entails protecting their privacy. The decision of the Tribunal to not release the images could also be a way of protecting the reading of the images by the second Tribunal.

The images of the performance in *SZQYU* are now contained on files in a memory stick, operating as memories of a performance that never convinced its audience. The performance in *NAOX* was a possibility never fulfilled. Both are cases of failed performance, whose legal memory exists in the archives or the scant words written about them in the judgment or correspondence kept on the case file. Performance scholar Herbert Molderings concludes that 'whatever survives of a performance in the form of a photograph or a videotape is no more than a fragmentary, petrified vestige of a lively process that took place at a different time in a different place.'[73] However, Auslander argues that the image 'is hardly a petrified remnant of some other event ... but exists rather as a lively, and forever unresolved process.'[74] These images are a remnant of a performance, but they still continue to do work in the Tribunal's archive. They are part of an unresolved process of adjudging the applicants' sexuality that even if seemingly resolved at the Tribunal's decision still has ongoing ramifications for the applicants themselves who must now operate in a world where they claim to be homosexual but the Tribunal has determined they are not.

## Conclusions: Receptions and Resistances

To go back to where this chapter started with the question of live versus mediatized sex acts on the legal stage, it could be argued that the Tribunal's refusal to watch a live sex act stems from the potency of the live, that it can be felt by the audience; whereas the screen intercedes to create a comfortable distance when watching the same act recorded. The Tribunal's engagement with the images of homosexual intercourse they contain is limited beyond the remark that 'the sexual activity depicted in the photos was engaged in ... for the sole purpose of strengthening the applicant's claim to be a refugee.'[75] What does sex 'for the sole purpose of strengthening the applicant's claim to be a refugee' look like? How can the purpose of sex be adjudged? This statement raises questions about 'the difference between actuality and simulation ... acting ... performance competence ... [and] *re-presentation*,' to use Bell's framing.[76]

Homemade porn is generally regarded as more authentic, and thus has a special appeal, because it contains ordinary or real people not actors who are, by implication, performing.[77] In some ways, authenticity 'is measured, interestingly enough, by performance *incompetence*.'[78] However, in this case, the Tribunal seems to be reading the images contextually. It would be difficult to infer the purposes of having sex from images themselves. Yet, by reading the images in the context of a refugee claim, the Tribunal is able to impute a purpose to the sex. It is not spontaneous sex, according to the Tribunal's reading, but sex created and choreographed for a specific purpose or in service of a viewing audience.[79] It is the premeditation of the act and the assumed lack of spontaneity that contributes to the lack of belief in the performance.[80]

It is also the competence of the performance. In *SZQYU*, the Tribunal 'accepts that [the applicant] has had intercourse with [redacted] on one occasion,' but perhaps because the sex lacked spontaneity and was instead undertaken for a particular purposes, it is deemed to be, to quote another scholar of pornography, an unreal 'elaborately engineered and choreographed *show* enacted by ... performers for a camera.'[81] In this sense, the performers are not 'engaged in real sexual activity.'[82] Of course, they are presumably sodomizing, but the way in which it is quite deliberately constructed leads the Tribunal to conclude that 'does not establish that [the applicant] is gay.'[83] In *NAOX*, the applicants' offer to engage in a live act of homosexual intercourse was taken as an indication that they were not shy, and thus when one expressed discomfort at answering questions regarding their use of lubricant in morning sex, the Tribunal was able to conclude that they were 'not a truthful or credible witness.'[84]

What underpins both these matters is resistance: resistance to engaging deeply with a performance of sexual intercourse, live or digital. In her study of refugee claims on the basis of sexuality, Jenni Millbank concludes that 'while the cases were replete with references to 'allegations' of gay identity as something easy to make and hard to disprove ... it could just as readily be argued based on our research that findings of the falsity of sexual identity in refugee determinations are easy to make and impossible to appeal.'[85] In these cases, appeals were successful on the grounds of jurisdictional error and unreasonableness. In *NAOX*, the Tribunal's decision is variously referred to as 'not made in good faith,' 'unreasonable,' and 'guilty of bias.'[86] What the appeals court found in both cases was a resistance to engage with the evidence and the performance of sexual intercourse. The Tribunal failed to look at the photographs or avoided witnessing in favour of recreating the act through words. This springs from a resistance towards confronting the performance of bodies in sexual intercourse—of seeing, facing, and even potentially touching these entwined bodies. When the photographs are finally witnessed, there is a resistance to articulating how the bodies look and how the images make the judging audience feel in an embodied sense.

An alternative judgment would explore these performances from a wider frame, asking larger questions of what prompts applicants to perform their sexuality and how these performances make applicants feel. The 'significant embarrassment' that applicants in *NAOX* feel in offering up their bodies for a performance of sexual intercourse is barely explored by the Tribunal, but may explain why they are subsequently uncomfortable with answering questions about their sexual practices. An alternative judgment might also confront the feelings of the Tribunal Member in engaging with the images of homosexual intercourse in *SZQYU*, exploring how the bodies look and also the Tribunal Member's sensory engagement with the images on screen through sight and through touch. An alternative judgment could also consider how records are to be kept and who is to retain them.

Fundamentally, the Tribunal in both instances resists accepting that the applicants are gay. The applicants are in a double bind: they have to perform to prove their sexuality, but by performing—or offering to perform—their sexuality is viewed not as real but rather a performance, with the connotation of faking it for the audience. The resistance that plagues these cases—both from the Tribunal but also the applicants themselves who are embarrassed to perform or request the Tribunal to not view images of their performance—hampers a more sophisticated engagement with the performance of sexuality.


## Notes

1.   *NAOX v Minister for Immigration and Citizenship* [2009] FCA 1056 (18 September 2009) [75].

2.   *SZQYU v Minister for Immigration; SZQYV v Minister for Immigration* [2012] FMCA 1114 (3 December 2012) [12].

3.   *SZQYU v Minister for Immigration; SZQYV v Minister for Immigration* [2012] FMCA 1114 (3 December 2012) [62] quoted in David Donaldson, 'Refugee case: the tricky task of proving to a court you're gay,' *Crikey*, 31 January 2013, accessed 1 June 2019, https://www.crikey.com.au/2013/01/31/refugee-case-the-tricky-task-of-proving-to-a-court-youre-gay/.

4.   Laurie Berg and Jenni Millbank, 'Constructing the Personal Narratives of Lesbian, Gay and Bisexual Asylum Claimants' *Journal of Refugee Studies* 22/2 (2009),195–6.

5.   Berg and Millbank, 'Constructing the Personal Narratives,' 95.

6.   Senthorun Raj, 'A/Effective Adjudications: Queer Refugees and the Law' *Journal of Intercultural Studies* 38/4 (2017), 453.

7.   Costas Douzinas, 'Rehearsals,' *World Rehearsal Court,* 2009, accessed 9 April 2019, http://worldrehearsalcourt.com/pdfs/wrc_rehearsals.pdf, 3.

8.   Philip Auslander *Liveness: Performance in a Mediatized Culture* (London: Routledge, 1999), 130.

9.   Auslander, *Liveness,* 115.

10.   Filmmaker Christian Delage and legal scholar Peter Goodrich write that 'film and now the plethora of digital forms of virtual relay are having a … drastic if not yet fully explored impact upon the preconceptions and forms of relay of legality': Christian Delage and Peter Goodrich, eds, *The Scene of the Mass Crime: History, Film and International Tribunals* (London: Routledge, 2013), 1. See also Kate Leader, *Trials, Truth-Telling and the Performing Body* (PhD thesis, University of Sydney, 2008), 192.

11.   Jack Balkin & Sanford Levinson, 'Law as Performance,' in *Law and Literature: Current Legal Issues*, eds. Michael Freeman & Andrew Lewis (Oxford: Oxford University Press, 1999), 729.

12.   Nicole Rogers, 'The Play of Law: Comparing Performances in Law and Theatre,' *Queensland University of Technology Law and Justice Journal* 8/2 (2008), 431.

13.   Julie Peters, 'Legal Performance: Good and Bad,' *Law, Culture and the Humanities* 4/2 (2008), 198. See also Peter Goodrich, 'Spectres of Law: Why the History of the Legal Spectacle has Not been Written,' *UC Irvine Law Review* 1/3 (2011), 808. This is discussed further in Julie Peters, 'Law

as Performance: Historical Interpretation, Objects, Lexicons, and Other Methodological Problems,' in *New Directions in Law and Literature*, eds. Elizabeth Ankler and Bernadette Meyler (New York: Oxford University Press, 2017) 193–209.

14.    Rogers, 'The Play of Law'; Peters, 'Legal Performance: Good and Bad.' 'Legal performance' could also capture performances in law-making chambers, legal offices, and other arenas that are subject to legal regulation. Other noteworthy texts on legal performance include Alan Read, *Theatre and Law* (London: Palgrave Macmillan, 2015); Peter Robson, 'Theatre and Law in the Twenty-first Century' in *Cultural Legal Studies: Law's Popular Cultures and the Metamorphosis of Law*, eds. Cassandra Sharp and Marett Leiboff (Abingdon: Routledge, 2015) 113–32; Marett Leiboff, 'Theatricalizing Law,' *Law and Literature* 30/2 (2018); Kate Leader, 'Closed-Circuit Television Testimony: Liveness and Truth-telling,' *Law Text Culture* 14 (2010), 312–36.

15.    Peters, 'Law as Performance,' 196.

16.    *Migration Act 1958* ss 91X, 501K.

17.    *NAOX v Minister for Immigration and Citizenship* [2009] FCA 1056 (18 September 2009) [75].

18.    Letter from Angela Leung, Legal and Policy Officer of the Administrative Appeals Tribunal, to author, 23 November 2018.

19.    *NAOX v Minister for Immigration* [2008] FMCA 1467 (31 October 2008) [49]; *NAOX v Minister for Immigration and Citizenship* [2009] FCA 1056 (18 September 2009) [77].

20.    *NAOX v Minister for Immigration* [2008] FMCA 1467 (31 October 2008) [140].

21.    *NAOX v Minister for Immigration and Citizenship* [2009] FCA 1056 (18 September 2009) [80].

22.    'Case 1' (17 November 2011), [38]; 1105875 [2011] RRTA 982 (17 November 2011) [51], [59]; *SZQYU v Minister for Immigration*; *SZQYV v Minister for Immigration* [2012] FMCA 1114 (3 December 2012) [12].

23.    'Case 1' (17 November 2011), [11]. This was recorded in the Case Note as follows: 'I received a message this morning to return a call from the Rep's office in regards to the case. I contacted the Rep's office ... I spoke with [redacted] who said that at the hearing on [redacted] that his client had handed a CD to the member. [Redacted] claimed this was done prior to the Rep entering the room and that his client only informed him after. [Redacted] was instructed to call the Tribunal and inform the member not to view it as it contains sensitive material.'

24.    It said so in the following terms, 'The Tribunal ... made no reference to the photographs of the applicants having sex. Before it could find that the applicants were not homosexual the Tribunal had to deal, amongst other things, with their allegation that their relationship had a physical dimension. It did this by concluding that neither of them had sex with a male, including each other. However, in order to reach that particular conclusion, it was necessary

that the Tribunal consider the evidence before it relevant to that subject ... It may be that the Tribunal did not consider ... the photographs because although the disc had been provided to the Tribunal at the commencement of [the applicant's] hearing, the applicants' advisers later wrote, in both cases, asking the Tribunal not to view what it contained ... The evidence of what was on the disc might have had a bearing on the outcome of the reviews in that the Tribunal's failure to consider it possibly deprived the applicants of a successful outcome to their review applications. A failure to consider such evidence amounts to a constructive failure to exercise jurisdiction and is thus a jurisdictional error': *SZQYU v Minister for Immigration; SZQYV v Minister for Immigration* [2012] FMCA 1114 (3 December 2012) [60]–[65].

25.   'Case A' (24/25 October 2013), [87].

26.   'Case A' (24/25 October 2013), [88].

27.   'Case A' (24/25 October 2013), [100].

28.   In the second edition of *Liveness*, Auslander notes that there are still 'ongoing discussions of performance in a mediatized culture': (London: Routledge, 2007) xiii.

29.   Peggy Phelan, *Unmarked: The Politics of Performance* (London and New York: Routledge, 1993), 146. Patrice Parvis makes a similar point that performance cannot be saved, recorded or documented, as it then veers into a recording: *Theatre at the Crossroads of Culture* (London: Routledge, 1992), 67.

30.   Auslander, *Liveness*, 44.

31.   The 'play' of the court is turned into 'replay' through video. See Cornelia Vismann, '"Rejour les Crimes!": Theater vs Video' *Cordozo Studies in Law and Literature* 13/1 (2001), 133.

32.   Carolyn McKay, 'Screening Testimony: Law and Performance in the Age of the Videosphere' (Seminar delivered at the Centre for Theatre and Performance, Monash University, 9 August 2018). See also Carolyn McKay, *The Pixelated Prisoner: Prison Video Links, Court 'Appearance' and the Justice Matrix* (Abingdon: Routledge, 2018).

33.   Sean Mulcahy, 'Screening Testimony,' *Art/Law Network*, accessed 9 April 2019, http://artlawnetwork.org/screening-testimony/.

34.   Sharon Kahanoff, 'The Will and the Way of the Apparatus,' *World Rehearsal Court*, 2009, accessed 9 April 2019, http://worldrehearsalcourt.com/pdfs/wrc_the-will-and-the-way-of-the-apparatus.pdf, 11.

35.   Elizabeth Bell, 'Weddings and Pornography: The Cultural Performance of Sex,' *Text and Performance Quarterly* 19 (1999), 173 (emphasis in original).

36.   Bell, 'Weddings and Pornography,' 174.

37.   Anselm Franke, 'Phantom Limb,' *World Rehearsal Court*, 2009, accessed 3 July 2019, http://worldrehearsalcourt.com/pdfs/wrc_phantom-limb.pdf, 2-3.

38.   Franke, 'Phantom Limb,' 5.

39.   Bell, 'Weddings and Pornography,' 174.

40.   Douzinas, 'Rehearsals,' 3.

41.   Linda Mulcahy, 'The Unbearable Lightness of Being? Shifts Towards the Virtual Trial' *Journal of Law and Society* 35/4 (2008), 465.

42.   Leader, 'Liveness and Truth-Telling,' 313.

43.   Leader, 'Liveness and Truth-Telling,' 314.

44.   Mulcahy 'The Unbearable Lightness of Being?', 487.

45.   Mulcahy, 'The Unbearable Lightness of Being?', 485.

46.   Mulcahy, 'The Unbearable Lightness of Being?', 484.

47.   Mulcahy, 'The Unbearable Lightness of Being?', 483.

48.   Richard Sherwin, *Visualizing Law in the Age of the Digital Baroque: Arabesques and Entanglements* (London: Routledge, 2011) 28.

49.   Anne Bogart and Tina Landau, *The Viewpoints Book: A Practical Guide to Viewpoints and Composition* (New York: Theatre Communications Group, 2005) 8.

50.   Auslander, *Liveness*, 129–30.

51.   *Romeo + Juliet*. Film. Baz Luhrmann. United State of America: 20th Century Fox, 1996.

52.   Mulcahy, 'The Unbearable Lightness of Being?', 485.

53.   Mulcahy, 'The Unbearable Lightness of Being?', 484.

54.   Kirsty Duncanson, 'Erotic Conversations about Contract and Consent at the Cinema' (Seminar delivered at the Criminal Justice Centre, University of Warwick, 26 October 2017).

55.   David MacDougall, *Transcultural Cinema* (New Jersey: Princeton University Press, 1998).

56.   Bell, 'Weddings and Pornography,' 181, 185.

57.   Bell, 'Weddings and Pornography,' 187.

58.   Judy Radul, 'Video Chamber,' in *A Thousand Eyes: Media, Technology, Law and Aesthetics*, eds. Marit Paasche and Judy Rahul (Berlin: Sternberg Press, 2011), 125.

59.   Sherwin, *Visualizing Law*, 34.

60.   Leif Dahlberg, *Spacing Law and Politics: The Constitution and Representation of the Juridical* (London: Routledge, 2017), 218.

61.   Radul, 'Video Chamber,' 129.

62.   Dahlberg, *Spacing Law and Politics*, 217-218.

63.   Sherwin, *Visualizing Law*, 7.

64.   Radul, 'Video Chamber,' 130.

65.   At the extreme end of the spectrum, see Mona Hatoum's *Corps Etranger*, where the artist filmed her skin and internal organs at close distance then broadcast them on screens for the audience to walk over and touch: Christine Ross, *The Past is the Present; It's the Future Too: The Temporal Turn in Contemporary Art* (London: Continuum, 2012).

66.   'Case A' (24/25 October 2013), [88].

67.   Dahlberg, *Spacing Law and Politics*, 219.

68.   Letter from Tina Bridge, Policy Officer of the Administrative Appeals

Tribunal, to author, 2 August 2018.

69.    Katherine Biber, *In Crime's Archive: The Cultural Afterlife of Evidence* (London: Routledge, 2019), 1.

70.    Biber, *In Crime's Archive*, 7.

71.    Letter from Tina Bridge to author, 2 August 2018. See *Freedom of Information Act 1982* s 47F.

72.    Biber, *In Crime's Archive*, 2.

73.    Herbert Molderings, 'Life is No Performance' in *The Art of Performance: A Critical Anthology*, eds. Gregory Battock and Robert Nickas (London: E.P. Dutton, 1984), 172–3.

74.    Auslander, *Liveness*, 44.

75.    'Case A' (24/25 October 2013), [88].

76.    Bell, 'Weddings and Pornography,' 182 (emphasis in original).

77.    Bell, 'Weddings and Pornography,' 186 (emphasis in original).

78.    Bell, 'Weddings and Pornography,' 186.

79.    Bell, 'Weddings and Pornography,' 174.

80.    Bell, 'Weddings and Pornography,' 183, 188.

81.    Linda Williams, *Hard Core: Power, Pleasure and the 'Frenzy of the Visible'* (Berkeley: University of California Press, 1989), 147 (emphasis in original).

82.    Bell, 'Weddings and Pornography,' 182–3.

83.    'Case A' (24/25 October 2013), [88]. Michael Kirby, in writing on the continuum of acting and not-acting, argues that acting appears 'at the point at which the emotions are 'pushed' for the sake of the spectators': 'On Acting and Not-Acting' in *Acting (Re)Considered*, ed. Phillip Zarelli (London: Routledge, 1995), 47.

84.    *NAOX v Minister for Immigration* [2008] FMCA 1467 (31 October 2008) [49]; *NAOX v Minister for Immigration and Citizenship* [2009] FCA 1056 (18 September 2009) [77].

85.    Jenni Millbank, 'From Discretion to Disbelief: Recent Trends in Refugee Determinations on the Basis of Sexual Orientation in Australia and the United Kingdom' *The International Journal of Human Rights* 13/2–3 (2009), 399.

86.    *NAOX v Minister for Immigration and Citizenship* [2009] FCA 1056 (18 September 2009) [80].

# 5

# Queering the Prison: Communication, Social Justice and the Expression of Genre Subjectivities in the Spanish Prison System

*Virginia Villaplana-Ruiz*

## More Than Words Can Tell

This chapter* has the form of a written dialogue for the author's art project in prison, the embodied text *Diaries of Intermittent Dreams*.[1] This is a text in dialogue with transgender people in jail, composed as an assembly of voices. The dialogue presented here takes place one week before Rudy's, Humberto's and Jeny's deportation from Spain to Venezuela. The place is Rehabilitation Centre for Social Integration and León Penitentiary Mansilla de las Mulas, Spain. As a writer, visual artist, and cultural researcher I address the notions of community and affective-sexual diversity through methodologies such as 'mediabiography' or co-learning. I conceive of writing as a negotiation between history and memory.

This project, linked to the educational programme of the León Penitentiary Mansilla de las Mulas and the Castilla y León Museum of Contemporary Art, explores the possibility of using art and community communication to overflow and transform the relationship between the inside and the outside (of the penitentiary institution, but also of the artistic and educational spaces and discourses). It thus raises the need to generate narrations and representations that break with stereotypes that exist around prisons and the prison population.[2] Two years after starting the workshop and launching the Hipatia magazine, it became possible to take advantage of the artistic-educational framework provided by the collaboration between museum and penitentiary institutions to facilitate access to the third grade for some of the women who were participating in the project. Alongside them and others from the León Penitentiary Mansilla de las Mulas, the co-learning process *Diaries of Intermittent Dreams* played a fundamental role through the practice of mediabiography, which I have devised and discussed elsewhere.[3]

Mediabiography is an interdisciplinary methodology that explores personal biographical archives through queer methods by analyzing the confluence between word, image, and memory.[4] In this process, we experiment with the creation of intimate and collective narrations.[5] When we began to work with this methodology, the first problem we faced was that most of these people had been arrested as *mulas*—people who were just passing through Spain and, therefore, hardly carried any images or personal memories with them. For this reason, I first proposed that they ask their relatives (with whom in many cases they had lost contact or only kept in contact in a very sporadic and cold way) to send them photographs or other objects of memories that were important to them at an affective level. Photographs and objects, I explained, would help them get out of the situation of identity annihilation that, after their time in prison, they were experiencing as resistance.[6]

A key aspect in the co-learning processes articulated through mediabiography is the process of writing. In the first work sessions of *Diaries of Intermittent Dreams*, the possibility of using writing (and specifically letter writing) as a tool for (self) knowledge both individually and collectively and for deconstructing and reconstructing identity was raised. To illustrate the fruits of this work, I first read a fragment of a text in which one of the participants in the project (L. M.) tells us that she felt great happiness when she was sent a photograph of her aged barely fourteen months ('because looking at her,' she assures, 'I return to my childhood').

Then I read another text in which one of the trans women with whom they have collaborated, Jeny, describes one of the first moments in which she was able to show and vindicate her sexual identity in the Spanish prison where she had been held. From these stories, from the photographs they had been receiving, and from the intense conversations they had during the sharing sessions, a series of key words or ideas (desire, freedom, reunion, realization, acceptance, life, future, longing, satisfaction, sharing…) were chosen, and with them, a kind of collective narrative that took the form of a mural that was displayed in one of the common areas of the León Penitentiary Mansilla de las Mulas was constructed. We cannot forget, I wanted to emphasize, that apart from taking into account the violence that is always suffered by those who are in a situation of deprivation of liberty,[7] trans men and women also need to deal with specific violence that the penitentiary system practices over their bodies and sexual identities.[8]

Within the framework of the project *Diaries of Intermittent Dreams*, other actions have also been carried out, such as the collaboration for several months with a radio programme of a radio station owned by the University of León (a programme in which they were free to deal with the subjects they wanted and which, often, was also used so that they could contact their families by telephone). Also, the production of a series of photographic reports in which an attempt was made to generate a situation of performativity that would allow them to represent their daily life. In relation to this last action, I wanted to comment on two things. On the one hand, the importance that the creation of photographic (auto)representations of the participants in the project and of the actions they carried out has had in all this process. We have to bear in mind that during a stay in a detention centre you can hardly access images of yourself and that in them the use of cameras is very restricted. In fact, in order to introduce our cameras we had to go through multiple bureaucratic procedures. On the other hand, the need to be aware that, in the end, institutions are constituted by people. If this project has been possible, it is because some workers from the institutions involved in it have listened to us and let us do it, even if sometimes they did not understand very well what we were trying to do.

After remembering that the group decided to work on a book of all their experiences as a way of closing the project, I ended my talk by recalling another one of the activities that was set in motion within the framework of *Diaries of Intermittent Dreams*: the film cycle that they called 'Your Favourite Film,' in which, as the name of the activity indicated, a member of the group and/or a resident of the centre chose the film that he liked best so that it could be shown in each session. The idea, I explained, was to set up a cinema-forum dynamic (accompanying the screening with a presentation of the film, a debate, etc.) that would make it possible to break with the rigid temporality that these spaces impose (the films are projected at ten o'clock at night, that is, after the hour in which the recount takes place) and would also make it possible to create an activity that could be managed autonomously and maintained over time (and that's how it was: what began as summer cinema, became autumn cinema and after winter and after spring... Thus, generating an activity that continued to be organized when the project ended).

Although throughout the process it was clear to them that they wanted to avoid the mechanisms of visibility and diffusion that are common in projects linked to artistic and museum institutions, the pressure they finally felt to tell and show what they were doing led them to take the decision to hold a press conference on this cycle of cinema. The result of the press conference confirmed their fears: the news published about the cycle had an impact on many of the mistakes and common places where people tend to fall when talking about initiatives related to the prison environment;[9] for example, insisting on calling them prisoners (refuting all the de-stigmatization and decodification work we were carrying out) or illustrating the information, as in the case of the review published by Diario de León, with a very aggressive photogram of the film *Amores perros* (a film that, in reality, did not even form part of the cycle). In my opinion, this example of how media logic works and how it constrains us shows that it is necessary to think and to develop analytical tools as well as discursive strategies and methodological practices to help us generate other forms of narration and communication; alternative devices of encounter and representation, alternative ways of doing things.

## Time as a Daily Routine, Transmigrants, Prisoners, and Law

Schools have their discipline, which may seem both severe and merciless to those with a sensitive nature. To such people we respond that schools are not made up of children, but rather they are made for them.

— The Criminal Child, Radio text, Jean Genet, 1949.

The architecture of this prison, its spatial distribution, is a powerful centre of seclusion. The formulas of the labyrinth and the panopticon coincide with the power of visual control technologies: surveillance cameras, public address systems, and restriction of access to spaces. The inmates move in the courtyard and have restricted access to move from one module to another, there are systems of double armoured doors, bars in the windows of their cells, regular prison controls, walls that not only confine the bodies, but also the look. Prison officers observe all their movements on the monitors. The women are being observed by cameras in all corridors and spaces of the prison. The limited vision is for them, the panopticon for power and authority.

The art project *Diaries of Intermittent Dreams* was born in this place because each of the groups of trans-women involved in the writing wanted to communicate their stories responsibly, and respect and be aware of the words, commitment, and confidence of each other. Because *Diaries of Intermittent Dreams* is more than an art project, it continues to be a meeting place. The project is for many of the trans-women a unique experience of making possible the learning of liberation and education, of social and artistic expression alongside the women and the transwomen who are deprived of their freedom in the penitentiary. Humberto speaks informally about the comments the guards make laughingly about Jeny's and Rudy's transexuality: 'Sweetcakes, they're looking for you; Sweetcakes, the police are looking for you; Sweetcakes, did you pick everything up? Have you got everything organized? And of course, some guards brand us for other things, you know what I mean, a sexual meaning.'

Humberto: Fortunately, Rudy's going soon. She's going to get out of here.

She has been in prison exactly three years and eight months. Now Rudy is going back to Venezuela.

Rudy: Yes! I'm getting out of here! And Jeny and Humberto haven't got much time left to go.

Jeny: I don't want … I don't want to go back to Venezuela … But I'm going back, too.

Humberto: In the end, we're going to have to go back. We have to think that, because they're going to send us back.

Jeny and Rudy are talking about the law under which a convicted criminal is returned to his or her home country in exchange for a commuted sentence. Articles 53.1 and 57.2 of the Spanish immigration law in reference to migrants who have been immersed in criminal proceedings and have been secluded in jail. In Spain, if migrant prisoners sign of their own free will that they want to go back to their home country, they are sent there and the sentence is commuted. Regular scheduled flights are used to carry out these legalized deportations back to Latin America.

Humberto: If we sign, it's a way to get out of this situation completely. And without even having to go there personally or signing, nothing. Just that everybody goes back to their country and gets their freedom and their life back.

Jeny: … Because this is exhausting, exhausting, exhausting … It's such a daily routine. Do you know what makes me so exhausted? The daily routine. Every day the same, get up, sleep, go down, sleep, go down again, go up all in the same place. Sometimes I just pass the time sleeping, and when we're granted a furlough pass, I get bored on the street, being there during the day like a little kid. The passes are good between 10 am and 1 p.m., returning here between 6 and 8. And what else can you do? Watch television and look out the window. But at least we can look out onto the street and enjoy our own thoughts.

Rudy: The good thing about this Rehabilitation Centre for Social Integration here in the prison is that it's in the city and we can watch people go by, cars going by in the street. And just people moving around. Because when we were in the Masilla de Las Mulas Penitentiary in León, you know. What could you see there? Walls and more walls. Then, when your sentence is just a third degree … It's a different world in the Rehab Centre than in the Masilla de las Mulas Prison. I can really say that even with all the bad things that have happened to us, it hasn't been all that bad. After being at the Masilla de las Mulas for one year we had the chance to come to the Rehab Centre to do a cooking course. And nobody thought we'd make it. Everyone thought we'd screw it up.

Jeny: Nobody thought we'd make it. They thought we'd be the first ones to screw up and have to go back to the Masilla de las Mulas Penitentiary.

Rudy: Because we're Latina transsexuals. They thought that we'd be jumping around, doing things we shouldn't and that kind of thing.

Jeny: Because we're transsexuals, they judge us, without even knowing us as people. Or our culture, or, what do I know? The way a person thinks. Because we all think differently and that's why no one thought we'd make it.

Rudy: Yeah. I'll tell you. There were twenty people who went down to do the cooking course and only five of us managed to finish.

Jeny: Right. Andrés, Rudy, César, Laudelina, and me. Only five out of more than twenty people. The others all got sent back up to Masilla within twenty days, fifteen days. Some were lucky enough to get deported back to their own countries. Like Hugo, this Argentinean guy who came down with us to do the cooking course on parole and they sent him back to his country. And Aurora, who got transferred to a prison up in Asturias. But the rest of the people in the course went back to the penitentiary and none of them got another chance to come to the Rehab Centre.

Jeny: … and fighting and dealing with it!

Rudy: After so much time, okay. Jeny has been luckier than me as far as work goes. Back at the penitentiary, as coordinator of the self-respect module, she got a salary; for better or for worse, the work kept her going. For me, the time I spent in there I wasn't so lucky. Then we came here to the Rehab Centre and we've been working in the kitchen and splitting one salary between the two of us.

Humberto: Jeny was in charge of the kitchen in the office and they paid her a salary that she split with Rudy.

Jeny: Half of my pay was for Rudy.

Rudy: Well, afterwards we shared it with Humberto.

Later, after working for a year, they passed an order to give me a job in the laundry after having worked for almost a year with no pay whatsoever. And now I've received three payments since they gave me the job in the laundry. Sure, all things considered it's not the salary that's important, but the job here in the prison is like my refuge. Far from everything. I'm never in the common rooms, never in the dining hall or in the courtyard. I'm always in the laundry from nine in the morning until two-thirty or three in the afternoon, depending on which guard is on duty. We go up to the cell to rest and then come down again at six o'clock. When I have money to go out and get on the internet, I leave the Rehab Centre for a while and, well, I go where I can make a phone call. And if I haven't got any money, well, I might even stay in the laundry until eight-thirty in the evening.

Rudy: This laundry room is designed to serve very few people. Because nobody thought that the prison Rehab Centre would get so full. Because there used to be thirty people max here, but now it's 'full.' You know? And on the days the laundry is full, there's more than one hundred people at the centre.

Jeny: You see, the washing machines aren't very big; they can only take about eight kilos of washing.

Rudy: They're not industrial machines; they're just normal washing machines like the ones you have at home. There are only two washers and two dryers and one of those doesn't work. So it takes longer to do the work.

Rudy: Around ten or fifteen a day. It depends on how many clothes there are to wash.

Jeny: The poor washing machines never stop. Even after they've done the roll call at night, the machines are still going. The washing machines never rest; they keep washing and drying clothes all day long.

Rudy: Now Humberto will be in charge of the laundry, and while Jeny's here, she'll get to keep the entire salary from the kitchen. Not that they're marvelous salaries or anything, but for those of us who are foreigners here, who don't have any family or roots here ...

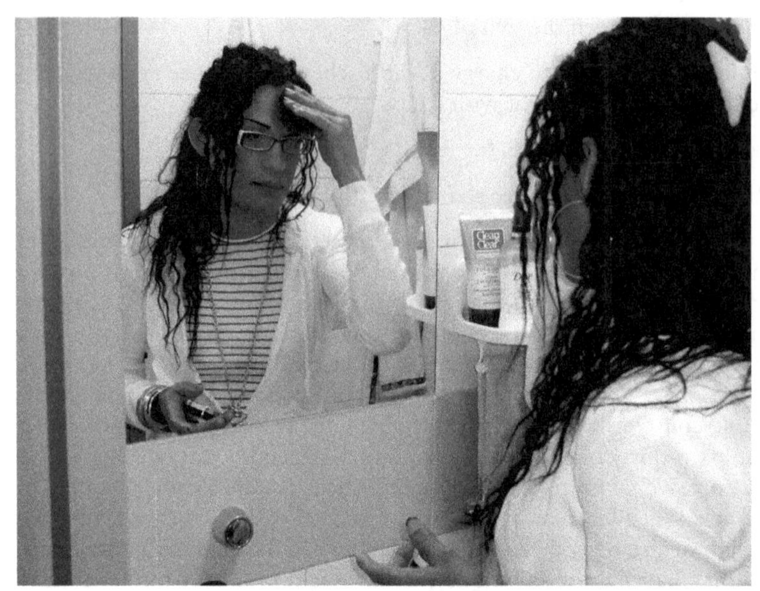

Fig. 1: *Portrait of Jeny, photo by Virginia Villaplana-Ruiz*

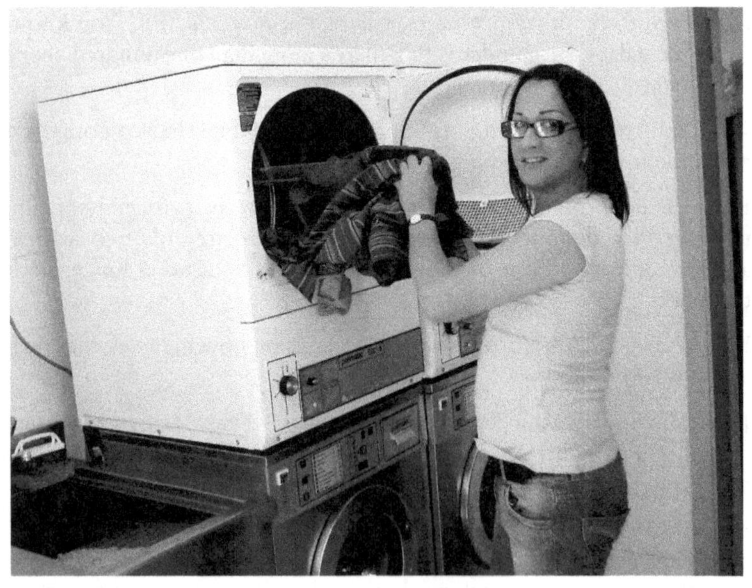

Fig. 2: *Portrait of Rudy, photo by Virginia Villaplana-Ruiz*

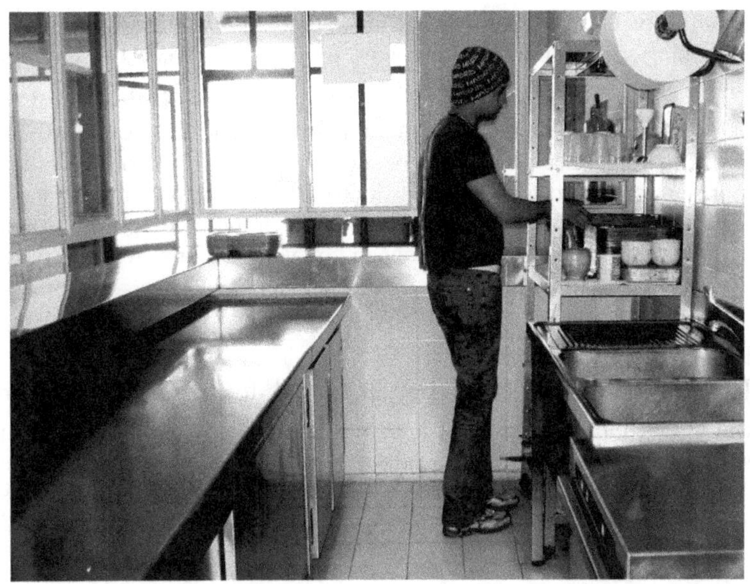

*Fig. 3: Portrait of Humberto, photo by Virginia Villaplana-Ruiz*

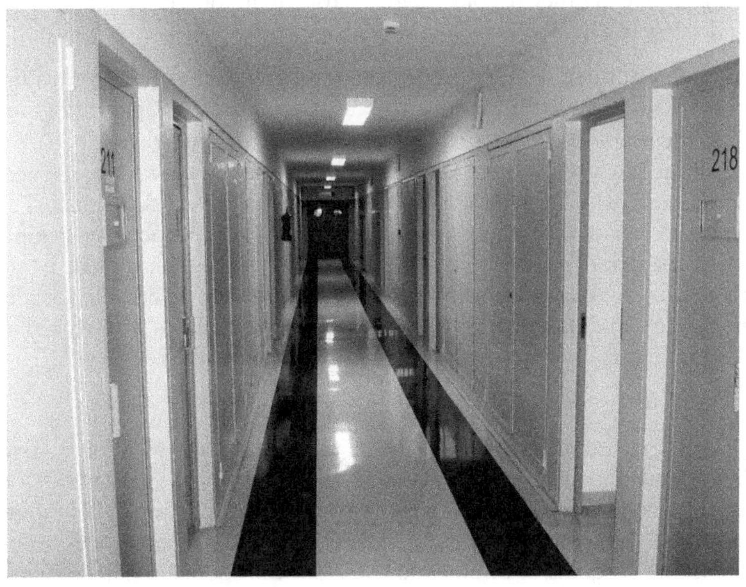

*Fig. 4: Prison cell corridor, photo by Virginia Villaplana*

Humberto: Hey, it's something, so that maybe someday you'll get something else and they'll let you work outside the prison because things change.

Later, if you want, when we start filming in the laundry, we can continue with this topic. But now it just occurred to me that for foreigners it's more important to have a job inside the Rehab Centre than to have one outside because outside of here it's much more complicated than it is for other people, especially when you've been convicted of a third degree felony.

Rudy: In prison, it's easier.

Jeny: Absolutely; it's much harder to look for work outside of here.

Rudy: Our idea when we got here with the cooking course—our goal was to finish the course and then look for work in a hair salon. Because we're hairdressers. But we couldn't because we don't have work permits and we fall under the Rights and Freedoms of Foreigners in Spain and so they don't let us work.[10]

Humberto: Although it's not always a problem because the Immigration Office isn't usually in charge of giving work permits; the one who deals with the permits is the warden and in the letter he sends it says right in the text whether they're going to give it to you or not. The prison officials and the warden have to make the decision.

Jeny: But of these permits ... of a thousand applications, they only take one. It's impossible for foreigners because in the case of Spaniards, they give them a work permit even though they fall under Article 10.[11] I think the law itself is what generates the bad blood between foreigners and Spaniards in prison with this whole subject of work permits. The way the law works it generates a lot of bad feeling between people from Spain and people from other countries, because on the one hand, there's discrimination when you go to look for a job to become socially integrated, and on the other hand, there are bad feelings with regard to commuting your sentences in exchange for leaving the country.

Rudy: Right.

Jeny: I remember the other day I was talking about it with Hans. Two laws come together here. The Immigration Law and the Penal Code, so there's a conflict because foreigners can benefit and this can work in some cases, but only if you take into account that the foreigners from outside the EU aren't going to be allowed back into Europe again until after ten years. It's a form of legalized deportation in this country in exchange for a commuted sentence. And for someone who wants this, it's a way out. On the other hand, it's the laws themselves which generate these differences within the prison population.

Rudy: The laws keep putting up obstacles for the people. Not for everyone, but for most of us.

Rudy and Jeny: Still, I can't complain. In prison we've met a lot of great people. Really good-hearted people who understood us. Sure, like I told you before, we tried to live in our world. We tried not to integrate completely into prison life. And if not to live in our own world, at least to follow our own way.

Humberto: Instead of hanging out in the courtyard, we decided to occupy our time and move things forward in a good way between the three of us.

Jeny: We wanted to spend the time doing things. In fact, I'm the first people who came to the museum, and that is very significant.

Humberto, and Rudy: Yes, but we were open to it. Because when someone talks to you about the museum, you don't really know what we're going to do until you get there and meet us. From the museum—I'm in the educational department—when I ask the prison officials if there are people signed up for an activity, in principle you don't necessarily sign up because you're interested, but rather because you have a certain attitude and you decide to go and participate, and then, whether it interests you or not, you stay. We're talking about keeping busy.

Jeny: Yeah, keeping busy doing things so that you stop thinking about it. Not just sitting around here because if you dwell on what happened before, you get a little crazy just rehashing the situation again and again.

Humberto: And because you can get depressed or something like that which makes you feel bad all the time, and that's the main thing. We avoided a lot of that. We had a lot of willpower even though we know that you can experience things in a really horrible way. We were really ready for this. And of course, it's clear that we all have things that make us sad, thoughts of our families and of people we left behind in our countries. This usually happens to everyone. But we always tried to rise above it.

Jeny: Yes, to try to keep your sense of self-worth up, high because if you let it fall, you fall into a depression, you get sick; there are drugs there and problems, so many things.

Jeny, Humberto, Rudy: Absolutely!

Rudy: Yes, because it's a world where everything gets maximized. And it's a very small world where the problems are very large. Even the smallest problem gets huge and the situation becomes too much for you. And if you don't have the strength of will to get through it, you sink. You sink and destroy yourself because you don't destroy the other people, you destroy only yourself.

Jeny, Humberto, Rudy: Right!

Rudy: Still, we're here serving a sentence and our family serves it with us, even though they're not in prison. Our families know that we're serving a sentence in a country that's not our own.

Jeny: Our families suffer more than we do.

Rudy: Our families know that we don't have anything or anybody and so they suffer. And we suffer thinking that they're there suffering for us. Our families suffer for the mistakes we made. So, if you don't have a tough, strong heart to get through this, both you and your family are going to go to pieces.

Jeny, Humberto, Rudy: Really, really strong! (Deep sighs of emotion).

Jeny, Humberto, Rudy: Yeah.

Rudy: Yes, but what happens is that because of our sexual orientation, we learned really young how to get over things and get through all kinds of obstacles. Because here, even though in a way there's not much discrimination against gays, in our country Venezuela this type of sexual discrimination is more evident and more latent. Here we can go out and take a walk up and down the street, come and go without being noticed at all. There's always someone who looks at us, but we really can walk around without being noticed too much.

Jeny: Not like in Venezuela. There they point at you in the street.

Rudy: If you go out in Venezuela, they point at you. For example, here I can go to the flea market in Madrid and walk around the entire market from end to end (laughter). From end to end without being afraid that people are going to laugh at me, or talk about me behind my back, or frighten me, or shout obscenities at me. Going to a flea market in my country is suicide.

Jeny, Humberto, Rudy: (Laughter).

Jeny: I'm going to tell you a little story. Look, Humberto, do you remember this story in Venezuela? (Complicit laughter between Humberto and Jeny.) Once in Venezuela. We lived in Guárico and Humberto and I and some other friends went to Barquisimeto to the flea market of San Juan, there they call it the street market. We went to the San Juan street market in December to buy clothes and me, because I'm the craziest of all, I wore my hair really, really short and I dyed it bright red. From the corner where the taxi left us to the point where we entered the flea market—Girl! That was really something!—the only thing they didn't do was throw hand grenades at us. They called me phospho-head, lit match, they ran at us throwing tomatoes and we couldn't buy anything. We had to go back out the way we came in. That was horrible. It was horrible, horrible, horrible. I'll never forget them throwing tomatoes at us from the stalls. It was scandalous; it looked like some celebrities were going down the street from the number of people who came to look at us. And the crowd screamed at us and turned their backs to us. That was horrible! It was horrible, horrible, horrible!

Jeny, Humberto, Rudy: But here you go unnoticed. Well, there's always someone who will look at you, but it's not in the same league. We really notice the difference in lifestyle between there and here a lot. It's different. Totally.

Rudy: Even in the mall where we work in Venezuela. We had to go with pants, high-necked shirts, covered up, not a lot of make-up, no heels. Because the directors of the mall didn't let us. And in fact, they've fought so hard against transsexuals in Venezuela that just a while back I called home and they told me that the hair salons where transsexuals work are all closed. The transsexuals who worked in the mall had to leave.

Jeny and Humberto: When we worked in Venezuela there was a discriminatory situation against transgender people that they didn't enforce at the beginning but then they did:[12] transsexuals couldn't go shopping at the mall; they didn't let them in or they made them leave, whether they were spending money or not.

Jeny, Humberto, Rudy: Well, like we told you. We adapted. As they say in our country, 'antiparabolic.' We tried to ignore what they said and what they screamed at us. We created a wall around ourselves and we moved forward. Because what happens in this type of situation is that they provoke you so that you'll fight back.

Rudy: But we didn't respond: not by arguing and not by answering back. Although there are days when you can stand just about anything that comes at you and others that you can't deal with it. Because despite the fact that we have, let's say, a different sexual orientation, it's not anything different for me. Everyone is free to choose who they want to sleep with or not. You know? And the fact that I sleep with someone who's the same sex as me doesn't mean that I'm not an intelligent person, with the right to work, the right to have a family, like any normal person. But for me it's not about being a normal person, because I consider myself to be a normal person.

I think that's the only thing that I'm going to miss about here, this kind of tranquillity. That's why I say that maybe someday in the future I'll come back to Spain. Although it's true that I won't be able to come back to Spanish territory or the European Union until the year 2019 because my deportation order and the commutation of the sentence depend on that.

## Violence, Art and Social Justice. How Do We Do It?

In art, science, literature, and in departments of life which we believe to be somewhat removed from our daily living we are hospitable to research, experiment, and innovation. Yet, so great is our traditional reverence for authority that an irrational fear arises in most people when experiment is suggested to them.

— Emma Goldman, Words as Weapons. Was my Life Worth Living? 1934.

Humberto: But I think that I won't last long in Venezuela. Of course I want to go back to Venezuela and be with my family, work, and I want to have a sex change operation. Because the first thing on my mind is to have that operation … But I … I hope to come back and set up a life far away from the bad blood that exists in Venezuela against homosexuality because I don't think it's logical that because we have a so-called 'different' sexual orientation we have to suffer discrimination from other people who don't have the guts to tell you anything. Nobody has the right to label someone else for anything. I think that whoever doesn't adopt the approach that you've explained so clearly, learned from childhood on: the right to freedom, to respect, to love, to an equal society, well, that person can't say very much. It's a basic question and it's related to the education that one receives.

Rudy: From childhood what they've taught you in school is that a man has to be a man and a woman has to be a woman. This is something that you see in how they've taught culture for millions of years. I'd like it if the world were different. I remember now. Do you remember the day that we showed the film *Beautiful Boxer* in the courtyard of the Rehab Centre with Virginia?

Jeny and Humberto: Yes!

Rudy: Yeah, that film tells it like it really is in the life of a transsexual. Because it's a constant battle. But it's not just that the transsexual world, the gay world, or the lesbian world fights to survive; everyone who feels different does it in a different way, to be free. This is what people should respect. That everyone fights for what he wants within certain limits because there are laws, but how good are the laws that we haven't shown too much respect for?

Jeny, Humberto, Rudy: (Laughter)

Rudy: The political and economic situation of each country and each family also have a lot to do with it. The reason why we took such a risky decision to disobey the law by running drugs inside our bodies. Why we risked wasting so much time being locked up …

At this moment of the interview, the prison warden came into the dining hall and the interview stopped. The warden, called Roberto, comes in to tell Rudy that his deportation will be within the next four days, without specifying the exact time.

Warden: (Joking about the topic) The plane's got a flat so I'm afraid that I don't know whether it will be possible to fly. But, well, we'll wait until tomorrow to see.

Rudy: My heart's pounding!

Warden: Okay, see you later! (He leaves the dining hall, closing the door behind him)

Jeny: (Joking) See you later! Have a good time! Happy New Year!

Rudy: Hey, girl, don't tell him that! Maybe I won't leave tomorrow!

Jeny, Humberto, Rudy: (Laughter)


The nervousness brought on by the situation subsides within the next few minutes.

Humberto: It's important to remember that we had to obtain the proper permits to tape here in the cenre. Institutions are nothing more than the people who are in them. With Virginia Villaplana, when we were thinking about this project and the way to put two institutions—the museum and the penitentiary—together through the *Diary of Intermittent Dreams*, we were thinking about this idea. Institutions are made up of the people in them. All this would have been impossible without this idea. Even this nice warden—don't you think so? He's involved. If we're here today taping and we've been able to show the films in the courtyard this summer, it's not because of us, but because it seems that they have an interest in culture. And, well, they've given us the permits to continue with a film series this autumn and winter. Look at how difficult it seems that a relationship exists between a penal institution and a cultural institution like a museum. A collaboration between a prison and a museum.

Rudy: Truthfully, it's like the first time in history. Maybe there are NGOs that work with prisons, but a museum? Art? Culture?

Humberto: I think the person who runs this prison has a goal: that the people who pass through here become more cultured. That they learn new things. That's why I say that institutions are really no more than the people who work in them. I mean there are prisons and prisons, museums and museums.

Rudy: Yeah, it depends on the prison, because before we were in the Cáceres Penitentiary (Extremadura, Spain).

Jeny: You're from Cáceres?

Rudy: We were there in Cáceres. First Jeny was there by herself for a year because they separated us after going into the Hotel Palace. And then after a year I met up with her without even knowing that I would find her there. When I got to the prison in Cáceres …

Jeny: And I yelled 'Surprise!' out the window to him!!!!

Rudy: When I got to the prison in Cáceres, we found each other again. But Jeny, because she was alone there, was inhibited about a lot of things. Apart from the fact that it was an old prison—it doesn't have showers in the cells, it has shower rooms—and there are a ton of people on drugs twenty-four hours a day; the courtyard, the dining hall, and the common rooms are filthy. There was no sanitation in this prison. The filth inhibited us. We met good people, there were some, but we really kept to ourselves.

In the Cáceres prison on 24 December, Christmas Eve, we got all dressed up. Jeny had been in prison for a year and she hadn't worn a skirt because she was afraid they would punish her or that the guys in the prison would say something to her, but with me at her side she felt freer and she had more strength to be herself. Then, she got to the cell, she put on a long skirt, we got all dressed up and we went to Christmas Eve mass. When we got to the gym, which was small, like fifty square meters, when we went in, there was a female guard who looked at both of us and said, 'Sit here. Women are always seated separately.' And she sent us to sit where the women were. She told us, 'We're going to sit you with the women because the men are on this side, on the right.' We sat down quietly, like two little angels who had never done anything wrong. Five minutes later the warden came in and saw us. He looked at us and said, 'What are you doing sitting on this side?' We told him, 'They told us to sit here.' He answered, 'That's because you confused them and they don't know who you are! Come on, get up and go over there!' But like that, in a bossy tone like I just used or worse. And we went to sit over with the men …

Well, it was the worst mistake that he made, sending us over to where the men were.

Because we got there and they put us behind all the men, at the end. The men started to approach us. They said, 'Merry Christmas!' and they kissed us on the cheek! And all the men came up to us. This man, the Director of the Rahab Centre went berserk, and I mean berserk… He came, found two more guards and sent them to grab the men who were coming out next to us. And if that wasn't enough, after mass we went to eat and as we were leaving the dining hall the warden reappeared and he grabbed Jeny and told her that as long as he was working there, she would have to dress properly. And Jeny asked him, 'How do you want me to dress? Like a man? Well, I'm not going to dress like a man because I don't feel like a man.'

But the sense of powerlessness was so huge that at that moment what I felt like doing was to knock his head around in one punch, you know? Because of how rude and how prejudiced he was.

Jeny: The only thing I did was sit down on a bench and swallow hard. And tell myself, 'My God! My God, control yourself!' I felt so nervous … 'Control yourself,' I said. Because if I had moved, I would have eaten him alive.

Rudy: Because it was awful. Right in front of everybody in the room.

Jeny: But what hurt him the most was that he thought I was going to stay quiet. But because I didn't stay quiet he felt like hitting me that day. And I told him again, 'I'm not going to dress like a man because I don't feel like a man.'

The turned his back on me and went away.

Jeny: 'Don't let this happen again,' I told him as he left.

Rudy: That day was terrible. Because it was after we had had such a good time. Then he came and ruined everything that way.

Jeny: Afterwards I went into the guards' office. And they told me, 'Be careful! Keep your cool.'

Rudy: In fact, up until that moment, we had had a cell with a window looking out onto the corridor. The window looked out onto the hallway where everyone walked by, the prisoners and the guards.

Jeny: From that day on, the warden made us move from that cell to the last cell next to the wall and with the window facing the courtyard. To the worst place in the prison so that nobody would see us. But the men still came up to the window at the back. They came up to us and gave us cigarettes through the window, but if they were caught, they got punished. Even so, they came up to us.

Rudy: Jeny had to live through this a whole year. I was only alone there for five months. And to apply to be moved to the prison at Masilla de Las

Mulas in León we had to make them understand that we were a couple. So that they would move both of us to León together.

Jeny: Because if not, when they move you one goes to Beijing and the other to the other side of the world.

Rudy: Humberto was also with us in the Cáceres Penitentiary, but it's different because of the way he is. Everyone knows he's gay, but because of the way he dresses and acts, he doesn't draw that much attention to himself.

Humberto: This is what happens in the gay world in prison. The gay men are usually accepted much more than the transsexuals, who are discriminated against just because they go around dressed like women.

Rudy: Humberto hasn't had too many unusual problems, but our experience in prison has been worse. A lot worse.

Jeny: I was just dying to get out of the Cáceres prison. When Humberto and then Rudy came after a year, I could relax. Because I wanted the trial to come up and for them to commute our sentence so that they could reclassify us and ship us off to another prison. In fact, when they moved us to the Masilla de las Mulas prison in León, the first thing I said was, And this?' I was surprised that everything was so clean and organized in the self-respect modules.

Humberto: Their new sentence was issued in October; they started the proceedings and within a week they moved them to Masilla. I had to stay in Cáceres because my sentence wasn't issued until three months later. My sentence was issued in July because I opted to have the extradition law applied to me so that they could commute my sentence. In July they moved me to the penitentiary in Masilla de Las Mulas in León. From that moment on I told them that if they were going to deport me back to my country, they could do it at any time, no matter where I was. If you're going to come look for me, then I'll go. They put me with my cousins Jeny and Rudy in León and they put me in the self-respect module, too.

Rudy and Humberto: Well, there are bigger prisons, like the ones in Madrid, Alicante, or Valencia.

Rudy: The thing is that the Masilla de las Mulas prison in León (Spain) is one of the newest. The cells all have their own showers and plus we were lucky enough to be admitted to a 'respect module' in jail. So when we got into the self-respect module, we lived in a different world, you know? The cleanliness, there were plants, the people sitting in a smoking area with a separate place for non-smokers, everything was really cool. There are workshops for drawing with paints and thread, drawing with glitter, workshops for making model ships, mirror workshops, metalsmithing workshops. You can keep yourself busy with arts and crafts.

Humberto: workouts, language classes ...

Jeny: When they moved us, it was like going from a public school to a private one. You totally notice the difference between things like that.

Rudy: Although in the beginning there was also some bad blood because it was the first-time transsexuals were admitted to the self-respect module in the Masilla prison. They wanted to give us a hard time and the seven team leaders bossed us around. Because there are seven cleaning teams; I think there are twenty-five people in each team. So the team leaders told the guys that if they saw them talking to us for too long, they would kick them out of the self-respect module. Because they can sanction you, kick you out of the module and send you to other modules that aren't the same as the self-respect modules.

So, if Jeny was talking to a guy, it wasn't like she was just talking to a guy; the team leaders thought she was doing something else.

If they saw me talking to a guy, I wasn't talking to try and be friendly; it was just that we were trying to do something else. This lasted for a month. The guys talked to us from a distance without getting too close and we felt isolated. But it wasn't their fault; they were being threatened with sanctions.

They have group meetings there with the group leader, the psychologist, and the counsellor. In one of the group meetings after they made all the proposals and plans for the module, seeing that Jeny felt pressured by everything that was going on with us, I spoke up. I explained it like this: 'Look, this is what's happening: they're saying that if the guys talk to us, they're going to punish them,' and the counsellor said, 'No, that can't be. You have to understand that you're the first transsexuals to come here and that's caused a bit of a stir.'

I told him, 'Yes, I understand that. It's normal. But to go from that to the point that the guys know they're going to be kicked out of the self-respect module if they come up to talk to us, well, that doesn't seem logical to me. Because if you catch me doing something I shouldn't do with a guy in the common areas, well, then you'd be right. But up until now we haven't done anything, and we haven't prompted anyone to do anything bad. Why are we being treated this way?' And from that moment on, the whole situation changed.

Jeny: That conversation changed everything. It turned the situation around.

Rudy: If we had stayed silent, the situation would have continued. But because we had come from the Cáceres prison where we were totally restricted and then to go to another place and have everything be the same… Well, we said to ourselves no, absolutely not! So we had to say something. We brought it up at the right time and the situation could be resolved. From then on, everything has gone marvellously.

Jeny: From there to there! The doors of the sun were opened!

Humberto: Later we became coordinators and secretaries of the general meeting.

Rudy: Yeah, I was the secretary of the meetings after that. They made me secretary and Jeny was the coordinator. Because there they have a meeting with the counsellor every day and on Saturdays all the inmates have a big general meeting with the coordinator, the team leaders, and the secretaries.

Jeny: Yeah, right. One Angel will go (Jeny gestures to Rudy with a wave of her hand).

Jeny: The other Angel will go (Jeny gestures to Humberto with a wave of her hand).

Rudy: Jeny will get out after me.

Jeny: The thing is, I don't want to go.

Jeny: I want to go because it's been a long time since I've been back to my country and I miss my family. But I'd like to stay or go together with Humberto.

Humberto: The thing is that if I ask them to apply the extradition law, the paperwork will get done quickly. Because I have a sentence and record review on September 12th and if I decide to go, well, I'll go. And if I ask them to reduce it to a third degree felony when they review my sentence and they start the deportation proceedings, everything will be really fast. So by the end of 2014 or at the most at the beginning of 2017, I'll be in Venezuela.

## Postscript to Collective Experience in the Diaries of Intermittent Dreams

Article 25.2 of the Spanish Constitution says that 'custodial sentences and security measures shall be oriented towards re-education and social reinsertion.' This conception of custodial sentences is related to the principle of prevention: the purpose of penalties is not to torment or undo the damage done, but to prevent further harm from occurring and social reintegration. We should ask ourselves: How is this social re-education carried out in Spanish prisons today?

Many of us have observed that social reintegration continues to depend on modes of respect and that these are based on obedience to moral norms, power relations, and 'corrective' educational programmes that also exclude the gender problems of women and men. They reinforce and victimize certain stereotypes such as in the case of migrant trans women prisoners, those who remain there for political reasons, or those women who, when they were on the street, already lived on the thresholds of social and economic exclusion (e.g. extreme poverty). The causes of the outside are reinforced on the inside and the forms of violence are maintained in both social spaces. Many of us have lived and learned that the right to re-education would exclude, according to this application, a good part of the exercise of personal freedom or simply self-expression as people. What the trans women have shared and communicated through dialogue with the group, the magazine, and the writing has to do with the desire to transform—to be nonconformist—despite the circumstances and to make use of their words in any situation but above all in a situation in which they are deprived of liberty.

We are aware that the Article 25.2 of the Spanish Constitution also adds that people deprived of their liberty will be entitled to paid work and to the corresponding benefits of Social Security, as well as access to culture and the integral development of their personality. Therefore the lack of willingness to address education (and re-education) and learning from a perspective that considers the awareness of race, sex, and social class is often rooted in the fear that prisons (those inside and those of the outside) become uncontrollable, they unleash emotions and passions. To an extent, we all know that when certain issues are passionately debated by people in the context of a prison it is possible for confrontations to occur, for ideas to be strongly expressed, and even for there to be conflicts with institutions or attempts to censor everyone's work. In the collective experience of the *Diaries of Intermittent Dreams*, we felt the need to say that freedom is something that cannot be stolen and that learning is part of a shared experience left in the memory of all. In the *Diaries of Intermittent Dreams*, the topics discussed by those women who have been deprived of their liberty during these three years make it clear to those of us who have read their words that violence against women extends from outside in and inside out. In their writings, women have been talking about the forms of violence that the prison reinforces, social exclusion, patriarchal domination, and the daily resistance that they undertake on a day-to-day basis. For them it is all about the recognition that things can be transformed daily with dialogue, and that is possible to share everything when initiatives are taken and you believe in group work.

*This chapter builds on the work supported by the research I+D+i MINECO PGC2018-095393-B-I00 (QUEERTEMP): Queer Temporalities in Contemporary Culture. Ministry of Economy, Industry and Competitiveness. General Direction of Scientific and Technical Research, Spain.

## Notes

1.   *The Diaries of Intermittent* Dreams (2014–2017) was a collaborative social communication art project between the León Penitentiary Mansilla de las Mulas and the Castilla y León Museum of Contemporary Art (Musac).

2.   Julia Sudbury, 'Celling Black Bodies: Black Women in the Global Prison Industrial Complex ,' *Feminist review* 70 (2002), 57–74.

3.   Virginia Villaplana-Ruiz, 'Tecnologías Creativas, Comunicación social y Expresión de subjetividades en el contexto de la cárcel,' in *Intersecciones. Cuerpos y Sexualidades en la Encrucijada*, ed. Lucas Platero (Barcelona: Bellaterra, 2012) 277–300.

4.   Kath Browne and Catherine Nash, *Queer Methods and Methodologies: Intersecting Queer Theories and Social Science Research* (London: Routledge, 2016), 2–25.

5.   Ann Reading and Tamar Katriel, *Cultural Memories of Nonviolent Struggles: Powerful Times* (London: Palgrave Macmillan, 2015), 205–25.

6.   Roger Matthews, *Doing time: An Introduction to the Sociology of Imprisonment* (London, Palgrave Macmillan, 2016), 174–204; Judith Butler, 'Rethinking Vulnerability and Resistance,' in *Vulnerability in Resistance*, eds. Judith Butler and Leticia Sabsay (London: Duke University Press, 2016), 12–28.

7.   Rita Segato, *La guerra contra las mujeres* (Madrid: Traficantes de sueños, 2016), 57–91.

8.   Adriana Estéves, 'La gubernamentalización necropolítica del Estado y la masculinidad hegemónica: dislocación y recomposición ontológica de los derechos humanos ,'*Derecho y Crítica Social*, 3/1, (2017) 45–74.

9.   Marcus Mahmood, 'Colllateral Consequences of the Prison-Industrial Complex,' *Social Justice* 31 (2004), 31–34.

10.   The law of foreigners is the name by which the Organic Law 4/2000 in Spain. The Organic Law 4/2000 of 11 January on the rights and freedoms of foreigners in Spain and their social integration has been amended three times since its adoption; in particular, it has been amended by Organic Laws 8/2000 of 22 December 11/2003 of 29 September and 14/2003, 20 November. All the reforms that have been indicated include Organic Law on greater significance,

which took place a few months after its entry into force by the Organic Law 8/2000 of 22 December. Some of the changes introduced by the latter law led to the filing of several resources of unconstitutionality against it. In the judgments 236/2007 of 7 November and 259/2007 of 19 December, amongst others, the Constitutional Court recognized that the requirement that the indicated law imposed on foreigners (that had legal residence in Spain) for the exercise of the fundamental rights of assembly, association, work, union, and strike, constituted an unjustified restriction and was therefore contrary to the Constitution, since according to the same, those rights reach all people because of it.

11.   In reference to the Article 10 of the Organic Law *4/2000,* 'work and the right to social security.' All foreigners who have been issued a visa or authorization to remain in Spain for a period of more than six months will obtain the foreigner's identity card, which they must personally request within a month of their entry into Spain or since the authorization is granted, respectively. Holders of a residence and seasonal work visa will be exempt from this obligation.

12.   Jeny and Humberto refer to the public and private spaces in Venezuela: parks, museums, restaurants, shopping centres, among others, are places that have experienced situations of stigma and discrimination against LGBTI persons by police officers, surveillance, or public order. Trans people do not have specialized services to accompany their gender reassignment process, which results in highly risky practices resulting from self-medication and access to clandestine aesthetic procedures. The protocol for gender reassignment is long, complex, and expensive. Faced with the absence of response in public services, the trans person makes undertakes the process without due professional accompaniment. In relation to the shortage of medicines to treat HIV and reagents for diagnostic tests, control, and monitoring of HIV: From 2009 to 2014 there have been episodes of stock-outs of antiretroviral drugs, especially in the year 2013, in which occurred up to 10 episodes of shortages of these medicines affecting mostly LGBTI people living with HIV and AIDS in Venezuela. See specially: 'Venezuela:Situación del acceso a la Atención y Tratamientos en VIH,a tan sólo 3 días antes del Día Mundial de la lucha contra el SIDA,' ACCSI, 29 November 2013, accessed 1 June 2006 http://www.accsi.org.ve/accsi/wp-content/uploads/ACCSI-y-RVG+-Situaciòn-del-acceso-a-tratamientos-antirretrovirales-en-Venezuela-para-noviembre-20131.pdf.

# 6

# Leelatu Fanzines in Confinement: Cutting Up, Pasting Together, Sketching Out

*María Ángeles Alcántara Sánchez (aka Gelen Jeleton),
Marisa Belausteguigoitia Rius,* Tania Gisel Tovar
Cervantes (Translator: Valerie Leibold)*

## Cutting, Illuminating, and Gluing Together in Prison

This chapter analyzes the work done with imprisoned women in the production of fanzines. We present the fanzine *Leelatu*, created in collaboration with 'Women in Spiral: Justice System, Gender Perspective, and Pedagogies in Resistance' ('*Mujeres en Espiral: Sistema de Justicia, Perspectiva de Género y Pedagogías en Resistencia*'), a project composed of academic faculty, artists, activists, lawyers, pedagogues, and students from diverse disciplines. Our approach is based on gender studies, from the field we call theory-based activism, structured with the intertwining of artistic, legal, and critical pedagogical practices. We work to contribute to the structural transformation of justice and penitentiary systems, in order to favour women's access to justice.

Since 2008, 'Women in Spiral' has carried out different projects with women imprisoned in the Female Centre of Social Reintegration of Santa Martha Acatitla (*Centro Femenil de Reinserción Social de Santa Martha Acatitla* [CEFERESO]), a prison in the Iztapalapa neighborhood, Southeast of Mexico City. The project focuses on a range of practices from artistic (murals, zines, documentaries, short films, prison dictionaries, articles, and artistic books) to juridical (*Amicus Curiae* briefs, analysis of privileges and sentence reductions, writs of amparos, reports, and penal code assessments). 'Women in Spiral' also created the Marisela Escobedo clinic of public interest with a focus on gender issues to work on their juridical processes.[1] These products came about through the work of the project's three working clusters: artistic-pedagogical, legal, and research. The diversity of the products we have orchestrated requires process facilitators. For the case of the creation of a zine in prison, we invited María Ángeles Alcántara Sánchez (aka Gelen Jeleton)—an artist, activist, and academic—to coordinate the production of a zine as a pedagogical, juridical, and artistic intervention with the intention of transforming disciplinary practices inside the academy and the prison complex.

In this text, we analyze the creation of zines as a mix of acts of resistance and of the reappropriation of voice and body, which favours an escape from gender rules and a type of feminine experience linked to an extended and monotonous time in prison, characterized by the persistence of repetitive feminized activities and the construction of a confined space under surveillance with rigorous control over the bodies of imprisoned women. We also propose a zine which goes beyond academic disciplinary borders and which contacts the most forgotten groups. In this way, we consider the zine to be capable of sketching out strategies of contact, cutting up long juridical sentences, illuminating human rights violations and gluing together what has been broken and shattered with so much violence in Mexico.

The following questions arise: What is the relevance of the zine medium in a space where freedom of expression has been severely limited? What forms of re-appropriation of space, women's time, bodies and voices in confinement are made possible through a zine? What artistic, pedagogical, and legal practices does the zine employ to magnify the right to speak, the right to free space, and the right to one's own body? If imprisoned women constitute one of the groups most affected by isolation and exclusion, how can the practices of sketching (out), cutting, and gluing intervene in their transformation?

This chapter is divided into three sections: the first outlines the *zine*, its definition and feminist trajectory. This section also contextualizes our work in prison as part of the project 'Women in Spiral.' In the second part, we introduce the zine work in prison, and the third and final section addresses theoretical and practical aspects of its making.

## The Zine and the Problem of Defining It

The zine has been a tool used by 'countercultures' as a political strategy to disseminate their interests and demands.[2] It proposes alternatives to hegemonic mandates and other forms of 'doing' and 'making,' with the objective of 'infecting' with a counter-capability. It is a quick and cheap method; it does not require previous knowledge and anyone can do it. Fanzines are put together to transmit different messages; for example, collages, made from cut up newspapers and magazines, change their original messages through reappropriation to communicate 'their own' messages,[3] which may be censured contrary to those promoted by the dominant system. It is difficult to define zines because this medium has already been characterized by escaping from definitions and classifications to invoke freedom of action and form. We will talk about the two words that compose its iteration in Spanish (fan-zine) and its manifestation from a feminist perspective.

The word '*fanzine*' is made up of two words: 'fan' and 'zine.' The word 'fan' is related to both an intense love towards something and an *amateur*, a person who loves something and practices it without any degrees or certificates which would authorize or accredit their involvement. (Fan)zines happen when a person shares their passion by 'publishing' their own zine. One of the origins of zines is in 1930s and 1940s science fiction publications which were called fan magazines or *fanegas*.[4] Around the 1960s, there was a turn in their content and they reflected a critical positioning in the underground scene.[5] The need for making zines comes from the need to find like-minded people with whom to share, and in the case of feminist zines with whom to intervene in the urgency of creating spaces for dialogue.[6] This inspires feminists to create their own culture as an act of resistance.[7]

Although the zine has adapted to different times and different needs, it tends to respond to a series of ethical and aesthetic guidelines that help us recognize it: zines are independent publications characterized by being self-determined, low cost, and constructed under the philosophy of DIY (Do It Yourself); which in feminist zines tends to be supplemented by DIWO (Do It with Others) and DIT (Do It Together). A zine can be 'everything' and 'nothing': everything if it is a tool of struggle, which is the case for feminist zines, and nothing because there is a stance in the zine world which draws from humility and the intention of separating it from what is considered relevant and important as well as 'valid and correct.' The harmony between 'everything' and 'nothing' marks the zine as a tool that is both very powerful and light at the same time. A characteristic of vanguard artistic predecessors of the zine like Dadaism and Situationism is their lightness and almost toy-like appearance to point out social problems with the intention of creating a paradigm shift through a form of education. In the case of zines with feminist ethics, their function has been largely to raise consciousness of gender violence, sexism, homophobia, machismo, racism, and classism.

In the world of femzines,[8] there was a need to use sources other than the generalized ones, which positions the sources of the feminist zine in the riot grrrl movement of the 90s with grrrlzines,[9] converting it also into a hegemonic discourse within counter-hegemonic trends.[10] Although riot grrrls continue to be a reference, they have given way to Latin American activism enacted at chicano and border cultures,[11] reflected in studies like Adela C. Licona's *Zines in Third Space*.[12] Here, she speaks of a 'third space' committed to narratives of queer, feminist zines made by people of colour in border areas.

**Leelatu: Taking Back: 'Do you really think you're going to make a magazine … if you don't know even how to read?'**

In 2008, a year of judicial reforms, the number of women in prisons multiplied in Mexico. By 2015 the number had tripled again, and with it the abuses. In this context of women imprisoned in overflowing numbers, women inmates made an unusual demand. In a prison where everything is bi-chromatic: blue for sentenced women, and beige for those who are awaiting the verdict, women in Santa Martha Acatitla prison made a call for colour. Thanks to relationships of inmates to activist groups, UNAM, through its Gender Studies programme (*Programa Universitario de Estudios de Género* [PUEG]), was able to intervene in this uprising. With this colourful move a complex and expansive project began, one involved with the taking over of the walls of the prison through a special artistic technic: muralism.

For five years (2008–13) 'Women in Spiral,' together with imprisoned women, took over prison walls in a process of pictorial, juridical, and visual expansion. This visual uprising on the prison walls registered different legal, emotional, subjective, material and daily representations of the life of women inside and outside prison. Over five years, four murals were created: 'The Cry' of women in prison (first mural), 'Strength' of the collective of women, the meaning of time and hope (second mural), 'The Paths and Shapes of Liberty' (third mural) and in the end, the closing one: 'Collective Actions for Justice' (fourth mural).

Faced with a lack of walls (they took over all the possible ones in public areas) and a need to keep on with the uprising of voice and representation, in 2014 the 'Women in Spiral' team and the women of Santa Martha Acatitla resorted to a new possibility of collective work. After having taken over walls, the women considered zines as an attractive possibility. As opposed to the weight, size, and format of murals, they were attracted to the low-cost, portable, and versatile characteristics of zines. Murals could not be seen outside prison, but paper could easily transport their voices of protest. That is how we moved from walls to paper.

While we were deciding the format and contents of our maga-zine-zine, one of the youngest women commented, 'Let's see if those who are outside don't say, "look at these *lelas* (fools) who want to be looked at as educated, they probably don't even know how to read."' To which Ana Lili, 'zinester' and muralist in prison, responded: 'Lela tú,' a combination between 'it's you who needs to read' and 'you're the fool,' a double entendre responding to the comment that imprisoned women were not other as uncultured and illiterate. The name *Leelatu* emanated from this dis/encounter.[13]

*Leelatu* is a zine which speaks from different skin colours and wounds. On some occasions it enters oppressive environments, and in others it transmits the sarcasm used by women to talk about the patriarchal Mexican juridical system (Fig. 5). This zine is full of cries and twists, of shouts and silences; in the words of Lulú, 'It's a weapon with a sharp tongue, but also it's *the voice that runs* because we need this voice to get out, to walk to the outside, to other countries, to other prisons' (Lulú, zinester and muralist of Santa Martha Acatitla; Fig. 6).[14] By means of the first zine *Leelatu,* imprisoned women expose the situation of hardship that they face every day: the passing of repetitive time, the prison odors and complicated maternities, their cry for justice and denounces of violations of human rights.

## Workshops: The Palapa

For seven years, the *palapa,* a small patio where women wait for their visit, was our workspace (negotiated on multiple occasions by the imprisoned women, because of scarcity of space). It was a sort of huge umbrella, a palm-roofed gazebo structure that worked as an expanded and open classroom (Fig. 7). A place of con-tagion,[15] but also of interruption of space and time of prison. This wall-less space, furnished with benches and tables, fosters the coming together of those who are on the inside and those who are on the outside, students, academics, and inmates.

With the guidance of Gelen Jeleton, imprisoned women became part of workshops on the making of zines with a gender perspective. These workshops fostered collective work, which produced a negotiation and reconfiguration of space, their bodies, and their emotions. Each of the workshops that took place in the prison was designed from a perspec-tive of the political culture of emotions,[16] which theorized from the restricted body through the experience of emotions in a critical way and through a gendered perspective. The work's methodology responded to the collective construction of a 'we.' In this collective, we were constructing a community, teaching a collectivity, and learning from ourselves.[17] Drawing from these three notions, we sought to construct a narrative and a creative space, where these women could re-configure, re-signify the prison space as well as their voice and body, to take a stand against their imprisonments in a collective and autonomous way.

Three workshops were planned, as explained in the art and justice 'Education and Awareness Manual.'[18] The first was the 'Gender Awareness Workshop: Doing and Undoing Gender.' It was made up of eight sessions with the goal of doing an exercise of recognition of the forms of confinement that they had experienced previous to the prisons experience, addressing signs of gender inequality.

The workshop on 'Transitions: from Gender to Artistic-Cultural Production' was the second one, and it was carried out in two sessions. Its main objective was to get comfortable with techniques, forms, and artistic formats that allowed them to claim their right to speak. The proposal was to strengthen a practice that would borrow from techniques of artistic production such as literature, autobiography, writing, and drawing to get closer to artistic activities and zine's critique.

The third workshop was called 'Cultural Production with a Gender Perspective: New Pedagogies from the Margins.' This workshop was the longest, spanning eleven sessions. Our goal was the creation of a cultural magazine in the format of a zine, as one of the strategies of resistance that allowed them to claim the right to their body and to speak in order to get some codes to deconstruct space and time in prison. In this workshop women delved into the zine environment, and particularly in DIY and independent publications constructed from a gender perspective. The outcome of the workshop was the creation of the first issue of the zine *Leelatu*, where the main topic was narrating, describing, and exposing life circumstances in prison: being forced to interact with others, water shortages, bad food, scarce visits, poor nutrition, precarious health, and dealing with their persistent hopes and wishes.

### The Zine in the Scene of Pedagogy: Interruption and Incarnation of Presence

These women positioned the zine as a practice that made their voices mobile from below, without leaving them exposed. Through the zine, they confronted the dynamics of control and nullification present in prison and interrupted enclosed and repetitive time. By doing so, they delved into zine manoeuvres to learn artistic techniques that enticed them into movement, dance, creativity, and claiming the right to their bodies and to speak in a collective way. In the words of Maye (inmate, writer, and workshop participant):

> We started three months ago with screen printing workshops, we learned to use stamps, we learned a bit of collage, of illustration, of bookbinding. And the objective of all of this is to express ourselves so that those who are on the outside know that there are women here who have something to say.[19]

One of the institutions which is furthest from being able to have interventions or be integrated/embodied is prison. The presence of a public university, of 'Women in Spiral,' and in particular the making of a zine with women inmates in confinement allowed for the construction of the margins as pedagogical borders and therefore as political territories in contact: a woman inmate in a university classroom and a student in a prison pedagogical scene.

The pedagogic scene that we want to build began with the creation of *Leelatu* in the space of prison interrupting the academic script and penitentiary discipline, while inaugurating practices that involve freedom, not possible in the space of the prison (critical viewpoints, consensuses upon prison violations and collective work).[20]

Zines require a certain form of presence; they call for the presence of the body and the representation of subjectivities and emotions in a space of repression and exclusion. The body that the prison produces is the body of punishment, which is minimized, disciplined, and surveyed. *Leelatu* made the body present precisely on the edge of prison discipline, by producing 'free' and voluntary time, and by doing it with other women, in the in-between spaces of the academy, at the borders of disciplines, confinement, protest and silence, wall and paper, between text and image. That is how the autonomous body appeared, within a fragile but certain freedom.

This commitment to autonomy in prison is above all narrative and it involves the body; it relies on women, students, and academics, and intends to produce a process of re-writing of their own story from these new textual, bodily, emotional, and collective pacts—which zines enable—where it is possible to take care and narrate ourselves, and write our own stories (make our own bio-graphy).[21]

## Zine-ing Time and Space

In prison, there are three daily roll calls (headcounts). One must drop everything and attend under threat of punishment (solitary/ the hole). These roll calls guarantee that women inmates are still present in prison. Bodies in prison are oxymoronic: they shout their presence with a 'here!', but they are not 'there' as autonomous subjects.[22]

The work of the zine held off one of the constitutive acts of the prison punishment system: the obligation to attend the roll calls. The roll call is interrupted when they work in the *palapa* with 'Women in Spiral.' Time then extends and becomes fluid. Within the contact of academia and prison, not only are prison routines altered, academic disciplinary forms are also interrupted. On the days we go to prison (Mondays for more than ten years), we have to use a full work-day so students negotiate being absent from other classes, a central aspect of the work.

During the months we worked on the zine, the women inmates exercised their power of action by interrupting prison discipline and making themselves present in public space rather than prison space. Rancière talks about this act of presence—appearing in improper spaces such as the academy in prison and vice versa—as the construction of the political subject, as an example of subjectivation that is becoming aware of oneself and the ways in which one belongs to a group. The political subject is therefore a *modus operandi* that appears and hides, while it also unites and separates regions, identities, functions, capacities.[23]

On the second fanzine, women reflected on labour inside prison. By visually unfurling, through cut-outs, multiple types of illustrations, they represented the many jobs they created as a community (water girl, basket girl, chapulinera,[24] tatoo girl, fortune teller, singer, braider) and they also saw how these jobs created and transformed their reality (Fig. 8). The making of the zine *Leelatu #2: Work,* allowed them to analyse their active contribution to the prison economy, their forms of organization and resistance to the prison institution's severe and persistent violations of labour laws and rights. *Leelatu #2: Work* visualized the mechanics of prison underground labour economy; it helped create a better understanding of the dynamics of the flow of money, bartering, and jobs/chores with which they obtain basic necessities to live in prison, with a huge amount of work.

Women counted the money spent in a day in prison. They looked for images and engaged in conversations about sexual division of labour and inequality. 'Free' time to invent and think, enabled them to design—parallel to monetary calculations—an alternative balance sheet of life in Santa Martha Acatitla, a life economy which calculated their moments of learning, of bitterness, but also of goal achievement and happiness (Fig. 9 and Fig. 10).

The legal arm of 'Women in Spiral' is made up of lawyers and students of law, pedagogy, political science, and other fields. Together they developed the Special Report on Labour 2015 where they highlighted legal obligations, national and international regulations, and especially violations to the women's labour rights. Additionally, the report offers an account of growing forms of informal jobs created inside prison. Despite the fact that the report focuses on general job conditions—formally recognized by the prison system—the testimonies while working on the zine gave an account of the existence of a variety of activities of self-employment which enable them to make a meagre income for their survival within the prison.

The report shows how women inmates have access to two types of activities related to work in the penitentiary: training and work per se. The second type can be divided into three categories: formal work, informal work, and institutional support. One of the main sources from which the special report drew considerations and recommendations, considered the women who worked on the zine. The combination of legal work tied to human rights and the work on the zine shaped artistic practices and the production of different types of knowledge. The fanzine produced information about rules, rights, institutional and labour practices which equipped the special report with detailed and current testimonies and information (Fig. 11).

**Method and Results: The Zine as a Tool of Liberation**

For the first zine which was focused on general conditions of life in prison, we had the support of the University Museum of the Chopo, who provided the material for the production (making and printing) of the zines.[25] Here is how we scheduled a series of workshops which enabled us to experience different techniques used in the zine narration. We planned three blocks of action: stamping and screen printing, layout design and book-binding, and distribution. These three blocks were developed through different workshops like: The Comic-Fan Workshop (*La comiquera taller*), which was a drawing and illustration workshop (Fig. 12); The Story-Telling Workshop (what if…) [*Taller de collage histórico (qué hubiera sido si…)*] which focused on the narration of possible stories from different perspectives by drawing on science fiction; and 'The Textile Printing and Screen Printing Workshop' to make image-symbols which we could stamp on different surfaces like patches, T-shirts, stickers, which would work along the zine and the exercises of self-representation like portraits (first zine) as well as the creation of icons painted on each other's skin which we called 'bodily memories' (second zine). To compose the section of 'Manifestos,' we used the game *cadáver exquisito,*[26] responding to a series of questions that defined our zine (with a later version agreed upon by everyone). In the layout workshop, we worked with the exercise of making perzines (zines which tell personal stories); so, we experimented with basic techniques of editorial design. In the book-binding workshop we finalized the zine, attending to matters like the size, number of pages, and colour. Lastly, in the distribution phase, we contacted people who made zines, editors, and distributors in Mexico City who connected us with what is currently being made and produced in Mexico City about zines, and inquired with whom we could built networks of solidarity and distribution.[27]

For this second zine, we did not get a grant so we relied on donations of material, using posters we made out of drawings from the first zine. The development process of *Leelatu#2: Work* was carried out with a similar organization as that used in the making of the murals: by assembling brigades, collective work, workshops on gender, and technical expertise. We created three brigades, one for sign painters (and poster makers), another for illustrators (drawings for texts and content), and the third one in charge of writing (narrations, poetry, interviews, titles). Each woman selected her own form of participation based on interest or willingness. Notwithstanding the animosity that prison injects into women, they switched roles to help each other.

When coming to consensus about the type of message that we wanted to communicate, the conversation was broadened by the diversity of voices and ways of thinking, while some insisted in not *victimizing* themselves, others felt a necessity to *complain and condemn*. Looking for the appropriate tone which could represent everyone collectively, was another one of the tasks. The collectivity was stated many times through the actions that constitute structurally the zine: doing and doing with others.

With the second zine, the women in the workshop participated in field work with a series of peer interviews about their labour conditions. They also undertook statistical work, comparing basic prices inside and the outside of prison. This research brought about some uncomfortable moments for some participants who were scared of future retaliation by the authorities. The sole event of analyzing labour and prices and bringing these comparisons to light made them feel frustrated and vulnerable. This condition made us interrupt and reconsider the direction of the zine. It led us to think about the methods and ways to narrate what we wanted, or to consider what we could use to make sure they felt safe and belonged to a team. Some of these methods brought us to the use of collage technic for the comparison of prices or using clippings of ads from coupon flyers from supermarkets (gathered on the outside), as the series of drawings and lists of official jobs. We used self-made drawings as well as a poetic-symbolic and fictional language.

We also had to work on the connection with the legal part of the project, which sometimes didn't work in synch with the artistic part, making for a difficult process of understanding of our legal, pedagogical, and artistic practices. With dialogue and using the research seminar as our forum inside the university, we could find solutions for almost all our concerns. Another complicated moment was the clearance and approval to bring cameras and video-cameras into the prison in order to record the video-zine (Fig. 13). Cameras are prohibited in prison, but strong arguments in favour of gender and pedagogical formation camouflaged our critical views and functioned as a productive way to solve the perverse prison norm of censure.

## The Zine as Camouflage

With the zine *Leelatu#2: Work*, we began with the idea of the metaphor of braiding, linked from an article suggested by Gelen Jeleton, which analyzed the role of women slaves in the foundation of a free space called Palenque in Colombia.[28] Palenque was founded by slaves who escaped Spanish slavery in Cartagena. The creation of this town was possible thanks to the braided hairstyles of the women slaves, in which they drew/recorded/mapped escape routes. These women in charge of domestic work had access to spaces which were less surveilled in the houses of the owners. From here they could identify routes of escape. Their braids were also used to hide seeds to harvest when they reached their freedom. With this history of braiding, routes, escapes, and sustenance, we started this second zine. On the first page, next to the manifesto, we drew a long braid that went through the entire zine, from the first to the last page (Fig. 14). Enhancing the braid symbolism, we added other readings about braiding, like the use of this traditional and identitarian hairstyle in indigenous cultures in Mexico, and braiding and threading narratives as affective strategies between women.

The camouflage capacities of the zine translates into an inoffensive appearance. Its artistic core, being a DIY project, hides its political-social and emancipatory weight. The use of tools like anonymity, pseudonyms, or collective signatures, as well as different masks allow us to say what cannot be said or is difficult to say inside prison.[29] All of these strategies contribute to *Leelatu* being a compendium of critical analysis of the prison, justice, and legal systems. The zine is dressed up as a cultural publication, converted into a radio-zine,[30] a video-zine-manifesto.[31] Camouflaged and full of artistic images, zines are the perfect tool for the visibility of women's voices in places under strong surveillance such as prison.

## Archiving, Registering, and Documenting: Archivo 'La Presa'

We are currently in the third phase of the third zine and its video-manifesto to which we are incorporating creation of an archive/publisher of artistic-pedagogic-legal activities. 'Archive and DIY Publishing as Liberatory Tools in Prison' is a research project that aims to create an archive of pedagogical practices carried out in women's prisons. We plan to delve into theory and practice with liberatory pedagogical tools that open internationally to a network of experiences with the creation of the *Archivo: La Presa*. It intends to build connections with like-minded research projects and networks through experiences like the magazine *Hipatia* and the project '*Archivio dell'arte irritado*,' to name some of the initiatives with which we have collaborated.[32]

The work done with *Leelatu* has been presented and exhibited in a variety of spaces like the University Museum of the Chopo (2014) and Forum 77 (2016) in Mexico City, in the Public Library of Valencia (2015), Bulegoa (2015) in Bilbao, Tabakalera in the festival *Feministaldia*, and in the exhibition *Giltzapekoak: Notes on Prison* [*Giltzapekoak: notas sobre la reclusión*] in the Koldo Mitxelena Kulturunea (2017) in San Sebastián.

What in the eyes of authorities looked like a workshop of cutting and pasting ended up being a pedagogy space in which women claim the right to speak. Through zine production, artistic, juridical, and pedagogical practices gave way to the demand of women inmates for access to justice. The zine is an instrument which transforms ideas into knowledges, and knowledges into images and texts. It is a medium through which women as subjects critical of their own experience express the ways they survive in a space as surveilled and punitive as prison.

*Marisa Belausteguigoitia thanks the UNAM (National Autonomous University of Mexico), in particular the DGAPA-[Dirección General de Asuntos del Personal Académico] and its program PASPA, for the support received during her sabbatical, which made it possible to write this article.

## Notes

1.     Marisela Escobedo Ortiz was a Mexican social activist who was murdered while protesting her daughter's murder, which happened in 2008.

2.     Countercultures are cultures which are not represented in hegemonic media. For more information see Stephen Duncombe, *Notes from the Underground: zines and the politics of alternative culture,* Bloomington: Microcosm, 2008.

3.     Techniques like *détournement* used by the Situationist International movement (1957–72) make it possible to take a product created by the hegemonic system/mass media, like an advertisement, to twist its meaning producing a critique.

4.     Translator's note: *Fanegas* were also a unit of measurement in ancient Spain, which referred to volume, capacity, and surface area.

5.     Underground: refers to diverse subcultures that went against the government like the Beat Generation, yippie culture, the punk movement, and others (Duncombe, *Notes from the Undeground*). With regards to the role of women in the underground scene, see Angela McRobbie and Jenny Garber [1975], 'Girls and subcultures,' in *Resistance Through Rituals: Youth Subcultures in Post-war Britain,* 2nd ed., eds., Stuart Hall, Tony Jefferson (New York, US Oxford, UK: Routledge, 2006) 172–184.

6.     Judith, Butler, 'Performatividad, Precariedad y Políticas Sexuales,' *Red. AIBR, Revista de Antropología Iberoamericana* 4/3 (2009), 321–36; GayatriSpivak, ¿Pueden hablar los subalternos?, (Barcelona: MACBA, 2009); Michael Warner, *Públicos y contrapúblicos,* (Barcelona: MACBA and UAB, 2008).

7.     For more information about feminist zines, their genealogies, and uses as a emancipatory tool, see Alison Piepmeier, *Girl Zines: Making Media, Do Feminism* (New York: University of new York Press, 2009), Teal Triggs, *Fanzines* (San Francisco: Chronicle Books 2010), esp. chapter on the designing of riot grrrl zines; Kate Eichhorn, 'D.I.Y. Collectors, Archiving Scholars, and Activist Librarians: Legitimizing Feminist Knowledge and Cultural Production Since 1990' *Women's Studies* (2010), 622–46; and Kate Eichhorn, *The Archival Turn in Feminism. Outrage in Order* (Philadelphia: Temple University Press, 2013). Other sources on feminist zines include Karren Ablaze, *The City Is*

*Ablaze!—The Story of a Post-Punk Popzine 1984–1994* (Leeds: Mittens on Pubishing, 2013), Lisa Darms, *The Riot Grrrl Collection* (New York: The Feminist Press, 2013), Andrea Galaxina, *¡Puedo decir lo que quiera!, ¡Puedo hacer lo que quiera! Una genealogía incompleta del fanzine hecho por chicas* (2017), accessed 1 July 2019, https://issuu.com/andreagalaxina/docs/puedo_decir_lo_que_quiera_puedo_hac, Gelen Jeleton, *Una Archiva del DIY: autoedición y autogestión en una fanzinoteca feminista-queer* (Doctoral Thesis, University of Murcia, 2016). Gelen Jeleton's thesis and some of her articles can be digitally consulted at her website '*Una Archiva del DIY: La fanzinoteca feminista-cuir*' http://archivodiymusicaydibujo.tumblr.com/tesisyarticulos, accessed 1 July 2019.

8.    Possible plays on words with 'fanzine' are varied, one of them is 'femzine,' used to refer to zines made by cis, trans, or feminist women. For example, in the English-speaking world, 'zine' is used to talk about what we tend to call 'fanzine' in a Spanish-speaking context. The word 'fan' at the beginning is not used either because it has become such a common word or because this absence highlights the fact that zines are not merely fan/amateur publications but instead something that is self-made. For example, close to these 'zines' could be what are called 'prozines' or professional zines.

9.    Grrrlzines: a feminist movement in the punk rock scene related to self-publishing and DIY which emerged in Olympia, Washington.

10.    Stephen Duncombe, 'I'm a Loser Baby: Zines and the Creation of Underground Identity,' in *Hop on Pop: The Politics and Pleasures of Popular Culture* (Duke: Duke University Press, 2003); Elke Zobl, 'Cultural Production, Transnational Networking and Critical Reflection in Feminist Zines,' *Signs: Journal of Women in Culture and Society,* 35/1 (2009), 1–12.

And it is important to emphasize the article *Why i never was a riot grrrl* (2013), in which Laina Dawes criticizes the riot grrrl movement for not including issues of race and class and for being a mostly white, middle-class movement.

11.    Concretely, we can refer to Gloria Anzaldúa and her text 'Speaking in Tongues: A Letter to Third World Women Writers' (1980), where we can find strong connections to the zine from a perspective of self-publishing and feminist DIY, for example when she advises us to 'forget the room of one's own' or when she says 'finally, I write because I'm scared of writing but I'm more scared of not writing … I write to record what others erase when I speak, to rewrite the stories others have miswritten about me, about you' (Gloria Anzaldúa, 'Hablar en lenguas. Una carta a escritoras tercermundistas,' *Esta puente, mi espalda: Voces de mujeres tercermundistas. En Los Estados Unidos,* eds. Ana Castillo and Cherrie Moraga (San Francisco: Ism Press, 1980), 219–224; citation in the Spanish translation).

12.    Adela C. Licona, *Zines in Third Space: Radical Cooperation and Borderlands Rhetoric* (Albany: SUNY Press, 2012).

13.    A fundamental characteristic of the zine is that it allows for

collaboration among women of very different educational backgrounds. In *Leelatu*, we worked with women who had just finished their Bachelor's as well as those who were beginning to read. This wide access constitutes a political/pedagogical act of resistance to power hierarchies in options of education and learning in confinement.

14.  La Presa, Mujeres en Espiral, UNAM and Museo Universitario del Chopo, eds., *Leelatu#1,* (Ciudad de México, 2014).

15.  In Spanish this is a play on words which can also mean 'with tact.'

16.  Sara Ahmed, *Cultura Política de las Emociones* (Ciudad de México: PUEG/UNAM, 2014).

17.  M. Belausteguigoitia, R. Lozano, and P. Piñones, *Manual de formación y sensibilización Arte y Justicia con Perspectiva de Género. Mujeres en condición de reclusión,* (Ciudad de México: INMUJERES, 2014).

18.  'Education and Awareness Manual: Art and Justice, with Gender Perspective. Women in Circumstances of Prison' ('*Manual de Formación y Sensibilización: Arte y Justicia, con Perspectiva de Género. Mujeres en condición de reclusión*'), available in Spanish as PDF at 'Mujeres en espiral,' 2014, accessed 30 June 2019, https://mujeresenespiral.com/artistico-pedagogico/.

19.  Maye Moreno, *Leelatu* [video-zine-manifesto] (Ciudad de México: Mujeres en Espiral, 2015).

20.  Diana, Taylor, *Disappearing Acts: Spectacles of Gender and Nationalism in Argentina's 'dirty war'* (Duke: Duke University Press, 1997), 28.

21.  Paulo, Freire, *Pedagogía de la Esperanza. Un reencuentro con la pedagogía del oprimido,* (México: SXXI editores, 1993).

22.  Diana Taylor, ¡Presente! La política de la presencia, (Dissertation, MUAC, UNAM, 2016).

23.  Jacques, Rancière, *En los bordes de lo político* (Escuela de Filosofía Universidad ARCIS, 2007), 2018.

24.  A Chapulinera is a woman who takes a basket of food to those who are punished in specially confined areas inside prison.

25.  This was part of the activities promoted by the exhibition *A DIY Archive (Una Archiva del DIY)* (2014) by Gelen Jeleton, framed in the exhibition cycle of the Fanzinoteca in The University Museum of the Chopo, Mexico City.

26.  A technique used by the surrealist movement in the mid-twentieth century, in which a piece of paper went around to different players on their turn, each player made their contribution based on a small mark left visible by the previous player, using a fold to cover the other part to keep it hidden. Later, it was unfolded to see the complete result.

27.  Among others, we depended on Iurhi Peña comic cartoonist, illustrator and creator of the publisher *Beibi Creyzy* together with Frosh Samo (Miguel Mondragón) as well as co-founder with Gelen Jeleton of the open traveling exhibition *Self-publishers: Let's Make Femzines! (Autoeditoras: hacemos femzines!)* (since 2015), a member of the publisher and zine archive of the

artist cooperative *Cráter Invertido* both in Mexico City.

28.   Jose Alberto Mojica, 'Palenque, un pueblo tejido en trenzas,' 23 August 2011, accessed 24 January 2019, http://joseamojica.blogspot.mx/2011/08/.

29.   Just as in some cases an individual signature is used to mark authorship and recognition in ways that are complementary and not contradictory.

30.   For example, the fiction radio programme *Mothers and Maternity in Prison (Mujeres y maternidad en reclusión)* (2016) edited by Amor Teresa Gutiérrez, which can be consulted at the following link: https://www.ivoox. com/mujeres-maternidad-reclusion-mexico-audios-mp3_rf_13244496_1.html, accessed 1 July 2019.

31.   The video-zine-manifestos from *Leelatu* can be accessed at the following links: https://vimeo.com/184403853 and https://vimeo. com/184401342, accessed 1 july 2019.

32.   Hipatia is an educational project from the DEAC and Museum of Contemporary Art of Castilla y León (*Museo de Arte Contemporáneo de Castilla y León*) (MUSAC) and women in the Mansilla de la Mulas prison in León (2007–11). 'Archivio dell'arte irritado' is a project with which we shared an exhibition in 2017, along with others. Projects we would like to get into contact with include: *Balm and Escape; Artistic Creation in the Penal Institution* [*Bálsamo y fuga. La creación artística en la institución penitenciaria*] (2017) curated by Mery Cuesta of the Foundation La Caixa of Barcelona; *The Condesa: No One Knows What a Body Can* [*La Condesa: nadie sabe lo que puede un cuerpo*] (2016), an activation project from the personal archive of Laura Dominique Pilleri, the first trans woman in Córdoba, Argentina who was granted permission to transfer from a men's prison to a women's prison; *Freedom in Her Mind* (2018) by Olivia Wright about publications edited by the *California Institute for Women*; *Frontera*, about women's prisons from the seventies; and *Tenacious: Art and Writings from Women in Prison*, a compilation of letters from women in prison in a zine format edited by Victoria Law since 2003.

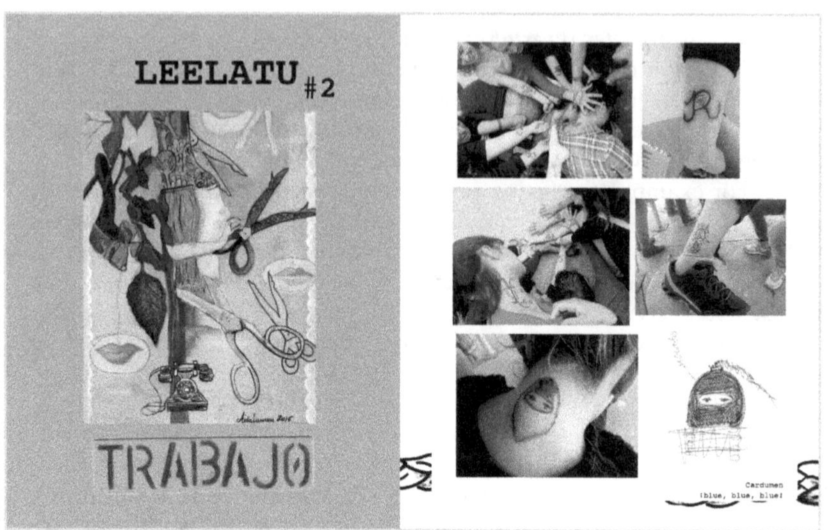



Fig. 5: Cover of the zine Leelatu #2: Work (2015) and photographic collage from the record of the session bodily memories during the Zine Workshop in Santa Martha Acatitla

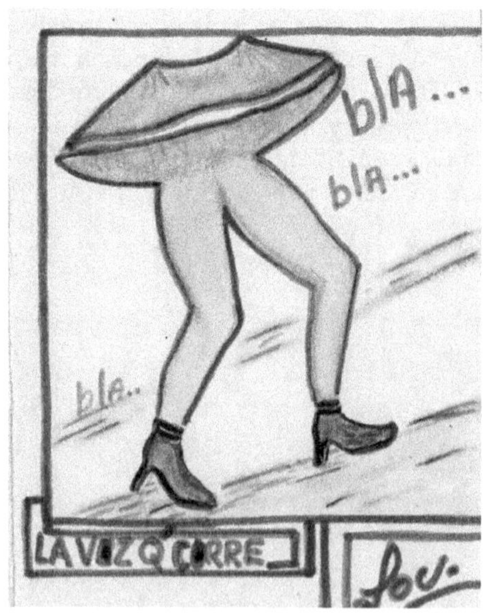



Fig. 6: Drawing of La voz que corre [The Voice that Runs], cover of fanzine-chiquito (perzine) by Lulú Lizárraga, fanzine Leelatu #1

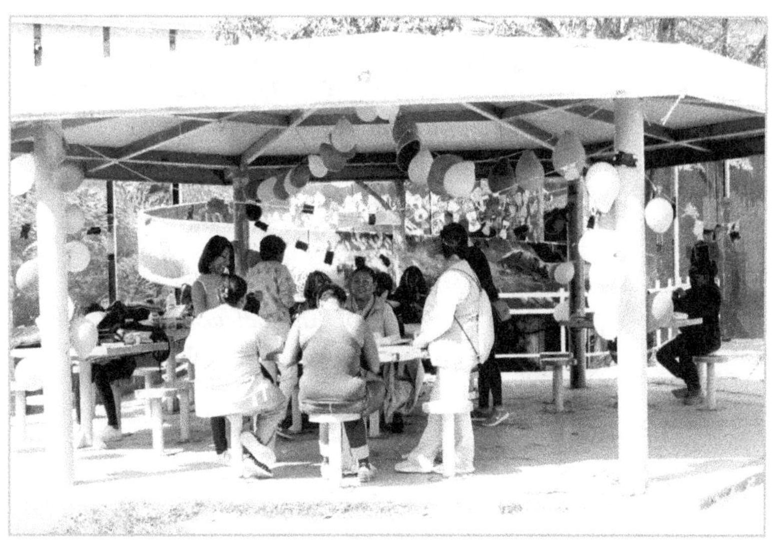

Fig. 7: *Photographic record of an activity during the Zine Workshop under the palapa, Santa Martha Acatitla (2015)*

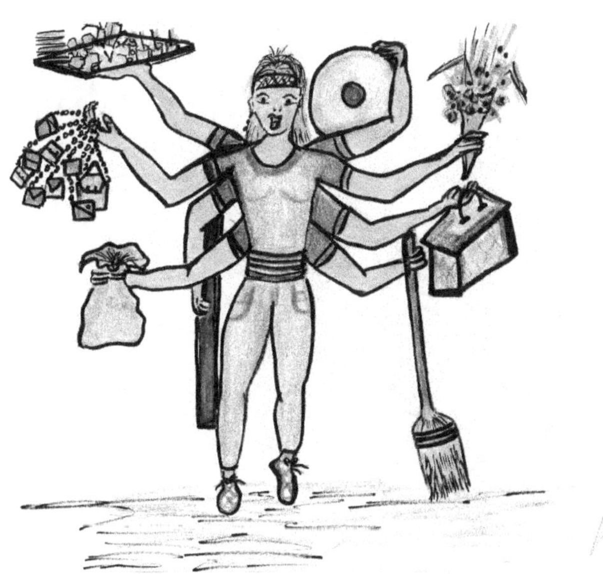

Fig. 8: *Drawing of Shiva, sticker design for the front of the zine Leelatu #2: Work (2015), by artist and zinester Lulú of Santa Martha Acatitla*

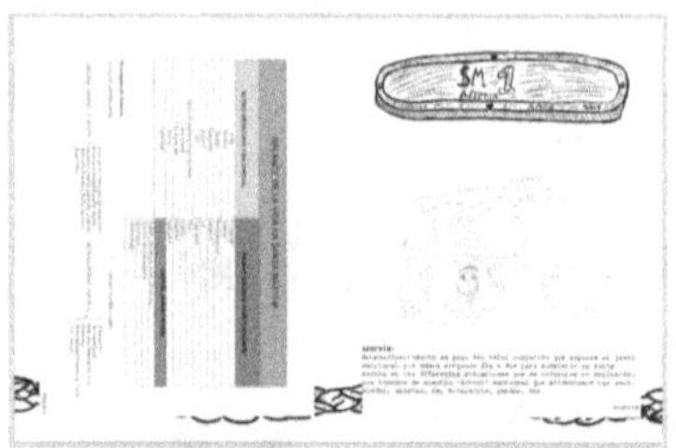

*Fig. 9: The Balance of Life in Santa Martha Acatitla and the coin: 'afectín,' illustration by Aurora (inmate of Santa Martha Acatitla) and her children during their visits. Leelatu #2: Work.*

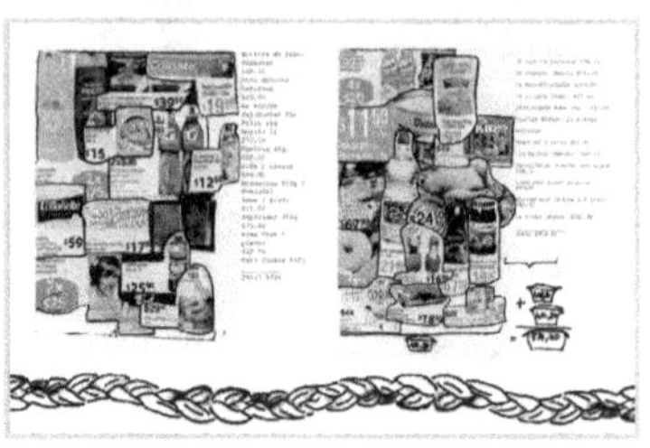

*Fig. 10: Price Balance Sheet in Santa Martha Acatitla, made from cut-outs of supermarket ads and such in comparison to prices inside prison. Collective collage illustration, Leelatu #2: Work.*

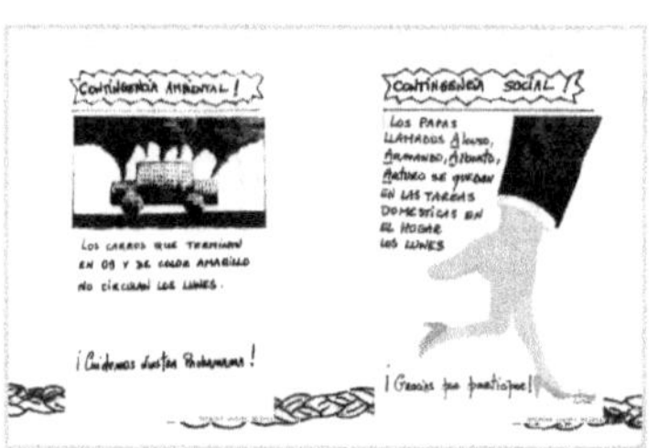

*Fig. 11: Drawing-Proposal about Domestic Work by Natacha Lopvet Mrikhi artist and zinester of Santa Martha Acatitla. Leelatu #2: Work.*

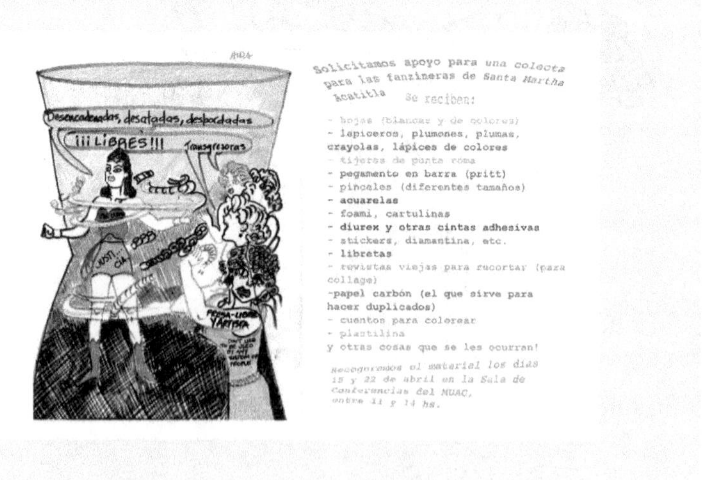

*Fig. 12: One of the posters made to collect material based on a drawing by Aimaluman (artist, inmate, and participant in zines) made in The Comic-Fan Workshop [La comiquera taller] for the first zine Leelatu #1 (2014).*

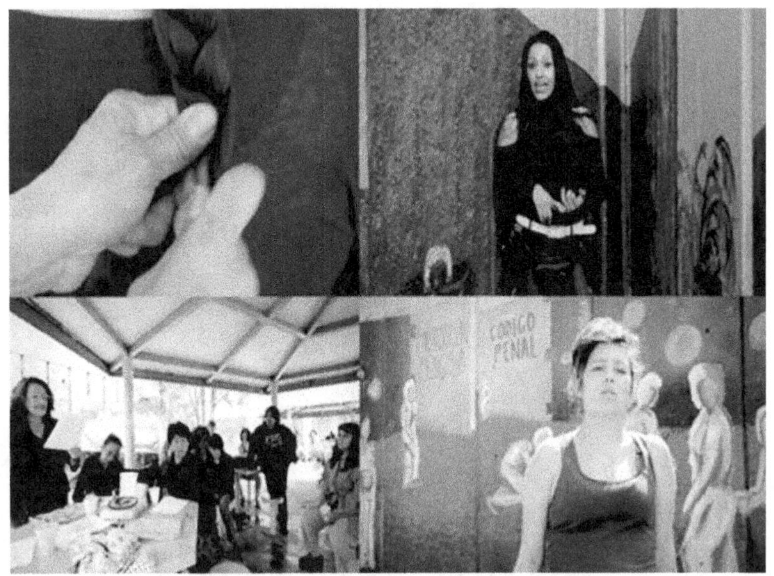

*Fig. 13: Sequence of stills taken from the video-zine-manifesto: Leelatu #1 (2014) y Leelatu #2: Work (2015).*

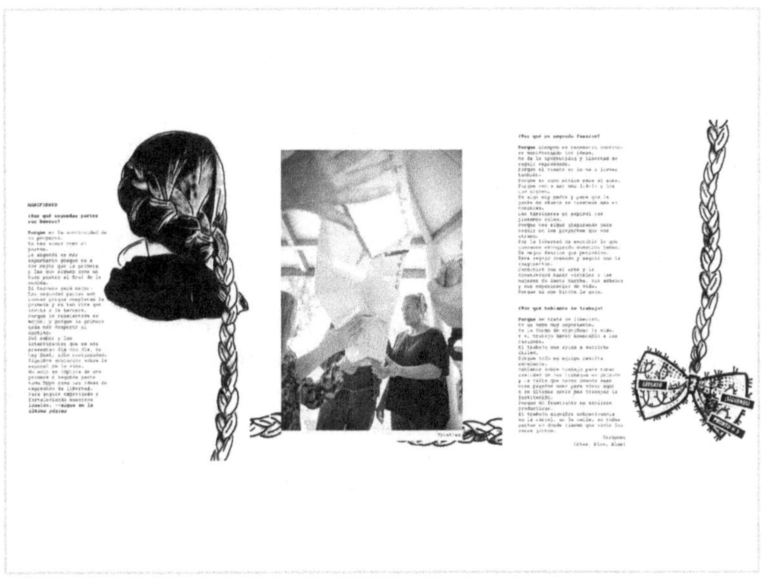

*Fig. 14: Braided manifesto in the zine Leelatu #2: Work.*

# 7

# Art Forms and Aesthetic Ordering in the Egyptian Revolution of 2011

*Radwa Othman*

## Introduction

At the end of March 2018, dancing scenes outside polling stations in the streets of Egypt dominated the media coverage of the three days of presidential elections in the country. Voters were captured holding the photo of President Abdel Al-Fattah Al-Sisi, while cheerfully dancing to pro-military and patriotic songs played by large speakers on trucks. A patriotic public sphere with an abundance of Al-Sisi's campaign posters became a spectacle. Public dancing scenes as a collective expression of joy have appeared in different critical moments of authoritarianism in Egypt, either to pass arbitrary policies or to fabricate a state of public satisfaction. For instance, a photograph dating back to the presidential referendum of 1999 shows a woman dancing in the streets of Egypt after former president Hosni Mubarak's rule over Egypt was approved by more than 93 per cent.[1] The artificial scenes of joy and dancing in public dominated the spectacle of Egypt with the protests of 30 June 2013 against the Muslim Brotherhood. Vast demonstrations supported by the army invaded the streets of Egypt asking for the downfall of then president Mohamed Morsi. However, these demonstrations were more like a carnival, a spectacle of fireworks over the skies of Egypt, with national songs playing, and public dancing while holding posters of General Al-Sisi taking place.

The demonstrations led to the military coup of 2013 that deposed Morsi as the army took power over Egypt. Subsequently, the regime started legitimizing authoritarianism through the enactment of different repressive laws and rationalizing the military coup through public and private media. It was important for Al-Sisi's coup to control cultural production in order to prevent autonomous narratives from reaching the public. The repressive policies of the military coup eliminated the existence of artwork by the opposition and, in contrast to grassroots political art of the revolution of 25 January 2011, dominated as spectacle leading up to the military coup in 2013. Accordingly, the prevalence of revolutionary art declined and pro-coup artworks increased.

In the post-coup era, Al-Sisi was portrayed as a saviour in uniform and the military establishment was propagated as the only solution that could save the country from terrorism and restore stability. In this light, civilian politics became sophistry and the military establishment and its generals were presented as the only true nationalists in Egypt who could save the country through their rule. At the same time, a personality cult was constructed around Al-Sisi, drawing on melodramatic discourse that portrayed him as the saviour of Egypt and protector of the nation through his authoritarian rule and repressive laws. Pro-coup art started to adopt a melodramatic nationalist rhetoric for the sake of creating an artificial joyous spectacle that interpreted the oppression of dissent as a glorified patriotic duty.

This chapter focuses on aesthetic ordering in Egypt. It particularly highlights the melodramatic discourse of revolutionary art in contrast to pro-coup art, to underscore the important factors and concepts that helped to create the melodramatic status quo and understand the relationship between art and activism after the revolution of 25 January. To understand the Egyptian melodramatic status quo, this chapter looks back to when art was used as a tool of activism in the revolution of 25 January, focusing only on the melodramatic artworks that dominated the spectacle. Meanwhile, it discusses the regime's control over aesthetics, in addition to the melodramatic pro-coup art that started to fill the void after the elimination of revolutionary art, which helped to aestheticize the military coup and legitimize authoritarianism. The chapter introduces different melodramatic revolutionary artworks in contrast to pro-coup melodramatic works of art, while questioning the effect of aesthetics on moralizing political tensions and rationalizing authoritarianism.

An understanding of the intersection between aesthetics and power is central to understanding and interpreting the revolution of 2011. Accordingly, the spectacle of Egypt at the time of revolution was formed by the melodramatic rhetoric discourse of social movements, revolutionaries, and media outlets. The avid attempts to aestheticize the revolution had participated in forming a utopian understanding of political change, and melodramatic victimization rhetoric prevailed over revolutionary art. This led to three interlinked phenomena regarding the relationship between art, law, and power: the moralization of political tensions, the depoliticization of the revolution, and the subsequent pro-coup discourse that reinforced authoritarianism.

What follows is an overview of recent cultural and political changes in Egypt. The chapter then discusses the meaning of melodrama in political discourse by reviewing the academic works of Jacques Rancière, Michael Blain, Murray Edelman, Walter Benjamin, and others. It also analyses the melodramatic victimization rhetoric in different artworks of the revolution in contrast to the pro-coup melodramatic patriotic-nationalist artworks. Finally, it illustrates the effect of aestheticizing the revolution on moralizing political tensions and rationalizing repression.

**Contextual Chronology**

In 2010, different political and social actors in Egypt were inspired by the Tunisian revolution and used social media to call for public demonstrations against the authoritarian government a year later.[2] These demonstrations were loaded with political, economic, and social grievances and led to the fall of former president Hosni Mubarak. The Egyptian revolution included youth movements, labour groups, activists, political parties, and Islamist movements, who had all agreed on the demand of deposing Mubarak and his government, without agreeing on a certain roadmap of what comes next. The protesting groups witnessed conflicts in political interests after the fall of Mubarak and the Supreme Council of Armed Forces' (SCAF) taking power over Egypt on February 2011 and until the presidential elections in 2012. The elections resulted in a victory for Muhammed Morsi, the Muslim Brotherhood candidate. Not surprisingly, the ruling military junta in Egypt, during the transition period (February 2011–June 2012), took advantage of the conflicts and division between different political actors, which obstructed the democratic transition process. The military seized control over the transition process, which was supposed to end in six months, by controlling key state institutions. The junta had covertly teamed up with the Islamist movements during the transition period, which facilitated the Islamists parties' victory in the parliamentary and presidential elections.[3] In return, the Islamists guarded and maintained the military's interests and the expansion of their power over Egypt.[4]

After Morsi's victory in the presidential elections in 2013, the Muslim Brotherhood tried to forcibly impose their control over the state and suppress opposition, which provoked the public. Public and private media outlets exploited the Brotherhood's shallow version of democracy and demonized their regime to the extent that, nationwide, the public marched in the streets on 30 June, in the biggest demonstrations Egypt had ever witnessed. The protesters called for the intervention of the military forces to end Morsi's rule of chaos and political instability from which the country suffered over the two years of his reign.[5] On 3 July, military forces seized power once again by deposing Morsi, who was the first civilian president in Egypt since the 1952 military movement,[6] which shifted Egypt's mode of governance from a monarchy to a republic.

The military's attempt to control public spaces started before the military coup in 2013, since the massive concrete walls that were erected by the military forces in November 2011 around the vital governmental buildings in the downtown area, to block the demonstration from reaching them.[7] These acts encouraged revolutionary artists and activists to draw colourful landscapes on the concrete wall through the 'No Walls' campaigns, challenging the government's control through their art.[8]

After the revolution of 25 January, cultural actors started to question the existence of the Ministry of Culture,[9] discussing its authority for producing what serves the political agenda of the state, the censorship of different arts, and its control mechanisms that suppress independent artistic movements.[10] Although the administration of arts did not change after the Egyptian revolution of 2011, during the revolution and transition period, art became a public product that could be found in the streets and outside usual formal and informal infrastructures without the dependence on the Ministry of Culture to provide artists with venues or means that are free from market pressures.[11] The Muslim Brotherhood was trying to control cultural production through the Ministry of Culture by posting their members in key positions across the institution.[12]

In contrast, after the military coup of 2013, the new regime of General Al-Sisi based its authority on suppression while adopting different legal methods, through passing vital laws that seize space through police control.[13] Al-Sisi's regime had propagated civil society organizations and social movements as chaotic actors, whose main aim is the collapse of the state that had participated in establishing the new mode of authoritarianism in Egypt by discrediting dissent. In November 2013, the Protest Law was issued to organize the right to demonstrations and public assemblies.[14] The law added what is known as 'secure zones' that helped security forces prevent any demonstrations taking place within areas of public governmental institutions, police stations, governors offices, or work sites[15]. If protesters convene in those places, security forces have the right to disperse them through different kinds of force. This made it nearly impossible for artists to use the streets once more as the theatre of their performances, as they used to express their demands through practicing art during demonstrations.

Additionally, the regime restricted the work of the civil society organizations that were described as 'seditious elements' by different media outlets and the government.[16] A new law gave the latter the right to prosecute different civil society actors in the same year, 2016; the law curbed the formation of new NGOs, put bureaucratic pressures on operating NGOs, and enforced their surveillance though intelligence and security services to make sure they were operating under the cloak of the new authoritarianism.[17] Different laws were passed to repress any potential opposition and to put public institutions (including universities) under the protection of the army.[18] In this sense, military tribunals became common for civilians who participated in sit-ins or peaceful protests.[19] The acts of silencing dissent and repressing potential opposition were not limited to the legalization of authoritarianism through passing different laws serving the regime. The regime also focused on propagating authoritarian acts through conspiracy theories and populist narratives that echoed through public and private media.[20]

It was important for the post-coup regime to dominate cultural production to eliminate any modes of expression that could have an autonomous narrative rather than the one propagated by the regime after the coup. Al-Sisi and the military establishment were propagated as the only solution that could save the country from terrorism and restore stability once more, which kept the regime away from public scrutiny or accountability.[21] Yet, the military establishment and its generals were keen on blaming opposition movements and the dissent for any economic failures or failed policies caused by the regime. In addition, the government implemented censorship policies that affected cultural production in Egypt and the new authoritarianism used different kitsch art to make up a spectacle of melodramatic populist nationalism that aestheticized the military coup and rationalized authoritarianism.[22]

## Art, Aesthetics, and Melodrama in Egypt

Jacques Rancière explains art as a work on the distribution of the sensible that affects people's perception of what is visible and under-standable and what is not. Art has a great influence on people. However, this influence is not necessarily in the intentions of art creators.[23] Rancière mentions that art is an environment of interacting events, space, and temporality, as art exists because 'it is an outcome of a complex set of relationships between what one is allowed to say, to perceive, and to understand.'[24] The meaning of political art is what is being understood by its audience and followers; they are the ones who can define art. Rancière explains that art can not be autonomous and there is no difference between art and the discourse of art.[25] Talking about the relationship between art and politics, he clarifies that not only do artworks affect our beliefs and perspectives, but also our minds and the milieu, where arts were produced, have a great effect on us. The effect is not limited to the moment, but it includes the past and the future, and our understanding of everyday life and the world we are living in.[26]

Politics, social causes, and different issues are being symbolized in the form of art and its discourse. Subsequently, art is a crucial element of the process of making a group of people politically conscious and shaping their ideas and political action. However, the potency of art's effect on a group of people is conditional on its availability and the intentions of people.[27] For instance, artworks by Pablo Picasso, Bertolt Brecht, and William Shakespeare that addressed war in an enthralling way participated in influencing the world's modern perception of war.[28] Discussing art and its relation to politics in the revolution of Egypt makes it important to touch on the aesthetics of the revolution, the melodramatic victimization rhetoric in revolutionary art, in contrast to the melodramatic populist-nationalist discourses of pro-coup kitsch artworks.

Firstly, the aesthetics of the Egyptian revolution got the attention of scholars studying the relation of arts to activism, discussing revolu- tionary/anti-regime poetry, chants, graffiti, and music.[29] Street art has received great attention by scholars and has been discussed as a tool to commemorate the martyrs,[30] to document the revolution,[31] and to help the dissidents in spreading their ideas.[32] Marwan Kraidy also discussed creative insurgency as an effective way of reassessing revolutionaries.[33] Scholars have done a great job in introducing the different kinds of art that were part of the political scene in Egypt, its history, the process of its production, and its power. However, Jessica Winegar has proposed a different perspective of aesthetics in the Egyptian revolution through the discussion of how aesthetic ordering dominated the spectacle and participated in the formation of a national utopia in the public mind set in terms of the meaning of revolution and socio-political change.[34] Martin Jay notes that aesthetic is 'identified with the seductive power of images, whose appeal to mute sensual pleasure seems to undercut rational deliberation' showing that 'the aestheticization of politics in this sense means the victory of the spectacle over (reason).'[35]

The discourses and practices of different political and social actors, who took part in the 18 days of protests and after the downfall of Mubarak, participated in the 'constitution of the sense of middle-classness' of the revolution.[36] The discourse of middle-classness is shown in the potent attempts, whether intended or not, of beautifying the public space through aesthetics. In this sense, revolutionaries started different beautification campaigns with nationalist messages, through cleaning the streets after demonstrations, painting curbs to renew them, and attempting to direct human traffic.[37] On the contrary, aesthetics limited political activism to political activities of the civilized non-violent middle-class, who are keen to clean the streets and express their beliefs through the arts. Marwan Kraidy discusses the attempts of coupling the two words 'creative' and 'activism' through activists, scholars, and journalists when studying arts in activism, showing that it gives the positive rhetorical impression about using art by ordinary people in their 'non-violent' and 'non-ideological' stand against oppression and dictators in the revolution of 25 January.[38] In this sense, other forms of activism tend to be less creative or even not at all; by coupling the two words 'creative' and 'activism,' creativity becomes restricted to aesthetics.[39]

On one hand, aesthetics engaged the public in political actions and cultivated support from the civilized middle-class youth, who were united in trying to change Egypt to the better through art and cleaning campaigns. On the other hand, aesthetics limited political change to an imagined patriotic utopia that fitted the interest of the counterrevolution in Egypt during the so-called transition period after the downfall of Mubarak, as SCAF and the media started asking people to stop the uncivilized acts of protesting and give their attention to the wheel of production.[40] The meaning of political action had turned out to be limited to civilized acts that aim to develop the country, instead of protesting the regime or expressing opinions in non-creative or uncivilized ways.[41] Thus, Egyptians encouraged and justified the death of nearly 1,000 anti-coup protesters, after the government had dispersed their encampments by force in August 2013, as Morsi supporters were not representative of the civilized utopian version of political change that was already constructed in the mindset of Egyptians during the successful attempts at aestheticizing the revolution. As Winegar says:

> When Morsi proponents set up their own encampments in Nahda and

Rabia Squares to protest the coup, they were quickly subject to the same aesthetic critiques (of their clothes, voices, styles, consumption) that they had levelled on others, with the additional accusation that their religiosity was vulgar and extremist.[42]


After Al-Sisi became president, the regime used the same melodramatic aesthetic discipline to encourage people to support the new authoritarian regime to bring stability back to Egypt.

Secondly, Egypt has been known for its production of melodramatic television serials that represent the everyday lives of ordinary people, and Lila Abu-Lughod shows that melodrama is produced as tool of constructing modern citizens and subjects.[43] Egyptian melodramatic serials have been an effective tool of representing moral lessons through featuring the quality of emotionality as a means of creating modern sensibility and moulding national community.[44] Such programmes have made the melodramatic genre a crucial part of the everyday social worlds of Egyptians.[45] Therefore, melodrama was a key component in the discourses of leftist and rightist groups in Egypt in terms of propagating their ideas and cultivating public engagement in political actions.[46] Melodrama in political discourse is an effective soft method of interpreting critical events in the way that the public are willing to hear in their most vulnerable moments.[47] Additionally, melodrama in the discourses of political movements has been studied as a tool of cultivating the political participation of people, as political movements approach activism as a heroic and moral action against villainous powers.[48] This is in addition to its great effect on rationalizing and justifying certain political and ideological acts that are believed to be necessary and heroic in the name of victims.[49] Melodramatic discourse achieves its targets by using exaggerated emotional rhetoric in understanding political conflicts, through the moralization of politics, while interpreting political conflicts in terms of *good* and *evil*.[50] Walter Benjamin (1998) introduced fascism as a meaning of aestheticizing politics.[51]

Melodrama of victimage rhetoric is the process in which social movements approach activism through two steps: the attempts at vilification of the opponent and the heroic action that must be taken by moral agents.[52] Subsequently, victimage rhetoric plays an important role in melodramatic political narratives to encourage their supporters, who are described as heroic protagonists, to take collective actions to defeat the opponents of movements, who are the villains.[53] Literary critic Bruno Bosteels (2010) explains melodrama in the discourses of the leftist groups in Europe after 1968, as a struggle of good and evil, by saying:

> The Left, too, frequently falls for a melodramatic figuration of politics by presenting itself in the guise of a radical disjunction between, on one hand, a pure social force such as the poor or the powerless, and, on the other, the corrupt machinery of the rich and powerful, protected by the State.[54]

In this sense, the melodramatic discourses of political movements approach political conflicts as a struggle between 'good' and 'evil,' instead of a struggle of interests and visions, to engage people in action, or sacrifice for causes and to turn them into ethical agents. The trap in which a great deal of revolutionary art fell into in the case of Egypt. As revolutionary artworks were moralizing political conflicts from the side of the vanquished through adopting melodramatic victimization rhetoric, this will be analyzed in depth in the coming section. Whereas, melodrama in the discourse of the pro-military coup is obvious in the different attempts to cultivate a personality cult around Al-Sisi after the 30 June demonstrations, using visual campaigns managed by the Department of Morale Affairs in the Egyptian army,[55] including songs proåduced by pro-Al-Sisi aspiring celebrities, and columnists glorifying Al-Sisi's 'physical strength and mental clout' in daily newspapers.[56]

### Revolutionary Art versus Pro-Coup Art

The crux of this section is the discussion of the melodramatic works of art that were produced in support of the revolution, in contrast to the art work that was aestheticizing the military coup to rationalize authoritarianism in Egypt after the 30 June. Both used melodramatic rhetoric expressions, though in different ways and with different targets. On one hand, different art works expressed the revolution with a victimization rhetoric that moralized politics. They were full of emotional exaggeration and melancholic narrations, which portrayed revolutionaries as vulnerable objects, who were killed by the villains and betrayed by the public. However, these kinds of artworks represent revolutionaries as heroes, and confine them to the side of the vanquished. The melodramatic art expression of revolutionaries was able to stimulate rage within the youth and, thus, guaranteed the permanence of demonstrations and confrontations with security forces. The melodramatic rhetoric interpreted political tensions in emotional terms, while expressing the revolution from the position

of the vanquished. As a result, rational critical attempts to interpret
the political failure of pro-democracy groups had been absent in the
discourse of revolutionaries. Accordingly, melancholy dominated the
spectacle and revolutionaries mourned their suffering through arts.
Mourning was not a temporary phase to overcome intense sufferings,
but the melodramatic victimization rhetoric turned out to be an enjoyable haven that justified the political failure of the fruitless attempts of
social movements in the post-revolution era. In short, the melodramatic
discourse helped revolutionaries to absolve themselves of responsibility
and blame others for their failure in achieving their political and social
demands.

Firstly, starting with Mustafa Ibrahim's poem *Ienni Raa'yto Alyoum
Men Barra* (Today I Saw) that clarifies the notion of the melodramatic
victimization rhetoric of revolutionary art clearly.[57] His masterpiece
(also known as *Al-Hussein*) is part of his anthology *Manifesto* that came
out in January 2013 and has had four editions. The poem includes:[58]

إن الحسين ملموم فوق جثته عساكر
Al-Hussein's body was under soldiers

بيدغدغوه بالشوم
beating him with rods

كل اما ييجي يقوم
whenever he tries to get up

وان البشر واقفة
and people are standing

تبكي بدال ما تحوش
weeping instead of fending them off ...

كل واحد منا يجري أو يجرى فلك بلك صيد ورا
every one of us runs with a thousand of hunting dogs behind him ...

كل الشوارع مصيدة ولكل البيوت
all the streets and houses are traps (for the revolutionaries)

الكوفة نايمة حتى من قبل العشا
Kufa is sleeping even before Isha

حطت صباعها في ودنها
it turned a blind eye

وسابتنا انت برة الباب نموت
and left us outside to die ...

يا حسين هتيجي تموت لمين
Hussein, For whom you will die ..

ارجع.
come back

كل اللي جاي عشانهم تفدى وتناضل ..
all of whom you are fighting and struggling for

راضيين يعيشوا عبيد .. 
are satisfied of being slaves ..
و المشهد الفاضل ه تموت ف آخره وحيد
and you will die alone at last

In Al-Hussien, the poet is using his rhetorical work to show his audience that the revolution is a conflict between the camps of 'good and 'evil.' While comparing it to the historical Islamic incident of the martyrdom of Imam Al-Hussein, the grandson of the Holy Prophet Muhammed, in a horrible dreadful massacre (Karbala battle), which led to the split between of Muslims into two camps: Shia and Sunni. Ibrahim narrates the tragedy of Karbala in a dismal melodramatic performance by comparing it to the confrontations between the security forces and protesters during the transition period under the SCAF. The events are being narrated through a camera lens that zoomed out from Karbala and in on the revolution. In his poem, Ibrahim is transforming the revolution from a matter of political conflict to a moral issue, while comparing it to a religious instance. In his narration, protesters are representing the *good*, while the regime and its security forces are the *evil*, as he compared them to the army that unjustly killed the grandson of the Holy Prophet. Moreover, Ibrahim narrates how protesters suffered and were treacherously killed, as happened with Al-Hussein. Moreover, the poet used an exaggerated melodramatic genre to show that the revolutionaries sacrificed their lives for a nationalistic cause and for the sake of the people, who are satisfied with living as slaves and will not defend the *good*. Additionally, in the beginning, he says that his words are about a time when people were ready to die for a cause, not for food or sustenance. The poem is a clear example of how revolutionary art was based on a utopian melodramatic victimization rhetoric of the good conflicting with the evil. Moreover, the evil camp did not only include the regime and its forces, but also the public who were not defending revolutionaries. In this sense, political conflicts became moralized and the revolution was limited to certain kinds of utopian and heroic actions. Also, the evil camp did not only include the regime and its forces, but also the public who were not defending revolutionaries.

Secondly, *Al-Naaehaat* mural of Alaa Awad is one of many murals drawn after the deaths of seventy-five Ultras Ahlawi youngsters,[59] who were massacred after a football match at Port Said stadium in February 2011. This incident was widely believed to be a retribution by SCAF and security forces to Ultras Ahlawy,[60] and their fans have been banned from attending football matches in Egypt to this date. The mural of Awad used Pharaonic motifs to show a melancholic melodramatic scene of ancient Egyptian women mourning and crying in a funeral, showing great sorrow, while the muses received the ascending souls of those young martyrs.

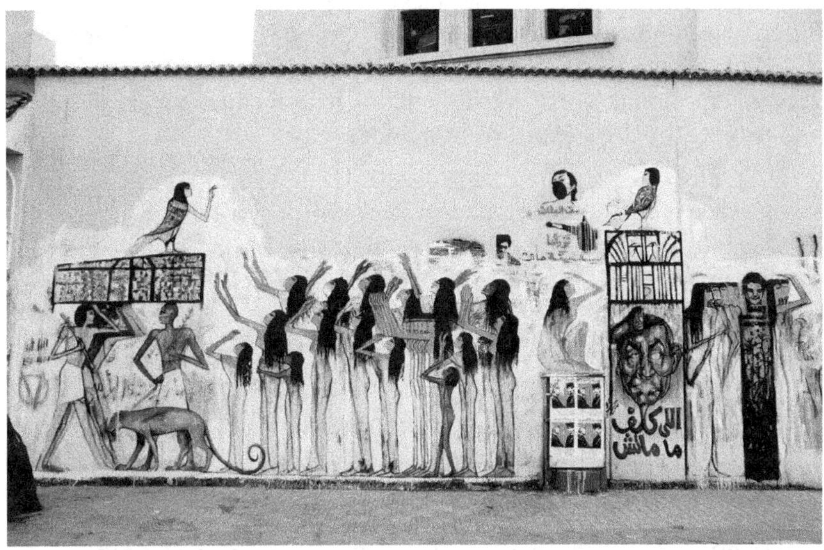

*Fig. 15 Al-Naaehaat mural in Cairo, Egypt. By the artists Alaa Awad, Awad, who works as a teacher of Fine Arts in Luxor https://www.facebook. com/155148504542884/photos/a.155149607876107.32565.155148504 542884/305702589487474/?type=3&theater (Accessed: 14 April 2018).*

Revolutionary graffiti murals were concerned with challenging the regime using 'authentic' visual narration of the revolution. Most graffiti murals commemorated the young lives taken by security forces in the post-revolution era. The victimization rhetoric was a key component of graffiti art, where an aesthetic appeal of the *martyrs* had been shown in the Egyptian spectacle in the transition period of the SCAF. Important to note that the word martyr is remarkable in illustrating the melodramatic discourse in the revolutionary art works, as it gives an honourable status for those who died supporting the revolution. Additionally, graffiti with melodramatic victimization rhetoric portrayed the martyrs as victims killed treacherously. Martyrs were recognized as the good people who were killed by the evil villains (the political regime represented by its security forces). In this sense, political and ideological conflicts turned out to be moralized and represented as a struggle between good and evil.

Thirdly, Ultras Ahlawy produced different melodramatic chanting songs addressing authoritarianism and the SCAF. They worked on documenting their songs by publishing them on their YouTube channel.[61] Although their conceptual songs lacked rhetoric, they were prevalent in different demonstrations in the pro-revolution era. One of their songs, called *Hikkaytna* (our story) and produced in June 2012,[62] used exaggerated emotional words to show how Ultras members were betrayed and trapped by the regime, as it includes:[63]

ولما الثوره قامت نزلنا في كل البلاد
and when the revolution started we deployed all over the country
متنا علي الحريه و سقوط رموز الفساد
we died for freedom and the downfall of corrupts
دبرولنا المؤامره بعد ما دبرولنا المستحيل
they hatched a plot against us
قتلوا اغلي الصحاب حلم قتلوا السنين
they killed our dearest friends, they killed what we had been dreaming of for years ...
في بورسعيد كالب لما العسكر فتحوا الباب
in Port Said there were dogs, when the military opened the door,
انطلقوا والفوضه عمت وقتلوا اغلي الشباب
they were released, there was chaos everywhere and they killed the most precious youths
منهم كان المهندسين والعمال منهم ولاد
the engineers, workers and children were among them
راحوا وكانوا منهم حكم لاغي في كل البلاد
they passed away while dreaming of ending your rule

The song portrays the members of Ultras Ahlawy as revolutionary agents who sacrificed their lives to a nationalistic cause. Additionally, *Gannet Al-Khaldeen* (Paradise of the Immortals),[64] another song by Ultras Ahlawy, narrates a scene in paradise where a *martyr* who got killed in recent political events is meeting with other martyrs, who were killed earlier. The song uses another melodramatic victimization discourse of aestheticizing the revolution and activists, while describing the recent martyr in a sacred expression by saying that there is 'no man like him' and that he was treacherously killed by security forces for revenge.

However, kitsch pro-coup art works were provided with a solid underpinning of populist-nationalist discourse to rationalize the military coup as a patriotic matter that must be supported by all nationalists.

This kind of discourse portrayed the military establishment and Al-Sisi as the heroes saving Egypt from the villains (dissidents and civil society). In this sense, unlike revolutionary art, the pro-coup artwork focused on using exaggerated victorious and artificial joyful themes to aestheticize the military coup. The political context of Egypt in the wake of 30 June 2013 embraced pro-state art to dominate cultural production in order to fill the void of a failed democratic transition. It cultivated support for the military coup and rationalized authoritarianism. The pro-coup camp focused on setting a specific definition to the meaning of patriotism, leading to support towards Al-Sisi and the military coup. Thus, the dissidents were portrayed as villains, who sought the downfall of the country, and the masses should accept the current state of exception and support authoritarianism for salvation.

Firstly, melodrama in pro-coup arts can be seen through the work of the Egyptian cartoonist and painter, Mustafa Houssein, in Al Akhbar daily newspaper. One cartoon shows Egypt as a provincial woman, happily hugged by Al-Sisi who is wearing a Superman uniform.[65] In this sense, Al-Sisi is the heroic saviour who has rescued his 'beloved' Egypt. Additionally, he has drawn a group of happy people who are encouraging and enforcing Al-Sisi,[66] who is wearing his military uniform, to take control over Egypt, with the title of 'Popular Consensus.' Both caricatures used melodramatic exaggeration to rationalize the military coup as a patriotic duty to rescue the country. In the first caricature, Al-Sisi is portrayed as a superman who has the potency to carry Egypt alone and with ease. While in the second caricature, it was too hard for only two ordinary men to hold the body of Al-Sisi to the chair of the presidency. The artist is showing the weakness of the masses in contrast to Al-Sisi's physical strength. In both caricatures, Al-Sisi is wearing sunglasses and looking forward with a poker face. This reflects his strict personality and shows that he has been forced into the patriotic hard mission of ruling Egypt.

Secondly, after the military coup in Egypt, Hussein Al-Gasmi the Emirati singer, produced seven Egyptian patriotic songs for different political events. The songs glorified the military establishment and supported the regime. Al-Gasmi's songs portray Al-Sisi and the military establishment as Egypt's eldest male who is saving it.[67] In his *Teslm Al-Aiady* (May Those Hands Be Safe) song,[68] produced after the military coup, he, in the name of the people, thanks the military establishment and General Al-Sisi for their 'sacrifices to the country' by saving it from the Muslim Brotherhood.[69] The lyrics of the song are written and tuned by Mostafa Kamel, Head of the Musicians' Union and sang by different popular singers, including Kamel. It includes:

الفـ ميت مليّون تحيه
Great Greetings
للمجند للفـريق
to the soldier, to the general
للعزيمة المليّة ميه
to the high determination
للى رسوملنا الطريق
to those who guided us through the way
منى ليك ابسط هديه
Accept -please- my simplest present
تحيه للرجال الجريـــئ
greetings to the brave man (Al-Sisi)

Al-Gasmi's songs for Egypt are known for their joyful tunes, dancing melodies, and their usage of melodramatic exaggeration to promote the military establishment and Al-Sisi.

Thirdly, in February 2018, the DMC media network, which is funded by the armed forces,[70] produced a dancing version of the military anthem *Qalu Aa* (What Did They Say?). The original version of the song discusses the army's role in fighting terrorism and glorifies its martyrs. Yet, the new version that was produced by DMC enforced a facetiously dancing melody to it, transforming the anthem into an artificially joyful song. Additionally, *Qalu Aa* was sung in different schools by students with the administrations and teachers supporting them.[71] Both songs *Teslm Al-A'iady* and *Qalu Aa* were broadcasted widely in the media during different political events including the presidential elections of 2018. In this sense, politics became militarized, and kitsch art was used to rationalize authoritarianism as a patriotic duty; while enforcing joyful melodramatic rhetoric to the spectacle in order to fabricate a state of public satisfaction.

Thus, pro-coup artwork adopted a joyful genre of the melodramatic rhetoric that interprets political conflicts through populist nationalist discourse. These kinds of art works, in addition to the joyful scene of the dancing women in front of ballot stations are one form of expressing patriotism in pro-coup discourse. The discourse in which the masses accept the rule of Al-Sisi and are happy with the current status quo. In short, the main purpose of this kind of melodrama in the discourse and artworks of the pro-coup camp is to produce a culture that rationalizes the military coup of 2013 and cultivates support for the new authoritarian regime through portraying Al-Sisi and the military establishment as true nationalists that have sacrificed themselves for the sake of the nation and rescued Egypt from the villains, by ruling it.

## Conclusion

Art has contributed to the constitution of an aesthetic interpretation of political tensions in Egypt after the revolution. This was accompanied by a focus on the melodramatic rhetoric that dominated the spectacle. On one hand, the revolutionaries' praise of creative activism and their attempts to aestheticize the revolution participated in forming a patriotic utopian understanding of political change in the public mind-set, where the revolution is limited to the civilized middle-class youths' means of expressing or protesting authoritarianism. Meanwhile, aesthetics dominated the spectacle and the melodramatic rhetoric was apparent in the discourse of different political actors, social movements, activists, and revolutionaries. Subsequently, revolutionary art works with a melancholic victimization rhetoric expressed political tensions as a moral struggle between the two camps of good and evil. In the discourse of revolutionaries, power relations between the two camps are flawed and revolutionaries are being vanquished by the powerful and undefeatable villains. In this sense, art activism depended on the lamentation of victims with a defeatist attitude, which resulted in depoliticizing the revolution, as political change had been limited to the aesthetic civilian acts and political conflicts were viewed as a struggle between good and evil. Even when the discourse of revolutionaries contained hope, it was implicated in interpreting victory with an exaggerated utopian discourse that aimed to encourage activists to sacrifice their lives for the sake of revolution in street battles against security forces. This was obvious when revolutionaries were raising slogans such as *martyr on demand* and *glory to the martyrs*. Aestheticizing the revolution in a melodramatic rhetoric became a sanctuary to revolutionaries in times of political failure. The victimization melancholic discourse of revolutionaries was a simple way of absolving themselves of responsibility, while justifying the political failure of pro-democracy groups as a matter of disruption in power relations between them and the villains.

Cultural structures and the administration of art did not witness a prominent change in the post-revolution era. However, it was important for the military coup to seize power over the spectacle in 2013 to aestheticize the military coup and legitimize authoritarianism. This was achieved with ease through the enactment of repressive laws and tightening control over official and private media outlets. Patriarchy had been transformed to something that is acquired by the military and Al-Sisi's rule over Egypt. This happened firstly through the same melodramatic genre to exclude Islamist movements particularly and pro-democracy groups generally from the political scene, through echoing patriotic populism discourses. Secondly, it manifested by turning political conflict into a struggle between the good and the evil or a war between patriotism and treason. The public had to choose between the two camps; either being a patriotic agent who supports the state by supporting its president (Al-Sisi) and the military establishment that ousted Morsi or being a conspirator and a traitor who is working in collusion with the West to spread chaos and vandalism across Egypt. Subsequently, opposing the regime was considered a chaotic expression of treason and opposing groups were obstructed by the public. In short, aestheticizing the military coup helped glorify the acts of authoritarianism through the melodramatic rhetoric's domination of the spectacle and the authoritarian regime of Al-Sisi asking the public to obey its policies even if they are based on repression and human rights violations. Pro-coup art works succeeded in forcing a way through the spectacle with its patriotic-nationalist rhetoric and participated in aestheticizing the military coup and rationalizing authoritarianism.

Finally, revolutionary art was a melancholic expression with a defeatist attitude of mourning the martyrs, while pro-coup art was focused on creating an artificial joyful expression of cheering the hero (Al-Sisi) to victory. The use of emotional excess and the acts of romanticizing the revolution that were key part of different revolutionary arts show how political tensions were interpreted and approached at that time as a moral struggle between good and evil. A rational discourse of understanding failure was absent in favour of the intense emotional display of mourning the innocent martyrs of the revolution with a melancholic victimization rhetoric. The aestheticization of politics had facilitated the military coup in 2013 and subsequent authoritarian rule, while private and public media presented Al-Sisi as the glorious leader who saved the country from the villains. The villains in the regime's discourse were not limited to the Islamists or Morsi, but also the dissidents who protest authoritarianism or criticize the president and the military establishment. The pro-coup kitsch arts used melodramatic-nationalist rhetoric to justify the regime's brutal crackdown on dissent and to convince the public that repression is an indispensable patriotic response to protect Egypt from the evil forces.

## Notes

1.     Hosni Mubarak's rule lasted for over thirty years (1980–2011) and the photo mentioned shows an Egyptian woman dancing and surrounded by the joyful public in the streets holding supporting posters with Mubarak photo, and the phrase 'Yes to Mubarak' to celebrate the approval of Hosni Mubarak in the 1999 referendum in the streets of Cairo. Photo Credit: MOHAMMED AL AL-SEHITI. Taken on 27 September 1999, https://www.gettyimages.com/detail/news-photo/people-celebrate-in-the-streets-of-cairo-27-september-1999-news-photo/107819623, accessed 22 April 2018.

2.     Rasha Abdulla, Egypt's Media in the Midst of Revolution (Washington DC: Carnegie Endowment for International Peace, 2014), accessed 17 January 2018, https://carnegieendowment.org/files/egypt_media_revolution.pdf.

3.     Marina Ottaway and Amr Hamzawy, *Protest Movements and Political Change in the Arab World*, (Washington DC: Carnegie Endowment for International Peace, 2011), accessed 19 January 2018, https://carnegieendowment.org/2011/01/28/protest-movements-and-political-change-in-arab-world-pub-42394.

4.     Zeinab Abul-Magd, 'The Egyptian Military in Politics and the Economy: Recent History and Current Transition Status,' *Chr. Michelsens Institute* 2 (2013), accessed 27 March 2018, https://www.cmi.no/publications/4935-the-egyptian-military-in-politics-and-the-economy.

5.     Nathan J. Brown, 'Egypt's Failed Transition,' *Journal of Democracy* 24/4 (2013).

6.     These were known as the Free Officers.

7.     Mona Abaza, 'Walls, segregating downtown Cairo and the Mohammed Mahmud street graffiti,' *Theory, Culture & Society* 30/1 (2013), 122–39.

8.     Marwan M. Kraidy, *The Naked Blogger of Cairo* (Cambridge, Massachusetts: Harvard University Press, 2016), 98–101.

9.     During Mubarak's era (1981–2011) the Ministry of Culture governed all cultural activities in Egypt through being the producer and distributor of all kinds of cultural services which would, subsequently, promote and serve state politics.

10.     Nadia Von Maltzahn, 'Governance of Culture in the Wake of the Arab Revolutions,' in *Arab Revolutions and Beyond: Change and Persistence*, eds. Belakhdar, Eickhof, el Khawaga, et al. (2014), 225, accessed 1 July 2019, https://www.polsoz.fu-berlin.de/polwiss/forschung/international/vorderer-orient/publikation/working_papers/wp_11/WP11_Tunis_Conference_FINAL_web.pdf.

11.     Maltzahn, 'Governance of Culture in the Wake of the Arab Revolutions.'

12.     Mohamad Elmasry, 'Unpacking Anti-Muslim Brotherhood Discourse,' *Jadaliyya*, 28 June 2013, accessed 15 June 2018, http://www.jadaliyya.com/

Details/28855.

13.    Amr Hamzawy, *Legislating Authoritarianism: Egypt's New Era of Repression* (Washington, Carnegie Endowment for International Peace, 2017).

14.    Mohamed Abdelaal, 'Egypt's Public Protest Law 2013: A Boost to Freedom or a Further Restriction?', *US-China L. Rev.* (2014), accessed 29 May 2018, https://papers.ssrn.com/sol3/papers.cfm?abstract_id=2440939.

15.    Patrick Kingsley, 'Egypt's Interim President Adly Mansour Signs 'anti-protest Law',' *The Guardian,* 24 November 2013, accessed 29 March 2018, https://www.theguardian.com/world/2013/nov/24/egypt-interim-president-anti-protest-law.

16.    Amr Hamzawy, 'Conspiracy Theories and Populist Narratives,' *Philosophy & Social Criticism* 44/4 (2018).

17.    Amr Hamzawy, 'Egypt after the 2013 Military Coup: Law-making in Service of the New Authoritarianism,' *Philosophy & Social Criticism* 43 (2017), 392–405.

18.    Hamzawy, 'Egypt after the 2013 Military Coup.'

19.    Hamzawy, 'Egypt after the 2013 Military Coup.'

20.    Hamzawy, 'Conspiracy Theories and Populist Narratives.'

21.    Hamzawy, 'Conspiracy Theories and Populist Narratives.'

22.    Re censorship policies that affected cultural production in Egypt, see Hessen Hossam. 'A battle for existence: How the combined forces of censorship and security shaped Egypt's music scene,' *Mada Masr*, 2 January 2018, accessed 29 August 2018, https://madamasr.com/en/2018/01/02/feature/culture/a-battle-for-existence-how-the-combined-forces-of-censorship-and-security-shaped-egypts-music-scene-in-2017/.

23.    Jacques Rancière, *Aisthesis: Scenes From the Aesthetic Regime of Art* (Lonsdon: Verso, 2013).

24.    Jacques Rancière, 'The Politics of Art: An Interview with Jacques Rancière.' *Verso*, 9 November 2015, accessed 25 February 2018, https://www.versobooks.com/blogs/2320-the-politics-of-art-an-interview-with-jacques-ranciere.

25.    Rancière, *Aisthesis*.

26.    Murray Jacob Edelman, *From Art to Politics: How Artistic Creations Shape Political Conceptions* (Chicago: University of Chicago Press, 2003), 5.

27.    Edelman, *From Art to Politics*, 5–8.

28.    Edelman, *From Art to Politics*, 5–8.

29.    Lina Khatib. *Image Politics in the Middle East: The Role of the Visual in Political Struggle* (London and New York: I. B. Tauris, 2013).

30.    Kraidy, *The Naked Blogger of Cairo*.

31.    Radwa Othman. 'Graffiti as a Means of Protest and Documentation in the Egyptian Revolution.' *African Conflict and Peacebuilding Review*, 5 (2015), 152–61.

32.    Mona Abaza. 'Walls, Segregating Downtown Cairo and the Mohammed Mahmud Street Graffiti.' *Theory, Culture & Society* 30 (2013), 122–39.

33.   Kraidy, *The Naked Blogger of Cairo*.

34.   Jessica Winegar, 'A Civilized Revolution: Aesthetics and Political Action in Egypt,' *American Ethnologist* 43/4 (2016) 609–22.

35.   Martin Jay, 'The Aesthetic Ideology as Ideology; or, What Does It Mean to Aestheticize Politics?', *Cultural Critique* 21(1992), accessed 12 June 2018, https://www.jstor.org/stable/1354116.

36.   Jay, 'The Aesthetic Ideology as Ideology.'

37.   Jay, 'The Aesthetic Ideology as Ideology.'

38.   Kraidy, *The Naked Blogger of Cairo*, 14.

39.   Kraidy, *The Naked Blogger of Cairo*, 14.

40.   Zeinab Abul-Magd, 'Understanding SCAF.' *The Cairo Review of Global Affairs* 6 (2012), 151–59, accessed 12 July 2018, https://cdn.thecairoreview.com/wp-content/uploads/2014/11/CR6-Abul_Magd.pdf.

41.   Winegar, 'A Civilized Revolution,' 619.

42.   Winegar, 'A Civilized Revolution.'

43.   Lila Abu-Lughod, 'Egyptian Melodrama—Technology of the Modern Subject,' in Media Worlds: *Anthropology on New Terrain*, eds. Faye D. Ginburg et al. (Berkley, University of California Press, 2002).

44.   Lila Abu-Lughod, 'Egyptian Melodrama.'

45.   Lila Abu-Lughod, 'Egyptian Melodrama.'

46.   Walid El-Khachab, 'Melodrama or Excessive Passion in Public Discourse', *Maraya*, 20 December 2017, accessed 20 August 2018, https://www.facebook.com/photo.php?fbid=10155853148137674&set=a.1015017 0052367674&type=3&theater.

47.   Elisabeth Robin Anker, *Orgies of Feeling: Melodrama and the Politics of Freedom* (Durham and London, Duke University Press, 2014).

48.   Michael Blain, 'Power, War, and Melodrama in the Discourses of Political Movements,' *Theory and Society* 23/6 (1994), 805–837.

49.   Blain, 'Power, War, and Melodrama.'

50.   Blain, 'Power, War, and Melodrama.'

51.   Walter Benjamin and J. A. Underwood, *The Work of Art in the Age of Mechanical Reproduction*, (London: Penguin Books, 1998).

52.   Michael Blain, 'The Politics of Victimage: Power and Subjection in a US Anti-Gay Campaign,' *Critical Discourse Studies* 2/1 (2005), 31–50.

53.   Robert D. Enford and Scott A. Hunt, 'Dramaturgy and Social Movements: The Social Construction and Communication of Power,' *Sociological Inquiry* 62/1 (1992): 36–55.

54.   Bruno Bosteels, *The Leftist Hypothesis: Communism in the Age of Terror* (2010), accessed 1 July 2019, https://arditiesp.files.wordpress.com/2012/10/bosteels_leftist_hypothesis.doc.

55.   Bel Trew, 'Welcome to the Department of Morale Affairs,' *Foreign Policy*, 15 January 2014, accessed 18 January 2018, https://foreignpolicy.com/2014/01/15/welcome-to-the-department-of-morale-affairs/.

56.   Kraidy, *The Naked Blogger of Cairo*, 84.

57.   Mustafa Ibrahim is an Egyptian young poet, who participated in the revolution of the 25th and was arrested among other protesters. He was praised by well-known Egyptian poets and writers, such as Ahmed Fouad Negm and Alaa Al Aswany; Omaima Sobhi, 'Manifesto—Mustafa Ibrahim,' *SoundCloud*, accessed 15 February 2018, https://soundcloud.com/amr-elfiqy/manifesto-mustafa-ibrahim/sets.

58.   'Mostafa Ibrahim,' *Poetry Translation Centre*, accessed 7 July 2018, https://www.poetrytranslation.org/poets/mostafa-ibrahim.

59.   Football fans of Al-Ahly club who attend matches and support their club by different means. Mostly known to be youths who chant for their club special songs during the matches. Ultras Ahlawy members used to protest the brutal acts of the Egyptian security forces of the Mubarak regime by singing their own political chants that mock the regime during football matches. While in the revolution, Ultras Ahlawy had a crucial role in confronting security forces in street battles. However, they became a viable revolutionary actor in the Egyptian political scene in the transition period of the SCAF.

60.   Fareeda M. Zikry, 'Ultras in Egypt: The Power of Organized Soccer Fans and Their Political Influence on the 2011 Egyptian Revolutions and Post-Revolution Era' (Master's Thesis, University of North Carolina, Chapel Hill, 2015).

61.   'Ultras Ahlawy 07 Media,' *YouTube*, accessed 12 February 2018, https://www.youtube.com/user/UltrasAhlawy07Media.

62.   Mhypar Awy, *YouTube*, accessed 21 April 2018, https://www.youtube.com/watch?v=ZjpH16W2Goc.

63.   *Dogs* is used by Arab people to humiliate others.

64.   'Ultras Ahlawy 07 Media,' *YouTube*, accessed 27 February 2018, https://www.youtube.com/watch?v=rW3xhdqj3J0.

65.   Caricature by Mostafa Houssien 'Don't be surprised … this is not an American movie, it's El-Al-Sisi Man rescuing Al-Mahrousa (Egypt) before its downfall,' *Al-Akhbar* daily newspaper, 10 October 2013, accessed 12 April 2018, http://www.almasryalyoum.com/news/details/531305.

66.   Public Consensus. Caricature by Mostafa Houssien, *Al-Akhbar* daily newspaper, accessed 16 April 2018, http://www.almasryalyoum.com/news/details/531305.

67.   'Hussain Al Jassmi Teslam Edenak,' *YouTube*, accessed 14 January 2018, https://www.youtube.com/watch?v=O-76xB2nhrw&index=10&list=PLehFR7UrVKjcgSGw_kMQWHMJtPtqyd-93.

68.   'Teslam El Aiady,' *YouTube*, accessed 29 June 2017, https://www.youtube.com/watch?v=RnVEzB2gJcY.

69.   Amina Khairy, 'Common Sense in Egypt: Teslam El Ayadi,' *Egypt Independent*, accessed 25 March 2018, http://www.egyptindependent.com/common-sense-egypt-teslam-el-ayadi/.

70.   Mada Masr, 'RSF Criticizes Takeover of Egyptian Media Outlets by Pro-state Businessmen,' *Mada Masr*, accessed 15 August

2018, https://www.madamasr.com/en/2017/09/06/news/u/rsf-criticizes-takeover-of-egyptian-media-outlets-by-pro-state-businessmen/.

71. Walaa Ali, 'Military Anthem Played at Egypt's Schools, Universities Nationwide,' *Egypt Today,* 4 March 2018. accessed 27 August 2018, https://www.egypttoday.com/Article/1/44390/Military-anthem-played-at-Egypt-s-schools-universities-nationwide.

# 8

# The Crime of the Pirate: A Case of Digital Resistance

*Fidèle A. Vlavo*

## Introduction

*The reform of criminal law must be read as a strategy for the rearrangement of the power to punish.*

— Michel Foucault

Following a historic trial launched in February 2009, a Swedish court condemned Fredrik Neij, Gottfrid Svartholm Warg, Peter Sunde Kolmisoppi, and Carl Lundström to one year of imprisonment for their involvement in copyright infringement.[1] The four defendants were behind the infamous file-sharing website 'The Pirate Bay' (TPB). Initially based in Sweden, this site was set up in 2003 to facilitate peer-to-peer file-sharing using BitTorrent technology. The website became so popular amongst Internet users that the administrators expanded the domain to address international demand. By 2008, TPB had built its reputation to become one of the most visited websites on the Internet.[2] As a response, entertainment companies and anti-piracy organizations, aided by law enforcement and national governments, embarked on a steady dismantling of the file-sharing website. For decades now, media corporations have lobbied for the control of intellectual property and the redeployment of copyright laws to digital media.[3] In many ways, the prosecution of TPB is the latest episode in a series of international vindictive court cases.[4] Like computer hacking or electronic protest before it, digital file-sharing has been subjected to a social and legal process of criminalization, and this trial is a compelling example of a display of power and control in the digital sphere.

This chapter takes the TPB trial as its case study to examine the criminalization of file-sharing. Its aim is to demonstrate that this legal action was against the practice, and was to protect the assets of media and private corporations. Indeed, many of these court cases are exemplary accounts of how legal systems are reformed to defend commercial interests, and how judgements are issued to discipline and educate Internet users. Central to the argument developed here is the assertion that the conflicts opposing users, corporations, and governments are not new phenomena. As will be discussed, legal cases have been used to regulate digital practices since the early days of the Internet. I relate this practice to Foucault's concept of *necessary illegality*, which contends that certain practices that were tolerated, if not encouraged, become the centre of legal battles the moment that they are perceived as a threat to financial gain.[5] Thus, I draw parallels between the TPB case and previous prosecutions to establish a historical, albeit recent, tradition of constructing digital crimes.

Borrowing from Foucault's discursive methodology, I begin the discussion with a textual reading of TPB's court proceedings and consider how the judges address the challenges of applying copyright law to digital media.[6] In particular, I focus on the strategies used to successfully convict the defendants. In the next part of the chapter, I read the verdict of the trial and underline the disputable assessments of the retributions and the sentencing. I argue that the prosecution displays most attributes of 'a strategy for the rearrangement of the power to punish,' for the purpose of promoting and protecting capitalistic interests.[7] In the last part, I revisit TPB's position within the rhetorics of digital piracy and performative resistance. I suggest that in the absence of technological restrictions, TPB may have transformed file-sharing into a politics of resistance. Indeed, the technological and discursive rejections of criminalization exemplify the type of renegotiations theorized in this volume. My aim here is to contribute to the scholarship on digital file-sharing by framing TPB as a creative movement that challenges the location of power within and beyond the law. While its abrasive aesthetics of opposition led to the conviction of its founders, TPB constitutes an effective, if temporary, space for a resistance that ultimately exposes the limits of law.

### Digital Illegality

File-sharing has attracted much academic attention. Social science studies have touched upon virtually every aspects of the practice, whether technological, political or ethical. Yet, most debates have soared concerning questions of legality and illegality. To be sure, little is written about file-sharing as a practice that enables the transmission of digital information without delict or infringement. The practice is also not readily discussed in relation to platforms and websites that operate in full legality. That is to say, file-sharing is examined, more often than not, within the framework of illegality. What is more, this legal focus is often combined with discussions of political economy. Thus, many academic studies have proceeded from legal battles between file-sharing services and media companies.[8] Indeed, it is only with the increase of music files download in the late 1990s that digital file-sharing becomes the target of legislation.[9]

In this context, the case of peer-to-peer file sharing services, Napster is a common point of reference and an example of the conflation between file-sharing and illegality. As one of the earliest digital file-sharing sites, Napster was condemned for copyright infringement in 2000.[10] The legal case brought forward questions examined in most early work on file-sharing, that is, its economic impact, and more specifically, its damage to the entertainment industry's business model. Following an injunction to cease activity, Napster's administrators could not defend the principle of 'fair use' and the site eventually shut down while filing for bankruptcy.[11] The point is that for over a year, the site had remained exempt from any scrutiny. What stirred the music industry was the prospect of high financial loss as companies were quick to blame declines in sales on peer-to-peer music sharing. Several analysts have supported that claim.[12] Others have refuted the argument, while they also demonstrated that records sales actually increased during the time of Napster.[13]

Oberholzer-Gee and Strumpf's study is often referenced for its conclusion that 'the estimated effect of file sharing on sales is not statistically distinguishable from zero.'[14] Yet, as Napster seemed to challenge the economic model of music distribution, media corporations as well as individual right owners decided to exercise their intellectual property rights to halt a potential loss of income. Despite divergences on the economic effects of file-sharing, these legal affairs led to the tightening of copyright legislation, often to the benefit of music and media companies. McChesney acutely frames the problem when stating that:

> Today copyright has become a huge market in which control over copyrights is frequently unconnected to the actual persons who created the original work—and the terms for copyright are extended after the fact, which makes no sense at all. Copyright is now something entirely

different: it protects corporate monopoly rights over culture and provides much of the profits to media conglomerates. They could not exist without it.[15] (original emphasis)

Over the years, more companies have engaged in lawsuits to halt the illegal distribution of copyright material, and more attempts have been made worldwide to regulate the circulation of digital content.[16] Yet, critics have also observed that legal victories over digital platforms have limited impact because new technologies are rapidly developed to counter legal restrictions.[17] One such technology is the BitTorrent protocol used by TPB, as well as other file-sharing websites. For this reason, websites owners argue that they cannot be made liable for copyright infringement.[18] This technology facilitates the retrieval and transfer of digital files from various locations without the need for the site to hold any files. This constitutes a radical shift from previous legal cases involving websites that provided users with digital storage and streaming functions.[19] In this instance, the indictment for copyright infringement is technically indisputable. By contrast, the BitTorrent protocol does not require platforms to host digital content, let alone copyrighted material.[20] Here is a case where a technology is devised to circumvent the law. This technological and legal opposition demonstrates that the structure of digital networks allows users to participate, and, when necessary, to regulate and control interactions. Therefore, file-sharing cannot be seen as an informal process and file-sharers cannot simply be perceived as greedy users.

This conceptual shift has also re-focused the discussion towards the behaviour and motivations of file-sharers.[21] In this process, the label of 'piracy' has provided a new context for analysis. In his study, Yar examines how the label has been used to frame a practice that increasingly requires social and political attention. For the critic, 'piracy' has been re-deployed by the copyright industry to extend potential criminalization. As he writes:

> The recasting of 'piracy' in a language of criminal violation amounts therefore to its 'moralization,' an attempt to create a normative consensus that it offends against the agreed standards of decent and acceptable behaviour. This has been necessary precisely because copyright violations have been rendered socially acceptable by their ubiquity and the widespread perception that they are not genuinely 'harmful' in the manner of 'real crimes' (such as theft of personal property, homicide, rape, assault and so on).[22]

Yar, therefore, exhorts us to scrutinize the criminalizing discourses channelled by the media industry and governments, and to recognize that 'the expansion of proprietary copyrights, and the criminalization of their violation, is part of a larger 'game' in which struggles to dominate the uses of information are being played out within the new 'knowledge economy.'[23] The arguments developed in this chapter respond to this call by providing a critical reading of the criminalization of file-sharing, as well as the opportunity to include a new reading of piracy. Indeed, early usages of the term may have carried a negative connotation, but recent social movements have explicitly recast piracy as a political exercise.

The phenomenon of TPB has proven to be key in shifting the debates. From its beginning as a file-sharing index site and until it became one of the most visited websites on the Internet, TPB operated in complete disregard of copyright and intellectual property laws.[24] The name of the site was even part of a process of re-appropriation where digital piracy and pirates are granted full legitimacy. This culture is epitomized by the term *kopimi* (read 'copy me') coined by the think-tank Piratbyrån (Pirate Bureau). This Swedish organization was set up as a counterpoint to the Swedish Anti-Piracy Bureau to advocate for a political defence of file-sharing practices, based on the philosophy of free circulation of information.[25] In 2005, the organization produced a lengthy publication in Swedish, titled *Copy Me*, which canonizes its ethos.

Since then, studies have examined the practice of TPB in relation to various issues, including copyright infringement, media piracy, intellectual property, and consumer behaviour.[26] Recent works have considered the practice of file-sharing as hacktivism, political participation, and sub-politics, with some positioning TPB as a key agent of change in media distribution and in the digital eco system at large.[27] In one such study, Patrick Burkart discusses TPB as pirate politics, or a form of 'cyberutopianism [that] covers the legal domains of free speech and access to information and culture,'[28] Pirate politics includes free speech and therefore file-sharing. In this politics, file-sharing is 'broadly perceived as private communication online, and as being very little like publishing.'[29] This position easily justifies file-sharing as a legitimate form of communication that should be protected against political and legal regulation. Thus, digital piracy is not merely a means for illicit media consumption; it is a politics that aims to counter the capitalistic control of digital media.

Indeed, as will be examined in the discussion that follows, none of the legal actions and new legislations have effectively resolved the main interrogations regarding the practice of file-sharing. First, the role of file-sharing websites in copyright infringement remains contested. The question is often the first point of contention between parties and constitutes a core challenge for defendants. Second, the evaluation of damages caused by the file-sharing platform remains inconsistent. In the case of a conviction, this lack of knowledge leads to arbitrary and disproportionate sentencing. Third, these trials and utilitarian sentences seem to generate more opposition and creative resistance than blind compliance from users. While studies have analyzed the TPB court case and attempted to explain the decision of the Swedish Court, little attention has been given to the debates and conflicts that took place during trial. As such, the case must be read and recognized as, yet another, example of the criminalization of file-sharing.

## Digital Complicity

In his account of generalized punishment, Foucault describes a central shift that reconfigured the political and economic life of the late 18th century. According to the historian, until then, European societies had relied on a widespread system of illegality, evidenced by a general non-observance of laws. These illegalities were the products of privileges granted to certain social groups, but also, of the reluctance or impossibility to press charges and prosecute offenders. For Foucault, illegality was 'so deeply rooted and so necessary to the life of each social stratum, that it had in a sense its own coherence and economy.'[30] This, Foucault argues, represented the 'margin of tolerated illegality.'[31] Since it promoted rapid economic growth, this margin was controlled and often supported by the bourgeoisie, but only to the point where it did not threaten property rights. The illegality of rights were tolerated, but not the illegality of property rights.

Using the example of pilfering in ports and warehouses, Foucault explains that increases in wealth investment and commercial entrepreneurship came to challenge this margin of tolerated illegality:

> With the new forms of capital accumulation, new relations of production and the new legal status of property, all the popular practices that belonged, either in a silent, everyday, tolerated form, or in a violent form, to the illegality of rights were reduced by force to an illegality of property.[32]

Foucault also describes the process through which these initially tolerated illegalities were criminalized:

> It proved necessary ... to control these illicit practices and introduce
> new legislation to cover them. The offences had to be properly defined
> and more surely punished; out of this mass of irregularities, sometimes
> tolerated and sometimes punished with a severity out of all proportion
> to the offence, one had to determine what was an intolerable offence,
> and the offenders had to be apprehended and punished.[33]

This process of regulation, or criminalization, that emerged more than two centuries ago is still active today. The legal action taken against TPB should be seen as an attempt to protect property rights through the reform of the law. Following past legal cases, the courts have associated the practice of file-sharing with the possibility of financial loss. From there, legislation was retrieved (in the form of existing copyright law) to confer file-sharing its criminal status.

One early attempt to control digital file-sharing occurred in the late 1980s, when a group a computer hackers was sentenced to jail for the unauthorized access of a private server. Following a brief lawsuit, in which they pleaded guilty, Robert Riggs, Frank Darden, and Adam Grant received prison sentences for accessing the network of BellSouth telecommunication company.[34] The case revolved around the unauthorized access and distribution of a computer file, the E911 document, which Riggs had retrieved from the private server. For this, the hackers were charged with 'computer fraud,' 'access device fraud,' and 'interstate transportation of stolen property.'[35] In addition, the Atlanta Three (the name popularly given to the hackers) were ordered to pay restitution fines to BellSouth.[36]

At the time, the outcome of the trial raised much criticism, in particular regarding the criminal treatment of the hackers. The main dispute was about the legal interpretation of the indictment. The hackers pleaded guilty to the charge of stealing property (BellSouth's electronic file), but as a digital file it was not taken away from the company; BelleSouth was still in possession of the E911. Hence, the hackers had not *stolen* the file, they had *copied* it.[37] However, the act of accessing and copying was redefined as theft, even though the 'victim' was still in full possession of the allegedly stolen item. This is how digital practices are discursively redefined to enable prosecution.

Fast forward twenty years later and the TPB owners found themselves in similar contention. Most administrators of file-sharing websites have argued that since their servers do not hold any material they cannot be made liable for contents shared via the platform. The TPB defendants also relied on this apparent technological immunity to challenge court orders. Yet, the indictment presented at the Swedish court was not for copyright infringement, but for *complicity,* more specifically: 'Complicity in breach of the Copyright Act' (Verdict: 1).[38] Since the perpetrators of the infringement could not readily be identified, the complicity charge was used to enable prosecution.

However, to be effective, the complicity indictment needed to circumvent an important issue raised during TPB hearings, that is, the possibility to be complicit in a crime for which no perpetrator had been identified. After all, the website itself was not illegal, and the prosecution established that the administrators had not infringed any copyright law (Verdict: 3). As explained previously, the BitTorrent protocol enables the uploading and downloading of digital content via torrent files that only contain meta information (including name, location, size, format). The sharing process remains peer-to-peer, that is, from one user to another, with no central server. This is why during trial, defendant Fredrik Neij could confidently declare that the website was a user-generated site and that 'it was made clear' to every user that the file-sharing service did not contain any copyright-protected material.' (Verdict: 27).

Identifying the actual perpetrators would mean locating those individuals that host the copyright-protected material on their devices and make them available to others; another point that the defence team made explicit,

> The link between the making available copyright-protected recordings or works and the alleged complicit actions is unclear on several points. It is not known who the uploader was, where he was based, or how he had obtained the original of the file he was sharing. Nor has there been any concrete indication of how the uploader and downloader were influenced by the operations of The Pirate Bay or by Fredrik Neij, other than that the filesharing service provided a filesharing model which is, in fact, legal. (Verdict: 28)

This point illustrates Foucault's argument that 'popular illegality' is tolerated due to an 'actual impossibility of imposing the law and apprehending offenders.'[39]

Because of this apparent impossibility, the Swedish District Court adopted a unique stand. While it recognized that 'the natural course of action would be to examine the principal offence first, and then move on to examining any complicity on the part of the defendants,' (Verdict: 36) it concluded that 'there is no requirement for the perpetrators to be known for liability for complicity to be considered.' (Verdict: 47)

This means that the charge of complicity only requires the prosecution to prove that a main offence of copyright infringement has been committed. Without this legal overturn of 'the natural course of action,' prosecution of file-sharing services such as TPB would not proceed; at least not until actual offenders could be brought to court.

This legal overturn proved to be crucial to the prosecution because the localization of the actual copyright infringers is made especially challenging by the BitTorrent protocol. Since torrents allow for various parts of the original file to be sent and retrieved from different sources, it is not possible to state that one source, or user, provided single access to another user; the sharing process is inevitably collective. This is why file-sharing technology is so efficient and so popular. In response to this technical loophole, copyright law does not require that full works be made available for the infringement to take place. In its assessment, the Swedish court concluded that the torrent files had been 'used for unlawful making available to the general public of the works [and] as such, the torrent files can be regarded as intended for use as aids in the offence' (Verdict: 54).

Here, the charge of complicity offers a rather flexible scope for prosecutors. First, perpetrators need not be identified before alleged accomplices can be charged. Second, the accusation is broad enough to encompass a variety of acts, including, in the case of TPB, 'making available to the general public copyright-protected sound and picture recording and works' (Verdict: 20). Third, the complicit act need not be a precondition for the main offence. As the court concluded, 'liability for complicity can apply even to someone who has contributed only insignificantly to the principal offence' (Verdict: 47). At this point, all of the necessary legal re-interpretations are in place to effectively criminalize file-sharing practices.

## Digital Discipline

Confronted with the inability to identify and prosecute copyright infringers, prosecutors have settled for the complicity indictment to outlaw file-sharing. The success of this indictment means that any other file-sharing websites can face legal action. The accusation also carries the legal count of 'aiding and abetting,' which enables the court to apply the same sanctions to culprits and accomplices (Verdict: 59). Consequently, TPB's conviction implied full liability for damage and compensation. Against this charge, the defendants re-stated that the website did not host any copyright-protected material and that they had no control over the material shared. This argument again proved ineffective and, aside from their year-long prison sentence, the defendants were summoned to pay retribution fees as if they themselves had committed the infringement. The total sum requested by all parties reached 30 million Swedish kronor (USD 3.6 million, EUR 2.7 million, GBP 2.4 million).[40]

During the trial, each media company formulated their own calculations for their damage claim. The Nordic film companies used a hypothetical license fee for the right to provide free downloadable material, whereas Swedish record companies and American film companies used estimation methods based on single downloading fees for individual media work (Verdict: 69). While the retribution costs were discussed at great length, there was no consensus regarding the appropriate means to assess income losses. Again, the Swedish District Court adopted a position that favoured the plaintiffs by confirming that

> under no circumstance, must a right be utilized without consent without the rightsholder being paid reasonable compensation. The right to such damages is not, therefore, dependent on whether it can be proved that the plaintiff companies have suffered any actual injury, and that the injury caused was the result of the unlawful utilization. (Verdict: 69)

This decision implies that TPB was to be sanctioned regardless of the corporations' inability to prove clear financial loss. The reference to 'reasonable compensation' implies that the retribution requested is not meant to equate financial loss, which often remains unknown. Instead, it is aimed to deter from future offences.

This kind of sentencing was already put in practice during the US trial of the Atlanta Three. In addition to prison sentences of between fourteen and twenty-one months, the defendants were ordered to pay a fine of USD 233,000 to BellSouth.[41] Yet, this sentencing was overcast by the outcome of another trial. At the same time, a fourth hacker, Craig Neidorf, was facing trial for the exact same offence in Illinois. This court case saw a radical turn of events, however. At the hearing, it emerged that the E911 document, allegedly stolen from BellSouth private system, was actually available to members of the public for USD 13. As part of the prosecution, BellSouth had estimated the worth of the file at USD 79,000.[42] As a result, Neidorf's legal case was dismissed and all charges were dropped.

Most importantly, Neidorf was not cleared of the charges of 'computer fraud' and 'interstate transportation of stolen property.' The court case was dismissed because his defence team successfully argued that the E911 document, central to the prosecution, was financially worthless. In other words, the trial was not judging the breach of BellSouth computer system. It was motivated by the need to sanction, based on the financial loss that BelleSouth had allegedly incurred. As an analogy, this mistrial would equate to the charges against a jewellery robber being dropped because the items that were stolen had little monetary value. What influenced the first condemnation was that the plaintiffs, BellSouth, had claimed considerable financial loss for the 'stolen' file. The sentencing was used as a punitive conviction to protect commercial assets. Hence, prison sentences and heavy fines are clearly meant as a public demonstration of control and an exercise of discipline.[43]

Initially, file-sharing lawsuits tended to be filed against websites, such as Grokster, Kazaa, and StreamCast.[44] However, individual users have now become the targets of media corporations, and hundreds of lawsuits are filed in the worldwide every year.[45] The disciplinary function of these prosecutions is latent, and some sentences have required users to pay up to USD 675,000 for downloading and sharing copyright-protected songs.[46] In all of these cases, the mechanisms leading to the calculation of the fines remain unclear. What is more, the assertion that peer-to-peer music exchange is having a detrimental impact on music sales is being consistently challenged.[47] Indeed, TPB defendants refuted the claim that media companies faced any damages; the evidence was that the sales of sound and pictures recordings did not decrease because of the alleged infringement (Verdict: 21). Similarly, the plaintiffs could not prove an 'adequate causality between the specified injuries and the actions of the defendants' (Verdict: 21). In the end, these arguments were all dismissed by the District Court. Nevertheless, the judges exercised some caution by reducing the plaintiffs' financial claims to a 'reasonable compensation.' (Verdict: 69)

This account of the TPB trial clearly demonstrates the process of criminalization of file-sharing. Many have argued that prior to the prosecution the downloading of copyright-protected media for personal use was not illegal in Sweden.[48] Thus, the government had succumbed to international pressure to implement new copyright legislation. Writing in *Wired*, Norton explains that:

> The politicians can tell police what issues to emphasize, but not what cases to pursue. So questions emerged in June when leaked documents appeared in the Swedish media that showed entertainment lobbyists with the MPA—the MPAA's international arm—had explicitly pushed for political interference.[49]

Swedish authorities have denied the claim that the MPA's have had any influence on law enforcement officials. Yet, these practices are far from novelty. In her analysis of the production of the criminal in the nineteenth century, Leps explains that 'the new propertied classes preferred to interpose a police force between them and thieves, strikers, or rioters who threatened their positions of wealth and authority.'[50] In this way, the mercantile elites can protect themselves using law enforcement authorities without ever exposing their implicit control of the rule of law.

The trial of TPB highlights this bias of law enforcement towards the media industry. Along with the court's usage of the complicity charge and the default ruling on compensation, the new Copyright Act issued in 2005 introduced the charge of 'broadcasting to the general public' (Verdict: 41). Since TPB could not be charged directly for infringement, this amendment was the way to indict its administrators. Swedish law also states that damages can only be paid for infringements committed in Sweden. Thus, all claims were assumed to have taken place in Sweden and foreign plaintiffs were compensated accordingly (Verdict: 21). In addition, changes to the Act also increased the maximum prison sentences from six months to two years, enabling the District Court to administer harsh sanctions.

These lawsuits against file-sharing services were many different attempts to discipline digital users, and despite opposition, these actions have succeeded. In his account, Foucault emphasized the ease through which 'popular illegality' could be turned into criminality.[51] Clearly, the non-observance of legislation never excluded the potentiality of prosecution. On the contrary, these laws were ready to be adapted and used to control any inconsistent behaviour. In this context, persistence in the practice of file-sharing becomes a politics of resistance. It is also the sign that digital platforms can become spaces of radical contention.

### Digital Resistance

Since its creation, TPB has operated with an explicit political stand associated with the culture of free sharing. As mentioned before, this position was at the core of the Piratbyrån organization that shared members with TPB. This movement which began as a reaction to copyright lobbying in Europe, eventually developed as a full-fledged political party that reframed piracy as a legitimate culture.[52] This stand also readily associates with the hacker culture whose ethics are equally rooted in the free circulation of information. In fact, Anonymous was one of the first movements to react to the dismantling of TPB, and to perform digital actions against media companies in retaliation.[53]

When Gottfrid Svartholm Warg set up TPB, he chose the name of the site in direct jest with the Swedish Anti-Piracy Bureau, and although, during the trial he denied that the name had any symbolism, the mockery had not been lost amongst frequent users. The site ran on the basis that intellectual property laws were not to be followed and that the free sharing of digital material was to be promoted. As explained by one operator, 'all of us who run the TPB are against the copyright laws and want them to change. ... We see it as our duty to spread culture and media. Technology is just a means to doing that.'[54] Therefore, the website became a space of contention where administrators and user could engage in digital resistance by sharing, or facilitating the sharing of, any material, in defiance of copyright law.

In several instances, TPB had to move its hosting servers to avert closure after receiving takedown notices (the owners also considered relocating the site to countries with looser legal enforcement practices, such as Russia and Argentina, Verdict: 25). Still, TPB was eventually moved back to Sweden, mostly because prior to 2006 (the year of the first arrest) the country was rather lenient regarding the legal prosecution of file-sharing services. In addition, Swedish people were known for engaging in file-sharing activities in mass and with little regards to possible copyright infringement.[55] Equally, many young people declared that any accusation of illegality would not alter their sharing practices.[56]

This battle between anti and pro piracy is also rooted in the affordances of digital technology. As many specialists have explained, the use of the BitTorrent protocol is key to a technology of file-sharing that does not require file storage from the service provider.[57] Unlike previous file-exchange technologies, sites do not need to host media content and the torrents do not contain copyright-protected material. As already mentioned, it is the reason why TPB was not illegal and its owners could not be charged with infringement. Thus, what anti-piracy groups have been trying to control is not only social and cultural practices but also technological affordances; the same affordances that they use and gain from. The issue here is that in order to protect economic interests, file-sharing is redefined as piracy, and the argument that many torrent files point to unlicensed material is often dismissed.

During TPB's trial, one defendant asserted that more than 70 per cent of the torrents circulating on the site did not point to copyright-protected material. This was compared to other platforms such as YouTube that facilitates much more infringement (Verdict: 199).

Yet, the difference between YouTube and TPB is paramount. YouTube tracks down, removes, and bans the sources of any copyright-protected material circulating on its site and administrators follow international legal guidelines to restrict access to specific content to specific countries. Most users are familiar with the notice that advises them that content 'is no longer available due to a copyright claim' or that it is 'not available in your country.' These warnings and takedown notices or lack thereof are the reasons why TPB defence in court was unsuccessful and why requests for compensation were granted. TPB's reluctance to control content was blatant.

TPB's political stand against copyright law was not just technical, using BitTorrent technology; it was also expressed through a creative use of the website. In a mode that could fit into Cammaerts's description of self-mediation, TPB used the space provided by its website to promote openly its piracy philosophy and to publicize its non-compliance with copyright legislation.[58]

One of the sections was specifically dedicated to provoking and mocking anyone attempting to disrupt the platform. This began with a direct message discouraging users from contacting the administrators about offensive material. TPB's argument was that users should focus on the material they found 'enjoyable' rather than those they deemed 'unpleasant.'[59] In addition, the site clearly stated that 'the only time The Pirate Bay will remove torrents is if the name does not reflect the content' (Verdict: 23). Ideally, for their defence, the TPB administration could have included a removal of 'torrents pointing to copyright-protected material' on its list. Instead, the site confirmed that 'any complaints from copyright individuals and/or lobby organizations will be ridiculed and displayed on the website' (Verdict: 23).

Indeed, some pages contained legal documents received from anti-piracy groups, which TPB posted alongside its responses. One such notice read as follows:

> We demand that you immediately disable the torrent and/or tracker and prevent further distribution of Apple's trade secret and copyrighted material. (Apple's counsel)

> We demand that you provide us with entertainment by sending more legal threats. Please?[60] (Pirate Bay administrators)

Many of the responses were inappropriate and some were offensive, but this provocative type of humour became TPB's signature communication strategy. To be sure, the aesthetics of mockery and sarcasm used in many replies functioned as a form of direct protest, but also, as a way to confirm an allegiance to pirate politics. This exchange with Warner Bros. is another example:

> [Warner Bros.] IMMEDIATELY REMOVE ALL TORRENT FILES OF BILLY CORGAN's UNRELEASED MATERIAL PLANNED FOR RELEASE ON WARNER BROS. RECORDS, INC. THE FOLLOWING LINK AND ALL BILLY CORGAN DOWNLOADS MUST BE COMPLETELY REMOVED: http://thepiratebay.org/search.php?q=3Dbilly+corgan

> [TPB] Sorry, but I can't remove search.php—our users would get upset if TPB suddenly lacked a search function. The problem here seems to be that the material is unreleased? If that is the case, you can easily fix the problem by releasing it. We'll be more than glad to help you distribute it—free of charge!—to our users.[61]

One of the determinant moments of the trial was the defendants' request for TPB to be considered under the Electronic Commerce Act. This Act proclaims that

> a service provider who supplies information cannot, under the provisions of the Act, be held liable for an offence which relates to the content of the information. The purpose of the Act is, instead, to place the burden of responsibility on the person who provides the information, and not on the person who simply supplies a route by which the information can be transferred. (Verdict: 28)

In a surprising twist, the District Court did agree that The Electronic Commerce Act was applicable to TPB as a file-sharing service, and as such, it could potentially be exempt from liability (Verdict: 55). However, the court focused on an additional requirement

> that the provider does not have actual knowledge of the illegal or infringing activity and, as regards damage claims, is not aware of facts or circumstances from which the activity is apparent. Further, in order to fulfil the prerequisites set out in the provision, the provider must, upon obtaining knowledge of such activity, act expeditiously to remove or disable access to the illegal or infringing material. (Verdict: 56)

This is where the ethos of piracy and the *kopimi* philosophy worked to the detriment of TPB. The defendants tried to argue that they had no knowledge that the site was used to share illegal content and that they could not monitor the activity of millions of users. Yet, their weakness for amusement and mockery was simply too potent. None of these derisive activities were actually examined during the trial, however, considering the notoriety of the website and the media exposure of the prosecution, it is difficult to conceive that a defence based on the defendants' unawareness would have succeeded.

In the end, TPB's performative irreverence became a double-edged sword. While it attracted millions of visitors and raised the website to become 'the world's largest BitTorrent tracker,' thanks to its open pirate politics, it also led to the downfall of its founders. Yet, the outcome of the trial remains open to interpretation either as a triumph of law over emerging socio-cultural practices or as the victory of free culture and technological affordances.

## Conclusion

One year after the first condemnation, the Swedish Supreme Court rejected the appeal brought by the defendants. This meant that the prison sentences and fines prevailed with no other recourse. As a result, TPB also faced closure. The site became officially inaccessible to UK users in May 2012, and was subsequently blocked in many countries worldwide.[62] Searches for the domain name return pages with the message 'Unable to connect.' Other searches direct users to the site ukispcourtorder.co.uk, which provides a list of blocked file-sharing websites, headed by TPB. The page also names the parties that obtained the orders, such as British Recorded Music Industry Limited and Phonographic Performance Limited. Thus, the blockade appears as a victory for the entertainment industry and anti-piracy lobbyists. The reality, however, is that any basic search for TPB also returns proxies that provide access to the site. One search result, 'Unblocking The Pirate Bay,' harbours the flagship logo of TPB and explains to visitors that: 'a proxy site allows you to bypass blocks setup by your ISP or network.'[63] In other words, for TPB, it is business as usual. Court orders have made hundreds of websites unavailable, yet not all of these sites have circumvented the blockades; most simply disappeared from the web. In contrast, TPB remains, and copies of the site can be downloaded, uploaded, and circulated via a file that fits onto a USB key.[64]

Ironically and perhaps counter-intuitively the remarkable endurance of TPB is linked to its owners' complete and assumed disregard for copyright laws and intellectual property. For this reason, TPB will remain a seminal case in the history of the Internet. The Swedish website has accomplished what many others attempted before it, that is, to politicize the practice of digital file-sharing. This success may seem paradoxical since all of TPB's key members were arrested, convicted, and imprisoned in the process. Yet, the most outstanding evidence is that TPB remains, at the time of writing, fully accessible.

From the many twists and turns of TPB's trial, it emerged that 'popular illegality' is both a strength and a downfall for file-sharing practices. On one hand, services providers can only escape prosecution by becoming the agents of media industries, and on the other hand, open resistance means that users are able to politicize their digital activities. Since then, many users have claimed allegiance and defiantly embraced digital piracy. Thus, sites such as The Pirate Bay 'have begun to appear less as a reactive force (i.e. 'breaking the rules') and more as a proactive one ('setting the rules').[65] In this light, further resistance should be expected from everyday digital users that are concerned with the capitalistic criminalization of socio-cultural practices.

*Funding:*

Part of the research for the production of this chapter was funded by the programme *Capital Semilla* of Universidad Iberoamericana.

## Notes

1.    Jemima Kiss, 'The Pirate Bay trial: guilty verdict,' *The Guardian*, 17 April 2009, accessed 30 November 2018, https://www.theguardian.com/technology/2009/apr/17/the-pirate-bay-trial-guilty-verdict.

2.    Ernesto, 'The Pirate Bay Enters List of 100 Most Popular Website,' *Torrentfreak*, 18 May 2008, accessed 30 November 2018, https://torrentfreak.com/the-pirate-bay-100-popular-080518/.

3.    Robert W. McChesney, *Digital Disconnect: How Capitalism is Turning the Internet Against Democracy* (New York: The New Press, 2013), 79–82.

4.    McChesney, *Digital Disconnect*, 79–80.

5.    Michel Foucault, *Discipline and Punish: the Birth of the Prison* (Harmondsworth: Penguin, 1977), 80.

6.    The document analyzed and referenced in this chapter is an English translation of the court proceedings and verdict, commissioned by the International Federation of the Phonographic Industry and not endorsed by the Stockholm District Court. References to the text will be annotated as: (Verdict: page number). *IFPI*, accessed 1 July 2019, https://www.ifpi.org/content/library/Pirate-Bay-verdict-English-translation.pdf.

7.    Foucault, *Discipline and Punish,* 80.

8.    Patrick Burkart and Tom McCourt, ' When Creators, Corporations and Consumers Collide: Napster and the Development of On-Line Music Distribution,' *Media, Culture & Society* 25/3 (2003), 333–50 ; Bernard A. Mantel, 'The Google Police: How the Indictment of ePirate Bay Presents a New Solution to Internet Piracy,' *U. Miami Bus. L. Rev.* (2012), 77–112 ; Alejandro Zentner, 'Measuring the Effect of File Sharing on Music Purchases,' *Journal of Law and Economics* 49 (2006), 63–90.

9.    Zentner, 'Measuring the Effect of File Sharing,' 68–71.

10.    Burkart and McCourt, 'When Creators, Corporations and Consumers Collide.'

11.    Burkart and McCourt, 'When Creators, Corporations and Consumers Collide,' 339.

12.    Rafael Rob and Joel Waldfogel, 'Piracy on the High C's: Music Downloading, Sales Displacement, and Social Welfare in a Sample of College Students,' *J. Law and Econ.* 49 (2006), 29–62 ; Zentner, 'Measuring the Effect of File Sharing.'

13.    Burkart and McCourt, 'When Creators, Corporations and Consumers Collide'; Felix Oberholzer-Gee and Koleman Stumpf, 'The Effect of File Sharing on Record Sales: An Empirical Analysis,' *Journal of Political Economy* 115/1 (2007), 1–42.

14.    Oberholzer-Gee and Strumpf 'The Effect of File Sharing on Record Sales,' 25.

15.    McChesney, *Digital Disconnect*, 80.

16.    These include the two unsuccessful bills Stop Online Piracy Act (SOPA) and Protect Intellectual Property Act (PIPA) in the US; the Digital Economy Act 2010 in the UK, and the Hadopi in France.

17.    Mantel, 'The Google Police,' 78; McChesney, *Digital Disconnect*, 126.

18.    The Pirate Bay, website, accessed 30 November 2018, https:// thepiratebay.org/about.

19.    Roger Parloff, 'Megaupload and the twilight of copyright,' *Fortune*, 11 July 2012, accessed 30 November 2018, http://fortune.com/2012/07/11/ megaupload-and-the-twilight-of-copyright/.

20.    George Siganos, Josep M. Pujol and Pablo Rodriguez, 'Monitoring the Bittorrent Monitors: A Bird's Eye View,' in *Passive and Active Network Measurement PAM 2009, Lecture Notes in Computer Science*, 5448, ed. Sue B. Moon, Renata Teixeira, and Steve Uhlig, Springer, Berlin, Heidelberg (2009) ; Scott Wolchok, and Alex J. Halderman, *Crawling BitTorrent DHTs for Fun and Profit*, 4th USENIX Workshop on Offensive Technologies, Washington, D.C. (2010).

21.    Mark Cenite, Michelle Wanzheng Wang, Chong Peiwen and Germaine Shimin Chan, 'More Than Just Free Content: Motivations of Peer- to-Peer File Sharers.' *Journal of Communication Inquiry* 33/3, (2009) 206-221.

22.    Majid Yar, 'The Global 'Epidemic' of Movie 'Piracy': Crime-Wave or Social Construction?' *Media, Culture and Society* 27/5, (2005), 687.

23.  Yar, 'The Global 'Epidemic' of Movie 'Piracy,' 691.

24.  Quinn Norton, 'Secrets of the Pirate Bay,' *Wired*, 16 August 2006, accessed 30 November 2018, https://www.wired.com/2006/08/secrets-of-the-pirate-bay/.

25.  Jonas Andersson, 'The Origins and Impacts of the Swedish File-Sharing Movement: A Case Study,' *Critical Studies in Peer Production* 1/1 (2011) 1–18.

26.  Mikko Manner, Topi Siniketo and Ulrika Polland, 'The Pirate Bay ruling-when the fun and games end,' *Ent. L. R.*, 20/6 (2009); Mantel, *The Google Police*; Tara Touloumis, 'Buccaneers and Bucks from the Internet: Pirate Bay and the Entertainment Industry,' *Seton Hall J. Sports & Ent. L.* 19 (2009), 253 ; Adrian Adermon and Chen-Yuan Liang, *Piracy, Music, and Movies: A Natural Experiment*, Working Paper, Department of Economics, Uppsala University (2010), 18; Joost Poort, Jorna Leenheer, Jeroen van der Ham, and Cosmin Dumitru, 'Baywatch: Two Approaches to Measure the Effects of Blocking Access to the Pirate Bay,' *Telecommunications Policy* 38/4 (2014), 383–92.

27.  Simon Lindgren and Jessica Linde, 'The Subpolitics of Online Piracy: A Swedish Case Study,' *Convergence: The International Journal of Research into New Media Technologies* 18/2 (2012), 143–64 ; Fenwick McKelvey, 'We Like Copies, Just Don't Let the Others Fool You: The Paradox of The Pirate Bay,' *Television & New Media* 16/4 (2014), 734–50 ; Jonas Andersson, 'For the Good of The Net: The Pirate Bay as a Strategic Sovereign,' *Culture Machine* 10 (2009) 74–5; Andersson, 'The Origins and Impacts of the Swedish File-Sharing Movement.'

28.  Burkart, *Pirate Politics,* 4.

29.  Foucault, *Discipline and Punish*, 3.

30.  Foucault, *Discipline and Punish*, 82.

31.  Foucault, *Discipline and Punish*, 82.

32.  Foucault, *Discipline and Punish*, 86–7.

33.  Foucault, *Discipline and Punish*, 86.

34.  Emmanuel Goldstein, 'Hacker view of the 'Legion of Doom' sentencing in Atlanta,' *The Risks Digest* 10/65 (1990), accessed 1 July 2019, https://catless.ncl.ac.uk/Risks/10/65.

35.  Bruce Sterling, *The Hacker Crackdown: Law and Disorder on the Electronic Frontier* (New York: Bantam Books, 1993).

36.  Sterling, *The Hacker Crackdown*, 270.

37.  Sterling, *The Hacker Crackdown*, 112–13.

38.  Also referred to as contributory copyright infringement or aiding and abetting a copyright offence. Verdict *The Pirate Bay Case* No B 13301-06, Stockholm District Court Division 5 Unit 52.

39.  Foucault, *Discipline and Punish*, 82–4.

40.  Manner et al. 'The Pirate Bay ruling,' 197.

41.  Goldstein, 'Hacker view of the 'Legion of Doom.'

42.   Sterling, *The Hacker Crackdown,* 127.

43.   Foucault, *Discipline and Punish.*

44.   Zentner, 'Measuring the Effect of File Sharing.'

45.   Yar, 'The global 'epidemic' of movie 'piracy,' 687.

46.   David Kravets, 'Supreme Court Lets Stand $675,000 File-Sharing Verdict,' *Wired,* 21May 2012, accessed 30 November 2018, https://www.wired.com/2012/05/supreme-court-file-sharing/.

47.   Oberholzer-Gee and Strumpf, 'The Effect of File Sharing on Record Sales.'

48.   Andersson, ' The Origins and Impacts of the Swedish File-Sharing Movement ;' Lindgren and Linde, 'The Subpolitics of Online Piracy.' ; Norton, 'Secrets of the Pirate Bay.'

49.   Norton, 'Secrets of the Pirate Bay.'

50.   Marie-Christine Leps, *Apprehending the Criminal: The Production of Deviance in Nineteenth Century Discourse* (London: Duke University Press Books 1992), 2.

51.   Foucault, *Discipline and Punish,* 83.

52.   Burkart, *Pirate Politics.*

53.   Fidèle A. Vlavo, *Performing Digital Activism* (New York, Routledge, 2018), 109.

54.   Norton, 'Secrets of the Pirate Bay.'

55.   McKelvey, 'We Like Copies.'

56.   Manner, et al. 'The Pirate Bay ruling,' 203.

57.   Siganos et al. 'A Bird's Eye View;' Moon et al. 'Crawling BitTorrent DHTs for Fun and Profit.'

58.   Bart Cammaerts, 'Protest Logics and the Mediation Opportunity Structure,' *European Journal of Communication* 27/2 (2012), 125.

59.   The Pirate Bay, website.

60.   Cathie Lomeli, 'The Hilarious The Pirate Bay's Legal Responses will make your ROLF!' *BeeBulletin,* 21 May 2015, accessed 30 November 2018, https://beebulletin.com/hilarious-pirate-bay-legal-responses/.

61.   Lomeli, 'The Hilarious The Pirate Bay.'

62.   British Broadcasting Corporation, *The Pirate Bay: BitTorrent Site Sails to Its 10th Birthday,* 9 August 2013, accessed 30 November 2018, https://www.bbc.com/news/technology-23587447.

63.   The Proxy Bay, *Can't Access The Pirate Bay? Try One of the Proxy Sites Below,* accessed 30 November 2018, https://proxybay.bz/.

64.   Ernesto, 'Download a copy of the pirate bay its only 90 mb,' *Torrentfreak* 9 February 2012, accessed 30 November 2018, https://torrentfreak.com/download-a-copy-of-the-pirate-bay-its-only-90-mb-120209/.

65.   Andersson, 'For the Good of The Net,' 64.

# 9

# The Pichadora Girl: Politics of Art Institutions, Legal and Extrajudicial Punishment, and the 'Pixo' As a Transgressive Social Practice

*Alexander Araya López*

## Pixo, Law, and Power

This chapter focuses on the relationship between street art, law, and power through the case of the pichação and particularly pixação (pixo), autochthonous calligraphy made with black ink and typically produced by (peripheral) urban youth. Its content varies from personal signatures (a raw form of branding or tagging) to more explicitly political messages. Through an analysis of discourses about this social practice in news articles, editorials and op-eds published in the Brazilian newspaper *Folha de São Paulo* (hereafter *Folha*),[1] I expand on the series of 'attacks' organized by pixadores (practitioners of pichação/ pixação) against several art institutions, particularly during the 28th São Paulo Biennial in 2008, which led to the arrest and imprisonment of a female pixadora.

This chapter contributes to this volume on art, law, and power in at least three ways. First, it demonstrates the importance of media narratives and discourses in shaping the perception of both artistic and 'criminal' activities. Second, through the example of the pixadora Caroline Pivetta da Mota, who became a major protagonist in 2008, it illustrates how women in the movement are considered as secondary players, with the practice mostly associated to normative ideas of masculinity. Finally, it shows how 'punishment,' when discussed in the public sphere, is positively analyzed by a plurality of voices, in opposition to (extrajudicial) 'punishments' that occur outside public supervision.

In terms of structure, first, this chapter defines the term pichação/ pixação, referring to the history of this 'movement' and describing the main discourses related to the practice and its producers. A second section summarizes the several anti-pixação strategies developed by public authorities over the last years. The third and fourth sections present a short history of the 'attacks' and the subsequent public debate regarding the arrest and imprisonment of the pixadora Caroline. The final section is dedicated to the conclusions and provides some recommendations for further research.

## The Difference Between the 'ch' and the 'x'

*Pichação*, derived from the verb *pichar,* refers to messages written on public and private surfaces, varying from political statements to interpersonal communication, such as love declarations. *Pixação* or *pixo,* on the other hand, is perceived by its producers as a countercultural movement, oriented towards both the transformation and appropriation of urban spaces through the *politics of transgression.* Characterized as an autochthonous form of writing, this calligraphy can be found in big cities such as São Paulo, Rio de Janeiro, or Belo Horizonte. The pixação seems to be a cultural practice of public writing combined with a radical politics of recognition. It is an adapted form of 'tagging' with a Brazilian socio-political twist.

The practice was allegedly born in São Paulo in the 1980s and is mostly developed by youth from the periphery or the urban favelas.[2] Pixação is described as 'essentially' illegal and unauthorized, a form of aggression against the broader society (*'os burgueses'*), and it is also highly valued by its producers given its *transgressive nature.* The emergence of these calligraphies was influenced, as seen in the documentary *Pixo* (2009), by the logos and covers of heavy metal, hardcore, and punk bands combined with Anglo-Saxon runes and subsequently adapted to the Brazilian context.[3]

Pixadores engage in their practice to forcefully include themselves in the aesthetics of the city. This aggression is thus perceived as the 'natural' response to the politics of segregation, stigmatization, and exclusion,[4] produced not only by political decisions but also by the capitalist system itself. In the words of Caroline Pivetta da Mota: 'It is the art from poverty, that exposes everything we feel, feelings that nobody wants to see, that the whole world closes their eyes to, because they don't want to pay attention to it.'[5] The popularity of the practice seems to entail a double movement: horizontally, spreading from the peripheries to the centre, and vertically, spreading from the 'low' classes to the middle and upper classes.[6]

Pixadores write on walls, windows, and even climb buildings aiming at high-visibility targets in order to get recognition (*ibope*)[7] as individuals and for the group of pixadores they belong to (*grife*). This status-economy is based on the creation of a personal signature that works as a logo, following the logic of spatial dominance characteristic of pervasive branding and advertising.[8]

Adrenaline rush (through 'crime'),[9] social protest, and social recognition are mentioned among the producers as the reasons to get involved in this practice. The adrenaline rush is linked not only to the creation of the pixação itself, but to other criminal activities that may result from its production (i.e. trespassing, violent encounters with the police or guards, stealing of materials, intimidation of witnesses, etc.) Similarly, Caldeira emphasizes how the omnipresent inscriptions in the city, which are visible in the most 'impossible' of spaces, constitute a central mark in the city (from the centre to the periphery), even if the majority of the population detests pixação and considers it a form of vandalism or a crime against private property.[10] According to her research, the violence, competitivity, aggressiveness and search for adrenaline rush are typical components of the idea of 'masculinity.' In the following pages, I will address how the case of the pixadora Caroline both confirms and defies this exclusionary narrative about the practice.

A sample of 682 articles from the period 2001 to 2010 was analyzed. These texts were collected directly from the website of *Folha,* which was one of the most widely-read Brazilian newspapers. The search was based on the keywords: 'graffiti' (including the Portuguese word 'grafite') and pichação/pixação. The discourse analysis was based on the methodology proposed by Tonkiss,[11] and the texts were coded aiming at: *a)* identifying key themes and arguments, *b)* looking for variation in the text, and *c)* paying attention to silences. The coding process was done with the assistance of the software for qualitative analysis AtlasTi. Additionally, in order to better illustrate the discussion of this chapter, I have included two secondary sources focusing on the Brazilian pixação: The documentary *'Pixo'* (2009) and a reportage by the TV show *Conexão Repórter* (2010).

Three different-yet-intertwined discourses have been identified in the newspaper *Folha,* targeting pichação/pixação and its producers: first, the medical-epidemiological discourse linked to hygiene and social prophylaxis. The pixadores are characterized as 'insects,' 'rats,' or 'little pigs' that 'need to be contained.'[12] They are considered 'dirty,' 'animalistic' in their territoriality and their practice is considered a 'plague.' Secondly, from a legal standpoint, pichação/pixação is considered a form of vandalism, a threat to common heritage and to the maintenance of social order (including its impact on the real estate business). Pixadores are judged as extremely illiterate, challenging the most basic notions of citizenship and heritage. Third, the criminogenic discourses, in which the inscriptions are related to the (re)production of social violence, with pixação being the gateway to more serious forms of crime (both committed by pixadores and by people 'negatively inspired' by the decay in the physical environment).[13]

In the last decade, through the (violent) actions of the pixadores, a fourth discourse that emphasizes the (counter-)aesthetic or artistic value of the practice has been emerging, demanding its recognition in art institutions. Moreover, it is necessary to point out that the pixadores separate themselves from other more commercial forms of graffiti and street art. They perceive the graffiti artists as *sell-outs*, considering that through their commissioned works they become 'traitors' to the transgressive ('countercultural,' 'deviant,' or 'rebel') origins of these urban practices.

Caroline Pivetta da Mota became a sort of symbol of the fight for this recognition of the pixação. Her case is of particular interest as she was held in jail for 53 days for not having a permanent address; hence, her imprisonment was discussed in several news articles and opinion columns. But before referring to her case, it is important to state that not unlike the graffiti and street art scene, the international recognition of pixação has contributed the emergence of what I call 'superpixadores,' a small group of pixadores with a differentiated status, associated with symbolic, economic, and political power. While the elite group of 'supergrafiteiros'[14] includes artists such as OsGemeos, Nunca, Nina, Speto and others, who are frequently invited to work abroad and are depicted in graffiti books and documentaries, I would argue that something similar is occurring to the pixação, particularly with pixadores such as Djan, William, 'Biscoito,' and Ricardo, who participated in an exhibition in Paris in 2009, in the Berlin Biennale in 2012, and in documentaries such as Pixadores (2014).[15]

## Anti-pixação Legislation, Clean Cities, Graffiti Workshops and the Police

In terms of legislation, pichação and pixação are considered illegal, except when their producers could offer the respective written authorization by the private owners or the local authorities. The *Lei de Crimes Ambientais* (Law 9.605), in its Article 65, proposes both fines and imprisonment—three months to one year—for those who are caught in the exercise of these practices. Law enforcers have also strategically (ab) used the former Article 288 of the *Código Penal Brasileiro* (Law 2.848), ascribing the cause of *illegal formation of gangs* to some pixadores (for example, in São Paulo and Belo Horizonte). The prison term for this type of crime is one to three years. Moreover, the law *Cidade Limpa* (Law 14.226) constitutes another effort to protect the urban landscape of São Paulo and establishes a series of restrictions to citizens and the local business owners.[16] In 2011, the government of Dilma Rousseff introduced the Law 12.408, which clearly separated the practices of graffiti from that of pichação/pixação. A first modification relates to the Article 65 of the *Lei de Crimes Ambientais* (Law 9.605), declaring the decriminalization of graffiti, under the condition of previous authorization. This law also forbids selling spray paint cans to minors, which now constituted a misdemeanour with an associated fine. Retailers may sell the product only to identified customers and manufacturers were required to include two labels on the spray cans: '*Pichação é crime*' (Pichação is a crime) and '*Proibida a venda a menores de 18 anos*' (Not for sale to persons under the age of 18). This is clearly a preventive reaction aiming towards *systematic predetection*,[17] and it could be argued that it represents a sort of pre-crime policy, considering that the act of possessing/acquiring a spray can is an irrefutable proof of 'future crime.'

Pichação, commonly made with blank ink or paint (*tinta*, in Portuguese), could be easily linked to the notions of 'dirt' and 'pollution.' The signatures and inscriptions are considered something that defiles the wall or the surface, altering its aesthetics and consequently damaging it (even in cases when it could be removed without any problems). In 2003, a news article reported a survey made in collaboration with real estate entities, estimating 'the total loss that the pichações cause to the city in R$ 8 billion, or nearly the annual city budget (currently R$ 11,4 billion).'[18]

Local authorities have implemented several strategies to tackle this problem, aiming at reducing the discontent of citizens. However, many of these measures have failed to contain the practice. These official campaigns against pixação have been continuous, at least in the case of São Paulo, where three different initiatives could be clearly identified: First, the *Projeto Belezura*, during the administration of Major Marta Suplicy (*Partido dos Trabalhadores*). Second, in 2005, several articles referred to some anti-pichação strategies adopted by Major José Serra (*Partido da Social Democracia Brasileira*), including the covering up of pichações (and a proposal to charge pichadores with the costs of removal), the placement of plants in walls (target-hardening),[19] stiff surveillance in particular areas of the city, and the successful arrest of six pichadores (who were later released under the promise of involving themselves in social projects).[20] At least one news article indicates that the removal of the inscriptions was not always successful, especially because the execution did not satisfy the needs or expectations of citizens. This quote illustrates the dissatisfaction:

**Anti-Pichação Plan Begins with Criticisms**

In place of stains of pichação, stains of concrete cover the walls of a stretch of the street Cardinal Arcoverde, in Pinheiros, West São Paulo.

The anti-pichação project of the Prefecture of São Paulo was released yesterday and surprised the residents, who hoped to see the clean walls. 'What they are doing is horrible, because they are only covering [the pichação] with another colour,' complained the merchant Emerson Bonfim Correia, owner of the bar and coffee Arrastão, whose wall, painted in deep blue, was the first to have the pichação removed with brushstrokes of paint in concrete colour.

Without believing that this attitude will prevent the actions of the pichadores, Correia said he will paint the wall blue, but he will not insist in case that his property is covered with pichação again. (Folha, 18 May 2005; news article by journalist Luísa Brito.)

The third campaign—however not directly aiming at pichação—is the law *Cidade Limpa,* signed by Major Gilberto Kassab (*Democratas*). The decree regulates a series of topics related to urban aesthetics, from dumpsters and public toilets to outdoor advertising.[21] As part of this project, some public surfaces were painted with an anti-pichação coating.[22]

In relation to the street art artists, policemen may even be responsible for judging the aesthetical qualities of any work in order to distinguish, arbitrarily, whether it is art or vandalism, or if they should bother to intervene or not.[23] In the case of pixação, police officers may have their own perception of the 'problem' and of the solutions implemented to fight it, as well as their own subjectivities and affections/emotions about the practice and its producers. Because they are in charge of the apprehension and processing of pixadores, who are frequently released later without any punitive measures, the use of alternative extrajudicial 'punishments' has been mentioned by several pixadores. In the documentary Pixo (2009), three pixadores explain the interactions with the police:

> *Djan:* It depends, there are policemen who prefer to beat us up, other policemen like to paint us, and others do both. Some will beat you, paint you and take you to the police station to sign the process, you know.

> *Zé:* They like to paint, no? Someone like me, bald, they like to paint hair here [Zé touches his forehead], paint it black. It's fucked up.

> *Pedro:* They made me drink the paint, and I was lucky because it was thin paint, and they made me bite the paint roller. So, I bit it and they said: 'No. Swallow it!.' And because it was made of foam, there was no way to swallow it. 'No. Swallow it.' So, I kept it in my mouth, and I chewed and chewed and chewed, and they let me walk away. (Documentary Pixo [2009])

The outcomes of these encounters with the police are not always as 'anecdotal' as the documentary shows. In 2014, the pixadores Alex Dalla Vecchia Costa, 32, and Ailton dos Santos, 33, were killed by the police in a violent encounter inside an apartment building. The families and friends report that their relatives were executed and that the sole interest of the 'victims' was in doing pixação. However, the police claim that the two men were 'robbers' caught in the act and resisted arrest.[24] Beyond violent interactions with the police, pixação is also considered as a *self-induced danger* because its producers not only risk their lives (i.e. accidental death by electric shock, falling, or being shot), but also their futures (by imprisonment). The practice is represented as a senseless and unproductive hazard, with no foreseeable positive outcomes in exchange. The impact of the action of pichadores in the lives of other inhabitants is depicted in several allusions to the criminal nature of the practice, with this notion of risk related to the vandalism against private property or to other more serious forms of victimization against citizens, like house robberies, drug dealing, and gang violence.[25]

Another of the strategies to fight pixação is the public and private funding of graffiti workshops. This conversion of 'pichadores' into graffiti artists not only implies the elimination of the 'grotesque' aesthetics of the pixação,[26] but its substitution for a more productive and more 'friendly' practice (considering the exclusionary, non-dialogical and 'antisocial' nature of the pichação/pixação). As Banet-Weiser (2011) suggests, there is a self-branding associated to street art production, and this could apply also for the pixadores.[27] One news article tells the story of Reginaldo, 16, a former pixador now in search of a 'better future,' who is attending graffiti workshops because it is important to 'preserve,' even if he has to walk forty minutes to get to the association where the training takes place.[28] Indeed, the idea of entrepreneurialism is present in this rehabilitation, considering that one article refers to the recent 'cool' fashion of decorating private dwellings with graffiti artworks (for example, images of superheroes in children's rooms).[29]

## The 'Attacks': A ('violent') Change in Narratives

Pixadores have claimed that the anti-pixação strategies and the violent interactions with the police (or the imprisonment) are just part of what pixação is, and they demand the recognition of their practice as 'cultural' and 'political.' Considering the convergence of cultural and criminal processes in contemporary social life, Ferrell proposes the 'criminological *verstehen*' as a valuable strategy of dismantling dualistic epistemic hierarchies, a task of sociological deconstruction.[30] The binomial 'crime as culture' (including, for example, the adrenaline rush and the culture of pleasure and excitement) and 'culture as crime' (referring to the public labelling of popular culture products as criminogenic) is interwoven with the mediated crime imaginary and the political agendas of the criminal justice system.[31] Criminological verstehen is a sociological approach necessary to defy the idealized notions of decency and community.[32]

In this sense, the 'attacks' organized by pixadores are complex events, considering that they could be read as a form of civil disobedience,[33] as both 'culture' and 'crime.' Indeed, some of these 'attacks' have been recorded by the participants, which are later broadcasted and shared online or included in documentaries. This relates to the concept of 'will-to-representation'[34] as proposed by Yar (2012), a capacity for mediated self-presentation that plays a crucial role in motivating the offending behaviour itself. Moreover, considering that the so-called 'pixação movement' is based on a status-economy, the *ibope* obtained by media coverage of these 'attacks' logically provides more prominence to the depicted participants.[35]

Following the news articles in *Folha,* the first of these series of 'attacks' was the pixação against the work of the artist Lenora de Barros in 2002.[36] After this, in 2004, the pichador (and later graffiti artist) 'Não'[37] wrote his signature in two pieces on exhibition in the 26th Bienal de São Paulo.[38] Four more attacks were reported in 2008: the first when a group of pixadores organized by Rafael Augustaitiz (a.k.a. Pixobomb) 'attacked' the building of the *Centro Universitário Belas*

*Artes* as part of his graduation project.[39] Secondly, Rafael Augustaitiz was also considered part of the leadership of an attack against the gallery *Choque Cultural*, aimed at fighting the commercialization of street art.[40] Third, a group of pixadores wrote all over the second floor of the Oscar Niemeyer building during the 28th Bienal de São Paulo, informally known as Bienal do Vazio,[41] with the subsequent arrestment of Rafael Vieira Camargo (a taxi driver) and Caroline Pivetta da Mota. After this intervention, the works of some graffiti artists placed in Avenida Paulista (a series of authorized murals commemorating the Japanese Immigration to Brazil) were written over (*atropelar*) by a group of pixadores, once more denouncing the commercial nature of graffiti.[42] According to Franco,[43] the walls of the Avenida Paulista have always been a contested space claimed by graffiti artists, pixadores, and the local government with selected muralists-graffiti artists.

### 'The Pixadora Girl': Discussing Art and Punishment in the Public Sphere

The 'attack' of the second floor of the Oscar Niemeyer building during the 28th Bienal de São Paulo, with the incarceration of Caroline Pivetta da Mota as an outcome was the tipping point for the debate about the artistic value of pixação. The fairness of the legal response was also a central point in this discussion. Caroline Pivetta, member of the group of pixadores *Sustos*, declared that they appropriated the empty space to propose their own art and in defence of those disenfranchised,[44] arguing that she identified herself with the void (*o vazio*)[45] proposed by the Biennial curatorship. After her arrest, she suggested that the hate against the pixadores was the *real* reason for her retention in jail.[46] The following quotes refer to the arrest of the pixadora:

> The incarceration of this young girl seems to me an absurd and cruel exaggeration. Yes, there is the law. But imagine the reader if the 'artists' of real estate speculation were in jail for each depredation of the public good that they sponsor, often in collusion with the government, to build this tragically horrible and inhuman city.

> That does not redeem other vandalisms, of course not. The arts of pichação can make sense as group ritual, catharsis, or therapy, but the result is socially and aesthetically regressive. There is no artistic value associated with the transgression inscribed on the dirty walls. It is, rather, the outbreak in cryptic language of a slightly digested Brazilian culture malaise. (*Folha*, 15 December 2008; opinion article by Journalist and

Columnist Fernando de Barros e Silva)

**The Pichadora Girl**

'IDEOLOGY, I want one to live.' This phrase by Cazuza might seem stupid. But it is not. We need, indeed, to believe in something. Even if it is something that almost the rest of the world finds silly, such as, for example, the pichação. Caroline Pivetta da Mota, 23, believes the same. So that when she was arrested, shortly after she wrote pichação with her friends in the Bienal de São Paulo, she screamed: 'Long live the picho!'

Right now, we can see the e-mails from our readers piling up in our mailbox. 'But writing pichação is a crime.' Yes, we know that. 'But pichação is not art.' About that we are not certain, but this is a very long discussion that won't fit in this column.

What interests us: Carol has been imprisoned for nearly fifty days in São Paulo. Attention. She was the only girl of the group. She is the only one that is imprisoned. The guys ran and they managed to get away. One of them was also arrested, but he is facing the process in freedom. We find it absurd that she is still imprisoned for writing pichação in a biennale of art whose theme was the void. If it is void, it could be occupied. And let's discuss pichação later, with calm. What we find with certainty is that everyone expresses themselves as they can. (*Folha*, 15 December 2008; opinion article by writers and journalists Jô Hallack, Nina Lemos and Raq Affonso.[47])

In various news articles and opinion columns, Caroline Pivetta was presented as a scapegoat, a 'victim' of the many years of public dissatisfaction regarding both the pixação and the failed strategies to contain it. The curatorship of the Biennial, highly criticized by the repression against the pixadores, responded with a 'right to reply':

**Caroline Case: Some Issues Not Considered**

WITH THE intention of opening new perspectives in the debate, sensational and passionate, created by the press in relation to the 28th Bienal de São Paulo and the imprisonment of Caroline Pivetta da Mota, 24 years old, we, the curators of the event, would like to bring some considerations and questions that seem to us pertinent to the question.

First, we should not forget that, contrary to the nocturnal and silent operation that is peculiar of pichadores, the event at the Bienal is far from being called an aesthetic and peaceful event: 40 youths invade the pavilion of the Bienal like an organized gang looting, tearing everything down, physically assaulting people, with the objective of, according to the online call of their leader Rafael Augustaitz (sic), writing pichação on the second and third floor, destroying all the works.

It was a peculiar gesture of this destructive group that, since the invasions to both the Centro Universitário Belas Artes and to the gallery Choque Cultural, uses the pichação as a means to erase and to damage the work of other artists.

Could it be that the art world does not realize the authoritarianism of that gesture, what it means regarding the censorship of the other? Is not it worrying to realize that the tactic of a former art student is to make a media phenomenon out of the erasing of other artists?[48] Yes, because the press and the Internet channels were warned three hours before the attack to the Bienal and they were ready waiting for the show! It was not, therefore, a filling of the void or a response 'em vivo contato,' what gives testimony that the curation never presupposed the use of violence. (*Folha*, 18 May 2008; opinion article by Ivo Mesquita and Ana Paula Cohen [Curatorship 28th Biennale *São Paulo*].)[49]

The incarceration of Caroline Pivetta was considered by some as an obvious case of Draconian punishment,[50] not only because she remained in jail for more than fifty days, but also because she was charged for damaging the Oscar Niemeyer building (considered a crime against *cultural heritage*)[51] and not under the legal framework that already punishes pichações.[52] Caroline Pivetta was also charged with the cause of illegal formation of gang (*'milicianos'*),[53] framing her arrest within organized crime (which includes criminal groups engaged in activities such as drug dealing and terrorism). The release of the pixadora was supported by public figures including the Minister of Human Rights, Paulo Vannuchi[54]; the Minister of Culture Juca Ferreira;[55] the former Minister of Justice Fernando Henrique José Gregori,[56] the former director of the Museo de Belas Artes, Paulo Herkenhoff,[57] and the art historian Jorge Coli.[58] The readers of *Folha* also got involved in the discussion through letters in favour and against the actions of the pixadores, the artistic value of pixação and the sense of justice represented by this case.[59]

In 2010, Moacir dos Anjos, the curator of the 29th Bienal de São Paulo, included the pixação as part of the official programme, granting it artistic recognition and proposing the need to rethink the limits between art, law and power. In his words:

*Folha*: Why to include the pichadores of the 28th Biennial in the 29th?
*Moacir Dos Anjos*: This is not an apology or a confrontation with the

previous edition. We want to include pichação or simply pixo, with 'x,' a spelling used by their practitioners to distinguish them from partisan political pichações that have filled the walls of the city for years. The pixo blurs and questions the usual limits that separate art from politics. This question is of great interest to the Biennial. Politics is understood here not as a space of appeasement of differences, but just the opposite. The space formed by the acts and gestures that open fissures in the conventions that organize common life. As philosopher Jacques Rancière puts it, it is the politics as a sphere of 'misunderstanding.'

*Folha*: Isn't this demagoguery?

*Dos Anjos:* It would be demagoguery if we were inviting pixadores as we invite many other artists. We know that this equality does not exist, and they also know that. What matters is to understand these differences and the limits and possibilities of this approach. Nobody is trying to dodge anything. The bet is on the explicit character of these questions, not on the easy answers. Our commitment is to demonstrate that the Biennale can be a privileged platform for the formulation of these issues. If we achieve this, we have already made an important contribution. (*Folha*, 15 April 2010; interview by journalist Fernanda Mena.)


The work of the pixadores in the 29th Bienal de São Paulo included the participation of Djan Ivson (the main narrator of the documentary Pixo) and Rafael Augustaitiz, who was responsible for the intervention (failed graduation project) in the Centro Universitário de Belas Artes. The arguments that the pichação was included in the 29th Bienal de São Paulo only because of the longstanding fight of its producers or due to the innovative vision of the curatorship can be contested; since it may be the result of the recognition achieved by pixadores in art institutions outside of Brazil. Despite of being invited, the participation in this Biennial was not smooth and had its own 'inner struggles,' for example, between pixador Djan Ivson and artist Nuno Ramos, with the conflict emerging because of some vultures kept in captivity in the work of the latter.[60]

It is important to note that in 2009, a group of pichadores was invited to take part of the exhibition *'Né dans la rue—Graffiti'* (Born in the streets) in the *Fondation Cartier* in Paris (among them, the pixador Djan). The documentary *Pixo* (2009) was also exhibited in this show dedicated to worldwide manifestations of graffiti and street art.[61] The Fondation Cartier is also credited in *Pixo* as 'cultural support.' The documentary has a length of approximately 62 minutes and the participation of Caroline Pivetta da Mota is barely one minute. In terms of published articles, the case of Caroline and the Biennial captured the most media attention, with approximately forty articles dedicated to this event. The 'attack' against the Centro Universitário de Belas Artes was mentioned in eighteen articles, while only thirteen articles were related to the 'attack' against the gallery Choque Cultural. The fact that she was a woman, unlike the majority of pixadores, was central in the debate about the fairness of her imprisonment and her right to express herself in a (radical) artistic way.

Moreover, in their 'right to reply' published by *Folha*, the curators of the 28th Biennale (Ivo Mesquita and Ana Paula Cohen) argued the need to 'save' Caroline not from jail, but from her original structural conditions. They criticized the government for not creating programmes of housing that could have benefited her, pointing out that her lack of a formal residence was the real reason why she remained under arrest. The other pixador captured during the 'attack' to the Biennale, Rafael Vieira Camargo, who later refused the charges and said that he was only a 'spectator,' faced his process in liberty. Other well know pixadores who organized the 'attack' were not prosecuted, even when they benefited from the popularity of pixação after Caroline's arrest.

Caroline Pivetta was the most important figure in the debate about the artistic nature of pixação in 2008 by drawing media attention to this 'artistic movement.' However, the subsequent acceptance of the practice in art institutions excluded her and other pixadoras. Indeed, pixadoras were not frequently included in the articles published by *Folha*, except for an anonymous school-teacher and pixadora (named only 'Piroboys') and the reference to a collective of pixadoras ('Dinha'). It could be argued that the artistic recognition of the practice could not have been possible without the arrest and imprisonment of Caroline Pivetta da Mota, although she distanced herself from the practice after her release.

In 2010, the TV show *Conexão Repórter*,[62] conducted by journalist Roberto Cabrini, focused on the 'sub-world' of pixação. Other episodes of this show have been dedicated to various topics including: paedophilia within the church, high-end prostitution, Spiritism, drug trafficking (including episodes on Cracolândia, a stigmatized neighbourhood in São Paulo), cannibalism, among other. Even considering the sensationalistic approach, the programme gave voice to some pixadores and corroborated the information published by the *Folha* (as well as the narratives identified in this study). The dangers of the practice were highlighted in this coverage as pixadores explained the risks associated to the practice, including imprisonment, death by accidents (i.e. electrocution, falls), injuries as an outcome of the interaction with rival pixadores (or with home owners), police brutality, etc. Both the motivation for joining the movement and for leaving the pixação were addressed by the journalist Cabrini. In his interviews with scholars and local authorities, it is clear that while pixação does not go unpunished, some judges prefer to give alternative punishments (such as community service), instead of prison terms.

Some pixadoras were also included in the reportage, named 'As Minas' (The girls), and they were described as 'young, pretty pixadoras,' 'who seem to be normal' and who wear 'high heels, jewellery, make-up.' These pixadoras are depicted as silhouettes, with a backlight highlighting their bodies and with close-up shots showing their hands shaking a spray can and their lips. One of them is described as 'married' to another pixador and a mother of a 3-year old, but her 'real vocation is to live on the edge.' The emphasizing of the idea of femininity (both through their bodies and their clothing) in *Conexão Repórter* works as a contrast to the characteristics attributed to the pixação as a (male) phenomenon: aggressive, violent, territorial, savage, disorderly. Only a short reference is given to Caroline Pivetta da Mota, indicating that she was contacted for an interview, but she refused to participate in the reportage. She is seen only in a short scene while sitting inside a car, while the journalist Cabrini explains that Caroline was sentenced to four years in semi-open conditions.[63] Indeed, only one pixadora escapes this narrative of femininity in *Conexão Repórter*, and she is shown wearing a hoodie and facing the camera while explaining the transgressive nature of 'pixo.'[64]

Furthermore, in 2012 a group of pixadores was invited to participate in the 7th Berlin Biennale. The group included only four pixadores: Djan, William, 'Biscoito,' and Ricardo. They are also the protagonists of the documentary *Pixadores* (2014), by director Amir Escandari. Caroline Pivetta da Mota did not take part in this trip to Germany.[65] While her arrest and imprisonment caused a long debate about 'art,' 'crime,' 'law,' and 'punishment,' the pixadora seems to be underrepresented or excluded from the subsequent national and international 'recognition' of the practice. Pixadoras, in general, are overlooked (or misrepresented) in the narratives about the practice, both in the articles published by *Folha* and in some audiovisual materials produced after the 2008 events. This outcome clearly benefits a small group of (male) pixadores, who are able to profit (both symbolically and economically) from the relative acceptance of pixação in established art institutions in Brazil and abroad.

## Conclusion

The power struggles against pichação/pixação in Brazil are not over. The main outcome of the series of 'attacks' coordinated by the pixadores over the last decade was the (temporary) inclusion of the pixação as part of the official programme of the 29th Bienal de São Paulo in 2010. However, at the street level, pixação remains highly unpopular, with a 'Datafolha' survey in 2017 estimating that 85% of the citizens in São Paulo are favourable towards graffiti artworks, but 97% of them are against pixação. Yet, 61% of the participants in the survey believe that strict punishments are not the solution to this problem.[66]

It is important to emphasize that the inclusion of the pixação in the artistic circles did not translate into the social recognition of the practice; especially considering the subsequent creation of 'new' laws that regulate the commerce of spray cans or distinguish graffiti from pichação (in 2011). In August 2010, the group of pixadores *Os Piores de Belô* ('The worst of Belo Horizonte') was arrested and criminally charged for illegal formation of gangs.[67] Several pixadores have been arrested and have died in controversial encounters with the police, private security guards and home owners. Also, João Doria (*Partido da Social Democracia Brasileira*), the Major of São Paulo between 2017–18, declared his opposition to pixação as a core part in his plan '*Cidade Linda*' (Pretty City), but his zero-tolerance policy caused criticism because it affected some celebrated graffiti artworks.

Pixação seems to be a practice intrinsically linked to the idea of violence, in the sense that the participants expose themselves 'voluntarily' to a series of situations that are potential 'risks.' Their agency should be understood as a way to respond to the 'other violence' that is imposed upon them (i.e. social exclusion, economic violence, criminality in general, sexual abuse, police brutality, etc.). In their willingness to experience violence and to accept the consequences of their actions (i.e. police abuse, death, imprisonment), male participants benefit from a narrative into which they have been socialized, a narrative that emphasizes aggressiveness and strength. In relation to the female participants, Caroline Pivetta da Mota in particular, the narratives associated to the pixação turn them into 'abnormal' participants. Even while her imprisonment helped to transform the public perception of pixação as a cultural practice, her 'womanhood' took priority in the discussion about the fairness of her punishment. Her extended imprisonment was hardly related to her socioeconomic conditions, or to the fact that she was allegedly a 'novice' in the practice. The role of other pixadoras seems to be secondary in the public debate about pixação.

It is possible to read the case of Caroline Pivetta da Mota from two opposing perspectives.[68] On the one hand, the debate on the media demanding the liberation of the pixadora can be interpreted as a form of political feminism, recognizing the abuse of the law and the excessiveness of the punishment in her case for a transgression that could be considered 'art' or a 'performance.' In this reading, Caroline is a 'free' agent who participated in a form of radical politics, appropriating the 'empty' space of the Biennale for (politically) expressing herself. On the other hand, the undertone of this perspective is a 'paternalistic' attitude, considering Caroline as a frail 'victim' who should not or could not be held in prison, but who should be 'protected' from the excessiveness of the legal system, because she was captured for being 'the only woman in the group.' In this subjacent narrative, Caroline needs to be saved from 'herself' and from the world of (male) pixo, a 'sub-world' in which she had no place to begin with. The idea of 'saving pixadores from themselves' is frequently mentioned in the news articles, editorials and op-eds analyzed for this study.

To conclude, there are two main reflections associated with the case of Caroline. Considering that pixadores 'attacked' several art institutions and included themselves by force *inside* the physical 'spaces of art' (museums, galleries, biennales), the outcome of labelling pixação as 'art' could be the result of these *spatial movement*. With this spatial migration, pixação could be accepted or rejected, labelled as aesthetic or anti-aesthetic, and subjected to more institutionalized discussions on taste. Instead of being 'disorder' outside, on public and private surfaces, pixação is finally finding its 'right' place and, therefore, could be recognized as a valuable artistic expression (because it has removed 'itself' from the public space). Inside the museum, the 'transgressive' nature of the practice reduces or loses its effect. After all, Caroline was arrested *'inside'* a museum, and not in the middle of a dark alley. Associated to this, her punishment was discussed in and tracked by the local media, which protected her from 'harm.' She was incarcerated for reasons that could be legally justified, although open to debate. Unlike pixadores, who have identified themselves as victims of irregular and extrajudicial punishments, the public discussion empowered Caroline as a symbol—more like a scapegoat—in two ways: as an artist who suffered unnecessary repression and as a low-income woman who suffered the injustice of the legal system. This seems to indicate that the punishment of the pixação follows two logics: *a)* one that is more 'circumstantial' in which law enforcers will decide the form and severity of the punishment *in situ*; and *b)* a punishment that is bounded by procedures and the legal system. The type of punishment to be exerted seems to be more a 'matter of luck' than the legally-bounded 'pursuit of due process.' This could theoretically explain why some pixadores die in ambiguous circumstances while others are formally processed and incarcerated (even if later they are prosecuted by laws aimed at punishing more serious forms of crime). As described above, the public discussion of the punishment in the case of Caroline positively impacted her chances of getting a 'fair' treatment.

Several new possibilities for research have been identified in this analysis. Scholars could focus on the alternative media produced by pixadores, in order to understand the inner market of cultural products and their status-economy. The role of women in the 'movement' needs to be addressed, particularly considering that the characteristics of the pixação are associated with stereotypical perceptions of 'masculinity.' The interaction between pixadores and the police, as well as the employment of extrajudicial punishments has been overlooked in current literature on the subject. Finally, the perception and subjectivities of the 'victims' of pixação could provide more insight about the impact that this transgressive practice has in the lives of local inhabitants.

## Notes

1.  This paper is part of a larger study that included the analysis of discourses about graffiti, street art, and other tagging practices (such as the 'pixo') and its producers in the local press in Brazil and Costa Rica. See: Alexander Araya López, 'Public Spaces, Stigmatization, and Media Discourses of Graffiti Practices in the Latin American Press: Dynamics of Symbolic Exclusion and Inclusion of Urban Youth' (PhD Thesis, Freie Universität Berlin, 2015).

2.  For more information, see Sérgio Miguel Franco, 'Iconografias da Metrópole: Grafiteiros e Pixadores Representando o Contemporâneo' (Master Thesis, Projecto Espaço e Cultura, São Paulo: FAUUSP, 2009). The documentary *Pixo* (2009) also describes this composition, but not excluding the participation of 'playboys' (youth from middle and upper classes).

3.  These runes are letters from the first alphabet used by Barbarian groups like Germanics, Scandinavians, and Anglo-Saxons.

4.  See, for instance, Teresa Caldeira, 'Social Movements, Cultural Production and Protests São Paulo's Shifting Political Landscape,' *Current Anthropology* 56/11 (2005), 126–36; Tristan Manco et al, *Graffiti Brasil* (London: Thames & Hudson Ltd, 2005); Franco, *Iconografias da Metrópole*.

5.    Documentary *Pixo* (2009). I have included this documentary to give voice to the pixadores, as it is a media text where they are speaking for themselves, in contrast to their partial inclusion in the articles published by *Folha de São Paulo*.

6.    Sérgio Dávila and Juca Varella, 'Pichadores ousam e chegam à classe média' (Pichadores Dare and Reach the Middle Class), *Folha de São Paulo*, 30 June 2003. However, considering the anonymous character of the pichação/pixação phenomena, it is not possible to provide an accurate description of the participants in terms of age, class, race, gender.

7.    *Ibope* is a slang word derived from the acronym for Instituto Brasileiro de Opinão Pública e Estadística. According to McCann (2004), *ibope* stands for audience and polls, it signifies 'star quality' and the mere presence of celebrities in an event 'give[s] it more *ibope*.' See: Bryan McCann, *Hello, Hello Brazil. Popular Music in the Making of Modern Brazil* (Durham & London: Duke University Press, 2004).

8.    In the documentary Pixo (2009), pixadores hunt for food in the trash cans of a local McDonald's during a night out, referring to the disposed hamburgers as McTrash (McLixo, in Portuguese). Although they apparently reject this 'commercialization' of public spaces, in terms of rhetoric and creative visuality, there is a potential for synergies between movements of street art—including pixação—and the commercial goals of both public and private business, as suggested by Stefania Borghini et al., 'Symbiotic Postures of Commercial Advertising and Street Art,' *Journal of Advertising* 39/3 (2010), 113–26.

9.    Joe Austin, *Taking the train. How Graffiti Art became an Urban Crisis in New York City* (New York: Columbia University Press, 2001).

10.    Caldeira, 'Social Movements.'

11.    Fran Tonkiss, 'Analysing Text and Speech: Content and Discourse Analysis ,' in *Researching Society and Culture*, ed. Clive Seale (London: Sage, 2004), 369.

12.    'A deprimente pichação de São *Paulo*' (The depressing pichação of São Paulo), *Folha de São Paulo*, 20 July 2003.

13.    George L. Kelling and James Q. Wilson, 'Broken Windows,' *The Atlantic Magazine*, March 1982. The 'Broken Windows' policing proposed by the authors has been heavily criticized, although it is still popular among criminology scholars.

14.    'Speto grafita con quixotes,' *Folha de São Paulo*, 7 June 2001. This article points out how the goal of some graffiti workshops is not to 'create supergrafiteiros' but to 'give access to culture' and transform the practice into 'a profession.' For a more detailed discussion on 'entrepreneurship' and 'self-branding,' see Sarah Banet-Weiser, 'Convergence on the Street,' *Cultural Studies* 25/4–5 (2011), 641–658.

15.    I have addressed this discussion on 'celebrity' and the difference between street artists and pixadores in Alexander Araya López, 'Conflicted

Celebrity in Media: Graffiti Artists and Pixadores in the Brazilian Press,' in *Becoming Brands: Celebrity, Activism and Politics*, ed. Jackie Raphael and Celia Lam (Toronto: WaterHill Publishing, 2017), 56–69. These street artists travel around the world and collaborate with established art institutions such as the Tate Modern in London. The participation of the pixadores in several international venues imitates this 'commodification' experienced by other 'street art' practices, while providing them with opportunities to monetize value from this acquired symbolic capital.

16.   This law, according to some of the news articles analyzed, contributed to the use of graffiti as a strategy to advertise products and services by local business, given the new restrictions regarding outdoor advertising.

17.   For a more detailed explanation of this concept, see Deborah Lupton, *Risk* (London: Routledge, 1999).

18.   'Prejuízo com pichação pode chegar a R$ 8 bi,' *Folha de São Paulo*, 30 June 2005.

19.   Target hardening refers to technological, structural or spatial components that difficult the access to one target, or delay/deter potential criminals. For an introduction to the literature about *Crime Prevention through Environmental Design* (CPTED), see Jeff Ferrell et al., *Cultural Criminology* (London: Sage, 2008); Neal Kumar Kaytal, 'Architecture as Crime Control,' *The Yale Law Journal* 111/5 (2002), 1039–139.

20.   'Prefeitura promete maior fiscalização em áreas visadas,' *Folha de São Paulo*, 5 June 2005.

21.   The law 14.223 *Cidade Limpa* is available in the website of the Prefeitura de São Paulo. The law does not mention pichação in its text.

22.   'Lixeiras e floreiras da avenida receberão produto antipichação,' *Folha de São Paulo*, 7 January 2009.

23.   Matze Jung, 'Mehr als optische Aufwertung. Graffiti in Rio de Janeiro—kreativer Widerstand aus den Favelas,' *Informationstelle Lateinamerika* 346 (2011), 7. See also Manco et al., *Graffiti Brasil*.

24.   Leo Martins and Letícia Naísa, 'A Polícia Militar Matou Dois Pixadores no Alto de um Prédio em São Paulo,' *Vice*, 5 August 2014, accessed 15 May 2017, https://www.vice.com/pt_br/article/gvxdv3/a-policia-militar-matou-dois-pixadores-no-alto-de-um-predio-em-sao-paulo.

25.   One article relates pichação to house robberies, arguing how these signs work as a code among criminals to get information about their targets: 'Pichação em casas vira código para assaltantes na zona leste,' *Folha de São Paulo*, 3 July 2006. The link between pichação and drug dealing/gang violence is reported in two articles: The first text is about the explosion of a homemade bomb close to a journalist team documenting pichação in a favela: 'Bombas caseiras explodem perto de equipe da Folha,' *Folha de São Paulo*, 14 June 2002. The second article relates a new form of tourism in favelas and explains how the pichação ADA ('Amigos dos amigos,' meaning 'Friends of friends') represents the drug dealing gang of the morro da Rocinha in Rio de Janeiro.

See 'Pacote turístico inclui passeio por boca-de-fumo,' *Folha de São Paulo*, 04 May 2008.

26.    For a discussion on how the aesthetics of pixação have been adopted by several business and corporations, see Ana Carina de Carvalho, A. C., and Angela Christina Salgueiro, 'Só poder pixar quem não é pixador: artifícios capitalistas de criminalização e capitalização no universe da pixação,' *Revista ECO-Pós* 18/2 (2015), 126–37. The authors suggest that there is value in the image and the aesthetics of the practice, but that the pixadores are considered a social 'problem' that needs to be controlled or eliminated.

27.    Banet-Weiser, 'Convergence on the Street.'

28.    'Buracos no muro' (*Folha de São Paulo*, 23 July 2001).

29.    'Na sala ou no quarto, desenhos enfeitam casas de descolados,' *Folha de São Paulo*, 23 June 2007.

30.    Following Weber's concept of *verstehen*, Jeff Ferrell et al. propose the necessity to create interpretation mechanisms of criminal and deviant practices based on the subjective, appreciative and emphatic understanding of the actions and motivations; Jeff Ferrell, 'Cultural Criminology,' *Annual Review of Sociology* 25 (1999), 177.

31.    Ferrell, 'Cultural Criminology,' 395–418.

32.    See the discussion on 'politics of dirt,' as proposed by Robbie Duschinsky, 'The Politics of Purity: When, Actually, Is Dirt Matter out of Place?' *Thesis Eleven* 119/1 (2013), 63–77. Duschinsky argues that 'dirt' (in our case, pixação) is more than 'matter out of place,' but refers to a process of assessment of self-identity, which includes perceptions of 'homogeneity' and 'essentialism.' For example, São Paulo as a metropolis or global city could not be easily reduced to a characteristic shared by an all-encompassing 'majority' of its 'citizens/inhabitants.'

33.    David Lefkowitz, 'On a Moral Right to Civil Disobedience,' *Ethics* 117/2 (2007), 202–33. Lefkowitz argues that dissenters might enjoy a moral right to engage in acts of civil disobedience, in the sense that these disenfranchised populations might 'act wrong' with the explicit goal of changing a law or policy that they consider 'unjust.' This is a more complex discussion, which requires a broader discussion on the idea of 'punishment' and 'harm,' following, for example, Joel Feinberg, *Doing and Deserving. Essays in the Theory of Responsibility* (New Jersey: Princeton University Press, 1970). To summarize, *if* the practice of pixação is a public disregard of the law motivated by moral principles, and the pixadores believe that the outcome of their actions will create a more just society, and *if* the practice is read as a protest and not as a form of 'harm,' then the State should refrain from 'punishing' their (political) actions because they are aimed at fostering public debate regarding a specific 'injustice.'

34.    Majid Yar, 'Crime, Media and the Will-To-Representation: Reconsidering Relationships in the New Media Age,' *Crime Media Culture* 8/3 (2012), 245–60.

35.    In the documentary *Pixo*, the pixador Djan Ivson states that he retired from pixação after 'some problems with the justice system' and that he now dedicates himself to 'document the practice.' He has previously been sentenced to community services for his pixações.

36.    'Obra de Lenora de Barros sofre pichação,' *Folha de São Paulo*, 17 October 2002.

37.    His real name is Diego Salvador.

38.    'Não,' pichador da Bienal, diz que também é artista,' *Folha de São Paulo*, 3 October 2004.

39.    'Pichadores vandalizam escola para discutir conceito de arte,' *Folha de São Paulo*, 13 June 2008. This 'attack' is also depicted in the documentary *Pixo*.

40.    The gallery Choque Cultural is a well-known spot for consolidated graffiti artists, including exhibitions by street artists such as OsGêmeos, Titifreak, Zezão, etc.

41.    The curator team of the 28th Bienal de São Paulo proposed a reflection on the 'vazio' (void) and for this reason the second floor of the Oscar Niemeyer building was empty. The 'attack' of the pixadores refuted this idea of the void space and proposed the (violent) appropriation of this space.

42.    'Pichadores agora destroem marcos do grafite em São Paulo,' *Folha de São Paulo*, 28 October 2008.

43.    Franco, Iconografias da Metrópole, 127–8.

44.    'Após mais de 50 dias presa, TJ manda soltar pichadora,' *Folha de São Paulo*, 19 December 2008.

45.    "Picho para o povo olhar e não gostar,' diz jovem presa na Bienal,' *Folha de São Paulo*, 05 December 2008.

46.    'Ódio a pichadores me deixou tanto tempo presa, afirma jovem,' *Folha de São Paulo*, 20 December 2008.

47.    The authors are writers of the former blog *O2Neuronio*, and their article was published in the section *Folhateen,* 15 Dezember 2008. [Available in: www1.folha.uol.com.br/fsp/folhatee/fm1512200813.htm]

48.    This refers to the 'attack' against the Centro Universitário de Belas Artes, early in 2008.

49.    'Caso Caroline: algumas questões não consideradas,' *Folha de São Paulo*, 18 December 2008.

50.    'Para ex-ministro da Justiça, punição foi 'draconiana,' *Folha de São Paulo*, 20 December 2008.

51.    'Grupo invade prédio da Bienal e picha 'andar vazio,' *Folha de São Paulo*, 27 October 2008.

52.    'Justiça condena pichadora da Bienal,' *Folha de São Paulo*, 26 September 2009.

53.    'Após mais de 50 dias presa, TJ manda soltar pichadora,' *Folha de São Paulo*, 19 December 2008.

54.    'Ministro defende libertação de pichadora e diz que Dantas ficou menos tempo na cadeia,' *Folha de São Paulo*, 15 December 2008.

55.   'Ministro pede a Serra que ajude a libertar pichadora,' *Folha de São Paulo*, 11 December 2008.

56.   'Para ex-ministro da Justiça, punição foi 'draconiana,' *Folha de São Paulo*, 20 December 2008.

57.   'Bienal age de modo cínico e intolerante ao lavar as mãos,' *Folha de São Paulo*, 15 December 2008.

58.   'O pais do homem cordial,' *Folha de São Paulo*, 14 December 2008.

59.   Five letters were found in relation to Caroline Pivetta (four against her actions and one in favour).

60.   'Pichador ataca obra com urubus na Bienal,' *Folha de São Paulo*, 26 September 2010.

61.   'Paris celebra pichação de SP,' *Folha de São Paulo*, 04 July 2009.

62.   *Conexão Repórter*, SBT (Sistema Brasileiro de Televisão), March 2010.

63.   'Justiça condena pichadora da Bienal,' *Folha de São Paulo*, 26 September 2009.

64.   Another former pixadora, 'Jessica,' is included in the episode, and she is described as a former drug addict, homeless, victim of sexual abuse, who is now married and became a mother. While some former male pixadores are also described as 'fathers' or 'married,' they are also referred as 'good employees,' a sort of description that was not used to describe women within the movement.

65.   This could also be a strategic move in response to the legal prohibition of engaging in any form of 'pixação' or 'criminal activity' after her release.

66.   'Doria sanciona lei antipichação e veta até grafite não autorizado,' *Folha de São Paulo*, 20 February 2017.

67.   'Pichadores mineiros são presos e acusados de formar quadrilha,' *Folha de São Paulo*, 25 August 2010. The article, written by journalists Rodrigo Vizeu and Leticia de Castro, points out that while in Minas Gerais the pichação is criminalized, in São Paulo is considered an art (in reference to the inclusion of the practice in the 29th Bienal de São Paulo).

68.   As mentioned by one of the anonymous reviewers, there is a need understand the gendered histories of crime and deviant behaviour in Brazil, particularly the patriarchal structures that banalize male deviance. In part, the imprisonment of Caroline Pivetta da Mota was justified because of her lack of a legal address, and therefore was not exclusively about her pixação. Considering that media coverage about the practice also relates it to 'criminal activities' such as robberies, organized crime, and drug trafficking, it is not possible to delineate any specific boundaries of these 'gendered histories of crime' or the notion of 'impunity.' Further research focusing on male and female pixadores and their interactions with the police and the legal system could close this gap.

# 10

# Street Art and the Properties of Resistance

*Marta Iljadica*

## Introduction

Graffiti writing and street art are significant not only for their inherent stylistic qualities but because they represent an exercise of creative powers which is inexorably bound up in the space in which this creativity occurs. The art—for both graffiti writing and street art are art forms in their own right—is public art, and for that reason the usual, somewhat banal, contest (actual or potential) between the creator and the owner of the material support of the artistic work is complicated by the addition of a public or publics that may claim 'ownership' of both the relevant creativity and the resulting objects, or instead seek to disclaim the creativity. The picture is further complicated by the more recent commercialization of street art in particular. This is a trend which can be seen in the proliferation of street art tours, the market for prints of works of street art and, indeed, the less savoury market for works cut directly from the walls on which their creator placed them. It is this form of the commercialization of street art—property owners cutting works from the wall in order to sell them and thereby depriving the community of their local art—which is the first issue considered in this chapter, the second being the destruction of art altogether by real property owners. This seemingly narrow focus on the work (or rather what is done to it) highlights, amongst other relevant matters, the tensions between uncommissioned public art, artists, real property owners, and different publics.

The undercurrent of the legal decisions discussed here is a concern with what public space is for and, specifically, who exercises control over the creativity found there. While the political and social aspects of this question are extensive, this chapter offers a consideration not of those, but rather of some of the specific tensions arising from within real and intellectual property law. It does so for two reasons. First, in order to discover and assess the legal strategies which have been, and might be, deployed, for resisting street art's commodification at the expense of its creators (and in so doing preserving their creators' personal autonomy and power) and, where relevant, preserving it for the communities where the work is found (recognizing the inhabitants of a city even where they lack private property rights). Second, in order to identify the limits of this strategy, which relies upon fitting street art, graffiti writing and any other creative interventions in public spaces—a form of creativity developed by and practiced by those (usually and at least historically) outside of the social mainstream of creativity—into established and only minimally flexible legal categories. In seeking to explore the ability of existing legal rules to preserve street art and similar works the chapter thus considers a 2015 UK case, *Creative Foundation v Dreamland*,[1] and for comparative reference, the 2013 and 2018 US cases of *Cohen I* and *Cohen II*,[2] concerning the removal of street art and/or graffiti and their respective property owners, artists, and, more indirectly, publics. These parts are concerned with examining the ways in which land and copyright rules respectively recognize the creative power of placement of artistic works.[3]

**Creativity, Commodification and Space: From Resistance to Property?**

The cases discussed below may usefully be placed within the context of two, though not the only, issues relevant to graffiti writing and street art. First, the examination of these cases and their engagement of intellectual and real property law must be understood in the context of the broader literature on graffiti writing and street art in public spaces including the distinctions made between the two forms of creativity, the significance of location and placement to creativity, and the interplay between creator, property owner, and community interests. Second, the cases ought to be read in the context of the relatively recent recognition of the economic value of this creativity. This in turn runs in two directions that are in tension with each other: from the creators seeking to exploit their own works (e.g. selling prints, challenging copyright infringements) to the exploiters of the creativity (e.g. advertisers, brands, street tour operators, local authorities keen to produce a 'creative city'). In resolving these tensions the law simultaneously punishes and assimilates graffiti writing and street art into real and intellectual property frameworks.[4]

## Creativity, Placement and Space

As Alison Young has explored in detail, graffiti writing and street art have a complex relationship to the legal regulation of space where responses range from prosecution for criminal damage to attempts to enact city specific policies (Melbourne being an example).[5] That it has been difficult for cities to embrace street art and graffiti writing in a coherent manner is perhaps unsurprising given that street art and graffiti are art forms which are defined by reference not only to their stylistic features, but more pressingly to the location in which the creativity takes place, 'the crucial "where" of graffiti.'[6] The aesthetics are bound up in placement producing the conception of graffiti writing as a 'crime of style.'[7] At the same time, using readily accessible street art as a business opportunity by holding street art tours serves to produce the so-called, problematic, 'creative city.'[8]

Street art has both spatial and temporal effects and, moreover, property law intervenes to at once 'outlaw and protect street art.'[9] The creativity is found on walls, on trains, often high up, and almost always in public places and it may or may not last.[10] As a number of works show in different ways,[11] graffiti writing, and street art exerts significant power especially in the new spaces that these aesthetic interventions in the city create. What also seems clear is that law, though not just the law, engages in the policing of the aesthetics of creativity on the street.[12] Of particular note is the way in which different types of legal rules (on public order, planning, crime for example) indicate a 'desire to control the city's perceived fecklessness and unruliness.'[13] A (legal) attempt to control street art may occur because a real property owner has decided to keep a work or because a local authority has decided to intervene to protect it but these decisions are taken against a background that requires setting aside some works as valuable. It is the seeming disorderliness of graffiti writing that this chapter returns to again in the context of the 5Pointz cases, and so provides a further example—this time in the realm of intellectual property law—of the kind of regulatory responses Young details. This highlights why copyright law's even very minor recognition of certain forms of creativity (namely, street art) is new without, as the case discussions below show, offering resistance to dominant legal narratives about creativity that is worthy of protection.[14] The cases need to be understood in this context.

Both street art and graffiti represent a challenge to the mainstream of creativity as well as the politics of public spaces. They do so not only by having their own stylistic features which are distinct from those of broadly socially-acceptable creativity (including specifically the kind of creativity ordinarily considered in copyright cases) but also because in their core form works are placed on property the creators do not own and without seeking permission from property owners, which in any event is not a viable or practical possibility. And, where there is permission, as in the 5Pointz case this permission is seemingly critical to the outcome. In cases where no permission is granted, the anonymity of the creator further complicates their legal position in terms of ability to vindicate their property rights (copyright).[15] Street art resists real property but the radicalness of that legal recognition should not be overstated. Graffiti writing may for example be contrasted with the practice of yarn-bombing and how the aesthetics of a work condition both social and legal responses to works where the latter is considered warm and welcoming and the former something to be eradicated.[16]

The difficulties raised only briefly here around the location of creativity and the difficulties and inconsistences in regulating aesthetic interventions raises broader questions about who the city is for.[17] In Lefebvrian terms we might consider the regulation of street art and graffiti in the context of the 'right to the city.' Such a focus means advocating for a response that takes seriously the experience of a city's inhabitants which in turn requires an understanding of political power derived primarily from place and the way in which non-legal norms serve to offer an alternative framework for regulating creativity and the places in which it is found. The cases discussed below show how creator, public, and other interests may be, perhaps unexpectedly, high-lighted within the resolution of private law disputes about street art. Nevertheless the cases are, fundamentally, about recognition of certain types of creativity, in certain locations and therefore vindicate (if they do so at all) narrow conceptions of what it means to inhabit the city.

## Creativity, Commodification and Property

It is useful at this point to note that this chapter is not based on some idea of a 'pure' form of creativity against which to set legally recognized creativity, nor does it seek to hark back to some idealized past. The graffiti writing of 1970s and 1980s New York (the focus on stylistic innovation, on pleasure, and creating spaces for those who were marginalized)[18] retains its echoes in contemporary graffiti writing practice. What is also clear is that creative interventions in the city and its public spaces have undertaken a shift so that the line between public and private creativity of street artists and graffiti writers has been blurred. In tracing this shift towards 'legal graffiti,' Kramer argues that considering graffiti writing only through the concept of 'resistance' is to tell only part of the story: train writing still occurs, but many writers have also turned graffiti writing into a career.[19] Any discussion of street art's commodification must therefore also include creators themselves making and selling prints.[20]

In light of this shift, combined with general public interest in street art, it is perhaps unsurprising that the intellectual property ramifications of these aesthetic interventions are coming to the fore. The relatively recent upsurge in interest, and the complaints to match, about copyright protection for graffiti mean that attempts by alleged infringers to make blanket statements as to the lack of copyright protection are ringing increasingly hollow.[21] There are thus two directions of travel in tension with each other when it comes to an account of aesthetic intervention, the recognition of property right and the question of who the city is for that this section briefly traces: from the creator (using property rights to protect the creator's own commodification of their work) and away from the creator (commercialization and exploitation of the creator's work without permission, but also local authority and other attempts to regulate street art and graffiti in an attempt to produce the 'creative city').[22]

On the first point, commodification emanating from the creator, it is important to note again that the creeping assimilation of street art and to a lesser extent graffiti writing into law's mainstream ought not to be confused with resistance, though there is a reading of the copyright disputes that certainly suggests the use of legal tools, justifiably, as a sword against alleged infringers. Instead, the recent uptick in cases, specifically relating to intellectual property, need to be read against the long, and often negative (in terms of state responses) history of uncommissioned creativity and the shorter more recent history in the acquisition of significant economic value of certain types of such creativity.[23] This is not to suggest that commodification is in and of itself a bad thing; indeed empirical research suggests that once works enter the commercial realm ordinary rules of copyright ought to apply (i.e. creators expect to be paid).[24] In fact, copyright law is only beginning to recognize what it ought always to have recognized—creativity embodied in a work that meets the originality standard—were it not hamstrung by overly traditionalist frameworks for recognizing creativity as an artistic work within the confines of copyright law.[25]

A relevant recent development is the recognition that the appropriation of graffiti and street art in advertisements is no longer, automatically, acceptable. British Airways incorporating a work of street art into a large advertisement placed in Shoreditch, London, an area already famed for its street art and graffiti writing, without compensating the creators whose work was incorporated into the advertisement is worthy of a news report.[26] One of the creators (MadC) is quoted as saying:

> My work has been in many videos and ad campaigns before but so far I have always been asked for permission first and, if it is a commercial project, been paid ... Of course, I am upset. It is very disrespectful towards any artist to use their work without permission.[27]

The alleged appropriators seem to have assumed, the charitable explanation might be, that public placement is an implied license to freely use works on walls.[28] It is thus unsurprising that street artists have turned to (the threat of) legal action to ensure the copyright in their works is respected.

There are also other means of commercialization besides straightforward reproduction. Ways in which commercialization occurs (though not the only ways) include the running of street art tours, local authorities protecting certain street art with Perspex or the auction of street art cut from building walls. Such acts may be understood as legitimation, but a 'spatial legitimacy' offered to street art in the apparently objective routes taken by street art tours instead 'curates' the streets.[29] The proliferation of street art tours thus suggests a certain taming of creative experience and the potential to change inhabitants' experience of the city. The difficulty arises when known tour paths in fact change the creativity and its placement (including we may surmise real property owners' inclination to keep some works and not others) and so it is the walking of the tour groups that potentially change what is placed on walls and not, as we might expect, the other way around.

Such nuances of creativity, space and movement are channelled, within property law, into the split between the physical object, such as wall or piece of wall, and the copyright embodied in that object: there is a clear and simultaneous affirmation of these distinct sets of property rights. Such a distinction is unremarkable in the realm of both real and intellectual property rights. And so while particular property rights might be challenged—certainly the internal normativity of the graffiti subculture offers a challenge to copyright law—the more general logic of property is not subverted, but rather strengthened when a creator employs the logic of property in response to an act of exploitation as we can see (indirectly) in the concern with real property rights in

*Creative Foundation v Dreamland* or the interference with moral rights in *Cohen I* and *II*.

## A Note on Comparison

The two examples here are not functionally equivalent. The 'Banksy case' was decided under English law; the '5Pointz cases' relate to US intellectual property law, specifically a moral rights rule which exists within federal copyright law and whose analogues in other systems differ in important ways. There is nonetheless an affinity between the cases in that both relate to works of street art (and graffiti writing) and indirectly ask whether such works ought to remain in the publicly accessible spaces where they were originally placed by their creators.

## The Banksy Case

*Creative Foundation v Dreamland* is a first instance judgment about the interpretation of a leasehold covenant to repair. On its face this is not an obvious context for a discussion of property law with respect to street art but it transpires that the interpretation of what 'repair' means in the land law of England and Wales is doubly interesting. First, the concept of repair is an unsettled one, and second, the judgment, in obiter, recognizes intellectual property rights in graffiti.[30] Moreover, the outcome of the case vindicates the rights of the creator and the local community seeking to preserve the work not through IP but through real property law.[31]

On the first technical point about the interpretation of the covenant to repair we see something interesting in the way street art forces a re-think of existing doctrinal categories. A consideration of street art forces a re-evaluation of the legal definitions of 'repair' and 'waste.' The leaseholder, Dreamland, had cut a Banksy work from the wall intending to auction it and subsequently repaired the wall. The problem for the leaseholder of course is that the wall itself belongs to the freeholder (the freeholder as we know had assigned the right to bring the action to the Creative Foundation community group who stepped into the freeholder's shoes here).[32]

Given the wall belonged to the freeholder, the resulting chattel—a piece of that wall embodying the artistic work—also belonged to the freeholder. To make this determination a different legal concept was in play: 'waste.'[33] An inventive argument was made by the defendant that the piece of wall was 'waste' as such it was the tenant and not the landlord who, because the tenant is obliged to remove it, was therefore entitled to its 'scrap' value.[34] This, of course, does not make much sense in the context of a potentially highly valuable work.[35] The court would not imply such a term where the chattel produced by the discharge of the obligation to repair had 'substantial value.'[36] An order was made for the delivery up of the piece of wall to the plaintiffs.[37]

But what is interesting is the observation made in the course of the discussion as to whether the chattel embodying the artistic work was 'waste':

> The answer cannot depend on the reasons why the Mural has substantial value (such as the fact that it is an artistic work or the identity of the artist), nor on the reason why *its removal is justified (such as the fact that it attracted graffiti)*. But in my judgment the fact that *the Mural has substantial value (both aesthetic and economic) is plainly a relevant consideration.*'[38]

What we see is both the distinction between acceptable and unacceptable creativity (street art and graffiti writing aesthetics are distinguished despite all of the creativity in question being placed on the wall without permission),[39] but also in the privileging of the artistic work as a commodity. The situation is complicated because this thing that somehow ought to be worthless in fact has both an economic value and, an aesthetic (social) value that militates against a description of it as 'waste.'

The case also raises broader questions about the preservation of the material object embodying the work and its relationship to public interests. Copyright in the work embodied in the disputed chattel (the piece of the wall) belonged to Banksy, the purported author of the stencil.[40] The case thus offers a neat study of the interface between real and intellectual property law; using land law to do the heavy lifting of moral rights protection so the creator is benefitted despite not having asserted their right to the integrity of the work themselves.[41] In other words the decontextualization of the work, which arguably destroys the work's power, is addressed through real property law rather than copyright.

It is the recognition not of the power of sensitive public placement and the community desire to keep the work (though that is in the background) but rather the potential economic value of the work that is critical to the recognition of property rights. The perceived value of the work changed local authority calculations about whether it ought to be preserved *in situ* (the desire to preserve rather than destroy being also a particular aesthetic intervention in public place). That graffiti writing and to a lesser extent street art will be destroyed is not considered unusual:

> Shepway District Council placed a sheet of Perspex over the Mural to protect it. It is not clear what authority the Council had to take this action. It proved to be a wise precaution, however, as *the Mural rapidly attracted attention from graffiti artists.* Graffiti were painted both on the wall alongside the Mural and on the Perspex. *The latter were cleaned off.*[42]

A similar distinction is made between street art and graffiti writing in the 5Pointz cases.

The Banksy case offers a helpful example of how the regulation of property rights in street art and its material support (wall/building) can represent explicitly or implicitly a variety of individual and group interests. One reading of the case is that it is a fortuitous meeting of public interests (in the preservation of certain cultural heritage) and private interests (the property owner or tenant; the copyright owner) whereby the local authority intervenes to preserve works considered valuable.[43] Local authorities have extensive powers to destroy graffiti writing and street art.[44] It is not clear that they are correspondingly empowered to preserve it.[45]

The outcome of the case meant that the interests of (a subsection of) Folkestone's public were able to inhabit the city in the way they desired.[46] Thus we see the recognition of economic value used to justify the preservation of a particular type of space for the community, against the leaseholder and in favour of the creator (assuming it is the location of the work and not just the work itself that is preserved).[47] The outcome of the case entrenches property rights and shows the limits of private, circumscribed, action; what appears a community 'win' and the vindication of the power of publicly placed creativity in no sense undermines the (potential) for commodification of creativity and the commercialization of public space. Thus, the power gained through the control of the chattel/the wall cannot be framed as 'resistance' insofar as no new legal relationships are imagined. The lack of exploitation is dependent on the relevant legal actor exercising their rights in concert with community expectations but could not be (legally) constrained by the community should the freeholder wish to act contrary to these expectations.

## The 5Pointz Cases

This part addresses a different type of legal question focusing on intellectual rather than real property, namely whether street artists can assert their moral rights, specifically by demonstrating that the destroyed works were works of recognized stature under VARA. The litigation concerning the 5Pointz site in New York has been ongoing since 2013. The first significant judgment in the case was handed down in November 2013. *Cohen I* related to a refusal of the grant of a preliminary injunction against the destruction of works on at the 5Pointz site. The works were destroyed and *Cohen II* (on the merits of the VARA 'recognized stature' provision) demonstrates the significant monetary consequences of that destruction. The discussion below considers these two judgments in turn. It is worth noting immediately that this is unlikely to be the end of the story given reports that the defendants are intending to appeal the USD 6,750,000 judgment against them following *Cohen II*.[48]

Notwithstanding that the cases concern the operation of intellectual rather than real property law, overlap may be found with *Creative Foundation v Dreamland* especially in considering the role of the community which in this instance is not thrust from background to foreground with the assignment of the right to bring proceedings or by references to local authority protection of the street art in question but rather forms a legal case where the artists themselves, through a fellow artist (and curator) brought the action against the property developer for the destruction of their works. The public is indirectly significant to the outcomes in two respects: first, providing the background to the mediation between intellectual and real property rights between the creators and the property developer, and second, in applying the 'recognized stature' test.

## Cohen I

The judgment denying the grant of a preliminary injunction is interesting for the way it treats public interests in the context of the relationship between real property—the interests in developing land which may serve both the interests of the property developer, the local government and so, potentially, broader public interests—and intellectual property, namely creators' right not to have their work (argued to be of 'recognized stature') destroyed, something that would serve both creator and broader public, including local community, interests in preserving works of street art *in situ*. The judgment demonstrates sensitivity to public concerns and the legal conclusion is not reached with much enthusiasm. On the determination of whether these are likely to be works of 'recognized stature'[49] the court begins with the observation that the 'recognized stature' provision is to function as a 'gate-keeping mechanism.'[50] The legal mechanics of this are in themselves interesting,[51] but suffice it to say that a fairly typical approach was taken to the question of what it means for a work to be 'recognized.' Weight was placed on expert evidence leaving little room for the appreciation of what is a form of subcultural creativity. It was thus difficult to demonstrate both that the works in question had stature *and* that their stature had been recognized by the relevant group.[52] The legal determination of the question of 'recognized stature' here may be contrasted with the more generous application of the tests in the detailed discussion of the merits in *Cohen II*.[53]

Yet what is perhaps more interesting here is the way in which the commodification of creativity (the artistic works displayed at 5Pointz) is highlighted. The court acknowledges that 5Pointz had become a 'major attraction'[54] (and note too that the 5Pointz works were created with the permission of the real property owner).[55] The following is also interesting:

> Cohen personally conducted hundreds of school tours a year, which sold out months in advance, for students from as far as Canada. As he testified, there were also corporate and VIP tours; moreover, 5Pointz is listed in Time Out New York 'as a New York must-see,' and is in 150 tour guide books.[56]

This makes it difficult to read the events as resistance as opposed to assimilation into the logic of both real and intellectual property law. Indeed, the broad narrative of the dispute as a contest between 'the bold and the bland,'[57] the boldness of street art against the 'banality of luxury skyboxes'[58] contains within it also a less obvious narrative of boldness contained. A distinction is made between desirable and less desirable forms of aesthetic intervention—and so between order and disorder—insofar as the court is alert to creative difference between 5Pointz and the site's previous incarnation as the Phun Factory which was much less tightly controlled. The description of the site pre-5Pointz adopts the language of disgust:[59]

> Starting in the early or mid-1990s, the exterior walls had become a place for *distasteful graffiti* by many *self-proclaimed aerosol artists*; it was then

known as the Phun Phactory. To *control this festering problem*, Cohen approached Wolkoff in 2002 to become the curator of the works that would be permitted to be painted on the walls. Wolkoff agreed.[60]

This dichotomy between acceptable and unacceptable creativity remained in the full discussion of the merits of the case when it came to trial.

Finally, if the preservation of the works was not the outcome of this stage of the legal proceedings there is a remarkable observation: 'The plaintiffs' works can live on in other media.'[61] The suggestion here is that the commons these works create extends beyond the physical surroundings and for the inhabitants of the city round 5Pointz perhaps the implication is that all is not lost. The outcome of *Cohen I* is presented regretfully in light of the mediation between public and private and between real and intellectual property interests. The defendant destroyed the works in the period between the refusal of the preliminary injunction and the handing down of the judgment paying no heed to the judge's warning that the merits were still to be assessed at trial which brings us to *Cohen II*.

## Cohen II

*Cohen II* is premised implicitly on a rejection of unruly creativity, namely graffiti writing, in favour of more tightly controlled (mostly, street art) creativity 'deserving' of preservation. The works were destroyed, often inexpertly so the underlying work was visible under the whitewash.[62] This section thus considers the way in which the court came to find that the majority of the contested works were works of 'recognized stature' especially in referring to the use of social media evidence, the privileging of street art over graffiti writing (which in turn is really a privileging of the 'curation' of space) and finally a note on other relevant factors including the use of an advisory jury perhaps as a proxy for public attitudes to street art.

The determination of 'recognized stature' turns on the meaning of community (which public produces the relevant acts of recognition) and here the use of social media evidence alongside evidence from blogs, newspapers, television etc. was considered.[63] It includes, too, evidence of 'academic and professional interest'[64] much expanded here, seemingly well beyond the typical approach involving evidence of art experts although that is also in evidence here.[65] In particular, the use of social media evidence for recognized stature is appropriate but it bears asking whether it would encompass the consideration of material shared only by graffiti writers in light of the narrow VARA case law on what constitutes an 'artistic community.'[66]

We thus see in *Cohen II* further evidence of the potential use of copyright law as a sword by creators who were previously marginalized by the law or did not or could not dispute the copying or other interference with their works. To that extent *Cohen II* is a victory for creator control. Acts of creative resistance would seem to be enabled because the result here suggests that individual creators are able to resist the commodification of their creativity and accepted forms of aesthetic intervention. Yet, at least with respect to 'recognized stature,' the reputation element introduces the availability for protection only where the radical potential of the artwork—its placement and its process of creation—is downplayed. Of course, legal walls already exist for graffiti writing and street art, what is interesting here is the judge highlighting one of the plaintiff's, Castillo, referring to street art as having 'become an industry' and 5Pointz having become an 'outdoor museum' where, distinguishing it quite beautifully from other museums, children can touch the paintings.[67]

Notwithstanding the distinctions made between different creative interventions, the position is more nuanced than the preceding discussion suggests: some of the destroyed works that were found to be works of 'recognized stature'[68] were, based on the appendix of photographs, graffiti writing rather than (the more typical, figurative) street art.[69] So to that extent it is not simply a question of aesthetics. The graffiti writing works in question are graffiti writing of a highly complex kind (unlike, seemingly, a tag or a throw-up which demonstrate more clearly a writing style because of the exclusion of colour, characters and other embellishment). The style also raises, amongst those outside the subculture, questions about how the work was produced and where, specifically whether it was produced with permission and in an orderly manner.[70]

The judgment explains the process of choosing works to be displayed at 5Pointz and how long the works are expected to last, referring to 'the site's rules and norms' which were explained to potential artists by Cohen who 'oversaw the site, kept it clean and safe, allotted wall space.'[71] Indeed the judge makes a number of references to the idea that 5Pointz was curated. The judgment distinguishes street art from graffiti writing and distinguishes curated and non-curated approaches to creativity (5Pointz versus Phun Factory).[72] In particular, reference is made to norms that arose to regulate how long those works lasted. What can be seen in the judgment is a concern with dividing art from graffiti writing and distinguishing the careful process of curation of 5Pointz from the (seemingly) more chaotic and therefore less desirable Phun Factory. For example, it is implied that the creators of that graffiti were a disorderly presence and they are thus excluded from the definition of the public:

> There was no control over the artists who painted on the walls of the buildings or the quality of their work, which was largely viewed by the public as nothing more than graffiti.[73]

What we have in this case then is not so much the clever use of existing legal rules, though there is also that, as the recognition by the law of an artistic practice that has seemed to conform and to move closely enough within the popular and legal imagination to warrant protection.

The court observes that every creator who testified to the court referred to 'going over' (fully or partially destroying someone else's work) was deeply disrespectful.[74] Yet what the judgment does not say, though it is almost certainly the case, is that this particular norm is a crucial one regulating the production of works within the graffiti subculture; indeed the lead plaintiff stated that 'respect in our game is everything.'[75] The norm undoubtedly also applied to the Phun Factory. But for the curation of 5Pointz the norm was not quite used in the same way—to regulate graffiti placement within the graffiti subculture in general—rather it was the foundation for the enforcement of a 5Pointz specific version of the rule by its curator: Cohen granted permission for all works and instituted a system of 'short-term rotating walls and long-standing walls.'[76]

What is also not explained in the judgment is that those norms are an extension of a strongly-felt and well-developed system of graffiti writing based on hierarchies of style and placement; the same norms that may have been in operation when 5Poitz was the Phun Factory. Perhaps more than the outcome, what is striking about this case is the re-imagining of a norm otherwise functioning through a loose sense of appreciation of hierarchy, and sanctions,[77] in a diffuse sense: we see the norm reinterpreted by an arbiter-curator. It seems unlikely—as *English* and other case law indicates[78]—that the norms of graffiti writers, adhered to in producing works without real property owners' permission, would elicit similar praise in the absence of such control. In *Cohen II* the 'going over' norm supports rather than contests the logics of both real and intellectual property.

There are further points to be made about the process of the decision-making in *Cohen II* in particular the use of an advisory jury.[79] The broader point to be made here is that procedural elements of these cases—such as the role of an advisory jury respectively—offers ways of taking into account interests beyond those of the parties. The judge elected not to let the jury know that their verdict would be advisory only: 'since 5Pointz had achieved worldwide community recognition, the Court was keen to learn whether the jurors, *as members of the community*, would view the works as having achieved recognized stature under VARA.'[80]. The judgment ends on a wistful note, invoking again, the importance of the public:

> The shame of it all is that since 5Pointz was a prominent tourist attraction the public would undoubtedly have thronged to say its goodbyes during those 10 months and gaze at the formidable works of aerosol art for the last time. It would have been a wonderful tribute for the artists that they richly deserved.[81]

### Street Art and Graffiti Writing: Properties of Resistance

This chapter began with a discussion of the context in which the Banksy and 5Pointz cases ought to be read including the relevance of placement and space, the different legal and social attitudes to types of aesthetic intervention in space as well as the tricky questions relating to the commodification of street art and graffiti writing and who may exert control over such creativity. Broadly, what a study of 5Pointz and perhaps to a lesser extent the Banksy case shows is that private disputes relating to *public* artistic intervention necessarily raise broader questions about the role of the public in disputes over public art, specifically the ways in which art can transform space to the point where it would be reasonable to expect the interests of the community to take precedence over private property rights.[82]

The outcomes of the cases mean that creators' interests are legally recognized but it remains an open question whether this welcome recognition comes at the cost of the assimilation of creativity associated with particular communities and their norms into the legal logic of property. This does not mean of course that the result ought to be viewed unfavourably but simply a call to look more closely at what the Banksy and 5Pointz cases may tell us about property, creativity and power especially given that the malleability of the law was not tested by creativity that was particularly unusual. That the argument for protection in the 5Pointz cases in particular was prefaced by unfavourable comparisons to graffiti writing should give us pause.

There are two further points to be made in light of the legal recognition of, especially, street art and if it indicates a move of this type of creativity into a more acceptable, commodified, sphere, where this leaves the idea that aesthetic interventions in public spaces might constitute resistance: first, that the counter-regulation of public spaces is ongoing and, second, that creators may choose to respond to attempts to exploit street art works with acts of refusal or withdrawal.

On the first point, namely the counter regulation of space through normative frameworks (i.e. recognition of intra-subculture 'property') offers a challenge to property relations that is written on city walls.[83] In both instances what we see on the ground as it were is a certain creative order. Indeed, already—which is what makes suggestions of unruliness so wide of the mark—is that within the graffiti subculture norms exist relating to the acceptability of certain surfaces and not others for the placement of graffiti writing.[84] More broadly, both *Creative Foundation* and the *Cohen* judgments may be placed in the context of the right to the city,[85] arguing that, notwithstanding the range of possibilities within real and intellectual property law for the preservation of street art, there exists an enduring power deficit that cannot be addressed through the application of legal rules. Rather, the resistance to commodification of art in/and public space is to be found in the subversive placement of art within the city itself. What the court was drawing attention to in *Creative Foundation v Dreamland*—the crowding of tags around the street art—is not just a wall attracting graffiti but in fact the visible playing out of non-legal normativity.[86] It is in that visibility that the power of street art and graffiti lies.

Street art is not only, or even primarily, a form of resistance to property rules. It is an assertion of a right that is not legal, that may be conceptualized as the right to the city. In resisting the real property rights of a building-owner, artistic works placed on walls without permission resist more fundamentally a whole swathe of things for which those property rights stand. And while the cases discussed above can vindicate individual creators' intellectual property rights, they cannot vindicate the right to the city, and the interests of the inhabitants of those cities who were in the background of both the Banksy and 5Pointz disputes.

The second point is that graffiti writers and street artists may simply elect to continue producing their creativity much as before by for example continuing to place works in public or recreating works if they are destroyed. More radically, resistance may be found in erasure. Creators may effect a withdrawal, an anti-aesthetic intervention, in situations where their work becomes the herald of gentrification and displacement. A prominent example (it is unclear whether it is the only one) is of Blu in the destruction of a mural in Kreuzberg, Berlin (on account of its precipitation of gentrification and exclusion)[87] choosing to whitewash their own works rather than allow them to be appropriated against their meaning. The aesthetic challenges to real property and the commercialization of public spaces are potentially thus continued not through more work but through the absence of the works used to produce the 'creative city.' Arguably even this action is 'bold, yet per se incapable of elaborating alternative pattern of valorization.'[88] Yet such a response remains a bracing one in light of the slow movement of, especially, street art into the legal fold.

## Conclusion

The two cases discussed above provide welcome, and still rare, consideration of graffiti writing and street art in the private law context. Yet though law can and occasionally does make room for street art (the rules of copyright can apply relatively straightforwardly to certain works of graffiti and street art as artistic works), law's imperialistic nature—its limited engagement with logics which are not its own, such as the discussion of norms considered in *Cohen II*—means that street artists and others whose creativity is subcultural rather than in the cultural mainstream, should not depend upon it for protection. And so the stories of these cases are not only ones of assimilation or long overdue recognition of a certain aesthetic style but also the product of creators themselves moving into the commercial realm. In other words, it is important to not think of legal recognition as something of which creators are merely passive recipients. The cases demonstrate how the application of legal rules can ensure that the creative power of artworks gained from the public placement is not disturbed. The excitement of the positive (in terms of recognition of placement and creativity) outcomes of these cases are undeniable, but they are not (necessarily) victories.

## Notes

1.    [2015] EWHC 2556 (Ch).
2.    Cohen v G&M Realty L.P. 988 F. Supp. 2d 212 (EDNY 2013) (*Cohen I*); Cohen v G&M Realty L.P. 320 F.Supp.3d 421 (EDNY 2018) (*Cohen II*).

3.    With regards to land, focusing on leasehold covenants in England & Wales in *Creative Foundation v Dreamland* and the broader issue of the recognition of property rights in the context of urban development in *Cohen I* and *Cohen II*.

4.    See e.g. Lucy Finchett-Maddock, 'In Vacuums of Law We Find: Outsider Poiesis in Street Art and Graffiti' forthcoming in *Art Crime Handbook*, eds. Duncan Chappell and Saskia Hufnagel (Palgrave Macmillan) available at https://papers.ssrn.com/sol3/papers.cfm?abstract_id=3066309.

5.    See e.g. Alison Young, 'Criminal Images: The Affective Judgment of Graffiti and Street Art,' *Crime, Media, Culture* 8/3 (2012), 297–314; Mark Halsey and Alison Young, '"Our Desires Are Ungovernable": Writing Graffiti in Urban Space,' *Theoretical Criminology* 10/3, 275–306; Alison Young, 'Negotiated Consent or Zero Tolerance? Responding to Graffiti and Street Art in Melbourne,' *City* 14/1 (2010), 99–114.

6.    Tim Cresswell, *In Place-Out of Place: Geography, Ideology, and Transgression* (Minneapolis: University of Minnesota Press, 1996), chapter 3.

7.    Jeff Ferrell, *Crimes of Style: Urban Graffiti and the Politics of Criminality* (Boston: Northeastern University Press, 1996).

8.    Sabina Andron, 'Selling Streetness as Experience: The Role of Street Art Tours in Branding the Creative City,' *Sociological Review* 66/5 (2018), 1036–57, using Shoreditch, London as a case study of the street art tour 'industry.'

9.    Finchett-Maddock, 'In Vacuums of Law We Find.'

10.    This is not a problem only for creativity such as street art and graffiti, see e.g. *Tate v Fullbrook* [1908] 1 KB 821. (Im)permanence is one of the hurdles to obtaining copyright protection in light if cases such as the much-criticized *Merchandising Corporation of America v Harpbond* [1983] FSR 32, cf. *Metix v Maughan* [1997] FSR 718: Marta Iljadica, *Copyright Beyond Law: Regulating Creativity in the Graffiti Subculture*, (Oxford: Hart, 2016), 100-2, and offering recent discussion of permanence, and contrasting examples, including of street art that is very difficult to remove because it is fixed with glue or cement: Enrico Bonadio, 'Copyright Protection of Street Art and Graffiti under UK Law' *Intellectual Property Quarterly* 2 (2017), 187–220, 190–2.

11.    e.g. Andrea Mubi Brighenti, 'At the wall: Graffiti Writers, Urban Territoriality, and the Public Domain,' *Space and Culture* 13/3 (2010), 315–32; Rafael Schacter, *Ornament and Order: Graffiti, Street Art and the Parergon* (London: Routledge, 2016).

12.    See e.g. on graffiti writing and street art discourses: Cameron McCauliffe and Kurt Iveson, 'Art and Crime (and Other Things Besides...): Conceptualising Graffiti in the City,' *Geography Compass* 53/2 (2011), 128–43.

13.    Alison Young, 'Cities in the City: Street Art, Enchantment, and the Urban Commons,' *Law & Literature* 26/2 (2014), 145–61, 146.

14.    As Finchett-Maddock describes it in the context of the 'art/law dichotomy': 'Individual property has the final say on the legitimacy of the

aesthetic value of street art and graffiti, through its division of our urban environment in terms of ownership, where you can and cannot create.' (Finchett-Maddock, 'In Spaces of Law we Find,' 12).

15.   This in turn raises questions about the operation of orphan works schemes: Bonadio, 'Copyright Protection of Street Art and Graffiti under UK Law,' 196–7. See, by contrast, the position of creators where works are commissioned: Bonadio, 'Copyright Protection of Street Art and Graffiti under UK Law,' 197–8.

16.   Leslie A. Hahner and Scott J. Varda. 'Yarn Bombing and the Aesthetics of Exceptionalism,' *Communication and Critical/Cultural Studies* 11/4 (2014), 301–21.

17.   e.g. conceptualizing the city as commons: Young, 'Cities in the City.'

18.   Iljadica, *Copyright Beyond Law*, chapter 1; Ronald Kramer, *The Rise of Legal Graffiti Writing in New York and Beyond* (Singapore: Palgrave Macmillan, 2016), 128. See also on graffiti writing the discussion in e.g. Kramer, *The Rise of Legal Graffiti*, 39.

19.   Kramer, *The Rise of Legal Graffiti*, 128. This will include for instance seeking permission to paint on walls: Kramer, *The Rise of Legal Graffiti*, 130.

20.   Luke Dickens, 'Pictures on Walls? Producing, Pricing and Collecting the Street Art Screen Print,' *City* 14/1–2 (2010), 63–81.

21.   Examples include disputes with fashion design house Roberto Cavalli and Moschino in the US: *Williams v Cavalli* No. CV 14-06659-AB JEMX, 2015 WL 1247065 (CD Cal 2015).

22.   See generally e.g. Cameron McAuliffe, 'Moral Geographies of the Creative City,' *Journal of Urban Affairs* 34/2 (2012), 189–206.

23.   This is not of course so straightforward given the fame of creators such as Basquiat during the hey days of 1980s New York graffiti.

24.   Iljadica, *Copyright Beyond Law*, chapter 10; Marta Iljadica, 'Painting on Walls: Street Art without Copyright?' in *Creativity without Law: Challenging the Assumptions of Intellectual Property*, eds. Kate Darling and Aaron Perzanowki (New York: New York University Press: 2017).

25.   See generally, Anne Barron, 'Copyright Law and the Claims of Art,' *Intellectual Property Quarterly* 4 (2002), 368–401.

26.   Jim Armitage, 'Corporate Vandalism? Anger as Brands "Steal" Street Art for Ads,' *Evening Standard*, 3 May 2017, accessed 1 July 2019, https://www.standard.co.uk/business/corporate-vandalism-anger-as-brands-steal-street-art-for-ads-a3529681.html.

27.   Armitage, 'Corporate Vandalism?'.

28.   Two-dimensional publicly placed works are outwith the scope of s. 62 Copyright Designs Patents Act 1988.

29.   Andron, 'Selling Streetness as Experience,' 7, drawing on Sarah Keenan's work on space as a relationship.

30.   The judge, Arnold J, is an intellectual property law expert.

31.   Marta Iljadica, 'Street Art Belongs to the Freeholder,' *Journal of*

*Intellectual Property Law & Practice* 11/2 (2015), 90–1.

32.   *Creative Foundation* [1].

33.   In turn, part of the determination of a tenant's property rights, was the distinction between fixtures and chattels.

34.   *Creative Foundation* [41].

35.   A valuation mentioned in the judgment, noting that there was no evidence of its accuracy, was £300,000: *Creative Foundation* [9].

36.   *Creative Foundation* [57].

37.   *Creative Foundation* [60].

38.   *Creative Foundation* [43], emphasis added.

39.   *Creative Foundation* [8].

40.   *Creative Foundation* [2]. Note also that the case was decided by an eminent intellectual property law judge who immediately identified the relevance of intellectual property law aside from real property.

41.   s. 80 Copyright Designs and Patents Act 1988.

42.   *Creative Foundation* [10], emphasis added. That the street art attracted graffiti is not unusual when viewed in the context of a contest or perceived hierarchy between graffiti writers and street artists: Iljadica, *Copyright Beyond Law*, chapter 1.

43.   On local authority removal and its regulation see e.g. Tatiana Flessas and Linda Mulcahy, 'Limiting Law: Art in the Street and Street in the Art,' *Law, Culture and the Humanities* 14/2 (2018), 219–241.

44.   Within public land law rules.

45.   The bolting of Perspex without the permission of the property owner might well constitute criminal damage.

46.   Finchett-Maddock, 'In Vacuums of Law We Find,' 11.

47.   Newspaper reports following the judgment indicated that it would not be; it may or may not still be in storage but the plaintiff has not stated where the work will be displayed: Katie Boyden, 'The Rise and Fall of Folkestone's Banksy and Whether it Will see the Light of Day Again,' *KentLive*, 23 March 2018, accessed 1 July 2019, https://www.kentlive.news/news/kent-news/rise-fall-folkestones-banksy-whether-1363178.

48.   An attempt to set aside the court's judgment in *Cohen II* has already been rejected: *Cohen et al v G&M Realty et al* 2018 WL 2973385 (13 June 2018).

49.   17 USC §106A(a)(3)(b) on the destruction of works. This provision sits alongside the more obvious moral rights: to attribution and integrity (i.e. interference with the work): 17 USC §106A.

50.   Quoting *Carter v. Helmsley-Spear, Inc.*, 861 F.Supp. 303, 315 (SDNY 1994): *Cohen I*, 215.

51.   See Marta Iljadica, 'Graffiti and the Moral Right of Integrity,' Intellectual Property Quarterly 3 (2015): 266–88.

52.   See *Cohen I*, 220; 221.

53.   This is not surprising given the stringent test for the grant of

preliminary injunctions.

54.   Quoting the lead plaintiff: *Cohen I*, 219.

55.   *Cohen I*, 215.

56.   *Cohen I*, 219.

57.   Joseph Heathcot, 'The Bold and the Bland: Art, Redevelopment and the Creative Commons in Post-Industrial New York,' *City* 19/1 (2015), 79–101.

58.   Heathcot, 'The Bold and the Bland,' 81.

59.   On the language of disgust using in relation to graffiti writing, e.g. Alison Young, *Street Art, Public City: Law, Crime and the Urban Imagination* (London: Routledge, 2013), 100–1.

60.   *Cohen I*, 218, emphasis added.

61.   *Cohen I*, 227.

62.   *Cohen II*, 434. The creators ought to have been given the chance to remove the works: USC §113(d)(2) but were not: at 437.

63.   Re use of social media evidence, see e.g. *Cohen II*, 437; what is less clear, in light of existing case law, is whether the court is correct to state that Cohen's careful choosing of works to be displayed (at 438–9) is acceptable evidence of 'recognized stature.' Referring to evidence of individual artists: *Cohen II*, 439.

64.   *Cohen II*, 439.

65.   The defendants' expert was criticized for setting the bar too high for recognized stature: *Cohen II*, 439.

66.   As described in *Carter*, 325; Iljadica, 'Graffiti and the Moral Right of Integrity,' 279–84.

67.   *Cohen II*, 433.

68.   'The Court was impressed with breadth of the artists' works and its social relevance: *Cohen II*, 433.

69.   *Cohen II*, 449–96.

70.   This is why the description of graffiti as a 'crime of style' by Ferrell is so compelling—the nature of the process imbues the aesthetic with criminality. There is an implicit recognition in the 5Pointz that the orderly placement of the work inoculates it against a finding that it is 'nothing more than graffiti'—it is writing but not perhaps seen as pure text with its associations of criminality.

71.   *Cohen II*, 433.

72.   A similar point is also made in *Cohen I* though less forcefully.

73.   *Cohen II*, 432.

74.   *Cohen II*, 433.

75.   *Cohen II*, 433. Empirical evidence indicates that this is a norm regulation the production of graffiti creativity: Iljadica, *Copyright Beyond Law*, chapter 9. The judgment also notes for instance that certain spots—those overlooking the train line—were the most prestigious: *Cohen II*, 434. This is unsurprising in light of graffiti writers' concerns with being 'up.'

76.   *Cohen II*, 433-4.

77.   Iljadica, *Copyright Beyond Law*, chapter 9.

78.    *English v. BFC & R East 11th Street LLC* 97 Civ No. 7446(HB) (SDNY 1997); 1997 WL 746444. The advisory jury in an apparently highly detailed verdict awarded damages in relation to works by 3 of the plaintiffs totalling 49 different works: *Cohen II*, 427–8. The court's findings did not exactly mirror the jury findings and the outcome of the case was to find the defendant liable in respect of 45 individual artistic works: at 428.

79.    In respect of all of the works the jurors considered both recognized stature applicability as well as the right of integrity (whether the work had been modified, mutilated etc.) such as to prejudice their reputation: at 431.

80.    *Cohen II*, 430, emphasis added.

81.    *Cohen II*, 447.

82.    Cathay YN Smith, 'Community Rights to Public Art,' *St John's Law Review* 90/2 (2016), 369–414, 383.

83.    See Brighenti, 'At the Wall.'

84.    Iljadica, *Copyright Beyond Law*, chapter 4. See also Brighenti, 'At the Wall.'

85.    i.e. as a 'right to claim presence in the city': Lefbvre quoted in Eugene J McCann, 'Space, Citizenship, and the Right to the City: A Brief Overview,' *GeoJournal* 58/2 (2002), 77–9.

86.    *Creative Foundation* [10].

87.    Andrea Mubi Brighenti, 'Expressive Measures: An Ecology of the Public Domain' in *Graffiti and Street Art: Reading, Writing and Representing the City*, eds. Konstantinos Avramidis, Myrto Tsilimpounidi (London: Routledge, 2016), 123-4.

88.    Birghenti, 'Expressive Measures,' 132.

# 11

# Regulating the Image of the City: Art, Law, and Power in the Built Environment of Delhi

*Swastee Ranjan*

## Introduction

Aesthetic adjudication of the city's built environment relies upon an interpretation of the material constituents of the city's surface. The city surface is not a totalized representation of the cartographer's map which flattens it to suit the dimensions of the medium. Instead, the city's surface is also the built environment of the city—its buildings, parks, roads, gardens, streets, houses, exhibition complexes, flyovers, street-lights, dustbins, amongst others. The visual aesthetics of the built environment, that is its appearance, is a crucial way in which these experiences are formed and encountered. Law, in its most instrumental sense, plays a pivotal role in determining the aesthetics of the built environment of the city, not only in the more formal processes of demarcating territorial limits, such as those that are found on the cartographer's map (the jurisdictional fragmentation of space), but also through its intervention in setting standards of beauty in the city. The city's aesthetic image or its surface is constantly invoked in law, so as to settle questions of what is deemed beautiful and legal and what is deemed ugly and hence illegal.

In this chapter, I explore the intersection of art, law, and power by mapping this legal intervention on Delhi's urban surface by arguing that law, through its authority over city spaces constantly transforms the built environment of the city. This form of aesthetic transformation guides urban design processes but more significantly accompanies several interventions that are often inscribed on the city's surface. In what follows I discuss two such aesthetic interventions which later became sites of juridical disputes. Through these disputes, the paper draws attention to the nature of aesthetic decision-making in the city which is both materially construed and subjectively determined by the aesthetic repertoire of the city itself. The concept of 'surface' has received considerable scholarly attention in recent years. Giuliana Bruno in her work on surfaces and visual arts understands the surface as a specific form of architecture, as a 'partition' that can be shared, as a site of 'habitation,' and most importantly as a context through which we understand and perceive our responses to our environment.[1] Accordingly, surfaces establish 'reciprocal *contact* between us and objects,' where the *contact* is 'tangible' and is a site through which we are able to communicate.[2] It is for this reason that she prefers to use surfaces instead of images, which allows us to experience 'how the visual manifests itself materially on the surface of things.'[3] Tim Ingold further extends this relationship between the surface and the visual as that which does not only warrant visual perception but also *haptic* perception. A surface welcomes a sensorial experience instead of merely the optic. Visual apprehension of the surface, he argues, suggests that the surface is 'simply the outer envelope of a form' which while helps in determining the status of an object privileges a scopic observation.[4] A haptic visuality renders the surface without limitations. It involves an affective understanding that overflows the object itself. So, while we are at the surface, we are continuously affected by its various complexities and multiple textures. Understanding the city's surface in this way compels us to consider the city not as a smooth site but instead as something that is striated, differentiated, complex, and multivariate. Our visual perception is only one form of apprehending this complexity and often works by locating the visual outside of the surface. Of importance here is the suggestion that the surface is not only a visual medium and instead, it defines and contours the material environment which in turn orchestrates our affective responses.

The following discussion is based on a perception of the material environment of commissioned art projects that often become sites within which aesthetic meaning is construed. This relationship between the material surface and its aesthetics contributes to a multi-textural understanding of the city and its lived spaces. In the following, I discuss two such aesthetic interventions which later became sites of juridical disputes. Through these disputes, the paper draws attention to the nature of aesthetic decision-making in the city which is both materially construed and subjectively determined by the aesthetic repertoire of the city itself.

In what follows, I focus on two legal judgements that show this interpretation of contextual aesthetics. I begin by evaluating a significant copyright case decided by the Delhi High Court, *Amar Nath Sehgal v Union of India* (decided on 2 February 2005).[5] The case concerned a damaged mural that was displayed in the lobby of an important public building, and while the court decided the sanctity of the moral right of the artist, I concentrate on the text of the legal judgement which constitutes the specificity of the mural by delineating the role that the public building plays. This construction of public building(s) as a site through which art is understood is highlighted as a way in which law engages in aesthetic adjudication. In the second instance, in *B.G. Verghese and Ors. v The Union of India and Ors.* (decided by the High Court of Delhi on 17 December 2004), the court discussed a dispute on the height of a national memorial.[6] The discussion of the height was not of aesthetic interest to the court, but as the judgement shows, the height was the precursor for determining the aesthetic landscape.

It is important here to note that in this paper, legal judgements are discussed as a specific site through which the material contours of city aesthetics are deliberated. The relationship of law and aesthetics by way of language, has been a subject of great interest to legal scholars. Although legal judgements can be seen within a similar context, I am interested in reading the legal judgement as it enunciates the material register upon which aesthetics are constructed.[7] My focus is on the ways in which law sheds light on this material register of the city and through its pronouncement, alters the visionscape of the city surface.

## Aesthetic Order and the Visible City

The relationship between aesthetic order and the city is by no means a novel idea, instead it has a long history in different disciplinary contexts. In urban theory, Kevin Lynch's germinal text, *The Image of the City*, discusses the ways in which city dwellers perceive and produce the image of the city. This is done, especially by concentrating on the 'apparent clarity or *legibility* of the cityscape,' by which Lynch means, 'the ease with which its parts can be recognized and can be organized into a coherent pattern.'[8] Lynch's concern is to enable an understanding of the city's image. His motivation in doing so is to help build a city (of the future) that 'not only offers security but also heightens the potential depth and intensity of *human experience*,' alleging that 'although life is far from impossible in the visual chaos of the modern city, the same daily action could take on new meaning if carried out in a more vivid setting.'[9] Potentially then, the city is the powerful symbol of a complex society. If set forth visually well, it can also have strong expressive meaning. He concludes that the imageability of the urban environment rests upon the perceptual clarity of elements in the city; he isolates, 'paths,' 'edges,' 'landmarks,' 'nodes,' and 'regions' as those specific image-orienting elements that are necessary to situate oneself in the city. The 'total orchestration of these units which ... knit together a dense and vivid image, and sustain it over areas of *metropolitan* scale' produces the modern city.[10] He reiterates that a modern city is complex and that these elements provide 'building blocks' for the urban designers to enable a better city—never a city that is complete, a point he concedes early in his book. Lynch's concern spawned a subdiscipline of cognitive mapping that sought 'urban design' as an important configuration in our experience of the city in totality, a realm that is imaginary at its best or is a complex order of these discrete elements. Lynch, however, never sought to go beyond these facile representations since there is no engagement with history (even while discussing landmarks), social culture, state or the law. This omission is glaring given that law plays a crucial role in not only creating the conditions of this physical environment by determining, for instance, its limits (zoning laws, territorial demarcations), but also in determining the constituency of its urban form (through municipal laws, like bye-laws). For Lynch, the 'image of the city' is the image that rests in the minds of its citizens. Yet, this image is orchestrated and determined by a series of legal interventions. As a visible representation, the image is also a series of encounters with an appearance and surface of the city, with its buildings, roads, and landmarks. The law, through its interventions, has sought historically to alter these appearances.

One such work that discusses the interventions between law and the image of the city, is Alison Young's work on street art and graffiti. Young explores the relationship between law and street art through a conceptual framework of 'legislated city.'[11] A legislated city, according to Young is a kind of spatial experience which is rooted in the regulation of time, space, and behaviour. It is a city of 'order and regularity' where 'a cartographic space of readily identifiable thoroughfares and buildings ... (is) governed ... by a grid of ordinances, regulations and statutory and common law.'[12] Moreover, legislative interventions work alongside the 'cartographies of timetabling and often produce an image of the 'city as smooth, compartmentalized, organized around boundaries' and functionality.[13] In this sense, law seeks to control the 'city's perceived unruliness.'[14] Walking on this smooth image of the city then allows for encounters with its material surfaces and objects such as street art. Street art in the city are experienced through an affective *or* 'enchanting' *encounter* with them.[15] Using the work of Jane Bennett, Young argues that the act of watching street art while walking in the city is an 'experience that *halts* the spectator's movement.' Young asserts that street art can be 'conceived of as a tangle in the smooth spaces of the city'—out of which arises the 'potential for enchantment ... a more complex and layered experience' of being in the city.[16] Law's encounter with uncommissioned art work relies upon their erasure as they constitute an 'affront to private property and to the norms of image production in city spaces.'[17] This affrontery persists since law seeks to control the ordering of urban spaces through a system of 'criminalization' and 'licensing' of private property. In her use of affective encounter, Young not only explains the status of such uncommissioned art work in the city but to its material inscription that threatens the image of the city. The affective encounter elicits a city that goes beyond the propertied characteristic inscribed on the object (through various municipal and local laws) and is used to understand the aesthetic materiality of the city's built surface.

In a similar vein to Young, Andreas Philippopoulos-Mihalopoulos uses the term, 'lawscape' to think about the intersections between city, law, and affect.[18] Lawscape is the 'interfolding of law and city in both a material sense and the immaterial sense, the hysteric ubiquity of the law in it has as a result the law's very imperceptibility.'[19] In thinking about the city as a lawscape, we think of urban spatiality as a space that is always co-existing with the law, this co-existence is co-constitutive and as such law cannot be without space and vice-versa. When considered in abstract, both law and space mirror their conceptual configuration. They are almost seen as eliding over the reality of their presence. Law in this description is not dealing with descriptions of space through metaphorical allusions such as territory, jurisdiction, and zone. Instead it is engaged in the materiality of *things* in the city that as inhabitants we encounter.[20] Yet, the success of the lawscape is precisely that we do not always encounter the law. It is the ability of the law to be dissimulated through the material configurations that makes it a worthwhile conceptual framework. For Philippopoulos-Mihalopoulos, this imperceptibility of law, is significant. I take the approach of material configurations of the art because the law in these instances is not aware of art's significance, either as a measure of the artist or the architect or as a measure of the art itself. Instead, in its ability to discard the role that these material configurations play in determining the aesthetic the law visibilizes them precisely as anchors of aesthetic deliberation. The legal judgements in deciding the moorings of these contentious art and architectural projects refer to material things, without recognizing the significance of their role. This chapter is an inquiry situated in visibilizing the role of law in enunciating the materiality of the city via an aesthetic repertoire.

## The Judgements

### On Heights

In *B.G. Verghese v Union of* India, a petition came to the High Court of Delhi in 2004 which complained that the construction of a national memorial dedicated to the service of the Police Force of India was obstructing the view of the *Rashtrapati Bhavan* (the Presidents' residence) by its extended height and was not contiguous with the aesthetic of the contextual landscape. The memorial was placed inside a large public park at the end of a road that serves as one of the main approaches to Delhi's central zone. This area was at the time of this case, under the Lutyens Building Zone (LBZ), a territorial delimitation inscribed in 1988 by the Delhi Urban Arts Commission (DUAC). The DUAC is a statutory authority and was created to 'advise the central government in the matter of preserving, developing and maintaining the aesthetic quality of urban and environmental design within Delhi.'[21] It also authorizes the 'location and orientation of buildings in Delhi' including administering Delhi's building bye-law regulations and setting up design criteria for all built constructions. The LBZ was largely built under colonial influence and houses significant public offices and embassies, including the President's home, Supreme Court of India, the High Court, the Parliament, and several other important public buildings.[22] The significance of the LBZ for this case is precisely because of specific height regulations that apply to this area and which becomes the object of contention for the claimants.

According to the claimants, the defendant, that is, the Government of India represented through the offices of the DUAC, had not complied with the guidelines laid down in the design criteria under the authority of the DUAC. The plaintiffs comprising of the members of the public as well as residents who lived near the unpopular memorial argued that any building of this kind should enhance

6 (23) the quality of the urban fabric — Individual architectural objects collectively become the image of a place and it is necessary to bear in the mind the *image of a place* while designing a structure in a complex

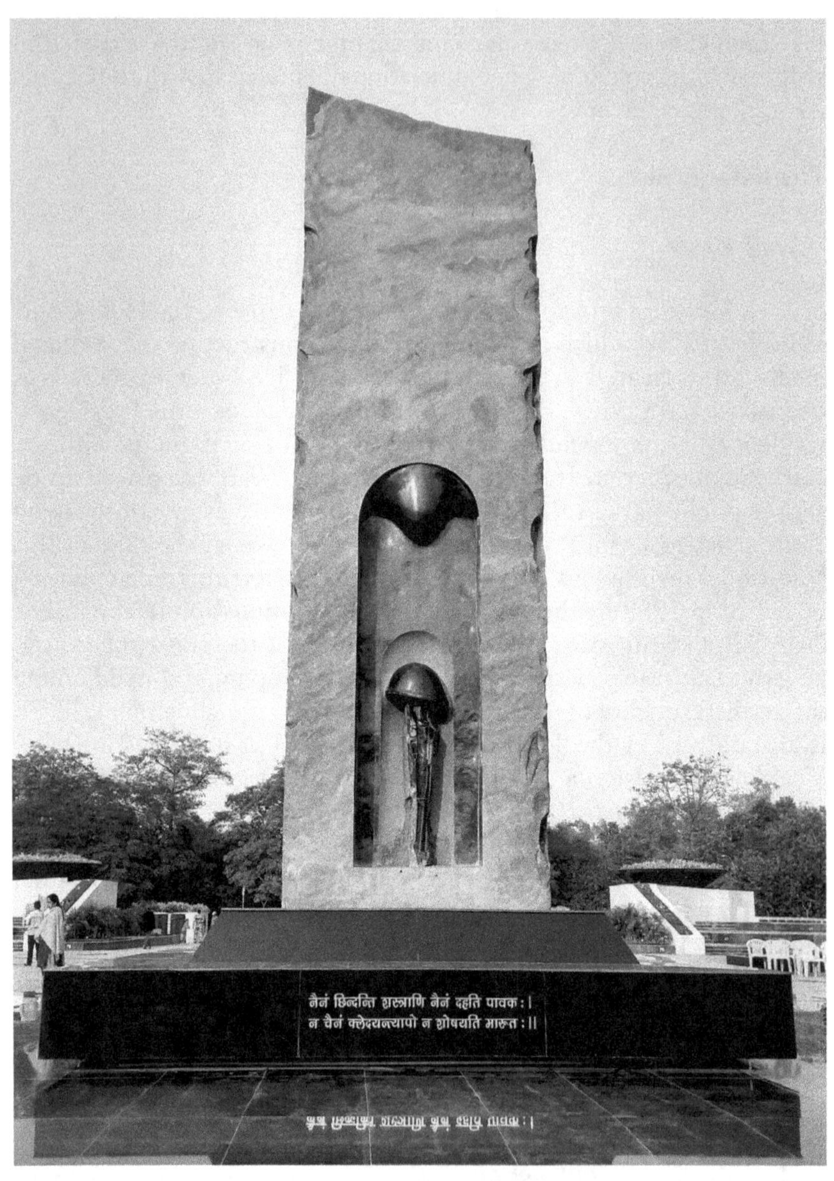


*Fig. 16: National Police Memorial, New Delhi*

urban scenario like Delhi. — The structure should respect the grain of the area and should synchronise with the texture of the surroundings. — *New structure in an urban setting should be viewed as a link with existing connections such as physical (pedestrian and vehicular), visual, architectural and historical connections.* — The new structure should acknowledge historical context of the areas in its proximity.'[23] (emphasis added)

The structure having been designed for the heart of the city was particularly bothersome as, the petitioners themselves submitted, it obstructed the view of the dome of the *Rashtrapati Bhavan* (the President's house). Here, the perception of the height was a hindrance to the aesthetic visual scape of the city. It also reflects upon the petitioners' interpretation of what constituted the 'image of the place.' The plaintiffs further argued that the height of the structure was being increased at the behest of a parliamentarian, who they alleged wanted it to be higher than 'India Gate' rivalling even the Rashtrapati Bhavan's dome.[24]

While the court deliberated upon the land use of the district park in which the national memorial was situated, and which would effectively establish if the memorial was under the LBZ and had to conform to height regulations; the more important thing the court noted was that there were no explicit rules regarding the construction of the national memorial in a district park according to the Master Plan of Delhi.[25] So, the burden of the defendant was then to establish the conceptual process through which the construction of the national memorial was undertaken. Hence, the role of the DUAC becomes pivotal since it commissions the orientation of buildings in Delhi. The court reviewed the series of communications that the commission had undertaken with the authorities on the design and building of the national memorial. The important aspect that emerges in this correspondence was that the limits on building height are also regulated by the department of civil aviation and any height construction above the prescribed thirty metres, had to be authorized by them. The architects and designers, established in court that the civil aviation authorities had authorized this height and hence, there was no plausible reason for it to be dismantled. The court in this review, however, notes that much of the construction of the national memorial was deliberated upon regarding the height of the structure instead of its aesthetic and artistic merit. It berated the DUAC for its incompetence in this regard. The court also dismissed the contest over the height of the national memorial being superior to the President's house as holding no consequence, since the latter had a national pre-eminence that could not be compared.

The outcome of this dispute also went through a series of ups and downs. The court initially (as in the present judgement) upheld the plaintiff's plea and stayed the construction of the national memorial. It later gave permission for horticultural activities as they would 'beautify the area and could not be harmful in any way.'[26] In 2005, the court asked the DUAC to review the height dimensions from the point of view 'of aesthetics, heritage and environment.' In early 2007, a Group of Ministers from the Indian Parliament decided that since the memorial had come under intense scrutiny, it would be better off being dismantled. Thus, the memorial was dismantled. The DUAC commissioned a new National Police Memorial, parts of which were opened in October 2016 at the same place, but far more congruent with the aesthetic landscape of the area.[27] The national memorial (Figure 16) itself was unveiled on 21 October 2018—the day is recognized as National Police Commemoration Day—by the Prime Minister of India.[28] The new memorial uses the foundation structure of the previous memorial but its design does conform to the height regulations.

I have had countless opportunities to see the police memorial before it was dismantled. It was a passing construction and held little academic interest to me, at the time. However, its design—of which we know little from the present case—was of a globe ensconced in pillar-like steel fortification. It was particularly jarring in the aesthetic landscape insofar as it was of exposed steel in midst of verdant gardens and low-lying buildings. It stood out, and while there is a subjective preference to what one might consider beautiful, the structure itself was manifest in the encounter. In this court case, the apparent discussion on height is seen as crucial to the construction of the national memorial. The reason why the height was of deliberate interest was, as is recorded in the case, a matter of the visual aesthetic landscape of the city surface. The residents wanted an unhindered view of the dome of the President's house, which according to them signified the aesthetic landscape. The claimant's argument that they could not 'see' the dome of Rashtrapati Bhavan already constitutes a framework within which an aesthetic engagement with the city surface takes place. Here the height of the memorial is discussed as a hindrance, that which inhibits a clear line of sight to the dome. Even though the present case is not solely about height, it illustrates an affective claim to the visual surface of the city represented in having a direct optic access to the dome of the President's house.

Although argued through the lens of a national memorial, the present case is an exemplary instance of stated preferences of the residential neighbourhood. It may be a sufficient presumption to state that heights are a matter of land use, yet as this case suggests the land use is not of intrinsic debate. Rather it is the construction of buildings, its very material dimension that attracted the attention of its residents. The height here, is a measure through which the *visibility of the object* is made possible. It is precisely this visibility that the court also uses to stake claims at aesthetic adjudication. The height is not a regulatory category alone, it is the determinant of the aesthetic landscape of the area. It is worth underlining here, that the interest of law in this case seems to be a matter of regulating the height. Yet what becomes clearer as the text progresses is that it is also about the affective response to the physical manifestation of the building.

*On Building*

*Amar Nath Sehgal v Union of India* is widely considered as a benchmark case on copyright law in India. Renowned artist, Amar Nath Sehgal had in the early 1960s been commissioned to display a mural at a public building called *Vigyan Bhavan*.[29] In 1979, during the redevelopment of the building, the mural was removed from the display area and stored in the warehouse. During the dismantling, parts of the murals were badly damaged including the artist's signature. The artist complained to the authorities about his objections with regards to their handling of the mural and requested that it be dealt with in an appropriate manner. The government did not return his request, where after Sehgal pursued the case under section 57 of the Indian Copyright Act (1957) which sets out the moral rights of the author. The case was filed in 1992, and ensued a thirteen-year legal battle after which the Delhi High Court in 2005 upheld the moral right of the author. The court relied upon an expansive interpretation of section 57 of the Indian Copyright Act and sought to establish that the author's right of integrity can protect outright destruction under the Indian law. Moreover, the court noted that the government had a duty towards the care of works that it owned.[30] There is little to deny that the upholding of the moral right of the artist is significantly altering for the practice of copyright law, but I want to take a different approach to interpreting the judgement. I want to argue that while reading the judgement, we ascertain how law itself encounters the mural—not through its artistic merit—and how there is less of a discussion on the representation of the art itself but through the *contexts* that make it an 'art.' This textual analysis discloses the rather unsaid corner of the judgement, where the material specificity of the art work is framed within the specific location of the art work. It is this material specificity that illuminates the ways in which courts also interpret national heritage. This analysis does not exclude the moral rights of the artist as divorced from the proceedings but instead argues that the constitution of these moral rights is based in not simply the art work but also in the work of context in which it occurs.

The judgement's opening paragraph sets the relationship of the art work to the building in which it was located. The judge writes:

> India was a nascent democracy. The world was divided into two camps… the first prime minister of this country … realised that to be non-aligned was the best policy…Fledgling India was asserting itself in the community of nations. International delegations were frequenting…large number of delegates had to be accommodated. A building was conceived to be the hub of international and national conferences. It was named *Vigyan Bhavan*.[31]

The judge then quotes the correspondence between the Prime Minister Nehru and his cabinet secretary where Nehru wrote:

> The central government as well as the State Governments are putting up many public buildings. Some of these buildings are big and imposing structures, like the building for the Supreme Court or theatre. … I think all these major buildings should encourage Indian artists to function in some way. Sculptors, painters, designers etc. should be asked to cooperate. There might occasionally be woven tapestries. This will cost very little in comparison with the total cost of the building.[32]

The purpose of introducing this correspondence has been to highlight the vision or the necessity that drives the relationship between buildings and their art works. The judge interprets this correspondence in these words:

> 5. The brick, mortar and concrete structure named 'Vigyan Bhavan' may have been an architectural feat, imbibing the science of construction, but the building was too lifeless. It needed a soul.[33]

I find this explicit excursion of reading the building as a composite of a 'science of construction' and 'having a soul,' a rather important reading of the built materiality. A comment such as this allows us to map the ways in which the judge and the court are mobilized to think of the artwork. Here, the 'soul of the building' is later equated to the commissioned mural. The external reference point to said art is the building itself. The underlying question in this assessment is whether or not the artwork could have existed as art without the building and without the historical significance attributed to it due to its geographical location? It may be a stretch to ask this question for the present judgement, but the script of the legal text also runs in to those interpretations that it doesn't necessarily engage with.

Further in this judgement, the judge notes:

> 7 ... research and untiring work, spanning over half a decade produced a piece of art—a bronze mural sculpture manifesting itself having 140 ft span and 40 ft. sweep on one of the walls' of *Vigyan Bhavan*. The wall was *no ordinary wall as it was the lobby of Vigyan Bhavan i.e the entrance*. The mural was a delicate balance between cultural and material aspects in national perspective and science of rural and modern India being its theme.[34]

From the above description, it may be clear that the mural's constitutive aesthetic is not what it seeks to represent or what it *is*, which can be a cause of debate but the surface of the wall on which it occupied itself. The importance and relevance of walls to an artistic piece here is mobilized to understand and appreciate the art itself, to qualify the art as a piece of cultural heritage. For the court, the intrinsic link between the building and art is collapsed as it deliberates upon the moral right of the author, yet this judgement is equally about the form of the building itself, about its lobby and its wall. Here, the law attributes to the specificity of the art project by suggesting the importance of the material frame of the building itself. In my reading, this attention to the building is of significance since it enshrines within itself the possibility of interpreting the mural's aesthetics. Indeed, in this case, the art and the material framing of art are constitutive of each other.

## Order and the Buildings of Delhi—The Corporeal City and Aesthetics

The most recent ratified building bye-laws of Delhi, known as the 'Unified Building Bye-Laws of Delhi,' incorporated for the first time, a chapter entitled 'Provisions for Public Art.' The chapter itself defines public art, the prescribed cost of such an undertaking, the dimensions of the artwork to be displayed, and the role of local authorities in commissioning such an art project. The annexure to the chapter is far more discursive in its content than the chapter itself. Entitled, 'Guidelines for Integration of Art in Building Projects,' it identifies 'the structure of the building' as an art form. It says:

> while trying to re-establish the relationship of art and built habitat, it has to be recognised that the prime form of man's art is the building itself... the proportion of buildings and their relationship to one another, the scale of public and private open space, the patterns created by openings and apertures, the materials used and their textures and finishes, the landscape and the environment should all be perceived as expression of art.[35]

Building bye-laws are rather prosaic laws determining the material surface of the city by prescribing the guidelines for the construction of buildings in the city. When one reads the building bye-laws, one is confounded by the extent of regulatory protocols that are put in place to enable an experience of the city that emerges from a series of detailed laws on specific components of the built environment.[36] These laws act to ensure the safety of the urban environment but are also composite directions on the *appearance of the city*.[37] Their inclusion in the building bye-laws of Delhi were the first statutory mandate regarding public art in India.

The building bye-laws, as discussed above, foreground the relationship between buildings, art and law rather neatly by smoothening its surface. By inscribing the building itself as an art form, the legislators and policy makers have deduced art as having a concrete material expression. 'What *is* public art?' in this instance has been defined through public buildings, through their material form. Yet, while discussing public art, this materiality, the reality on which it is inscribed receives scant attention.

Elizabeth Grosz, in her work on *Architecture from Outside* points at the intersection of corporeality/materiality, bodies (both real and imaginary) and cities:

> The city can be seen as a body prosthesis or boundary that enframes, protects and houses while at the same time taking its own forms and function from the bodies it constitutes. Simultaneously, cities are loci that produce, regulate and structure bodies. This relation is not one of mutual determination nor a singular, abstract diagram of interaction. ... *The corporeality, or materiality, of the city is of the same order of the complexity of bodies.*[38]

Grosz writes that representation of the city in any form must consider its corporeal dimension. This understanding allows us to reveal the nature of city itself, that which seeks to frame lived experience, however significantly, it is that which also allows lived experience to order the city. If the legal texts, as I have shown above, discusses the material dimensions of art itself, then this is not merely constitutive of aesthetics but also of an inscription that invokes affective responses. This inscription is accessible through an encounter with the material surface. The surface is corporeally determined and is the site at which art *emerges*. The art is not here for its own sake but for what it does to the urban environment.

## The Text Bleeds—Building with Laws

The material surface of the city on which I led this discussion over-spills every imaginable territorial demarcation. The legal judgement enunciates the city through a network of institutional demarcations: the DUAC, the DDA, the *Vigyan Bhavan* amongst others. Yet, all of them only presents the city's material surface in its most fragmentary sense. The material surface of the city is ever flowing, ever receding, ever emerging. The way the law works through these specific judgements frame the material surface is an acknowledgement of power. For law, the necessity in framing art through the material surface is to authorize the art as belonging to that corporeal realm of the city. The legibility of the city's materiality allows the law to demarcate things with order. Here, the building of *Vigyan Bhawan* is inscribed with a law of its own corporeality—the rules of exit and entry, rules of behaviour, rules of time, and more. The law of building is not merely codified in the building bye-law but also emerges in the encounter with the building itself. The commissioning of the mural for that lobby space enshrines the lobby with the power of nationalism, one would have been compelled to have an affective response towards the nation. Similarly, it may be that the object of height preceded the deliberation around the national memorial, yet the national memorial had it been built would have had similar laws, with aspects like one could not walk through it, one could not enter anytime they pleased amongst others.[39] The legal judgements concerned only hint at the elusive nature of corporeality. It is only ever able to visualize the building in relation to it appearance, its façade. Yet, the built environment is more than what the legal judgements suggest, they are more than the frames for art. They are also art in so far as they provoke the law of affective encounter. For Alison Young, this is the site of 'enchanted encounter'—a *haltness* that processes affective response. The intersection of art, law, and power is precisely in this corporeal affective encounter that is often subsumed under the image of the city. The image of the city seeks to frame this encounter without recognizing that perhaps this corporeal affective encounter will always defy any enframing. It is perhaps this defiance that makes legal texts such as the ones discussed above, significant especially as they help trace the differing aesthetic repertoire of the city suggesting that any claims of universal standardization of aesthetic integrity are ultimately incomplete.

*I am extremely grateful to Lucy Finchett-Maddock, Sabrina Gilani, Pratiksha Baxi and Eleftheria Lekakis for their critical feedback, comments and support for this chapter.*

## Notes

1.   Giuliana Bruno, *Surface: Matters of Aesthetics, Materiality and Media* (London: University of Chicago Press, 2014), 3.
2.   Bruno, *Surface*, 3.
3.   Bruno, *Surface*, 3.
4.   Tim Ingold, 'Surface Visions,' *Theory, Culture and Society* 34 (2017), 101.
5.   *Amar Nath Sehgal v Union of India and Ors*; MANU/2005/DE/0216.
6.   *B.G. Verghese v Union of India; MANU/2004/DE/1288.*
7.   For more on the relationship between law and language especially through the legal text, see Peter Goodrich, *Languages of Law: From Logics of Memory to Nomadic Masks* (London: Weidenfield and Nicolson Ltd, 1990); Peter Goodrich and Yifat Hachamovitch, 'Habeas Corpus: A Semiotic Analysis of Common Law Cartographies,' in *Tracing the Semiotic Boundaries of Politics,* ed. Pertti Ahonen (Berlin, New York: Mouton de Gruyter, 1993), 175–202. For Goodrich and Hachamatovich, engaging in a semiotic analysis of law allows us to identify those material structures through which law seeks to structure our everyday life and more importantly ensure that *law* itself continues. This perpetual inheritance of law ensures that law is not only seen as immaterial but also commits to law being from an outsider perspective. While this paper has not presently discussed this, it is important to note that a legal judgment often empowers itself with jurisdictional discretion which allows it to mandate over aesthetic considerations as if it itself is not wholly implicated.
8.   Kevin Lynch, *The Image of the City* (Cambridge, Mass.: MIT Prressm 1960), 2-3.
9.   Lynch, *The Image of the City,* 4.
10.   Lynch, *The Image of the City,* 108.
11.   Young in their work has characterized street art as 'situational art.' This 'situational art' emphasizes the nature of 'placement of artwork' and its integral association to viewing experience in the city; the artist's aim in

creating image over 'commercial or informational concerns'; and finally, the 'illegality of the work either as a result of placement without permission or through assumptions brought by the spectator.' In her book, Young also uses the word 'uncommissioned' to suggest these characteristics. In this paper, I refer to commissioned art projects instead of street art, that which is authorized and legitimized by the state with appropriate permissions. Alison Young, *Street Art, Public City: Law, Crime and Urban Imagination* (London: Routledge, 2014), 8, 42.

12.    Alison Young, *Street Art, Public City,* 42.

13.    Alison Young, *Street Art, Public City,* 42–43.

14.    Alison Young, *Street Art, Public City,* 43.

15.    Alison Young, *Street Art, Public City,* 45.

16.    Alison Young, *Street Art, Public City,* 45.

17.    Alison Young, *Street Art, Public City,* 122–3.

18.    Andreas Philippopoulos-Mihalopoulos, *Spatial Justice: Body, Lawscape, Atmosphere* (London: Routledge, 2014); See also Andreas Philippopoulos-Mihalopoulos, 'Atmospheres of Law: Senses, Affects, Lawscapes,' *Emotion, Space and Society* 7 (2013), 35.

19.    Philippopoulos-Mihalopoulos, 'Atmospheres of Law,' 35.

20.    This paper understands 'materiality' following use of the word by Philippopoulos-Mihalopoulos, who in another context describes it as 'something that is stuck underneath our nails not outside of us ... [and] to deal with materiality is to deal with all these things that theory has been careful to avoid for fear of getting its hands dirty: bodies, space, objects are the stuff that gets under ones nails and is hard to get rid of. Mind, time or history, on the other hand are things that pull one's head above the ground, at a safe distance from being affected by it.' I extend this understanding to the objects that constitutes the lawscape of Delhi. See Andreas Philippopoulos-Mihalopoulos, 'Critical Autopoiesis and the Materiality of Law,' *International Journal for the Semiotics of Law* 27 (2014), 389.

21.    See *B.G Verghese v Union of India*, para 6[23]. For more on the history of DUAC, see, their website at, http://www.duac.org/content_page. aspx?Id=HISTORY&language=ENGLISH. Last Accessed on 22 August, 2019.

22.    For a discussion on Lutyen's Building Zone, refer to M. N. Buch, 'Lutyens' New Delhi—Yesterday, Today and Tomorrow,' *India International Centre Quarterly* 30 (2003), 29; Jane Ridley, 'Edwin Lutyens, New Delhi, and the Architecture of Imperialism' *The Journal of Imperial and Commonwealth History* 26 (1998), 67; Ashok Kumar Jain, 'The Significance of Shahjahanabad and Lutyens' Delhi' *International Journal of Environmental Studies* 73 (2016), 651.

23.    *B.G. Verghese v Union of India (2004)* was a Public Interest Litigation and the court spent considerable time, in establishing the standing of the petitioners engaging with the classical concept of 'person aggrieved' (see paragraph 2). Public Interest Litigation (PILs) are cases where cases affect

the general community as well. They are petitioned through representatives.

24.   War memorial dedicated to Indian soldiers is located on an axial road on whose end is the Rashtrapati Bhavan. This road between the India Gate and the President's House was designed by Edwin Lutyen and is considerable ode to the grandeur of the British Raj. The axial road is referred to as *Rajpath*. India Gate comes under the Lutyens Building Zone.

25.   The Master Plan of Delhi is a statutory law which lays down all development codes which needs to be implemented. Delhi has had four major master plans—1962, 1982, 2001, and 2021. Each of these master plans 'function' as a blueprint, a road map for 'developing' Delhi in a particular socio-economic context which frames with respect to the 'needs' of the people. Laws and regulations around the built environment consist of Building Bye-Laws, Special Area Laws, Nuisance laws, Environment Laws, Commercial and Industrial regulations.

26.   'HC Allows Work on Police Memorial,' *Architexturez*, 12 October 2004, accessed 27 January 2019, https://architexturez.net/pst/az-cf-30499-1097609535 .

27.   Somreet Bhattacharyal, 'Police Memorial Thrown Open to Public,' *Times of India,* 22 October 2016, accessed 27 January 2019, https://timesofindia.indiatimes.com/city/delhi/Police-memorial-thrown-open-to-public/articleshow/54985980.cms.

28.   Bharti Jain, Richi Verma, 'PM Modi to unveil National Police Memorial, museum on October 21,' *Times of India*, 19 October 2018, accessed on 28 January 2019, https://timesofindia.indiatimes.com/city/delhi/police-story-sacrifices-etched-in-stone/articleshow/66279258.cms.

29.   *Amar Nath Sehgal vs Union of India and Ors. Vigyan Bhavan* when translated to English is Science Building. It was built as a convention centre and is a popular place for hosting public events.

30.   MTS Rajan, 'Case note. Moral rights and the protection of cultural heritage: Amar Nath Sehgal v. Union of India' *International Journal of Cultural Property* 10/1 (2001), 79–94.

31.   *Amar Nath Sehgal v Union of India and Ors.*

32.   *Amar Nath Sehgal v Union of India and Ors.*

33.   *Amar Nath Sehgal v Union of India and Ors.*

34.   *Amar Nath Sehgal v Union of India and Ors.*

35.   Delhi Development Authority Gazette Notification, *Unified Building Bye Law for Delhi 2016*, published on 22 March 2016. accessed 31 July 2019. https://dda.org.in/ddaweb/gazette_notification.aspx#, 477.

36.   The origins of the bye laws in Delhi can be traced to the colonial regime whose interest in Delhi's urban environment was not only to secure its control over the territory but to improve the spatial conditions of the subjects. This included improving basic infrastructures of water, sanitation, health, amongst others. After India gained independence in 1947, much of this rationale sustained itself in its myriad institutions especially the local

municipalities and hence bye-laws continued as instruments of furthering these rationalities. In Delhi, the building bye-laws are read alongside the Master Plans of Delhi which are statutory legislations that are committed to developing the city to accommodate its burgeoning needs. So, the most recent master plan of Delhi ratified in 2007 sets as its vision of making Delhi a 'global metropolis' and a 'world class city.' The building bye-laws on the other hand, are an instrument through which the vision is actualized and it is the guidelines prescribed in them that changes the city in its most visceral form, that which influences the way in which we 'encounter' the city's material environment.

37.    At around the same time, the chairperson of the Delhi Urban Arts Commission which is a statutory body that advises the government of India on matters of maintaining the aesthetic quality of urban and environmental design within Delhi, and which also formulates the bye laws wrote an editorial opinion in a prominent newspaper of India lamenting the neglectful role that aesthetic plays in determining the vision of the city. See P. S. N. Rao, 'Prioritising Aesthetics: Cities Need to Be 'Art Smart,' *The Indian Express*, 4 June 2016, accessed 1 July 2019, http://indianexpress.com/article/india/india-news-india/prioritising-aesthetics-cities-need-to-be-art-smart-2833456/.

38.    Elizabeth Grosz, *Architecture from the Outside: Essays on Virtual and Real Space* (Cambridge: MIT Press, 2001), 49.

39.    On my recent visit to the park, the rules of entry were in full force. For instance, the entry gates were manned by police officers, the periphery of the park had CCTV and there was a police post stationed outside.

# 12

# Performative Agoras: The Use and Misuse of Public Space

*Daniel Hignell-Tully*

## Introduction

The agora, as a public space that exists between the functional institutions of the city—its banks, courts and shops—offers an ill-defined horizon dedicated to the autonomous movement between Self and Other that is the basis of *being*.

Such a movement is conducted by way of a concomitant emergence of ethics, a primordial responsibility that exists—if we are to differentiate between Heidegger's *dasein* (presence, or being-*there*)[1] and Levinas' face-to-face encounter (which we might in contrast describe as a being-*with*)[2]—as a prerequisite of community.

The unification of self through a co-constructive interaction with Other is a procedural act unfolding within shared space. It is what Gilbert Simondon, logically extending Levinas' position, described as 'individuation,' the process by which we interrogate, negotiate, and perform our individual and collective lives. It is here, within the referential space of the agora, that the Self may 'attain presence, a being-in-the-world, through signification.'[3] As such, the agora might be considered a horizon in a definitive sense; it is the boundary, the mark at which being, as a noun, is transmuted into a verb. Rather than an appended liminal space between clearly defined states—a line between heaven and earth, night and day—it represents instead a threshold of another kind: a watershed, a death, the point of emergence or first resonance that is 'both the opening and limit that defines an infinite progress.'[4] It is the point at which being 'becomes,' a horizon of infinite potentiality. The agora does not, however, exist in a vacuum, but rather as a functional space within the wider social system, and as such is subject to an imposition of order as determined by those that govern that system. In practical terms, this imposition takes the form of law and, more specifically, legislative frameworks such as Public Spaces Protection Orders (hereinafter PSPOs).

In this chapter, the apparent tension between philosophical considerations of shared space and the reality of the UK government's denotative policies concerning such locations is explored. Drawing upon philosophers and theorists such as Plato, Simondon, and Michel De Certeau, I will seek to analyse the language, implementation, and affect of PSPOs and to argue that their usage fundamentally overlooks the innate character of the agora as a space of performed dysfunction (or perhaps, *transfunction,* since it expresses a beyond, rather than a negative move away from). I will examine the tension inherent in the demand for autonomy and creativity in theoretical narratives (including the government's own rationale for the development and upkeep of public parks), and the implicit reliance on unspecified, normative behaviours within the community as a means of mediating shared space. By engaging with the utility of space in both the arts and social anthropology, I will argue for a greater need for the agora to reflect the full range of a community's membership; a membership for whom the act of sharing space is itself a vital and (co)constructive social drama through which people explore new modes of being, and new roles within their community. I will suggest that it is ultimately the misuse of such spaces and their utility by an explicitly transnormative (read: beyond-normative) Other fundamentally outside their architects' experiences and intents, that allows for the autonomous navigation of difference through which a community can maintain the political resonance required for self-governance.

I begin by discussing the nature of the agora and its roots as a sociopolitical space, exploring how it has developed, and circumvented its function over time. I then examine how the agora serves as a space for individuation, focussing on its inherent dialogic properties and their affordances, and in doing so expanding upon Heidegger and Levinas's contrasting approaches to being. Using the notion of the performative, I suggest that the act of navigating agoric space is itself a means of exploring and extending potentiality, and argue that it is through such a navigation that we actively construct the cityscape—and the Self—through our mutual sharing. Lastly, I discuss how PSPOs are implemented, and how they conceptually and pragmatically both engage with, and circumvent, the inherent nature and social-affordances of the agora.

## Unpicking the Agora

> What'd you say just a minute ago? They had to wait and save their money before they even thought of a decent home. Wait? Wait for what?! Until their children grow up and leave them?... You know how long it takes a workin' man to save five thousand dollars? Just remember this, Mr. Potter, that this rabble you're talking about, they do most of the working and paying and living and dying in this community. Well, is it too much to have them work and pay and live and die in a couple of decent rooms and a bath? Anyway, my father didn't think so. People were human beings to him, but to you, a warped, frustrated old man, they're cattle. Well, in my book he died a much richer man than you'll ever be.[5]

George Bailey's impassioned speech in defence of his father's Building and Loan—a seminal moment in Frank Capra's 'It's a Wonderful Life'—articulates the perpetual state of tension inherent in shared social spaces. Focussing upon building and loans manager George Bailey's ultimately failed attempts to escape his hometown, the film implicitly ties selfhood to the agora; its protagonist's life and well-being is positioned as fundamentally reliant on the very shared space he so longs to escape.

It was arguably the ancient Greeks who first noticed that cities were more than mere congregations of houses, and in doing so constructed an appropriate location for the vivacious nature of humanity. Arguably, the Greek agora was more in line with the ethos of Bailey's adversary, the arch-capitalist Mr. Potter: a space bordered by the revered institutions of the state—the court, the sanctuary, and the temple; and from which political and religious declarations could be issued hierarchically to the masses. In addition, the agora served as the city's permanent market space, and would have been lined by statues of the gods, always present, ever overseeing the city's inhabitants.[6]

If the agora started out as a functional space of trade and governance, it was not long before it took on a new life as a means of not only receiving dictates, but sharing ideas. With the term itself derived from both the Greek for an 'assembly of people,' and a 'place of speaking,'[7] it seems wholly unsurprising that it would become a favoured location for philosophers to engage with the demos. Socrates used this forum to question the people of Athens as to the meaning of life, and it was here that a young poet, Aristocles, was inspired to burn his life's work and reinvent himself as the philosopher we now know as Plato.[8] What Socrates had first identified as a place of dialogue, Plato responded to as a place of self-invention, literally becoming a new man when faced with Socrates' interrogation. Perhaps contrary to its architects' intent, the agora provided a fundamental shift in public engagement with city governance. Not only did it facilitate the sort of dialogue that might imbue a city's inhabitants with political acumen—the opportunity to hear philosophers discuss the very meaning of collective life—but its inclusion in city planning actively redesigned the relationship between Greek governments and their citizens. In Athens, the inclusion of the agora went hand in hand with 'a further descent of the seat of government from the rugged slopes of the Acropolis to the level land at its north foot';[9] what had served, for hundreds of years as a burial ground, became 'the civic centre of the city-state.'[10]

Whether by design or by accident, the agora has come to embody the geo-specific nature of its architecture; it occupies physically and philosophically the spaces between the institutions of the city. Given how fundamental the agora was to Plato's identity, it seems perhaps surprising that he rails against the value of such transitory space. In *Republic*,[11] Plato divides the means of production between the city's occupants, with each member assigned a specific role with little room for divergence. When Plato divides up his city dwellers into their core functions (the farmer, the mason, the weaver and the shoemaker) he does so as a form of moral regulation that mirrors the differentiation found in nature. Only by isolating mankind according to each individual's function can the city-state maintain the justice of specialization. Wherein, 'each individual should always be put to the use for which Nature intended him, one to one work, and then every man would do his own business, and be one and not many; and so the whole city would be one and not many.'[12]

For Plato, the kinds of dialogue which the agora promotes—the same dialogue that leads to his conversion from a poet to a philosopher—risks the corruption of the city-state, an erosion of its natural justice. The city-state, so reliant on the specific non-transferable skills of its inhabitants, should be a space of pure uncontaminated functionality—the farmer who takes up masonry at the weekend spends less time farming, and as such is a less valuable member of his society. And yet, as many of Plato's critics point out, his utopian vision, whilst 'a masterpiece of economy,'[13] ignores the distance between the community's interlocutors that allows a state to be something more than the buildings from which it is built. Plato's pupil, Aristotle, points out that the inhabitants of a state cannot help but infringe upon each other's selfhood, and indeed, that such infringement is integral to the formation of a state:

even supposing that such a community were to meet in one place, but that each man had a house of his own, which was in a manner his state, and that they made alliance with one another, but only against evildoers; still an accurate thinker would not deem this to be a state, if their intercourse with one another was of the same character after as before their union.[14]

For Aristotle the city-state is always a place of change, wherein its inhabitants' characters are informed by their geographic union. In an explicitly functional society such as Plato's, the space between where we sleep and where we work would be filled only with dysfunction, a habitat for the least productive members of the state. Where Plato had extolled the functional equality inherent to clearly articulated participants working towards a common goal, Aristotle pointed out that some activities simply take more time than others, resulting in an inequality where some of society's members are far more able to engage with the dialogic nature of the agora than others. If the agora was originally a space for political discourse—for governments to speak, and even potentially listen, to their people—it is only those who are not currently contributing to the broader functions of the society that will have the means to explore such a dialogue.[15] In contrast to Plato, Aristotle's fear was not dysfunction in and of itself, but the risk that the agora, as a space for political discourse, would facilitate a democracy for the few, wherein democratic involvement was conversely linked to an absence of social function.

## Paths of Individuation

Thankfully, the reality of the city-state is a world away from both Plato's utopian vision and Aristotle's democratic hell. People are inherently dysfunctional, and no degree of economic streamlining can compromise the most enduring quality of human experience—diversity. People rarely if ever define themselves by a single, overriding function, and there are few social roles that do not benefit from a healthy tension between specialization and diversification. Farmers do not always farm, weavers do not always weave, and as such social spaces are filled with the broad spectrum of the city's inhabitants as they embark on the multitude of narratives and roles that make up their individual and collective lives. Social spaces are more than the gaps between functional spaces, they serve as a means by which inhabitants can explore the broader facets of being; a point overlooked by the highbrow musings of Aristotle and Plato, but which served as the basis for Capra's 'It's a Wonderful Life.' George Bailey's Building and Loan, or perhaps more likely, his affordable housing development 'Bailey Park,' stand in for the agora, insofar as they represent spaces between the functions of capitalism, in which people can explore who they are beyond the limits of their professions or respective social standings. Indeed, when Bailey describes his nemesis, Mr. Potter, as being poorer than his father, his meaning is clear. Potter is poor precisely because of his Platonic functionality: he is such a good capitalist than he has no time to be a good human being.

If we are to define the agora as a shared space beyond function, we must therefore acknowledge it as a location in which selfhood emerges, an infinite horizon; a threshold to the beyond-self rather than a demarcated limit, and one upon which we can determine who we are through our reflection in the eyes of the Other. This process, the very interaction by which Plato was born, amounts to what Simondon calls 'collective individuation.'[16] For Simondon, the distinct functions proffered by Plato cannot exist, for the process of individuation is never complete. Indeed, 'birth' is too concrete a term to describe Plato's own transition from poet to philosopher, for what occurs is an ongoing, systemic emergence of being *from* being: 'individuation is not produced by one sole operation, limited in time; the living being is itself partially its own principle of individuation.'[17] Individuation is not simply the means by which 'people' become 'farmers,' or even by which farmers express their individuality by demonstrating a penchant for colourful hats. Rather, it is itself a relation to the world and the collective which originates from neither. Individuation is an emergence from nothing, or more accurately, from nothing concrete; the process of becoming, undertaken collectively, is a sharing that takes place *from* life, and which serves as the basis for the becoming of self.

With this in mind, the agora (expanded from its Greek root to now denote the shared space between the concrete functionaries: houses, factories, courts that make up the city-state) is the place where people act out alternative ways of being beyond the often arbitrary status provided by the exterior forces of class, profession, or lineage. It is precisely because of its dysfunction that the agora allows its inhabitants to play out new roles; to act within this space is rarely done from necessity, but instead as a form of creativity. To act is to play, to construct new planes of potentiality. It is here that living as play, as art-making, feeds directly into the mutability of being. The agora is not a parade, where we publicly share who we are or who we wish to be, but the threshold upon which *being*, which is, after all, a verb, not a noun, unfolds.

The agora is a canvas upon which our actions, lacking the urgency of specific function, can serve to actively enliven what is possible. Social interactions, ways of moving or speaking can be undertaken without fear that they might be unproductive or lack achievement. Indeed, it is the plasticity of the agora as a space of dysfunction that allows its occupants to challenge any existing social or ethical consensus, to disrupt, as the philosopher Jacques Rancière puts it, 'the distribution of the sensible.'[18] In its capacity as a transfunctional space, the agora redefines its occupants as carriers of potential Otherness; artists among artists, collectively reimagining the world.

By this logic, the agora can be considered as stemming directly from Levinas's concept of being. For Levinas (and arguably it is this that differentiates his thought from that of Heidegger), being is a process that emerges from our co-construction with an 'infinite' Other, via face-to-face interactions.[19] It is through the concept of the infinite that we can best contrast these philosophers two approaches. Martin Buber points out that Heidegger's '*mitsein*,' though ostensibly meaning 'being-with,' is characterized more in terms of '*beistand*,' or 'standing next to one.'[20] Heidegger's self is in fact an individual 'on a finite journey culminating in the non-relational event, death'[21], and whilst 'the journey is conducted alongside other *daseins*, such interpersonal relationships are 'secondary to the vertical end/terminus which each one faces alone.'[22]

In contrast Levinas's encounter, which builds upon Buber's position, is always an encounter with the infinite, made concrete in the face of the Other. The alterity of the Other is absolute, rather than existing as any form of hetero-reference within the self, the Other is 'infinitely transcendent, infinitely foreign'[23] and as such 'approachable only ethically.'[24] For Levinas, being-with is not a shared togetherness of individual entities (communion) but a co-constructive movement, an interaction with that which is fundamentally not-self (community). We find in the face of the Other not only an insurmountable foreignness, but, by virtue of the mutual and primordial co-construction that both informs and pre-dates Self, an ontological responsibility.

Levinas promotes the idea that being relies upon a shared responsibility born of our mutual and inter-reliant development in shared space: a first ethics that determines not only how we act, but who we become. Whilst in its initial concept as a space for hierarchical proclamations from a government to its people, or from a merchant to his customer, the agora may have served a discrete function, its power lies in the fact that, as with any shared space, its use-value soon extends beyond that which could ever be conceived hierarchically. It is the being-with of shared space, regardless of any pre-existing role, that affords a city's inhabitants the capacity to autonomously develop their social environment, their specific ethical contract.

For the theorist Michel De Certeau, it is the act of walking, itself the precursor to all of our 'working and paying and living and dying,' between and beyond the imposed order of the city-state that makes it more than simply a collection of buildings. De Certeau acknowledges the presumed functionality of the city, but suggests that:

> If it is true that a spatial order organizes an ensemble of possibilities (e.g. by a place in which one can move) and interdictions (e.g. by a wall that prevents one from going further), then the walker actualises some of those possibilities. In that way, he makes them exist as well as emerge. But he also moves them about and he invents others, since the crossing, drifting away, or improvisation of walking privilege, transform or abandon spatial elements.[25]

The act of walking serves as a literal means of enacting potentiality, the physical manifestation of the Self's ability to explore, extend, and otherwise surpass any prior limitations imposed upon being. To walk is to see things from a new angle, at a new time, a movement that is both constructive and reflective (in so far as it changes our understanding of any prior state). What is more, walking is emergent (in so far as potentiality is formed from the myriad of contrary and overlapping acts of the community as a whole), pointing beyond the Self and towards the inherent dysfunction of the Other. Rather than ontologically-complete actors contributing to a common life via the sum of their distinct functions, De Certeau's walkers face one another in a Levinasian manner; it is the infinite and ineffable nature of an ongoing dialogue with a never-complete Other that allows the self to write its own ethical discourse as a prerequisite of being. In attempting to impose a top-down ethical framework upon the agora, legislative solutions such as PSPOs overlook a fundamental truth. Agoric spaces are already ethical by default, and any imposed code of conduct risks impeding the discourse by which ethics emerge.

## Performative Negotiations

How we interpret the plans laid down at our feet, how we 'improvise' within the cities constraints, is the very basis for how we share space. Indeed, such spaces embody the essential flaw in Plato's prioritization of explicit function—people are unpredictable. However much the farmer strives to follow the paths her lineage has placed before her, however hard she tries to emulate existing modes of practice, of being, she cannot help but deviate from perfect functionality, for she is imperfect. Her biology, physicality, environment, experience, all of the incalculable myriad of elements that bring her into being only serve to point towards a single fact: to express, to individuate is always to emphasis difference. As De Certeau makes clear, 'enunciatory operations are of an unlimited diversity. They therefore cannot be reduced to their graphic trail.'[26]

The outcome of such unlimited diversity, such a prioritization of difference, is that our exposure to Other unfolds as a form of performance. By its very nature collective individuation amounts to theatre, in which the agora serves as the stage. It would be a mistake, however, to consider it merely a space for acting out existing social roles. When De Certeau describes the impossibility of reducing expression to a 'graphic trail,' his suggestion is that it is the acting out of being in shared space that forges the nuance and difference that might later come to constitute selfhood. Again, the allusion to artistic creation is more than simply a metaphor. As with paint upon a canvas, or notes upon a score, the graphic trail produced within shared space amounts to more than a mere sum of its parts, and points to a mode of expression and potentiality beyond the given. It is no accident that terminologies drawn from the vernacular of art are used so often by those who critique social space. As I have previously explored,[27] art-making is fundamental to being. It is by considering sociality as a form of creative ecological engagement replete with many, if not all, of the same qualities inherent in the production of art, that we can best interrogate the specific nature of shared space. What Simondon describes as an acting out, and De Certeau as a graphic trail, for Brandon Labelle amounts to a public negotiation in which shared space 'is a volatile stage where the individual body takes a step, and then another, to ultimately negotiate the movements of others as they shuttle past.'[28] For Labelle, the shared space of the sidewalk represents a point of change enacted by our mutual engagement with the exteriority we uncover there. The performance of becoming is not a performance *to* an Other, but a performance *with* them in the process of individuation. Our movement through the agora is not a deliberative motion towards a fixed goal (even if that goal is the extension of Self). Rather, it is the agora itself that acts as a threshold between the finite and the infinite, where the interior, by necessity a limited and defined space, encounters the exterior, the beyond Self which lies literally outside of comprehension or subsumption. It is in both the perception of dysfunction and the exploration of dysfunction that the community can achieve the sort of equality that Plato so longed for—a fraternity of man born not of a considered communion in pursuit of a common goal, but from the holistic and multi-faceted emergence of Other that is the signifier and symptom of potentiality. The shared public spaces that comprise the agora are, for Labelle as they were for Aristotle, more than simple paths between the institutions they append. It is in these spaces that the city comes to life, for a city is always more than the sum of its parts. It is precisely because the agora affords us the opportunity to stray from the imposed, delineated and monochromic functions of the dominant social or economic system—just as the imagination allows us to stray from the biological functions of the body—that it is so pivotal to the life of the city. The courthouses, job centres, banks and shopping malls might determine what a city has—its capacities and functions—but it is in the shared space of the agora that the rabble, ill-formed and mutable, determine not only what the city is, but what it will become.

## How We Share Space

That the agora harbours some degree of value to its inhabitants is rarely lost upon the governments and councils that oversee modern cities. In the United Kingdom, there has been a renewed interest in the value of city parks in particular, thanks largely to a longstanding investment by the National Lotteries Heritage Fund.[29] Estimated to be used regularly by over 37 million people, and numbering 27,000 in total, the UK's parks contribute a significant portion of the social space available to the public.[30] The stated aims of such investment points to an understanding of the complex issues surrounding diversity. The Heritage Fund has lauded city parks' ability to 'tackle many of today's greatest challenges, from childhood obesity to our changing climate,'[31] whilst simultaneously acknowledging the broad spectrum of participants who engage with such spaces, wherein 'households with children, people living in urban areas and those from black and minority ethnic communities use their parks the most.'[32] It is interesting to note, however, that though a great deal of research has been published detailing the value of parks, and the demographic make-up of those who use them, there is little reference to the *manner* in which people use such spaces. The promotion of 'active parks'—those with a tangible programme for engaging with the health benefits of green spaces, such as the provision of 'green gyms, health walks, pram-active and fitness classes'[33]—are often framed as a means of reducing certain modes of abstract behaviour, bound together under the term 'anti-social.' The over-riding problem with such an analysis of city parks is often that governments seem unable to galvanize the holistic and open-ended nature of the data such research provides. Though those surveyed cite walking, nature, and peace and quiet as the most important attributes offered by parks,[34] the majority of public space initiatives appear to focus on less woolly affordances, such as sports provision or children's playgrounds. As useful as these aspects are in themselves, such a disparity has led to the Parks Alliance stating that 'parks deliver a range of benefits to society, but in our experience, these are not properly understood or acknowledged,'[35] and the government admits that 'traditional accounting methods for assessing the value of parks and open spaces fail in our view to fully capture the impact of access to high-quality green space on physical and mental health.'[36]

Part of the issue is that data collection in general tends to overlook the self-constructive nature of public performance, even as the public themselves articulate that very theme. If governments struggle to appreciate quite what walking, or a desire to be in 'nature,' might entail, it is precisely because these activities are themselves abstract undertakings for which any beneficial outcome is always secondary, even tangential. Walking through the park might well improve your mental health, you may even recognize this as an outcome, but the act of walking within the agora is a performance undertaken in pursuit of the emergence of being, and takes place prior to the formation of Self.[37] Legislation of the agora, as exemplified by the implementation of PSPOs, may well attempt to engage with some of this vagueness, particularly in their focus on localized geo- or community specific regulations. However, it is the autonomous nature of such spaces that makes it so hard for governments to define in advance their use value—they are, as highlighted by the Joseph Roundtree Foundation (JRF), 'a self-organizing public service.'[38] The JRF suggests that social spaces demonstrate the public's aptitude for self-organization, arguing that 'groups may be self-segregating in their use of different public spaces at different times, with social norms affecting how and whether people engage with others.'[39] Here however it is the concept of a 'social norm' that is both deeply problematic, and all too often co-opted by the state in its attempts to govern the agora. Spaces that foster collective individuation, do so because they provide a shared horizon upon which a self can freely interact with an Other; an exteriority that is deeply and inexhaustibly foreign to any existing understanding of the world. It is only through our performed navigation with the Other that the

Self is put in a position of compromise by which *being* can take place. To return to Plato, his transformation from poet to philosopher could not have occurred had he already known the teachings of Socrates; it is only through the difference offered by his teacher's words that Plato was able to reinvent himself. It is the fact that we cannot recognize in advance what might constitute the Other that allows for the reshaping of being, the expansion of our epistemology. In contrast, even the most loosely applied PSPO must presuppose certain conditions concerning both the existing utility of an area and its occupants, not least by determining what normative conditions may look like. As with any imposed system, the result is such that what should be a self-regulating system is artificially organized from above which, in the long term, may compromise (through lack of practice) the system's ability to self-regulate at all.

If the Other, as per Levinas's definition, is unknowable, this unknowability invalidates the notion of a social norm as a definitive or ultimate goal of the community. To experience the Other is to experience something fundamentally outside of our existing ontology, and the desire for shared spaces to reflect some kind of normalized identity may result in the perception of difference as a threat to our selfhood. As much as the agora provides the means by which we can explore difference, being faced with a social group whose actions we cannot understand, or which do not meet our pre-emptive social norms, risks promoting tribalism over an engagement with the Other. By way of an example the JRF reminds us that though 'public spaces are a particular and distinct resource for young people looking to socialize with others… young people are sometimes perceived as having antisocial intentions, which in many cases is simply not true.'[40] Indeed, if the nature of the agora is that it provides a space between the more functional aspects of the city it intersects, and if it is precisely because of this inherent lack of defining purpose that being, and thus community, can emerge, then terms such as 'social norms' or 'anti-social' are redundant. Any pre-emptive, hierarchically imposed rules of behaviour are liable to result in a stratified community, 'in which some groups are routinely privileged over others,'[41] for the simple reason that within a truly self-governing agora, social norms are always in flux. The promotion of fixed norms directly opposes the affordances that the agora should offer, and as such, 'the government's emphasis on crime and safety in public spaces is depriving them of their historic role as a place where differences of lifestyles and behaviour are tolerated and co-exist. What is considered 'anti-social behaviour' may vary from street to street, from one public situation to the next, or from one person to the next.'[42]

## Public Spaces Protection Orders

On face value, the creation of PSPOs exists as a response to the issues of Otherness and self-governance inherent to the agora. Introduced as part of the Anti-social Behaviour, Crime and Policing Act 2014, the orders serve as a means to prevent anti-social behaviour in a location-specific fashion, seemingly acknowledging that the nature of such behaviour might differ from place to place. Deliberately vague in their implementation, the orders allow communities to define their own criteria for socially normative behaviour, so long as they meet two main conditions—that the activity to which the order relates has a 'detrimental effect on the quality of life of those in the locality,'[43] and that the effect of the activity concerned 'is, or is likely to be, such as to make the activities unreasonable.'[44] The power that this bestows upon a local authority is not inconsiderate: orders last for 3 years but can be renewed indefinitely, new prohibitions can be added to an existing order, and the area they cover can be expanded once they have been introduced.[45] As with the Anti-Social Behaviour Orders (ASBOs) that predated them, the implementation of PSPOs has not been without criticism. On the one hand such broad and sweeping powers provide local people with the autonomy to decide for themselves when and where specific activities should be prohibited; on the other, groups such as Liberty consider the orders to be 'too widely drawn, with vague definitions of what can be criminalised, and carry disproportionately punitive sanctions.'[46]

Such vague definitions, however much localized autonomy they may promote in theory, in practice risk serving as a means of discrimination against any group that does not meet an abstract set of standards. If the law is too flexible the potentiality exists that it can be bent to deter certain types of people from participating within the wider social dynamic. This tension is addressed by the inclusion of a set of guidelines that local authorities are obliged to follow, and which underscore the desire for localizing autonomy rather than promoting discrimination. The orders are thus described as 'council-led, and rather than targeting specific individuals or properties ... provides for restrictions to be placed on behaviour that apply to everyone in that locality,'[47] and are presented as one of a range of possible tools used to mediate social space. Options such as 'awareness-raising campaigns about the impact of certain activities on others, improved community engagement, or offering support to those exhibiting certain behaviours'[48] are preferred over the blanket implementation of legislation, with a view, ostensibly, to providing local communities with the broad range of tools and approaches required for meaningful self-governance.

A question might arise, however, as to what the provision of such an order (even on the assumption it is implemented in line with its guidance) means for the fundamental nature of the agora as a space of dysfunction. If, from a philosophical perspective, the agora is the horizon upon which we can explore and enact being, and if this is achieved through the sort of negotiation and confrontation discussed so far, PSPOs compromise confrontation as a matter of course. As a device intended to mediate, in a quite literal sense, shared space, such orders are by default hierarchical, and serve to intervene in any dialogue that might emerge from their locations. PSPOs are fundamentally intermediary, disrupting (in the hope of reducing) conflict and as such frustrating the communicative cycle that exists between Self and Other, the very process of collective individuation. The agora, as a 'place of speaking,' relies on dialogue, and whilst it might be argued that legislating socially normative behaviour prevents any one voice dominating its peers, such a position fails to appreciate the emergent nature of normalcy. To fully comprehend this, we might return to the analogy of walking. Despite the inherent diversity of the human body, walking becomes socially normative when it is repeated, by multiple people, in broadly the same way. Walking achieves its definition—that is, its status as walking, not running, or dancing—when the community co-constructs traits relating to speed, angle, hand-position, and so forth. This behaviour emerges over time from the multitude of ways of being found in the collective dysfunction of the agora. The dialogic nature of the space, its location between and beyond its participants' existing social roles, means that 'normative' is simply the current abstracted state of the ongoing process of self and collective individuation. As was so succinctly demonstrated by the artist Richard Long's work, 'A Line Made By Walking'[49]—comprised of a simple line of trampled grass born of the artist's repeated movements across a field—entrenched norms are simply the outcome of repeated behaviours, the composite result of the act of being, the act of forging new paths through shared space. To prioritize the abstracted results of our collective negotiations over those negotiations themselves is to stultify them, and in doing so to actively delegitimize any future negotiation. To a certain degree this happens anyway; social norms already dominate the potentiality of space, enacting the very issues PSPOs seek to mitigate. The process of collective individuation, whilst born of dysfunction (the exploration of the space beyond any explicit social function), unfolds in a somewhat contradictory fashion, since it harbours a specific function in regard to the community as a whole. To enact new modes of being is to explore difference, to prioritize alternative behaviours that exist in conflict to, and as such unwork (a term coined by Jean-Luc Nancy to describe the required process of self-deconstruction inherent to the community)[50] the existing social norms that govern collective behaviour. In a very real sense, such an unworking acts as an autonomous ground level mediation of social space in a far more cohesive fashion that even the most optimistic interpretation of the PSPOs' guidance. Indeed, all of the criteria that apply to the issuing of such orders can equally be applied to the cyclical construction and subsequent unworking of social norms. They are 'carried out in a public space,' are 'persistent or continuing in nature' and, crucially, as a form of conflict, have 'a detrimental effect on the quality of life of those in the locality.'[51] Whereas an autonomous unworking relies upon the specific and temporally-bound state of the community in that moment, PSPOs must define in advance the contours of the community to which they relate. This leads to a situation where there is a potential disjunction between guidance, intent, and enforcement; between the law, the spirit of the law, and the perception of the law. In Brighton, by way of example, a complex situation has arisen wherein the local council enforces PSPOs in direct contradiction to their own legal framework; by targeting specific at-risk social groups, namely the homeless. Whilst their rationale for this falls outside of, and even directly contradicts, the general guidance concerning PSPOs' implementation, it nonetheless falls within the wider social expectation of the law as articulated in local right-wing newspapers. For some, the council's actions are perceived as legal because they chime with their world view and are undertaken by the council (who are themselves considered synonymous with the law). The outcome of this sums up the fundamental issue with such legislation. Rather than articulating autonomously-defined norms (for better or worse), in practice PSPOs prioritize certain positions regardless of whether or not they have legal or social legitimacy.

Put simply, legislated normative behaviours are anti-social, since they intervene and reduce the performed conflict *that is the nature of sociality*. By stultifying the process of being, social norms restrict the productive dysfunction by which individuals can explore being, and reduce the wealth of exposure to the Other by which we might expand our limited ontology. To prioritize stultification over becoming, reason over difference, is to create a shared space that denies the very fabric of collective individuation. Just as Capra's Mr. Potter sought to denigrate the 'rabble' in 'It's a Wonderful Life,' to confine them to an abstract condition of 'rabbleness,' the application of order to the agora risks abstracting and cementing the very worst aspects of social normalization—it normalizes a fear of difference, fundamentally undermining the performance of individuation that is at the heart of our collective identities.

## Conclusion

> Every explicit attempt to fix social relationships or social symbols is by implication a recognition that they are mutable. Yet at the same time such an attempt directly struggles against mutability, attempts to fix the moving thing ... representing it as stable or immutable or at least controllable to this end, at least for a time. Rituals, rigid procedures, regular formalities, symbolic repetitions of all kinds, as well as explicit laws, principles, rules, symbols, and categories are cultural representations of fixed social reality ... whether these processes of regularization are sustained by tradition or legitimated by revolutionary edict and force, they act to provide daily regenerated frames, social constructions of reality, within which the attempt is made to fix social life, to keep it from slipping into the sea of indeterminacy.[52]

The extent to which PSPOs—or any other ritual, formality, rule, or explicit law for that matter—succeed in normalizing behaviours, or protecting citizens from undesired, even dangerous interactions, is not the subject of this chapter. Rather, the concern is the subsidiary effect of such impositions, and the degree to which they compromise the integrity and value of the agora. To truly perceive such an effect, I have argued that we need to consider the agora as, first and foremost, a space of collective performance. To individuate, to explore who you are, is to act out new roles upon a shared horizon, and to explore ways of being beyond those attached to social function—being a farmer, a parent, a pauper or a king—to which you are in some way already wed. Furthermore, I have argued that the application of enforced order upon the agora is counter-productive and unnecessary, since any attempt to police shared space inherently imposes restrictions upon the act of sharing and compromises its ability to self-regulate. Although, as I have explored, the agora may well have been designed as a hierarchical space for governments to dictate to their people, to consider the agora in such a way is to overlook its defining characteristic: dysfunction.

To dictate what kinds of behaviour are acceptable in such spaces—to impose and reify social norms—is to undermine the agora by turning it from a location of becoming and emergence into a location of abstract function. Rather than allowing a community to explore the dysfunction of what it *might* be, the agora comes to demonstrate what *it is*. We recognize in our social norms the limits of being as stated by the community prior to our arrival. As Aristotle suggested, the city-state is more than a collection of buildings, and it is in the agora that we find, reflected in the faces of the Other, the act of being that brings the city to life. The desire to force that life to reflect our existing prejudices, our long-standing bias as to the value of certain types of difference, risks undermining the very interactions on which the city-state relies.

Ironically, it is arguably in the failure of PSPOs that we see the most compelling defence of the dysfunction of the agora they purport to mediate. According to Liberty, Orders have been introduced that outlaw 'swearing,' 'amplification,' 'gathering in groups of 2 or more,' 'rough sleeping,' 'aggressive begging' and even doing 'anything annoying.'[53] Not only are many of these actions hard to define, and even harder to police, but as has been exemplified in Brighton, they also disregard the government's own guidance regarding the provision of such orders.[54] The vagueness of the legislation, however, allows local authorities to override such guidance in all but name.[55] Such inconsistencies in the implementation of PSPOs point to the fundamental argument that underscores this paper, namely the practical impossibility of placing such orders upon the agora. It is precisely because the agora allows for such 'unlimited diversity,'[56] that local authorities are able to circumvent the spirit of the law. The PSPO project fails, regardless of their continued usage, not because they are being implemented incorrectly by local authorities, but because the ability to implement them incorrectly is itself a defence of the very life of the agora that such orders seek to dispel. As a space of dysfunction, the agora relies on the autonomous navigation between self and Other in the performance of being. The attempt to impose restrictions on this activity is itself a form of navigation, a movement that invalidates any social benefit inherent to mediating shared space. Indeed, the desire to eradicate anti-social behaviour by mediating social interaction is ironic for its lack of efficaciousness: reducing the diversity of performed drama by which we engage with Other is a distinctly anti-social endeavour.

## Notes

1.   Martin Heidegger, John Macquarrie, and Edward Robinson, *Being And Time* (Malden: Blackwell, 2013).

2.   Emmanuel Levinas and Phillippe Nemo, *Ethics and infinity* (Pittsburgh: Duquesne University Press, 2011).

3.   Gilbert Simondon, in David Scott, *Gilbert Simondon's Psychic and Collective Individuation* (Edinburgh: Edinburgh University Press, 2014) 150.

4.   'Jacques Derrida,' Stanford Encyclopedia of Philosophy, 16 April 2018, accessed 15 December 2018, https://plato.stanford.edu/entries/derrida.

5.   Frank Capra, *It's A Wonderful Life* (Hollywood: Paramount, 1946).

6.   Homer Thompson, 'The Agora at Athens and the Greek Market Place,' *Journal of the Society of Architectural Historians* 13/4 (1954), 9–14.

7.   'Agora,' Online Etymology Dictionary, accessed 07 June 2018, https://www.etymonline.com/word/agora.

8.   Joshua J Mark, 'Agora,' *Ancient History Encyclopaedia*, 02 September 2012, accessed 10 June 2018, https://www.ancient.eu/agora.

9.   Thompson, 'The Agora at Athens.'

10.   Thompson, 'The Agora at Athens.'

11.   Plato, *Republic* (Hertfordshire: Wordsworth Editions, 1997).

12.   Ernest Barker, *Greek Political Theory* (London: Methuen, 1947) 166.

13.   Jacques Rancière, 'The Order of the City,' *Critical Inquiry* 30/2 (2004), 267.

14.   Aristotle, *Politics*, Great Books of the Western World, book 3, vol. 9 (Chicago: Encyclopaedia Britannica, 1952) 478.

15.   Rancière, 'The Order of the City.'

16.   Scott, *Gilbert Simondon's*.

17.   Gilbert Simondon, in Scott, *Gilbert Simondon's*, 33.

18.   Jacques Rancière, *The Politics of Aesthetics* (London: Continuum, 2000).

19.   Emmanuel Levinas and Phillippe Nemo, *Ethics and infinity* (Pittsburgh: Duquesne University Press, 2011).

20.   David Novak, 'Buber's Critique of Heidegger,' *Modern Judaism* 5/2 (1985), 125–40.

21.   Novak, 'Buber's Critique of Heidegger.'

22.   Novak, 'Buber's Critique of Heidegger.'

23.   Anselm Kyongsuk, Toward a Dialectic of Totality and Infinity: Reflections on Emmanuel Levinas,' *The Journal of Religion* 78/4 (1998), 571–92.

24.   Kyongsuk, 'Toward a Dialectic,' 571–92.

25.   Michel De Certeau, *The Practice of Everyday Life* (London: University of California Press, 1988), 98.

26.   De Certeau, *The Practice of Everyday Life*, 99.

27.   Daniel Hignell-Tully, *Scoring other: The Social-function of Art-making*

(PhD thesis, University of Sussex, 2017, http://sro.sussex.ac.uk/id/eprint/68361).

28.   Brandon Labelle, *Acoustic Territories* (New York: Continuum, 2010), 87.

29.   *Written evidence submitted by Heritage Lottery Fund*, 2016, accessed 10 December 2018. http://data.parliament.uk/writtenevidence/committeeevidence.svc/evidencedocument/communities-and-local-government-committee/public-parks/written/39448.html.

30.   Written evidence submitted by Heritage Lottery Fund (2016).

31.   *State of UK Public Parks* (London: Heritage Lottery Fund, 2016), 1.

32.   *State of UK Public Parks* (2016), 2.

33.   *State of UK Public Parks* (2016), 23.

34.   'Public Parks, Seventh Report of Session 2016–17' (House of Commons, 2017), 12.

35.   The Parks Alliance, in 'Public Parks, Seventh Report of Session 2016–17' (House of Commons, 2017), 20.

36.   'Public Parks, Seventh Report of Session 2016-17' (House of Commons, 2017), 21.

37.   Since individuation is an ongoing process, there is no concrete position from which we take up the defined mantle of 'a walker.' To 'walk' describes only a physical process, implicating fully neither the 'walker' (who is always something more than a device 'for' walking) nor the complex navigation of conceptual, geographic, and social space that the act necessitates. To walk is not simply to re-present a fixed identity or way of being (such as declaring 'I am a walker,' or pointing to a desire or requirement for walking), but to explore being as a performance of selfhood beyond the confines of the singular body—its outcome is explicitly tied to the specific and relational process undertaken at that time, in that place.

38.   Melissa Mean and Charlie Tims, in Ken Worpole and Katharine Knox, *The Social Value of Public Spaces* (York: Joseph Roundtree Foundation, 2007), 2.

39.   Worpole and Knox, *The Social Value of Public Spaces*, 2.

40.   Worpole and Knox, *The Social Value of Public Spaces*, 2.

41.   Worpole and Knox, *The Social Value of Public Spaces*, 2.

42.   Worpole and Knox, *The Social Value of Public Spaces*, 2.

43.   Anti-social Behaviour, Crime and Policing Act 2014, chapter 2 (2014), 59, accessed 01 May 2018, http://www.legislation.gov.uk/ukpga/2014/12/part/4/chapter/2/enacted.

44.   Crime and Policing Act (2014).

45.   Anti-social Behaviour, Crime and Policing Act 2014, chapter 2 (2014), 59, accessed 01 May 2018, http://www.legislation.gov.uk/ukpga/2014/12/part/4/chapter/2/enacted.

46.   Campaigning Against Public Space Protection Orders (2018), accessed 05 June 2018, https://www.libertyhumanrights.org.uk/campaigning/public-space-protection-orders-0.

47.    Public Space Protection Orders: Guidance for Councils, (Local Government Association, 2018), 2.

48.    Guidance for Councils (2018), 5.

49.    Richard Long, A Line Made by Walking (1967), accessed 01 May 2018, http://www.richardlong.org/Sculptures/2011sculptures/linewalking.html.

50.    Jean-Luc Nancy, The Inoperative Community (Minneapolis: University of Minnesota Press, 1991).

51.    Anti-social Behaviour, Crime and Policing Act 2014, chapter 2 (2014), 59, accessed 01 May 2018, http://www.legislation.gov.uk/ukpga/2014/12/part/4/chapter/2/enacted.

52.    Sally Moore, in Victor Turner, *The Anthropology of Performance*, (New York: PAJ Publications, 1987), 78.

53.    David Mulcany, *PSPO Watch: Hometown Zeros (2016)*, accessed on 05 June 2018, https://www.libertyhumanrights.org.uk/news/blog/pspo-watch-hometown-zeros.

54.    In the case of 'rough sleeping,' for instance, the guidance has been updated to explicitly state that 'PSPOs should not be used to target people based solely on the fact that someone is homeless or rough sleeping, as this in itself is unlikely to mean that such behaviour is having an unreasonably detrimental effect on the community's quality of life,' *Public Space Protection Orders: Guidance for Councils* (2018), 7.

55.    Brighton Council, for instance, have prohibited 'maintaining a fire,' 'urinating,' and 'occupying any vehicle, caravan, tent or other structure,' and in doing so publicly stated their intent is to target 'ethnically defined Gypsies and Travellers,' a social group that is legally defined as homeless. *Public Space Protection Orders (2018)*, accessed on accessed on 11 May 2018, https://www.brighton-hove.gov.uk/content/leisure-and-libraries/parks-and-green-spaces/public-space-protection-orders.

56.    De Certeau, *The Practice of Everyday Life*, 99.

# 13

# Twitter as a Space of Resistance to Brexit: Stories of Belonging and the Concept of Affective Citizenship in #1DayWithoutUs

*Photini Vrikki*

## Understanding Affective Citizenship through #1DayWithoutUs Narratives

As digital tools and platforms mediate more and more of our everyday lives, few would disagree with the idea that we live in a progressively digital age. Our communication, our information, and other forms of digital technology are increasingly governing the contemporary forms of our lives and our affective spheres.[1] Some have followed through to argue that the rising role of digital media indicates a shift from a world of top-down power structures into bottom-up structures that are more horizontal and democratic.[2] Yet, social media platforms are harbingers of certain volatility systems, of an uncertainty that affects not only the ways in which we connect to each other, but also the ways in which we tell stories of political participation and of our common lives. It is thus important to understand how digital technologies grant us access to politics as they unravel in front of us instantaneously; each tweet, post, hashtag, is now perceived as an attempt to belong, or alternatively, as an attempt to be an active citizen who can voice their concerns and support to the causes they worry about or believe in.

This chapter argues that the dismantling of the power systems—and more specifically, the legal systems of citizenship in the UK—may not be as underway as formerly suggested but that social media, and specifically Twitter, may be stretching the notion of a rigid legal citizenship through 'stories of belonging,' as explored here through the case of the #1DayWithoutUs movement, a resistance movement after the British vote to leave the European Union in June 2016 (Brexit). Here, I look more specifically at the affective space that was created on Twitter through #1DayWithoutUs narratives and how they can be considered as a process through which stories tell what is *good*, what is *important*, and what is *meaningful* to a changing United Kingdom. Through this approach, the chapter aims to explore the ties between citizenship and affect, as well as the relationship of fluid collective identities on Twitter. It precisely addresses questions regarding a legal system and understanding of citizenship in relation to affective citizenship as manifesting on social media.

Protests against Brexit have been prevalent in 2017 and 2018 and appeared on social media platforms under popular hashtags, e.g. #1DayWithoutUs, #MarchForScience, #MarchForEurope that have demanded the recognition of all the people who voted to remain in the EU and the acknowledgement of migrants' contributions to the country. Such protests should not be perceived as just a reaction to the referendum's result, but more so as a solidarity politics that has attempted to reshape notions of belonging in the twenty-first century and thus question the requirements of citizenship and political participation as it is defined by the power structures that govern us. The instantaneity of disinformation flows on social media also invites us to look at 'more systematic disruptions of authoritative information flows' that tend to normalize the collapse of the public sphere into a constant questioning of the traditional flows of information and of belonging, such as our media structures and state structures.[3] Yet we need to consider the importance of structures of citizenship and their potential to develop into a more fluid and diverse framework that can be applied more inclusively and further than electoral politics.

The sections that follow offer a different perspective into a *sense of belonging*, and suggest that it is an amalgam between citizenship, social media, and affect. This chapter contextualizes and explores its case study, the resistance movement of #1daywithoutus through the three frames above. The first section discusses the ways in which the state uses affect to impose itself on its polity, and make specific references to the ways in which the British state has used affect throughout the years leading to Brexit. Following that, a section discusses how affect can also have impact on and activate the agency of citizens, granting them with an identity that can be fluid, ephemeral, and multifaceted. The third part of the chapter deals with the notion of affect and networked communities, suggesting that social media create a space for affective and effective participation in contemporary political events. The fourth section grapples with fluid collective identity and suggest that combined with affect and the storytelling processes of social media, this identity is what might be producing an affective citizenship that is more ambiguous but also open for a post-Brexit UK. The final sections analyse #1daywithoutus narratives in terms of how post-referendum resistance movements in the UK discuss what it means to be a (affective) citizen of a changing Britain.

## The Affective British State

In legal terms, British law covers concerns related to the UK's nationality and citizenship cases. UK citizenship is divided into six classes with each one of them covering a different category of citizens. Two of the British nationality categories are considered 'active' citizenships that can be gained at birth, by naturalization or by registration if the person covers all the eligibility criteria, while the rest four categories—British overseas citizen, British subject, British national (overseas), British protected person—have certain limitations to their citizenship status. Questions about the right to remain in the country and the cultural or social implications of 'a good citizen' even though not covered by law in the UK have been part of the public discourse for decades.[4] This debate entered even more mainstream discussions as soon as the referendum was announced in 2015 by then Prime Minister (PM), David Cameron, who in his campaign for re-election committed to hold an in-out referendum on UK membership of the EU through the Conservative Party's manifesto. Since then, and after a near 51.9% of the voter-turnout voting in favour of leaving the EU in the referendum in June 2016, citizenship has become a core issue for the country.

In October 2016, the new PM Theresa May in her talk to the Conservative Party muddled the waters even more regarding post-Brexit citizenship. More specifically, during her talk she said: 'if you believe you're a citizen of the world, you're a citizen of nowhere. You don't understand what the very word "citizenship" means.' May was suddenly proclaiming that citizenship was something confined and limited, aligned with British localism, enveloping herself and her party in an affective anti-immigration rhetoric that was tediously used by the Leave campaign in the weeks leading to the referendum. This statement resonated poorly with a large group of people who reside in the UK. These were people who felt rooted in their communities, who felt a sense of solidarity with the society and the culture they created together with migrants who lived in the country, either they held UK citizenship or not. Twitter flooded with reactive comments, while *The Independent* published an article on the 'Prime Minister's attack on global elite as ' "citizens of nowhere' condemned as "quite evil"—"It could've been taken out of *Mein Kampf*",[5] and *The Guardian* called her speech a 'rejection of Enlightenment values.'[6]

It is, however, worth noting that Theresa May was not the only PM making such affective remarks and distinctions between *home citizens* and *outsiders*. Fifteen years earlier, then PM Tony Blair suggested that his Labour government ought to devote effort to relieving the public's worries about the country's Muslim population. He said, 'The vast bulk of the British people are not racist. It is in their nature to be moderate. But they expect government to respond to their worries. They can accept migration that is controlled and selective. They accept and welcome migrants who play by the rules.'[7] What those rules were—or still are—is still ambiguous, but what became clear was that not all migrants were welcome and that for one to be British one should reject what did not resemble the British national identity, culture, and values.

The use of such affective rhetorics in political leaders' speeches has been commonplace since Aristotle's time.[8] Conveying feelings of fear, vulnerability, and disbelief has been a weapon that has allowed the state to remain in charge and governments to hold power even if in some cases, such as here, meant that they attack certain communities. Fear against the Other and of the unknown, has been a political strategy that has gained even more traction in contemporary politics through mass communication tools.[9] In the case of Brexit, migration was one of the big issues. As Leave campaigners had argued, by allowing too many migrants to enter the UK, the country's cultural and social fabric was altered. This fear of the migrant Other that discourses of the Leave campaign mobilized unveiled how political forces use affect to influence the polity.

Scholars looking into the ways in which affect is utilized by the state suggest that 'it is the lack of residence that allows fear to slide across signs, and between bodies.'[10] Inasmuch, the power of affective state politics relies on the fear of specific bodies defined as the 'outsiders' of a community. In the case of Brexit, those bodies were migrants residing in the UK. As Fortier puts it, 'the prescription of sentiment—of feelings for the nation, for the community, for the neighbour, for the Muslim, for the suicide bomber, for minorities—is also what race and ethnicity are about.'[11] In this context of affective identification, citizenship becomes something broader than can be defined in a legal framework. It becomes a word that incorporates what it means to be a diverse community, which comes in direct conflict with what PM May and Blair insinuated or argued in their speeches. Both PMs' arguments are indeed evidence that the definition of *citizenship* can be revisited and adjusted so as to fit specific political purposes. As Lister has argued in her work on feminist perspectives into citizenship, its interpretations are so diffused that the notion 'runs the danger of meaning what people choose it to mean.'[12] All these make clear that affect is often employed by the state to rule and exclude while in the meantime changing the meanings of *belonging*.

## The Affective Citizen

In 2007, in his notable work *Cultural Citizenship*, Toby Miller suggested that 'We are in a crisis of belonging.'[13] While his argument focused on television consumption, his concerns about *belonging* are relevant concerning social media use by citizens today. A crisis of *belonging* can be identified in the presence or absence of a legal UK citizenship: if you are not a citizen under the law, you do not *belong*. Yet, how can then the gap of *belonging*, which was animated by the EU referendum, be filled when even more ambiguity enters everyday life as its impacts become all the more real? I suggest that the answer lies in the concept of affective citizenship and in embracing this ambiguity as a characteristic that makes the concept of citizenship more inclusive, evading the rigid structures of the state. In Fortier's words:

> The 'affective subject' becomes the 'affective citizen' when its membership to the 'community' is contingent on personal feelings and acts that extend beyond the individual self as well as beyond the 'private' realm of family and kin, but which are also directed towards the community'[14]

Affective citizenship then, does not only exist outside the legal boundaries of the state, but also outside the boundaries of a confined identity, definitions of community, strongholds of specific identities such as gender, and nationality. Thrift defines this attribute of affective citizenship as *a maelstorm*.[15]

This brings to mind the notion of a *dutiful citizen* proposed by Bennett in 2008. Bennett suggests that we are currently experiencing a shift from the habits of a *dutiful citizen*, who felt obliged to take part in government-centred endeavours and considered voting as their moral obligation for sustaining democratic governments, to an *actualizing citizen* type, where voting loses its significance to habits such as volunteering, consumerism, and activism. The actualizing citizen type does not usually identify with a political party and does not trust mainstream media, leaning instead towards networked and digital technologies.[16]

Similarly, in the British context, the idea of *fractured citizenship* has been present since the Second World War. Three registers of British citizenship are suggested: first, legal frameworks that construct it politically, inclusive of social rights and responsibilities of citizens.[17] Secondly, British citizenship is the sense of *belonging* to a structured community on the ground, with the only difference to the first kind being not having a citizen status. Finally, it is a *differentiated* citizenship, owned by those who are labelled as the *good citizens*, because they engage in voluntary work and other participatory civic actions. It is particularly these ideas of *belonging* and affective citizens who try to circumvent constrains of rigid citizenship and instead identify with the community they feel they belong to through the digital platform of Twitter that this chapter grapples with.

There is an expanding body of literature that agrees on the concept of a crisis in civic engagement because of the deterioration of traditional participation roles and of an increasing detachment of youth from traditional governance systems such as voting.[18] However, this does not necessarily mean the death of democracy or of social structures. As Dalton has extensively discussed, 'citizen norms are shifting from a pattern of duty-based citizenship to engaged citizenship,' under which political activity is preserved, albeit in new forms.[19] He attributes these changes in citizen norms on the rise of an educated, politically skilled polity who explore and experiment with 'more direct means of influencing policy makers.'[20] This form of *engaged citizenship* grows forms of political action that are more direct and participatory such as 'contacting, working with collective groups, boycotts or contentious actions.'[21] Under this new umbrella, citizens are engaged in civic duties that extend further than, but do not dismiss, electoral politics. Similarly, Zerilli argues for political communities that share common feelings that essentially broaden legal authority notions, like legal citizenship.[22] Going back to the main argument of this chapter then, regarding the importance of affective citizenship not all the communities that reside the UK conform to the rigid notions of *national citizenship*. Citizenship is only a part of what makes someone feel like they are part of the country.

**Affect and Networked Communities**

In a different context, that of the lesbian public cultures, Ann Cvetkovich (2003) sets out a link between citizenship and affect by arguing that 'it is important to incorporate affective life into our conceptions of citizenship and to recognize that these affective forms of citizenship may fall outside the institutional practices that we customarily associate with the concept of a citizen.'[23] Scholarship published in the last decade has certainly given much attention to the ways in which affect influences politics; indicating a growing influence of 'affect publics' as a concept which impacts both the vernacular and political realm.[24] Indeed, as previously discussed, debates regarding the role and influence of affect in politics have been growing evermore in the era of digital omnipresence.

Yet, even though affect's impact on the public and private realms has been tantamount, discussions surrounding politics have tended to form their arguments based on reason.[25] By making *rationality* the only line of analyzing civic life, political analysis has remained trapped in conventional and stereotypical notions of the means people organize and participate. Papacharissi has specifically stressed the predicament of 'philosophy, political theory, and common sense' to 'view emotion and reason as two opposite forces that must somehow be reconciled so that people can function as informed citizens.'[26] Likewise, Habermas has emphasized the importance of rationality for democratic politics, romanticizing archaic systems of public participation, believing that a public sphere that depends on media that invoke and depend on emotions would lead to a crumbling democracy and public manipulation.[27] Habermas stressed the importance of civic systems that would be able to withstand and prevent unsubstantiated claims made by authoritarian systems that have traditionally relied upon affective mastery and emotional control.[28] Certainly, Habermas' concerns are valid in an era where emotional manipulation and misinformation governs a large section of public rhetorics and discourses. However, a static sphere in which reason alone controls the public sphere cannot be entirely participatory and engaging. In the same vein:

> Participation is fundamentally a social act, based in human communication, and contingent on sociality. All too often analyses ignore the importance of sociality in stimulating and maintaining participation, how interactions with others actually serve to support (or not) participatory activities.[29]

I argue that, in addition to public life, the sociality and interactions that Dahlgren describes above can also be found in digital and social networks such as Twitter. I support this through Ross's point that affect is 'contagious' in local, national, and international levels since it sources from emotions that are part and parcel of intimate interactions between citizens.[30] This *contagion* spreads even more through platforms such as Twitter, which are defined by their spreadability.[31] More importantly, and as Papacharissi argues, 'networked technologies enable affective processes that reflexively drive or nullify publics,' creating spaces for people with different views to find like-minded people.[32] Twitter is a platform that allows users to easily contribute to a collective informational space and, regardless of its ephemeral and instantaneous qualities, it may be opening a connecting space for people to find like-minded others.[33] Hence, it can promote networks of *affective flows* that are created, negotiated, and modified. We cannot hence talk of affect as separate from the technology it is linked to.[34] We should instead talk about affect as part of the flow of technologies and the 'one-time system' of networked communication that gives the world and events around us meaning.[35] Affect here gains a political character that presents social media users as emotional individuals, who can also be part of a collective and rational community.[36]

Following Anne-Marie Fortier and Sarah Ahmed, this chapter does not attempt to point to the differences between affect and emotions or rationality, but instead on how affect can be part of the UK's political culture post-Brexit.[37] I discuss affect as a 'non-conscious experience of intensity,' which allows feelings to be *felt* and therefore be interpreted into emotion.[38] According to Deleuze and Guattari, affect and emotion are not entirely the same elements and this is evident through their argument that any action is foreshadowed by affect.[39] They make clear the distinction between personal emotions and affection as co- and interdependent, instead of distinctive. For them, affect is negotiated in an aggregate of space-time chunks 'some events ... are regular and ordinary, whereas others ... singular, marking turning points in a system's history.'

As Papacharissi suggests, 'emotion is subsumed within affect, and perhaps the most intense part of affect,' but it goes further than just giving meaning to experience, as feelings do.[40] Affect not only helps us make sense of the everyday, it also encompasses 'regimes of expressivity' linked to 'resonant wordings and diffusions of feelings/passions' while at the same time it communicates emotions.[41] In this context, technologies that are steered by affect can promote networks of 'affective flows' that are created, negotiated, and modified through communication and networks of 'the affective economy, of consumerism, branding ... and more generally, culture.'[42]

Affects' fluidity and flexibility can be used both for and against state and power structures. Here, I argue that the key to sustaining these communities is through feelings of belonging and solidarity, however ephemeral or fading those may be. These networked communities become themselves 'a record or trace' of what they are at the same time on online platforms. Commenting and reacting on social media, individual users grow 'feelings of community' which may either lead to an on-the-ground community and/or to an online community.[43]

In this chapter, Twitter is explored as an affective space for storytelling post-Brexit referendum. Turning to Berlant's theory of intimate publics, and to the role that sentimental narratives have in forming collective action in 'intimate publics' may elucidate the extent to which these narratives have in preserving the voices of those involved in these actions.[44] Therefore, the focus will be on (re)telling the affective stories of the public, rather than identifying the coordinates of the affect, in an attempt to reveal affective citizenship narratives that have been forming after the referendum. What is at question here is the process, the *what* and the *why* certain stories are told and shared, not the *how* the movements came to be. Focusing on the intimate storytelling processes of #1DayWithoutUs makes the affective coordinates of the community more clear.

This approach commences with a broad and extensive report of tweets and the narratives they formed for the *One Day Without Us* action. Working with empirical data from social media offers the chance to present a powerful account of alternative linearities to the traditional single closed sequences of narrative logic; one that unveils the multiplicity of narrative paths on Twitter and the stories of this action that were open and formed through diverse narratives.[45] The narrative analysis of tweets unveils the dynamics of the stories told and reveals the dominant narratives of these actions' stories on Twitter. By analyzing the affective dimensions of the referendum on the political and identity narratives of UK citizens and migrants, this chapter aims to stimulate new discussions about social media's role in contemporary social movements, and how they can provide a springboard for a fluid *citizenship* and *engagement*.

## Building a Fluid Collective Identity for Affective Citizenship

In investigating how affect is used to create these narratives online, I underline how affect might be both the fuel and the vehicle of resistance and of collective action against Brexit. For Melucci, collective action is the result of purposes (purposive orientation), resources (constructed by means of social relationships within a system), and limits (opportunities and constrains) and it should not be defined within the constrains of values and beliefs; it should consider the interactive and negotiating relationship of the actors within the ecosystem and their own definition in connection to it.[46] In this *collective action*, actors construct a 'we' through the sense, the possibilities, the limits, and the environment in which the action takes place. Hitherto, what Melucci suggests that the process of 'constructing' an action system is what *defines* a collective identity.[47] Collective identity as a process includes a network of active relationships between the actors who interact, communicate, influence each other, negotiate and make decisions. Therefore, emotional investment to the moment and its causes is compulsory in defining 'collective identity' since it allows individuals to feel part of a group. 'Identification processes shift to human action, to culture and communication, to social relations and technological systems,' and for that the process of collective identity is constructed in multiple steps and levels.[48] Based on this, collective identity can both be loose and multifaceted and allow for individual difference; it does not need to be coherent, rigid, and homogeneous. As I argue, a fluid collective identity allows affective citizenship to arise.

Movements such as post-referendum actions in the UK depend on their definitions being multiple, diverse, and all-embracing and can exist regardless the existence of a definitive strong collective identity, which can instead be replaced by a collective identity in constant process. By looking at collective identity as a process, we can trace how it can both be fragmented but held up by its elements of common purpose, aims, and will for social change.[49] Following Tajfel's oft-quoted definition of identity as 'that part of an individual's self-concept which derives from his knowledge of his membership in a social group (or groups) together with the value and emotional significance attached to that membership,'[50] I propose a conceptual move from the conventional notions of collective identity to a new notion that depends on also sharing that knowledge and values online; not one that evades the characteristics of collective identity, but one that combines them with fluid identity notions present in social media networks. The logic of these two collective actions advance models of information sharing that allow individuals to position themselves as present in the movement, while at the same time, avoiding the distinct entanglements that form a collective identity and a clear *we*.

Indeed, there is no single agreed definition of collective identity in social movement studies, but there are a number of academics whose work has tried to discuss collective identity in explicit terms. In Snow's words, the essence of collective identity

> resides in a shared sense of 'one-ness' or 'we-ness' anchored in real or imagined shared attributes and experiences among those who comprise the collectivity and in relation or contrast to one more actual or imagined sets of others. Embedded within the shared sense of we is a corresponding sense of collective agency. ... Thus, it can be argued that collective identity is constituted by a shared and interactive sense of 'we-ness' and collective agency.[51]

Similarly, McDonald's approach proposes that collective identity is subjective and we should avoid leaning on the collective identity paradigm by focusing on collective action as 'the public expression of the self.'[52] By focusing on the individual's perception of collective identity, he urges researchers to 'explore what may be an emerging paradigm of contemporary social movement, one constructed in terms of fluidarity rather than solidarity, and in terms of the 'public experience of self' rather than collective identity.' However, I would argue that we should first look into the processes (leading to the product), and then discuss it as the result of those processes if necessary. What the case of #1daywithoutus and the post-Brexit referendum backlash more broadly has indicated is that we cannot look at collective identity in contemporary social movements as an entirely stand-alone product, but only as a process. This process is contingent on the affective paths discussed earlier and the fluidity of social media platforms. Emotions and shared sentiments between anti-Brexit supporters form identity processes that depend and are formed through homophilic trends and have to do with the ideology of the movement, its values, or its aims. Following Melucci, collective identity for these movements can be seen as a network of flowing affective relationships and their emotional engagement to the movement.[53]

### Unpacking #1DayWithoutUs on Twitter

The purpose of the analysis of the Twitter data forming #1DayWithoutUs story is not to offer a holistic analysis of the events as they appeared on Twitter, but to examine the affective patterns in which certain kinds of stories show up on Twitter. The aim is to look into the narratives that shaped 1DayWithoutUs on Twitter to understand what they represent and what they suggest regarding contemporary citizenship in a post-Brexit Britain.

I use Narrative Thematic Analysis (NTA) to unveil the narratives of these two actions. This is a combination of qualitative and quantitative approaches that relies heavily on narrative analysis.[54] The process begins from a bottom-up perspective that starts from reading and coding tweets into narratives, then moves on to grouping those stories into micro-narratives, and finally creates narratives by combining sets of narratives that complement each other. While in early versions of NTA the process would start with interviews in order to narrow down the thematic approaches of the social media data, in the case of this dataset (#1daywithoutus) the size was more manageable and thus the process begun by reading and coding the tweets into themes/stories directly. This 'thematic' method allowed for a creation of meaning making that was built from the data by comparing and contrasting the tweets to each other and allowing micro-narratives to be formed through the classification of tweets into themes. As the analysis below shows, there are seven micro-narratives building the bigger narrative of 1DayWithoutUs: *1)* mainstream media and politicians (MSMs and politicians); *2)* NHS and universities (NHS & Universities); *3)* Showing solidarity; *4)* Definitions of a migrant (Who's a migrant?); *5)* EU referendum; *6)* Content dissemination (photos, videos, quoted tweets); *7)* Aggressors.

The focus is on the analysis of 35820 tweets posted under the #1DayWithoutUs hashtag, collected between 28 November 8:43 pm and 22 October 2017 11:17 am through Twitter's Streaming API. With an eye to unveil the micro-narratives of this action as it appeared on Twitter, originally posted tweets posted under the hashtag are the focus of the analysis. Therefore, the dataset was limited to tweets sent out from a single user and excluded retweets and quoted tweets. This allowed for a focus on the qualitative analysis of the tweets instead of their quantitative aspects. After this process, the dataset was shrunk to 5282 tweets. This number represents all the tweets that were read and coded, and excludes tweets that were identified as tweets posted by bots (n=580).

Here, I choose not to include or reveal tweets, and instead to paraphrase them or talk about them discursively. This has a twofold purpose. First, it safeguards the identities of the users who tweeted under the hashtag and may have no familiarity with the ways in which Twitter data are used for research, hence becoming the subject of research project without being aware of it. Second, it follows the ethical parameters of allowing these users the benefit of the doubt, meaning that they may have changed their minds regarding the opinions they tweeted about a year or so ago. Indeed, as researchers, our role is to protect the subjects of our research while producing rigorous research.

In this context, and following the aforementioned parameters, I believe to have cultivated a safe space in which both the researcher and the researched are benefitted equally, either in terms of data quality or participant safety.

## #1DayWithoutUs: A Resistance Narrative Against Brexit

Twitter's use during #1DayWithoutUs first year (there was a second action in 2018) has brought to light other means of communication for protest movements in the UK: the kind of protest movements in which written online communication becomes vital to the movement. In this section, I argue that some of the dimensions of #1DayWithoutUs identity can be examined by analyzing the resistance narratives that constructed it on Twitter, especially with regards to the personal and collective stories of users. I first discuss the kinds of stories, the micro-narratives, told on Twitter under the hashtag. Then, I examine the dynamics between the micro-narratives formed, highlighting the several forms of *belonging* they unveil, and finally conclude that #1DayWithoutUs's identity is formed through the combination of several micro-narratives that together form a collective way of thinking about citizenship in a post-Brexit UK.

The seven micro-narratives that formed #1DayWithoutUs on Twitter were different in sizes and may have had different affective influence on the action (Figure 1). Starting from the 41% of the tweets that were used in order to disseminate content (e.g. photos of people taking part in action, videos of supporters expressing solidarity, quoted tweets that usually offered support to the protesters), it becomes clear that Twitter was largely used to transmit information from the on-the-ground to the online and vice-versa. Photos, videos, and other information added to others' tweets, allowed for a visual extension to the textual stories tweeted under #1DayWithoutUs. The big percentage of the stories under this micro-narrative also illustrates how visual content and the representative nature of seeing others' favourites, placards and group gatherings online has become important for protest movements: sharing photos, videos, and commenting on others tweets places you in an environment in which even if you are participating online, you still feel part of the action.

Similarly, the 28% of stories express solidarity, illustrating that the collective feeling of 'togetherness' can be traced on Twitter. These stories expressed an affective sense of belonging and support, while a lot of them relied on the 'every person deserves to be safe, happy, healthy and equal' slogan. A lot more were suggesting that the UK was and still is a country 'for everyone,' that welcomes refugees and migrants, and in which 'diversity is our strength.' Others just plainly expressed their solidarity to #1DayWithoutUs through encouragement and emotionally charged messages, such as suggesting that they were hurt by the government's actions. Others argued that the day was a day to 'celebrate the contributions of migrants,' either those were cultural benefits, such as the foods, cultures, and languages introduced to the country, or financial benefits, such as the businesses run by migrants or how many of the migrants in the UK hold minimum wage jobs that sustain big businesses. Yet, one of the most important solidarity themes were the tweets using #notabargainchip, which described how EU migrants should not be the negotiations' trick between the UK government and the EU. Most of them suggested that a migrant is 'not a "bargaining chip," but a human being,' conveying feelings of unity. Lastly, some of the solidarity stories expressed their appreciation to the cause and their pride towards the existence of the movement itself and of the migrants' bravery to go into action.

In sum and before moving into the analysis of the rest of the five micro-narratives, I would argue that this engagement of individuals tweeting in solidarity, and expressing thus affective meanings of identity, illustrates the construction of a new kind of citizen. Twitter demonstrates here that the physical does not form *the community* in the traditional sense of a community anymore, but the community is also empowered and enhanced through the number of users who set themselves as part of the discussion on such platforms. Adding to the discussion on Twitter, automatically made twitterers part of a community that had affect at its core. Most of these tweets can therefore be described as representing a collective action that is affective, characterized by its fluidity and by its trait of bringing personal stories and the experiences of the movement's members together in such ways that they created common narratives.

Another 10% of tweets mentioned their solidarity by emphasizing the importance of migrants in the NHS and the universities of the country. Suggesting that one of 'academia's strengths is its cultural diversity' some users pointed towards the importance of migration for higher education institutions while some universities specifically celebrated #1DayWithoutUs by posting their personnel's diverse profiles on Twitter. Similarly, other stories told of how important migrant nurses and doctors are to the NHS, and how these migrants are the backbone of the national health system in the UK. In these stories, I also found stories from healthcare professionals themselves, who proclaimed their belief in the UK and its health system, but were worried about their jobs and the NHS after the EU referendum. Brexit was mainly what concerned 5% of the tweets, with lots of them passionately in support of the EU nationals' rights, defining free movement, and calling for solidarity between the Leave and Remain voters. This solidarity called for a unity between the two poles in order to overcome the difficulties that would arise during the Brexit process and the understanding of the reasons the referendum happened all along, such as economic anxiety and the widening gap between rich and poor. Even though these kinds of tweets were very limited, they are important to note, since they show that there is still some presence of the 'dutiful citizen'; the one who still has faith in the electoral system.

These stories were also complimented through the 7% of the stories that debated, questioned, or stated the definition of 'migrants.' A number of the users under the hashtag, told stories about how their parents or grandparents were migrants and how themselves could be considered as migrants of second and third generation. They described themselves, detailing what their regular routine looked like on that day and how their mundane everyday lives were nothing different to other migrants in the UK. Others described how as migrants living in the UK for decades or for a few years felt like home; what they do for a living in the UK; and shared their stories of migration and belonging. The proliferation of this particular discursive notion of who is a migrant and what it means to be one created what can be defined an affective area of identification, in which people shared their common stories and common lives, regardless of their country of origin.

It is important to remember that the technologies, networks, and media #1DayWithoutUs engaged its members and supporters in, were a lifeline for the construction of community feelings between activists and their supporters. This affect dimension implemented a social awareness in and through which the sense of who they are in response to the state was socially bestowed and socially sustained both on the streets and online. Second, in order to support the idea that #1DayWithoutUs was a movement that had affect at its core. This affect—apart from social, cultural, and technological dimensions—also relied on Twitter as a device that could, and still can, cultivate a collective sense of belonging and meaning.

Finally, the 6% of tweets under the #1DayWithoutUs hashtag were stories against the movement and in their majority in favour of the UK leaving the EU. These users called the action 'nonsense,' 'undignified,' and 'bullying attempt by the globalists' who wanted to intervene in the UK's politics and sovereignty. In these stories, racism, nationalism, and notions of colonialism were prevalent. Despite the gloom of these stories, it is important to include them as part of the movement's narrative. They come to represent those voices that did not fit with the rest of the stories but, however, had a presence in the narrative of the story and were influenced by the rhetoric and discourses of the campaign to leave the European Union. Just as Twitter was used as a tool for social justice and advancing the movement's messages, it was also used by aggressors who did not share the same views.

The social movement narratives I have discussed here are deployed for a number of seemingly contradictory purposes. I do not maintain that Twitter's use for social movements is positive or can only benefit the movement and its politics, because that is not the case. Of course, Twitter could be a platform for social movement communication, but we cannot disregard that communities that challenge social, cultural, and political norms through social media are subjected to unsolicited aggression, threats, and abuse from users that use the same platforms. In this environment, the rapport of #1DayWithoutUs' effectiveness was firmly debated and took up two purposes. First, it integrated diverse experiences, instead of surrendering to the restricting and restricted patterns of *collective identity*. Instead of enclosing #1DayWithoutUs into the conventional norms of collective identity, the stories of its supporters on Twitter, were unveiled as telling affective stories that imagined a community, one which did not entirely depend on a homogeneous collective identity, such as citizenship but was instead linked to stories of different identifications, announcements, definitions, etc.[55] Second, the telling of these stories cultivated loosely connected, heterogeneous, and shared stories that formed a different kind of affective citizenship. Social media storytelling does important identity work here, since it escapes from being dictated by dominant narratives of collective identity meanings and moves into incorporating affect as an essential part of belonging which are usually set up top-down in the UK. Examining the stories users tweeted about and the kinds of stories they told, this chapter unveils the importance of contemporary culture that emanated from the experiences and affective stories of this resistance movement.

## Towards an Affective Citizenship

To make sense of the 1DayWithoutUs narratives and trace this social movement's affective role, Twitter becomes the affective space where 'collective action is a 'form' which by its very existence, the way it structures itself, delivers its message.'[56] The concept of identity deployed here is not essentialist or traditional, but contextual. That is to say, the adopted concept of analyzing 1DayWithoutUs's affective dimensions does not advocate for a single idea of a citizenship or group that is unveiled from within specific dimensions. As Polletta and Jasper argue, collective identity is 'an individual's cognitive, moral, and emotional connection with a broader community, category, practice, or institution.'[57] It is a perception of a shared status or relation, which may be imagined rather than experienced directly, and it is distinct from personal identities, although it may form part of a personal identity. In this affective citizenship framework, the identity of who *belongs* here is not consolidated but is progressively aligned to feelings of solidarity, identification, and shared experiences. *Belonging* here counts on the processes of transformation and of different identities that coexist in the UK and comes to contradict what current and former Prime Ministers have defined as national identity.

Twitter's storytelling process, as social interaction, creates an affective environment for users who tweet under #1DayWithoutUs. Through identifying and *co-creating* the story of the movement on Twitter, the users construct a *We* that is assembled through affect and a sense of solidarity: told and retold, *my story about migration* becomes *our story about migration*. These expanding identity narratives are the ground on which the idea of a fluid affective citizenship can be based. Individual tweets tell what kind of feelings the individual holds, their aspirations and motives. If Twitter enables and encapsulates a new form of *citizenship* that is more affective, one must understand this is not a closure of traditional civic identities, a final realization or dialectical move from social structure to anarchy. Within this new narrative space where political, social, and cultural dissemination becomes feasible, and the actual level of sharing practices is culturally driven and cross-culturally manifold, tools such as Twitter form a space that affords communities and citizens new possibilities of expansion, change, and development. As this chapter has discussed, affective micro-narratives and storytelling are essential dimensions of #1DayWithoutUs and its activities to express, connect, broadcast, and mobilize the members of the public towards a more affective citizenship. Examining both the opportunities and vulnerabilities of affective storytelling on Twitter, I argue that #1DayWithoutUs can be best seen as influencing the problematic balance between clarity and frailty, empowerment and uncertainty, that the Brexit negotiations have been enveloped in.

This chapter has illustrated that the sharing of the affective stories that constructed the narratives of the movement became an activity that sustained, nourished, and deepened the relationships between Twitter supporters and those on the ground.[58] I have argued that the importance of Twitter in the construction of #1DayWithoutUs's identity narrative is not entirely technological. Twitter cannot and should not be defined as a sole technological device or as a precise collection of signifiers attached to one platform; instead it is described as a new space of communication flows that allows the world and events such as #1DayWithoutUs to use it to tell their resistance stories; creating a sense of 'togetherness and collectivity.'[59] #1DayWithoutUs rose on Twitter as a collection of stories that explicitly demonstrate that 'technology is gradually becoming a second nature, a territory both external and internalized, and an object of desire' which we do not 'need to make transparent any longer, simply because it is not felt to be in contradiction to the "authenticity" of the experience.'[60] Twitter to some extent, produces and reproduces, stores away and conveys a national identity whose grammar develops in the stable but also fluid space of social media where it is transferred and transmitted as a new form of affective citizenship; one that departs from the rigid notions of legal citizenship.

Through narrative analysis, tweets as a new kind of everyday, interactive stories have disclosed new concepts for narrative functions and architectures for a citizenship that might work for those who hold a citizen status and for those who 'legally' do not but 'affectively' do belong in the UK. This forms a departure from social movements that retained their collective notions through the physical occupation of spaces, their solidarity, their protest values and cultures, etc.; some of these processes (and some new) ones are also enacted and portrayed on social media platforms such as Twitter.

In view of this, we can draw on the importance of the relationship between law, culture, and power. The popularity of identity-aligned social movements after the EU referendum in the UK, emanates from their function in creating different notions of individual and collective identities for its residents, specifically during a time in which bigger frames—such as nations and governments—have to some compelling extent, lost their ability to adequately create trustworthy structures. Twitter has succeeded in curtailing this by providing #1DayWithoutUs supporters with alternative spaces to make sense of them and identify with a sense of togetherness. Their stories furthered the formation of affective citizenship and the social affiliations that materialized this identity, allowing intrinsic identities to remain viable and attainable. This chapter has argued that the modern means of communication have succeeded in throwing out the idea of a citizenship as just a state structure. Citizenship has entered the everyday discourse of communication. *Citizenship* and *belonging* are now part of the mainstream discourses of interaction; creating identities that are not exclusively lawful, personal, or collective, but largely affective.

This new language of *belonging* eventually creates a new kind of shared multifaceted national identity. This same language allows people to become active actors of meaning in the story of Brexit—even if their activity was translated as social media engagement or/and physical protest. The collected tweets this chapter has analyzed formed stories and narratives of affective resistance; of the struggles and successes experienced by the many individuals whose lives were influenced by migration and eventually by Brexit. By appealing to and exploring the processes through which these stories are told through social media, Twitter offers us a glimpse into the voices of this community and specifically of those who identified or stood against Brexit, while creating and affirming an affective identity that exists somewhere between solidarity and adversity. But what makes #1DayWithoutUs collective identity storytelling unique and a significant contribution to the growing literature that looks into social media and social change is the opportunity social media storytelling offers us to look into the process. This refers to the narrative dynamics between the movement's participants/activists/supporters collective identity and to the subversive stories told from their adversaries, placed between and with those stories of support. This interpretation of collective identity storytelling results in collective narratives that challenge and redraw the boundaries of traditional collective notions in general, presenting it as a storytelling process rather than a consolidated and stable entity.

Realizing that 'citizenship' can no longer represent what it once did for people who reside in the UK, and that in its place there is a language of belonging, togetherness, social media content, that comes with digital platforms, the boundaries between law and affect blur. What matters is who uses that narrative and for what reasons. This appertains on questions of power, leadership, and organization. While Brexit is an ongoing political phenomenon, what is really at stake is much larger, as this chapter has illustrated. A people which is isolated from its own struggles is far less free to choose and act as a collective than one that has managed to situate itself in language and discourse, even if that discourse is on Twitter. This is how and why the entire social media framework of social movements can now be considered as owning political dimensions.


## Notes

1.    Anthony Giddens, 'Risk and responsibility,' *The Modern Law Review* 62/1 (1999), 1–10; Zizi Papacharissi, *Affective Publics: Sentiment, Technology, and Politics* (Oxford: Oxford University Press, 2015).

2.    Clay Shirky, *Here Comes Everybody: How Change Happens When People Come Together* (London: Penguin, 2009).

3.    W. Lance Bennett and Steven Livingston, 'The Disinformation Order: Disruptive Communication and the Decline of Democratic Institutions,' *European Journal of Communication* 33/2 (2018), 122–139.

4.    Carol Johnson, 'The Politics of Affective Citizenship: From Blair to Obama,' *Citizenship Studies* 14/5 (2010), 501.

5.    Rob Merrick, 'Theresa May Speech "Could Have Been Taken out of Mein Kampf," Blasts Vince Cable,' *The Independent*, 5 July 2017, accessed 16 Jul 2018, https://www.independent.co.uk/news/uk/politics/theresa-may-mein-kampf-adolf-hitler-nazi-vince-cable-liberal-democrat-conservatives-a7825381.html.

6.    Jeremy Adler, 'Theresa May's Rejection of Enlightenment Values | Letters,' *The Guardian*, 9 October 2016, accessed 16 July 2018, https://www.theguardian.com/politics/2016/oct/09/theresa-may-rejection-of-enlightenment-values.

7.    Tony Blair, 'Speech Delivered to the Confederation of Industry on Migration,' 27 April 2004, accessed 10 January 2007, http://www.pm.gov.uk/output/pages5708.scp.

8.    Jonathan Charteris-Black, *Politicians and Rhetoric: The Persuasive Power of Metaphor* (Basingstock: Palgrave, 2005).

9.    Engin F. Isin, 'The Neurotic Citizen,' *Citizenship Studies* 8/3 (2004), 217–35.

10.    Sara Ahmed, *The Cultural Politics of Emotion* (London: Routledge, 2013).

11.    Anne-Marie Fortier, *Multicultural Horizons: Diversity and the Limits of the Civil Nation* (London: Routledge, 2008), 89.

12.    Ruth Lister, 'Investing in the Citizen—Workers of the Future: Transformations in Citizenship and the State under New Labour,' *Social Policy & Administration* 37/5 (2003), 13.

13.    Toby Miller, *Cultural Citizenship: Cosmopolitanism, Consumerism, and Television in a Neoliberal Age* (Philadelphia: Temple University Press, 2007), 1.

14.    Anne-Marie Fortier, 'Proximity by Design? Affective Citizenship and

the Management of Unease,' *Citizenship Studies,* 14/1 (2010), 25.

15.   Nigel Thrift, 'Intensities of Feeling: Towards a Spatial Politics of Affect,' *Geografiska Annaler: Series B, Human Geography* 86/1 (2004), 57–78.

16.   W. Lance Bennett, 'Changing Citizenship in the Digital Age,' in *Civic Life Online: Learning How Digital Media Can Engage Youth*, ed. W. Lance Bennett (Cambridge, MA: MIT Press 2008) 1, 14.

17.   Matthew Grant, '"Citizen of the World"'? Think Again: British Citizenship after Brexit,' *Democratic Audit*, 21 November 2016, accessed 1 July 2019, http://www.democraticaudit.com/2016/11/21/citizen-of-the-world-think-again-british-citizenship-after-brexit/.

18.   Eleftheria J. Lekakis, *Coffee Activism and the Politics of Fair Trade and Ethical Consumption in the Global North: Political Consumerism and Cultural Citizenship*, (Basingstoke: Palgrave, 2013), 47; W. Lance Bennett, W.L. Chris Wells, and Deen Freelon, 'Communicating Civic Engagement: Contrasting Models of Citizenship in the Youth Web Sphere,' *Journal of Communication* 61/5 (2011), 835–56.

19.   Russell J. Dalton, 'Citizenship Norms and the Expansion of Political Participation,' *Political Studies* 56/1 (2008), 76–98, 76.

20.   Dalton, 'Citizenship Norms,' 85.

21.   Dalton, 'Citizenship Norms,' 86.

22.   Linda M. G. Zerilli, '"We Feel Our Freedom": Imagination and Judgment in the thought of Hannah Arendt,' *Political theory* 33/2 (2005), 158–88.

23.   Ann Cvetkovich, *An Archive of Feelings: Trauma, Sexuality, and Lesbian Public Cultures* (Durham: Duke University Press, 2003), 11.

24.   Andrew Chadwick, *The Hybrid Media System: Politics and Power* (New York: Oxford University Press, 2013); Francesca Polletta and James M. Jasper, 'Collective Identity and Social Movements,' *Annual review of Sociology* 27(2001), 283–305.

25.   Jonathan Charteris-Black, *Politicians and Rhetoric: The Persuasive Power of Metaphor* (Hampshire: Palgrave, 2005).

26.   Papacharissi, *Affective Publics*, 10.

27.   Jürgen Habermas, *The Structural Transformation of the Public Sphere*, trans. Thomas Burger (Cambridge, MA: MIT Press, 1989) (original work published 1962).

28.   Craig Calhoun, *Habermas and the Public Sphere* (London: MIT Press, 1992).

29.   Peter Dahlgren, 'Parameters of Online Participation: Conceptualizing Civic Contingencies,' *Communication Management Quarterly* 6/21 (2011), 87–109.

30.   Andrew A. G. Ross, *Mixed Emotions: Beyond Fear and Hatred in International Conflict.* (Chicago, IL: University of Chicago Press, 2014), 3.

31.   Jenkins, Henry, Sam Ford, and Joshua Green, *Spreadable Media: Creating Value and Meaning in a Networked Culture* (New York: New York

University Press, 2018).

32.    Papacharissi, *Affective Publics*, 24.

33.    Jennifer Earl and Katrina Kimport, *Digitally Enabled Social Change: Activism in the Internet Age*, (Cambridge: MIT Press, 2011), 73.

34.    Donna Haraway, *Simians, Cyborgs and Women: The Reinvention of Nature* (New York: Routledge, 1991).

35.    Bruno Latour, 'Network Theory | Networks, Societies, Spheres: Reflections of an Actor-Network Theorist,' *International Journal of Communication* 5 (2011), 15.

36.    John Protevi, *Political Affect: Connecting the Social and the Somatic* (Minneapolis: University of Minnesota Press, 2009), xvii.

37.    Fortier, 'Proximity by design?'; Ahmed, *The Cultural Politics of Emotion*.

38.    Brian Massumi, *Parables for the Virtual: Movement, Affect, Sensation* (Durham: Duke University Press, 2002).

39.    Gilles Deleuze and Félix Guattari, *A Thousand Plateaus*, trans. Brian Massumi (Minneapolis: University of Minnesota Press, 1987) (Original work published 1980).

40.    Papacharissi, *Affective Publics*, 15.

41.    Melissa Gregg and Gregory J. Seigworth, eds., *The Affect Theory Reader* (Durham: Duke University Press, 2010), 8.

42.    Elizabeth Wissinger, 'Modelling a Way of Life: Immaterial and Affective Labour in the Fashion Modelling Industry,' *Ephemera: Theory and Politics in Organization* 7/1 (2007), 250–69, 247.

43.    Jodi Dean, *Blog Theory: Feedback and Capture in the Circuits of Drive* (Cambridge: Polity, 2010), 22.

44.    Lauren Berlant, *The Female Complaint: The Unfinished Business of Sentimentality in American Culture* (Durham: Duke University Press, 2008), 41.

45.    Alice Bell, *The Possible Worlds of Hypertext Fiction* (Basingstoke: Palgrave Macmillan, 2010).

46.    Alberto Melucci, 'The Symbolic Challenge of Contemporary Movements,' *Social Research* 52/4 (1985), 789–816.

47.    Bert Klandermans and Dirk Oegema, 'Potentials, Networks, Motivations, and Barriers: Steps Towards Participation in Social Movements,' *American Sociological Review* 52 (1987), 519–31.

48.    Klandermans and Oegema, 'Potentials,' 521.

49.    Joshua Gamson, 'Must Identity Movements Self-Destruct? A Queer Dilemma,' *Social Problems* 42/3 (1995), 390–407.

50.    Henri Tajfel, *Human Groups and Social Categories: Studies in Social Psychology* (Cambridge: Cambridge University Press, 1981).

51.    David Snow, 'Collective Identity and Expressive Forms,' *University of California, Center for the Study of Democracy*, 2001, accessed 1 July 2019, https://escholarship.org/uc/item/2zn1t7bj.

52.    Kevin McDonald, 'From Solidarity to Fluidarity: Social Movements Beyond "Collective Identity"—The Case of Globalization Conflicts,' *Social Movement Studies* 1/2 (2002), 109–28, 111.

53.    Alberto Melucci, 'The Process of Collective Identity,' *Social Movements and Culture* 4 (1995), 41–63.

54.    Vrikki, Photini, 'The Story of Occupy Wall Street: Narratives of Politics and Identity on Twitter,' (PhD thesis, King's College London, 2017), 126.

55.    Benedict Anderson, *Imagined communities: Reflections on the Origin and Spread of Nationalism* (London: Verso, 1983), 15–16.

56.    Melucci, 'The Symbolic Challenge of Contemporary Movements.'

57.    Polletta and Jasper, 'Collective Identity and Social Movements,' 285.

58.    Zizi Papacharissi, 'On Networked Publics and Private Spheres in Social Media,' in *The Social Media Handbook*, eds. Jeremy Hunsinger and Theresa Senft (New York: Routledge, 2014),144–58.

59.    Zizi Papacharissi, *A Networked Self* (New York: Routledge, 2011), 58–62.

60.    Erkki Huhtamo, 'Encapsulated Bodies in Motion: Simulators and the Quest for Total Immersion,' *Critical Issues in Electronic Media* (1995), 159–86.

# 14

# Everyday Resistances: Walking and Talking the Hostile Environment

*Lizzy Willmington*

## Introduction

Times of political upheaval are often thought to provoke new forms of resistance. Whether through direct actions, legal challenges, or community art projects, they are visceral responses to a diverging politics. Critical interjections are invaluable in developing an understanding of and for these moments through an analysis of systematic injustices, inequalities, and oppressions. They situate current turmoil within a broader historical context and deeper political comprehension. Official truths are exposed, opening up opportunities for subversion and alternative accounts. Exploring political upheavals through the creative brings opportunities to imagine beyond these points rather than within them. This is a radical endeavour in and of itself. As Graeber states: 'It's not so much a matter of giving "power to the imagination" as recognising that the imagination is the source of power in the first place.'[1] Critical and creative spaces can allow an imagining of what is possible—creatively, politically and democratically—when such possibilities appear determinedly foreclosed. These spaces can provide important sites of critique, capture moments and enhance movements of civil disobedience, and model new forms of participation and being together. Utilizing the tools provided in creative practices allows a less restrictive and more imaginative development of this process. This process offers an opportunity to push the boundaries of what is possible while working together in a new way.

Through the act of collective participation, rather than observation, a shared understanding can develop for social change. This motivates an approach that challenges traditional understandings of spectatorship 'in ways that refuse to be dissuaded and empowered by the notion that forging institutions and institutional imaginaries are the exclusive terrain of the elites.'[2] This process can be explored through many forms, as Cooper's work demonstrates.[3] This chapter will focus on how participatory art practices can create critical and engaged spaces of dialogue and resistance. The term *participatory art practice* infers that 'people constitute the central artistic medium and material.'[4] This brings an evolving, interconnected, and fluid quality to the work. The aim of the chapter is not to instrumentalize the language and methods of participatory art to produce good socially included citizens as 'a form of soft social engineering' to accept and cope with their daily existence.[5] It specifically challenges this. It also challenges the notion that only citizens can be part of creating understandings of society, how they want it to be, and contribute to its making. Instead the motivation is to encourage spaces where citizens and non-citizens work and create together. It is to generate critical spaces to understand and challenge the structural and everyday practices of racist immigration policies with citizens and non-citizens through participatory art methods. This is specifically in the context of the 'hostile environment' agenda of the UK government and the recent provocation of this legal and political anti-immigration policy through a participatory art project, *The Hostile Environment Tour* as part of the *Who Are We? Project* at the Tate Exchange 2018. It is through this methodology that a move from spectatorship to participation will be explored within the context of the current immigration policy of the United Kingdom, and the subversive potential of art in its countering.

First, the hostile environment policy will be introduced, with its legal and political history of internalizing the border in the UK. *The Hostile Environment Tour* and its participatory practices of walking will follow. It will be framed within a discussion of creating a critical space for resistance to the hostile environment. Cooper argues, 'critical work doesn't just show what is wrong, it also scoops out space (destabilises a settled landscape) for other kinds of work as well.'[6] *The Hostile Environment Tour* will be argued as an example of a critical intervention that scoops space out where new forms of resistance can take place, unbounded by dominant modes and 'accompanied by a utopian rethinking of art's relationship to the social and of its political potential.'[7]

This argument deviates from the conceptualization of the border and detention regimes as spectacles. This understanding is helpful to illuminate how the border and detention regimes are utilized to hyper-visibilize and invisibilize certain aspects which construct a narrative that serves its own purpose.[8] However this analysis does not take into account how spectators are part of these spectacles, and contribute to building or dismantling these regimes, or indeed the often blurred lines between these two roles. The expansion of the UK's 'internal border' controls through the hostile environment is argued as complicating the role of the spectator further as it is enacted within everyday essential services and requires participation of citizens within these roles for it to be successful.

## The Hostile Environment

Five months before the 2010 General Election David Cameron, then leader of the Conservative opposition, pledged to reduce annual net migration from the hundreds of thousands to the tens of thousands. This would become the cornerstone of the incoming immigration policy. Cameron stated, 'I think we should be focusing on the pressure on our public services, on health and education and housing,' further laying the blueprint for the upcoming wholesale state reform.[9] The justification for this approach was to demonstrate that the government was concerned with the impact of pressure on public services during a time of austerity. The wrong kind of immigration was considered the cause of this, with increasing and more open hostility towards people considered migrants. This networked approached to immigration controls connected different government departments and supported a 'mandate of renewal,' with the introduction of twenty-seven bills in the 2015 Queen's Speech.[10]

The narrative that followed created and sustained a distinction between people who were wanted by and for the country, and those who were not; the shift would bring 'good immigration, not mass immigration.'[11] The new Home Secretary and Minister for Women and Equalities, Theresa May, addressed the government's approach to immigration in November 2010. Wanting to attract the 'the brightest and the best,' would support the belief that 'settling in Britain should be a cherished right' which would be upheld 'by weeding out those who do not deserve to be allowed in.'[12] May declared, 'I want a clear way to control who can settle in Britain—that is a historic privilege that we should not fritter away lightly.'[13] The repetition of the wanted/unwanted dichotomy through bogus colleges and sham marriages, for example, versus genuine people who came to Britain through the right routes with good intentions, was used to support and justify the promise made to manage immigration. Skilled and wealthy migrants who came through the correct channels were welcomed, the others were not. As such, a major tactic of the government's immigration reform was to prevent access to public services, employment, and benefits for people who were undocumented, to ensure this target. Restrictions were already in place but the new Cameron-led Coalition Government wanted to make these rules tighter, believing it would deter people from coming to or staying in the UK. Following the Prime Minister's instructions, different departments were brought together in 2012 under his lead. The aim and subsequent achievement of this group has been to create an inter-departmental and cross-Whitehall approach to shared responsibility for immigration control, rather than solely that of the Home Office.

The UK has a strong self-image of international generosity through its international aid commitments, boasting the second largest bilateral donation towards the Syrian crisis for example.[14] 'But just as we are generous to those who need our help, the UK will be tough on those who flout our immigration rules or abuse our hospitality as a nation.'[15] This approach is used to demonstrate that the UK government is fair and generous regarding overseas conflicts and fulfilling commitments within the international community and as regards the 'migration crisis.' This creates a contested claim that there are sufficient resources within the region to support the largest number of newly displaced people the world has ever seen.[16] It suggests that anyone who moves on from neighbouring countries is an economic migrant, and therefore not entitled to international protection as they have entered the country illegally.[17] The message is the UK is playing by the rules for those who are willing to play by these same rules, and therefore deserve to settle. This means they must be tough with those who do not. The problem with this logic is the government makes these rules and these rules keep changing.

The architect of the new immigration reforms, Theresa May stated: 'The aim is to create here in Britain a really hostile environment for illegal migration.'[18] The purpose and effect of this statement, and subsequent legal and policy developments, has an internal and an external message. Firstly, to create a daily life in the UK that is so unlivable for people who are considered undocumented as to encourage 'voluntary returns' and identify people for removal, either 'voluntarily' or forced. It is in effect a coercive self-deportation tactic. Secondly, it is a deterrent message to people considered 'would be migrants,' to prevent people attempting to come to the UK. This is all part of the approach to try to tackle the belief that 'migrants think our streets are paved with gold,' the title of a newspaper article written by Theresa May and her French counterpart at the height of fears of people coming to the UK from Calais in 2015.[19]

## The Border Inside

The hostile environment creates an everydayness to border controls incorporated into regular workloads which Vaughan-Williams describes as the 'banalisation of the border.'[20] This externalization of legal responsibility blurs the lines of accountability while also removing processes and procedures to prevent rights abuses and injustices. The ubiquity of immigration controls within the public, private, and third sectors, and increased surveillance in everyday life can be understood as a 'border on every street,' a mobile border, or people taking the space (and violences) of the border with them, which disproportionately impacts upon communities of colour.[21] The normalization of the daily performances that uphold the internal border encourages the belief that rights are entwined with responsibilities, and entitlements to state services with belonging in the UK.[22] Understandings of the ideal law-abiding citizen are narrowing as such discrimination towards racially targeted people assumed to 'not to be playing by the rules' is increasing.[23] All this to emphasis the omnipresence of the border, and the differential impact it has, depending on someone's immigration status.

The prominence of guarding the borders of the nation and national identity is evident in the UK's agenda for national and global security.[24] While this is not new, it has accelerated in recent years. The notion of belonging in the UK has become increasingly tied to whiteness. The work of Étienne Balibar can help us to understand the justification for and interconnectedness between upholding both borders; he writes, 'the 'external frontiers' of the State have to become 'internal frontiers' or—which amounts to the same thing—external frontiers have to be imagined constantly as a projection and protection of an internal collective personality.'[25] For Balibar, the collective remembering of a singular national identity serves to reproduce the nation, and within this, ethnicity is created as a 'closed' identity to create a dominant—read white—'naturally homogenous' identity. Therefore anyone outside this dominant ideology is 'not authentically national.'[26] The external and internal borders of a nation are guarded both materially and symbolically, which 'enable[s] the state to some extent to create public consciousness.'[27] The dominant discourses frame these 'imaginary segregations and prohibitions' as something that is permissible in the public and legal imagining.[28]

While the Immigration Acts of 2014 and 2016 have furthered the criminalization of immigration, categorizing ever more people as illegal, it is not that straightforward. As Dauvergne explains, 'the problem with "illegal" as a rhetorical solution is, of course, that 'illegal' is not neutral.'[29] It requires a fixed understanding of the law and of 'othered' identities, 'the two are necessarily entwined.'[30] Legal binaries create a paradoxical interdependence and encourage an essentialized and othered understanding of the subject.[31] This process neutralizes the complexities and differences in circumstances, histories, and life stories. The mapping of identities further reinforces and demarcates hegemony, making those who are considered to fall outside the legal category hyper-visible.[32] Bigo explains, 'by analyzing the conditions under which the authority of truth is given to a discourse that creates the immigrant as an 'outsider, inside the state' we can begin to effectively challenge them.'[33]

## Collective Amnesia

The accumulative act of collective remembering is constructed in conjunction with a collective forgetting or amnesia. Critically evaluating official narratives and highlighting those suppressed has a rich history. The work of Walter Benjamin helps us to articulate how 'our accustomed concept of history' wields power over contemporary understandings. He argues for the necessity to be vigilant in our unlearning of the dominant narratives that create a singular truth, to expose its benefactors and listen to the 'echo of those who have been silenced in the voices to which we lend our ears today.'[34] Listening to these silenced voices awakens a pluralized history. If we hear these stories we would not ask how the violences people suffer today 'are "still" possible,' as we would learn this has always been so for the oppressed, to use Benjamin's words.[35] He argues that real and radical potential lies within the exposure and dismantling of history's constructions that give power to the mechanisms of oppression and give rise to the voices of the oppressed. The hostile environment has long-standing and far-reaching roots in colonial and imperial practices, and it is through a strategic and forced 'collective amnesia' that we in the UK can be told, and believe, undocumented people are creating a crisis.[36] El-Enany explains, 'this rhetoric is entirely divorced from an understanding of British colonial history, including the country's recent imperial exploits, which have destabilized and exploited regions and set in motion the migration of today.'[37] This process demonstrates how 'the mystification of the past underwrites a mystification of the present.'[38]

A contextualization of the current 'migration crisis' within a historical and colonial configuration, both internationally and within the UK, is needed.[39] The purpose of this contextualization is to understand how 'the migrant' and 'the refugee' have been historically produced as political categories through the process of decolonization, and how it is acceptable to attribute different rights to different categories of people within a state.[40] Restricting the conception of a political community to a national territory—and the rights that are entwined with that—is essential to contemporary European identity, purging itself from the shared and broader history of imperial communities.[41] To historicize the concepts of citizen, migrant, and refugee within a national framework rather than a framework of empire allows people to be labelled as 'being in, or out, of place and their movements facilitated (as citizens) or constrained (as refugees or migrants) as a consequence.'[42] This historically sanitized framing shapes how the British population understands people who arrive to the UK from across the world.[43] Ware argues, 'it is in this context that economic migrants, refugees and asylum seekers are liable to be seen as undeserving beneficiaries of social resources, claiming and receiving welfare entitlements at the expense of the majority ('indigenous') populations.'[44] This demonstrates a resentment to a perceived decline of racial privilege among the poorer social groups in predominantly white societies and homogenizes the working class as white, erasing working class people of colour. Further, this legitimizes resentment towards migrants as the cause of the genuine declining material conditions people face and blocks a more nuanced discussion around class and inequality. This establishes the suppression of the discussion of race within Britain, which Ware contests, highlighting the continued discussion of race, and racist legislative restrictions, and therefore removal of rights, to those who can claim British citizenship.[45] The restrictions of who can settle in Britain have fallen sharply along racial lines.[46]

## The Hostile Environment Tour

As soon as you walk through the door and into the exhibition you see it—the hostile environment. From the entrance the hostile environment snakes around the whole exhibition floor, identified by ten plain cardboard plinths immersed within the activity of people and projects taking place around the space. Here the audience is greeted with a placard detailing a synopsis of the hostile environment and the meeting

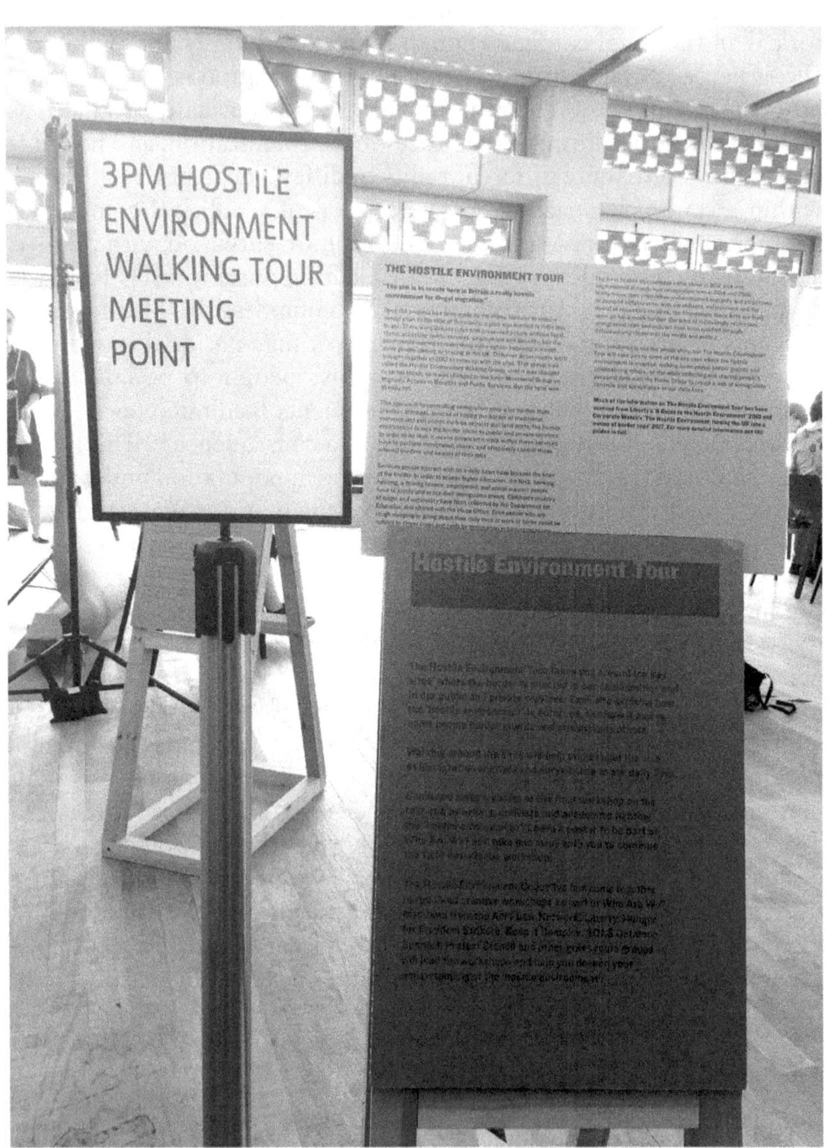


Fig. 17

point for a tour. Stepping through the door you become enthralled by the energy and activity of the *Who Are We? Project*, within the web of the hostile environment. Each plinth explains what is happening in different sectors of society, and are pulled together with the clear style of the plinths and hazard tape mapped out across the floor to show the larger and connected impacts of the policy. The space held many amazing projects and groups who are working in solidarity with and support of people who migrate. The curation of the plinths demonstrated that though there is a great wealth of solidarity and challenge, the law and its hostilities are never far away. Within the exhibition, people and projects would largely carry on without interaction or interruption from the hostile environment, but everyone came across it, whether by choice (stopping and reading the plinth text or joining the walking tour or poster workshop) or by coercion—walking through the installation, encouragement to join the walking tour, engagement with it as it moved, or stopping other performances to accommodate it. Everyone engaged with it at some point during their time in the exhibition space.

*The Tour* utilized traditional symbols and methods of a gallery, with plinths, the objects of focus placed on top of them, and a walking tour conducted to explain them. Each plinth held a double-sided A4 text explaining how the hostile environment was being enacted at different 'sites,' or places and services that are woven into the fabric of society and the everyday.[47] While *The Tour* was materially modest, it held multiple meanings and forms, attempting to produce something that held to the notion that 'they may be simple in means, but they are rich in ends.'[48] Working as the liaison between *The Hostile Environment Collective* and *Who Are We? Project* team, I was involved in lengthy creative and planning discussions. During these we focused on how we could do justice to the creative process, yet not portray the subject matter as too performative or reproduce it for the sake of a creative outcome. The subject matter stands on its own, both in terms of content and importance; what could we add? We focused on the key information, how it was presented and who would be involved in communicating this during the project. As such, it worked as a visual installation—understated at first, but pervasive.

With an audience it took on a different dimension—this is the intention of the Tate Exchange. As a space of interaction and collaboration, artists and audiences work together to develop, create, and talk through art. This approach blurs the separation between these two roles. While not a new understanding, such a big and dedicated undertaking is relatively uncommon in such an institution. The dichotomy between the spectator and the spectated, the viewer and the viewed, has long been complicated, breaking down the 'voyeuristic separation.'[49] Mulvey's analysis criticizes the reproduction of the gaze as depicting desire through the male gaze upon the feminine object. In doing so, Mulvey argues the audience, or spectator, follows and attains the male protagonist's enjoyment and gaze upon the woman. This analysis has provided a useful language to understand the spectatorial relationship, through defining the roles and the attribution of agency and passivity. In other words, the designation of who gets to speak and drive the narrative. However, it has been criticized for reproducing the male-female, subject-object binary, as well as refusing the agency of both the audience spectator and the spectated. Participatory art practices fundamentally challenge the separation within this duality, blurring who creates and contributes to the artistic process and outcome. This interactive approach develops a shared opportunity to 'capture the collective imagination.'[50] Instead of assuming the passive or active engagement of the audience through the content of an art work,[51] the meaning of participatory art falls on the process and method of interaction and production.[52] The outcome of the art work depends on the participation of those who engage with it.

The exhibition interacted with the people, as much as they interacted with it. In a solitary walk through or talking in small groups, engagement with the information would be interspersed with other projects happening in the space. People reading and processing the texts came to understand how the hostile environment is taking hold of key social establishments throughout the country. At two points during the weekend a walking tour took an impromptu group around the sites. The Head of Advocacy at Liberty led the first walking tour, and a former detainee and I led the second.[53] Lasting about an hour, a space of sharing knowledge, narratives, and experiences was created. The act of walking can initiate a new way of engaging with the given environment, a method of generating a shared and interlinked knowledge.[54] A group walking practice allowed a new understanding of the hostile environment and the group's relationship to it. This process shifted the walking group from engaged audience or spectator to active participant. While the walking tour was led by campaigners and activists, the interactive process drew on the whole group's knowledge. Everyone was familiar with the content by one name or another, through administrative tasks in their own role or institution, or through the news.

Responding to the exhibition theme, production of people and places, *The Tour* demonstrated how the hostile environment is making some people border guards and criminalizing others, all the while collecting and sharing people's personal data with the Home Office. During the walking tour we discussed how this is being done through the criminalization of migrants and the collaboration of citizens in implementing immigration controls as well as the collecting and sharing of personal data.[55] Each of these rely on the entwining of immigration controls with other social support systems to function and create a web of immigration controls and surveillance in daily life. *The Tour* highlighted how services which people interact with on a daily basis have become sites of the border. People who provide these services are to act as border guards. Implemented through the Immigrations Acts of 2014 and 2016, these measures are all interwoven. They are used by the Home Office to update the contact details of people they have lost contact with and to identify new people they believe to be undocumented. This is done in order to restrict or prevent access to services with the aim of forcing voluntary returns or pursue forced removal from the country.

Below follows a summary of the issues we discussed during the walking talk. We stopped at each plinth detailing the legal and policy changes in each particular institution and the effects on those impacted by these changes. While discussing each site individually, we elaborated on the three key themes that have emerged through the hostile environment policies.

*The Criminalization of Migrants*

We discussed how the existing rights of migrants have been restricted or removed, creating more situations where people are left unprotected by the law. This has been implemented through a swathe of new offences, including working while undocumented, which carries up to a six month sentence, and earnings confiscated as proceeds of crime,[56] and driving while undocumented, which could carry a custodial sentence and having their vehicle impounded.[57] People from a European Economic Area (EEA) country who are rough sleeping have been subject to detention and deportation.[58] An important aspect we considered was people being stopped, searched and detained. In 2015 the Independent Chief Inspector of Borders and Immigration found immigration enforcement officers only had warrants to enter the premises for 43% of the raids.[59] Street stops and raids are one of the most violent and public acts of the hostile environment. For some

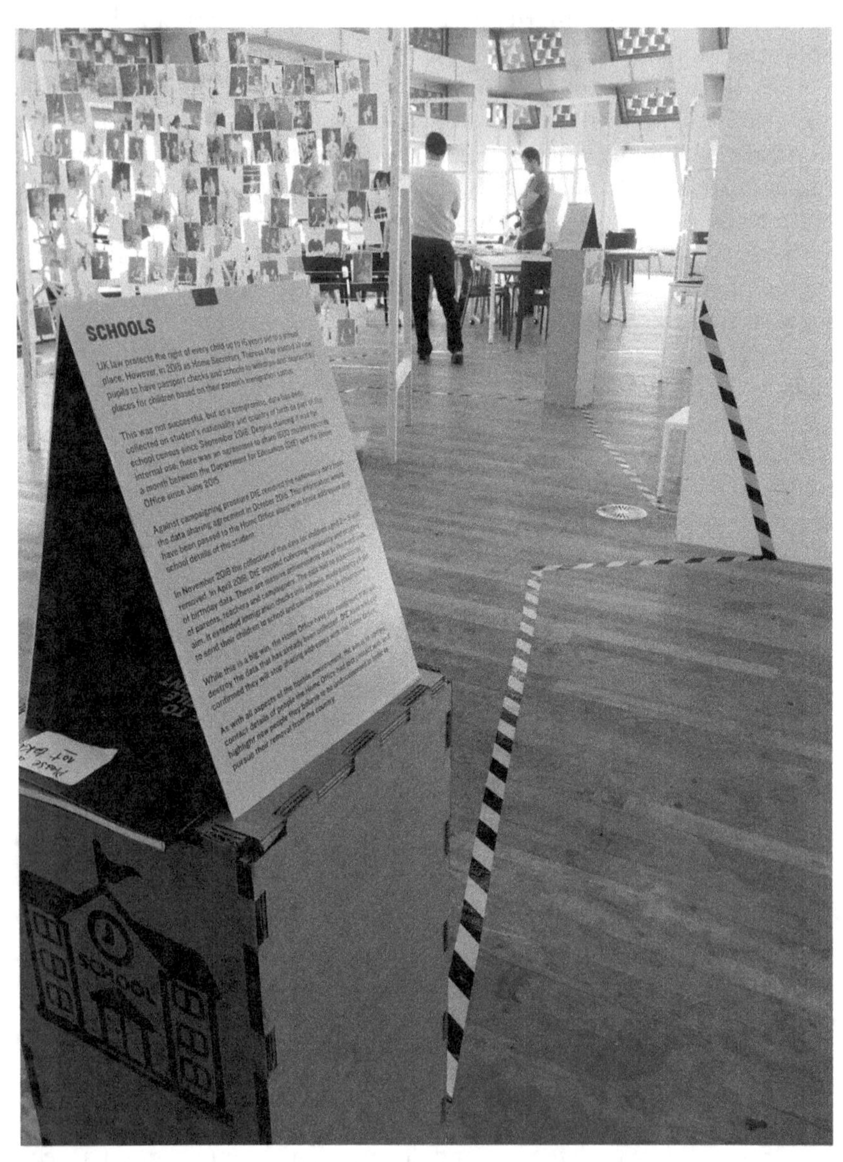

SCHOOLS

UK law protects the right of every child up to 16 years old to a school place. However, in 2015 as Home Secretary, Theresa May wanted to ask pupils to have passport checks and schools to withdraw and deny school places for children based on their parents' immigration status.

This was not successful, but as a compromise, data has been collected on student's nationality and country of birth as part of the school census since September 2016. Despite claiming it was for internal use, there was an agreement to share 1500 student records a month between the Department for Education (DfE) and the Home Office since June 2015.

Against campaigning pressure DfE removed the nationality and country of birth data sharing agreement in October 2016. This information would have been passed to the Home Office along with home addresses and school details of the student.

In November 2018 the collection of this data for children aged 2–5 was removed. In April 2018, DfE stopped collecting nationality and country of birth data. These are massive achievements due to the campaigning of parents, teachers and campaigners.

While this is a big win, the Home Office have not confirmed they will destroy the data that has already been collected. DfE have not confirmed they will stop sharing addresses with the Home Office.

As with all aspects of the hostile environment, the way of collecting contact details of people into the Home Office had dire consequences and highlights how people they believe to be undocumented as well as pursue their removal from the country

SCHOOL

Fig. 18

it is their first encounter with immigration enforcement; for others it is one of their last events in the UK. Having been made possible because of collaboration between the Home Office and private and public sectors sharing data, increasing surveillance and refusing people services, employment, and housing, it pushes people into informal and vulnerable employment and housing. After raids, people can be detained indefinitely in immigration prisons. Many people have ongoing cases and the majority of people are released back into the community because the Home Office does not have grounds to remove or detain them.

*The Collaboration of Citizens*

By highlighting the ways public, private, and third sector actors collaborate with the Home Office, we also identified how individual employees play a role in collaboration, and how this expands the reach of the Home Office. We discussed services in which this happens, and how. For example, the Greater London Authority (GLA) and homeless charities commissioned by the GLA work in collaboration with Immigration and Compliance Enforcement (ICE).[60] Employers and landlords are encouraged to cooperate with the Home Office by complying with or arrange ICE raids on employees or tenants in order to avoid fines, criminal sanctions, or being closed down.[61] Similarly, in order to implement the hostile environment in the NHS and higher education, a change of culture is needed.[62] This has a strong financial element, where front line service staff must ask patients for proof of immigration status before they receive treatment. If they fail to do so they face charges at 150% of the cost, which must be paid for before treatment. If higher education institutions do not fulfil Home Office requirements, they could lose the licence needed to recruit international students. As such, they are very willing to comply, even to go beyond Home Office demands to monitor international staff and students to ensure no reputational or financial damage. Through these discussions people became aware of how the hostile environment was impacting access to and the running of vital daily services as a whole, and also how it was present in their own workplaces and lives. This allowed an opportunity to touch on how even small acts of resistance and solidarity within their roles as front-line service workers or students for example, could frustrate the hostile environment and support people whose lives are difficult because of these policies. This process shifted the positioning of the walking group from spectators of the hostile environment, even if unknowing spectators, to active participants in either implementing or resisting the policy.

*The Collection and Sharing of Data*

The final theme we drew out was the collection and sharing of data. Through specific examples we discussed how this less well-known strategy underpins the ability of the Home Office to implement the hostile environment. The Independent Chief Inspector of Border and Immigration highlighted the quality of data used to implement the hostile environment policies as a major concern.[63] We discussed how large scale data sharing with private organizations su ch as the DVLA and banks has been in effect since 2011 and was extended through Memorandums of Understandings (MoU) to fulfil the restrictions set out in the 2014 Act.[64] CHAIN is a London-wide database of information regarding people rough sleeping. It is run by St Mungo's and funded by the GLA. Information is shared with ICE teams. MoUs have been in place to share data between other government departments, such as the Department of Health and Department for Education. NHS Digital is a database that holds personal information on patients that is routinely collected. There has been an agreement to share data on a mass scale from NHS Digital to the Home Office on request. This data is shared without medical professional or patient knowledge. In May 2018 data sharing on a mass scale was halted due to huge campaigning efforts inside and outside the NHS, though only implemented in November 2018 through legal proceedings. However, data is still being collected by NHS Digital through front line staff, and the Home Office can request it for people they believe have committed a serious crime and who they aim to deport. Data has also been collected on pupils' nationality and country of birth up to the age of 16 as part of the school census since September 2016. The Department for Education shared 1500 pupils' records a month, with details of country of birth, nationality and home address, with the Home Office since June 2015. In November 2016, the collection of this data for children aged 2–5 was stopped and in April 2018 the DfE announced it would stop collecting nationality and country of birth data.

## Disrupting the Everyday

Who participated in the project was fundamental to the shape the narrative took while being explored on the walking tour. *The Hostile*

*Environment Tour* was enacted by a group of activists, artists, and academics who were already active in resisting the hostile environment and came together for this project. This was to highlight the existing everyday resistances taking place to challenge and disrupt the ideological and material functioning of the hostile environment. The central participation of someone who is undocumented and was detained as a result of the hostile environment shifted the dynamic of the walking tours. An open space was created with, what seemed like, genuine engagement between all the participants. Focusing on both the experiences and the critical analysis of the internal border regime of someone who has experienced them first hand, as well as the critical analysis by the Head of Advocacy from Liberty and myself, a PhD researcher on the topic, challenged peoples' assumptions and ignorance. People asked questions and shared their experiences throughout *The Tour*, providing opportunities for the group to learn from each other and create a space of critical and interested enquiry amongst the group. For most people it expanded their understanding beyond the one or two sites they knew about; for others there was alarm at the breadth and depth of collaboration between organizations and the Home Office, saying they were going to ask more questions of the organizations they worked with. Each day brought spontaneous and new groups, different and unplanned perspectives. The purpose of *The Tour* was to make a space of engagement and to offer a fuller understanding of the hostile environment. Sharing the intimate experience of talking and walking encourages participation and 'allows us to occupy the space for an extended period of time while engaging with the spatial and cultural practices that constitute it.'[65]

During the week, two screens displaying filmed testimonies from *Detained Voices* were located at the street stop site. These films displayed the stories and experiences of people who have been in detention and understand the violences of the internal border regime. *SLEEP, the game where you try and get a night's rest* (made by another author in this collection, Dann Hignell-Tully), joined *The Tour* for a day, and was located at the rough sleeping plinth to engage in the frustrating snakes and ladders of access to support as a homeless person. A poet in residence joined and wrote a poem during one of the walking tours, which she performed to the group at the end.[66] This allowed collaborations with other projects that discussed detention and public safety protection orders, building an understanding between these and the hostile environment.

After the walking tours, we ran a poster-making workshop. Stencils with the symbols on the plinths representing the different sites of the hostile environment were provided along with other materials to create posters. This was an opportunity to process the information and discussions that were taking place. Some posters responded to the hostile environment as curated in *The Tour*, some were anti-detention posters to take to the next *Shut Down Yarl's Wood* demonstration, while others were personal migration stories or exploring migration generally. Some posters were taken away by the participants, providing an opportunity to continue the discussion with other people. Other posters made their ways to the advertising spaces of bus stops. This was to promote the hostile environment, as the government has been doing since 2010, in a disruptive way, shifting the narrative and perspectives of the everyday understandings of the hostile environment produced by the government; and to help 'lead us to think about how movements produce new forms of knowledge and strategy that help us to see from below.'[67] It disrupted the everyday nature of the 'banalisation of the border,'[68] embodying the notion of a 'disobedient object' as something which aims to embody 'upending the terms of public debate.'[69] The government has promoted and advertised the hostile environment through speeches, interviews, news articles, posters in NHS buildings, and of course laws and policies. Posters were placed to literally advertise resistance to these. A bus stop is part of the everyday function and design of the street, and the advertising spaces have also become so. To change the messaging within the bus stop frame, utilizes an everyday space to communicate a message of challenge in plain view, making the bus stop a site of resistance. It is a challenge to the hostile environment, but also to the public—to open your eyes and see what is happening every day and in plain view. This is a challenge to spectatorship and the silos of everyday life, and the brutalities of border violence that have become normalized into the fabric of the everyday.

The aim of *The Tour* as an exhibition, a walking tour and a poster making workshop, was to disrupt the perspectives portrayed through mainstream media of the people who are actually impacted by the hostile environment. With the tropes of fairness, morality, and illegality reproduced throughout political and media debates, different perspectives are essential to break these down. The project represented a 'time in motion, rather than accumulated,' both in terms of the development of the project over the week, the wider programme of events, the interactions and creations, but also in terms of the subject of the project.[70] Having real stories and accounts gives life and activates the laws; how they are implemented, by whom, and to what effect. An emotional complex battle ongoing in current struggles was embodied in the plinths of the exhibition. Posters that made their way out of the Tate Exchange could be considered part of something unfinished, as disobedient objects or wilful subjects.[71] To put the hostile environment under the spotlight is to identify its aspects and traits,[72] and its impacts; it is an attempt to encourage the people who engaged with the exhibition to see the expanse of the hostile environment policy and its proximity. The proximity to their own lives and the potential impact on those around them.

## Conclusion: Spaces of Resistance

Exposing how official truths, as well as modes of inclusion and exclusion, are produced, opens up opportunities for subversion and alternative accounts. Those who are impacted by the hostile environment should be at the centre and can be supported in solidarity by others. Reclaiming and articulating one's own story challenges dominant modes of knowledge or 'truth' production. As James Baldwin explains, 'the victim who is able to articulate the situation of the victim has ceased to be a victim: he or she has become a threat.'[73] Indigenous peoples, people of colour and other dissenting voices have been resisting dominant narratives and mappings of law and legal identity throughout history. Grassroots movements are creating shared common understandings and aspirations for a better world. Further, as Lamble states 'if violence is socially produced, then responsibility must be socially enacted.'[74] Direct action, campaigning, advocacy and everyday support work, both creatively and legally, forge a radical rethinking of how the world is organized, mounting challenges and demanding accountability. Academic engagement with these spaces is growing, as is the involvement of people who are impacted by border violences in academic spaces. This demands an ethical, reflexive approach to research, activism and collaboration.[75] This means centring and working with people who are on the receiving end of brutal immigration policies, rather than about them. It is also the case with creative spaces, and arguably needs to be further developed in all these spaces.

As the success of these policies will only work if front-line employees comply by carrying out internal border controls, it is important people know what is really being asked of them and how they can resist it. By employing a participatory art practice to critique and communicate what the hostile environment is, how it is implemented and by whom, it can pluralize. It formulates, and hopefully instigates, a participation

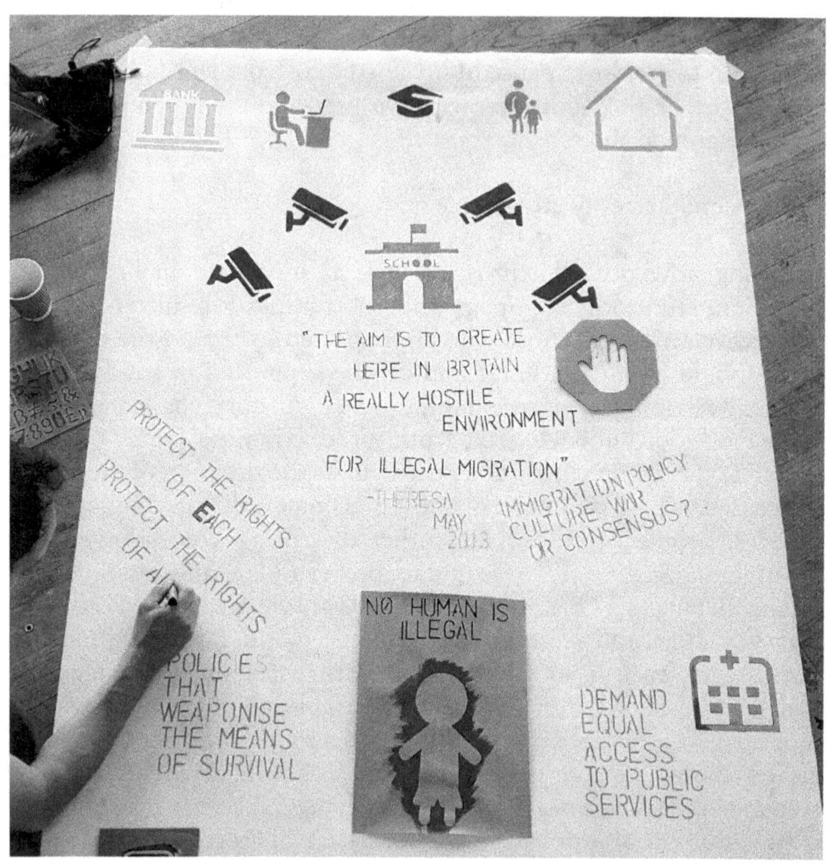

BANK
SCHOOL
"THE AIM IS TO CREATE
HERE IN BRITAIN
A REALLY HOSTILE
ENVIRONMENT
FOR ILLEGAL MIGRATION"
-THERESA
MAY
2013
IMMIGRATION POLICY
CULTURE WAR
OR CONSENSUS?
PROTECT THE RIGHTS
OF EACH
PROTECT THE RIGHTS
OF ALL
POLICIES
THAT
WEAPONISE
THE MEANS
OF SURVIVAL
NO HUMAN IS
ILLEGAL
DEMAND
EQUAL
ACCESS
TO PUBLIC
SERVICES

*Fig. 19*

of resistance against it. *The Tour* provided alternative narratives, stories and realities that already existed, a different standpoint to the official narrative. It is an acknowledgement that there is a pluralism and to 'read *for*.'[76] What *The Tour* did is critical *reading for* with a playful and participatory methodology. This space opened up the possibilities for interaction and exchange and allowed the participants to approach the subject with a playful and open mind that is often challenging to bring to difficult topics of discussion: 'While play suggests subjects' willing engagement in creative, open-ended practice, what is also important is the *aspirational surplus* play identifies.'[77] There is a shift in those involved. Perhaps this is an outcome of play, or this goes beyond play. While it does not change the laws of the hostile environment, it generates possibilities of challenge to the workings of it, and to those who are required to perform roles in, or simply prescribed to be spectators to it. However, as I have argued, the function of spectatorship is a complex one and removes the agency of the spectator. With insight into one's role, one can choose how to participate either by resisting or by supporting its production, even through inaction.

What these processes should make clear, however, is the role critical academics, artists and activists can play in exposing official truths and imagining a future beyond our current moment. This is continuous and should receive attention before and beyond the point of crisis. Further, political upheaval should not be understood as an aberration from long term histories of colonialism, imperialism, and neoliberalism but rather as the logical intensification of their harmful consequences. Many of these concerns discussed in this chapter are contemporary manifestations of historical issues, and have long been confronted by indigenous peoples and people of colour who have used art and activism as a tool to challenge dominant political and legal narratives. With more people needing and choosing to migrate than ever before, global trends by states towards curbing migration are not ceasing. Existing rights are being removed from people, criminalizing them and the everyday activities and services needed to live. To tell the stories of everyday impacts and everyday resistances is to challenge the increasingly narrow understanding of belonging. The hostile environment relies on the compliance of residents and citizens to implement border controls, but through challenge and dialogue a more intersecting understanding of who belongs can develop. While creative spaces may have limitations in terms of their impact for substantive legal and policy changes, they offer a space to break down boundaries and develop experimental ways of thinking, learning and participation. This may allow for a challenging of the everyday enactments of border violences and encourage the boundaries to be pushed in notions of race, migration and belonging.


## Notes

1.    David Graeber, 'On the Phenomenology of Giant Puppets,' in *Disobedient Objects*, ed. Gavin Grindon and Catherine Flood, 1st ed. (London: V&A Publishing, 2014), 77.

2.    Davina Cooper, 'Can Projects of Reimagining Complement Critical Research?' *Social Politics and Stuff*, 20 April 2018, accessed 1 June 2019, https://davinascooper.wordpress.com/2018/04/20/can-projects-of-reimagining-complement-critical-research/. Emphasis in original.

3.    See Davina Cooper, *Everyday Utopias: The Conceptual Life of Promising Spaces* (Durham: Duke University Press, 2013).

4.    Claire Bishop, *Artificial Hells: Participatory Art and the Politics of Spectatorship* (London: Verso Books, 2012), 2.

5.    Bishop, *Artificial Hells*, 5, 14.

6.    Cooper, 'Can Projects of Reimagining Complement Critical Research?'

7.    Cooper, 'Can Projects of Reimagining Complement Critical Research?' Bishop, *Artificial Hells*, 3.

8.    Alison Mountz, 'IN/VISIBILITY and the SECURITIZATION of MIGRATION Shaping Publics through Border Enforcement on Islands,' *Cultural Politics* 11/2 (2015),184–200; Cetta Mainwaring and Stephanie J. Silverman, 'Detention-as-Spectacle,' *International Political Sociology* 11 (2017), 21–38.

9.    Rosa Prince, 'David Cameron: Net Immigration Will Be Capped at Tens of Thousands,' *The Telegraph*, 10 January 2010, accessed 15 January 2018, https://www.telegraph.co.uk/news/politics/6961675/David-Cameron-net-immigration-will-be-capped-at-tens-of-thousands.html.

10.    Jon Burnett, 'Entitlement and Belonging: Social Restructuring and Multicultural Britain' (Institute of Race Relations, 2016), 3.

11.    David Cameron, 'In Full: Cameron Migration Speech,' *BBC News*, 14 April 2011, accessed 15 January 2018, https://www.bbc.com/news/uk-politics-13083781.

12.    Theresa May, 'Immigration: Home Secretary's Speech of 5 November 2010,' *GOV.UK*, 5 November 2010, accessed 17 January 2018, https://www.gov.uk/government/speeches/immigration-home-secretarys-speech-of-5-november-2010.

13.    May 'Immigration: Home Secretary's Speech of 5 November 2010.'

14.    Theresa May, 'Home Secretary Statement on Illegal Immigration in Calais,' *GOV.UK*, 14 July 2015, accessed 20 January 2018, https://www.gov.uk/government/speeches/home-secretary-statement-on-illegal-immigration-in-calais.

15.   May, 'Home Secretary Statement on Illegal Immigration in Calais.'

16.   UNHCR, 'Figures at a Glance,' UNHCR | UK, accessed 19 August 2018, http://www.unhcr.org/uk/figures-at-a-glance.html.

17.   Frances Webber, 'Brexit, Refugees and the Hostile Environment,' *Europeanrights.eu*, 19 December 2017, accessed 08 July 2018, http://www.europeanrights.eu/public/commenti/BRONZINI8-Webber_-_ELDH_Brexit_refugees.pdf.

18.   James Kirkup and Robert Winnett, 'Theresa May Interview: "We're Going to Give Illegal Migrants a Really Hostile Reception"' *The Telegraph*, 25 May 2012, accessed 10 January 2018 https://www.telegraph.co.uk/news/uknews/immigration/9291483/Theresa-May-interview-Were-going-to-give-illegal-migrants-a-really-hostile-reception.html.

19.   Theresa May and Bernard Cazeneuve, 'Migrants Think Our Streets Are Paved with Gold,' 1 August 2015, accessed 2 August 2015, http://www.telegraph.co.uk/news/uknews/immigration/11778396/Migrants-think-our-streets-are-paved-with-gold.html.

20.   Nick Vaughan-Williams, 'The UK Border Security Continuum: Virtual Biopolitics and the Simulation of the Sovereign Ban,' *Environment and Planning D: Society and Space* 28/6 (2010), 1077.

21.   Rachel Robinson, 'A border in every street,' *Liberty*, 3 April 2014, accessed 1 June 2019 https://www.liberty-human-rights.org.uk/news/blog/border-every-street; Frances Webber, 'You Have No Rights! The Creation of the Bad Immigrant' (Talk given at Cumberland Lodge, Windsor 2018); Sarah Keenan, 'A Prison around Your Ankle and a Border in Every Street: Theorising Law, Space and the Subject,' in *Routledge Handbook of Law and Theory*, ed. Andreas Philippopoulos-Mihalopoulos, (Abingdon, Oxon; New York, NY: Routledge, 2018).

22.   Burnett, 'Entitlement and Belonging: Social Restructuring and Multicultural Britain.'

23.   G4S, 'Protecting National Interests. Strengthening the UK Border, Safely and Securely,' found at www.g4s.com (G4S, 2009), 2. For example, see JCWI, '"No Passport Equals No Home": An Independent Evaluation of the "Right to Rent" Scheme,' *Joint Council for the Welfare of Immigrants*, 3 September 2015, accessed 1 June 2019, https://jcwi.org.uk/sites/default/files/documets/No%20Passport%20Equals%20No%20Home%20Right%20to%20Rent%20Independent%20Evaluation_0.pdf.

24.   DFID and HM Treasury, 'UK Aid: Tackling Global Challenges in the National Interest' (London, November 2015).

25.   Etienne Balibar, 'The Nation Form: History and Ideology,' *Review (Fernand Braudel Center)* 13/ 3 (1990), 348.

26.   Balibar, 'The Nation Form,' 357.

27.   Balibar, 'The Nation Form,' 348.

28.   Balibar, 'The Nation Form,' 357.

29.   Catherine Dauvergne, 'Making People Illegal,' in *Critical Beings:*

*Law, Nation and the Global Subject*, ed. Patricia Tuitt and Peter Fitzpatrick (Aldershot, Hants, England ; Burlington, VT: Ashgate Publishing Limited, 2004), 84.

30.    Catherine Dauvergne, 'Making People Illegal,' in Tuitt and Fitzpatrick, *Critical Beings*, 84.

31.    Patricia J. Williams, 'On Being the Object of Property,' *Signs* 14/1 (1 October 1988), 5–24, http://www.jstor.org/stable/3174659.

32.    Sarah Keenan, 'Subversive Property: Reshaping Malleable Spaces of Belonging,' *Social & Legal Studies* 19/ 4 (2010), 423–39, http://sls.sagepub.com/content/19/4/423.short; Dean Spade, *Normal Life: Administrative Violence, Critical Trans Politics, and the Limits of Law* (Brooklyn, NY: South End Press, 2011).

33.    Didier Bigo, 'Security and Immigration: Toward a Critique of the Governmentality of Unease,' *Alternatives: Global, Local, Political* 27/1 (2002), 66, https://www.questia.com/library/journal/1G1-84338226/security-and-immigration-toward-a-critique-of-the.

34.    Walter Benjamin, *On the Concept of History*, trans. Dennis Redmond, *Global Rights*, 2016, accessed 1 June 2019, https://www.globalrights.info/wp-content/uploads/Dennis-Redmond.pdf, para. II.

35.    Benjamin, *On the Concept of History*, para. VIII.

36.    Charles W. Mills, 'White Ignorance,' in *Race and Epistemologies of Ignorance* (New York: State University of New York Press, 2007).

37.    Nadine El-Enany, 'The Iraq War, Brexit and Imperial Blowback,' *Critical Legal Thinking*, 14 July 2016, accessed 1 June 2016, http://criticallegalthinking.com/2016/07/14/iraq-war-brexit-imperial-blowback/.

38.    Mills, 'White Ignorance,' 31.

39.    Gurminder K. Bhambra, 'The Current Crisis of Europe: Refugees, Colonialism, and the Limits of Cosmopolitanism,' *European Law Journal* 23/ 5 (2017), 395–405; Nadine El-Enany, 'Aylan Kurdi: The Human Refugee,' *Law and Critique* 27/1 (2016), 13–15; Nadine El-Enany, 'Things Fall Apart: From Empire to Brexit Britain,' *IPR Blog*, 2 May 2017, accessed 1 June 2019, http://blogs.bath.ac.uk/iprblog/2017/05/02/things-fall-apart-from-empire-to-brexit-britain/; Stephen Small and John Solomos, 'Race, Immigration and Politics in Britain: Changing Policy Agendas and Conceptual Paradigms 1940s–2000s,' *International Journal of Comparative Sociology* 47/3–4 (2006), 235–57.

40.    Bhambra, 'The Current Crisis of Europe,' 403.

41.    Bhambra, 'The Current Crisis of Europe.' 404.

42.    Bhambra, 'The Current Crisis of Europe.' 400.

43.    Small and Solomos, 'Race, Immigration and Politics in Britain,' 237.

44.    Vron Ware, 'Towards a Sociology of Resentment: A Debate on Class and Whiteness,' *Sociological Research Online* 13/5 (30 September 2008): para. 5.8, accessed 1 June 2019, http://www.socresonline.org.uk/13/5/9.html#.

45.    Ware, 'Towards a Sociology of Resentment,' para. 3.6.

46.    Ambalavaner Sivanandan, *A Different Hunger: Writings on Black*

*Resistance* (London: Palgrave Macmillan, 1982); El-Enany, 'The Iraq War, Brexit and Imperial Blowback'; Bhambra, 'The Current Crisis of Europe.'

47.    The information in *The Tour* was supported by Corporate Watch's *The Hostile Environment: turning the UK into a nation of border cops* (2017) and Liberty's *A Guide to the Hostile Environment. The border controls dividing our communities—and how we can bring them down* (2018), which was placed around *The Tour* for people to read further.

48.    Gavin Grindon and Catherine Flood, 'Introduction' in *Disobedient Objects*, ed. Gavin Grindon and Catherine Flood (London: V&A Publishing, 2014), 12.

49.    Laura Mulvey, 'Visual Pleasure in Narrative Cinema,' *Screen* 16/ Autumn (1975), 6–18.

50.    Alan S. Brown and Jennifer L. Novak-Leonard, 'Getting In On the Act. How Arts Groups Are Creating Opportunities for Active Participation,' The James Irving Foundation, October 2011, accessed 1 June 2016, https://irvine-dot-org.s3.amazonaws.com/documents/12/attachments/ GettingInOntheAct2014_DEC3.pdf, 3.

51.    Mulvey, 'Visual Pleasure in Narrative Cinema'; Robert Hariman and John Louis Lucaites, 'Photography: The Abundant Art,' *Photography and Culture* 9/1 (2016), 39–58.

52.    Bishop, *Artificial Hells*; Brown and Novak-Leonard, 'Getting In On the Act. How Arts Groups Are Creating Opportunities for Active Participation.'

53.    We met during the Hunger for Freedom strike, a month long all out strike that took place in Yarl's Wood detention prison in early 2018 demanding structural policy change regarding detention. See DV, 'The Hunger Striker's Demands, *detained voices*, accessed 1 June 2019, https://detainedvoices. com/2018/02/22/the-hunger-strikers-demands/.

54.    Kate Moles, 'A Walk in Thirdspace: Place, Methods and Walking,' *Sociological Research Online* 13/ 4 (2008),1–9, accessed 1 June 2019, http:// journals.sagepub.com.abc.cardiff.ac.uk/doi/pdf/10.5153/sro.1745.

55.    Corporate Watch, 'The Hostile Environment: Turning the UK into a Nation of Border Cops' *Corporate Watch*, 8 April 2017, accessed 1 June 2019, https://corporatewatch.org/ the-hostile-environment-turning-the-uk-into-a-nation-of-border-cops-2/.

56.    Immigration Act 2016,' sec. 34.

57.    Immigration Act 2016, sec. 44.

58.    The Immigration (European Economic Area) Regulations 2016 legislates that an EEA national may be removed (regulation 23[3]) if they misuse the right to reside (regulation 26). While it does not explicitly state that the misuse of the right to reside includes rough sleeping it has been used in this way. It is interpreted as not exercising one's treaty rights, and therefore considered to be a misuse of rights. This was found to be unlawful in December 2017.

59.    David Bolt, 'An Inspection of How the Home Office Tackles Illegal

Working October 2014—March 2015,' *GOV.UK*, December 2015, accessed 1 June 2019, https://assets.publishing.service.gov.uk/government/uploads/system/uploads/attachment_data/file/547674/ICIBI-Report-on-illegal-working-December_2015.pdf, 24.

60.    Corporate Watch, 'The Hostile Environment: Turning the UK into a Nation of Border Cops,' 14.

61.    Immigration Act 2016, s.39 and s.35.

62.    Corporate Watch, 'The Hostile Environment: Turning the UK into a Nation of Border Cops,' 6.

63.    David Bolt 'An Inspection of the "Hostile Environment" Measures Relating to Driving Licences and Bank Accounts January to July 2016,' *GOV.UK*, 2016, accessed 1 June 2019, https://assets.publishing.service.gov.uk/government/uploads/system/uploads/attachment_data/file/567652/ICIBI-hostile-environment-driving-licences-and-bank-accounts-January-to-July-2016.pdf.

64.    Ss. 46–47 and ss. 40–43 of the Immigration Act 2014 relate to driving licences and bank accounts. Independent Chief Inspector of Borders and Immigration, paras 5.9–5.19 and 6.11–6.21.

65.    Moles, 'A Walk in Thirdspace: Place, Methods and Walking,' para. 4.1.

66.    Laila Sumpton, 'Hostile Environment Procedures, Poem by Laila Sumpton' Who Are We?, 26 June 2018, accessed 1 June 2019, https://whoareweproject.com/edinthebox-2-2-2.

67.    Gavin Grindon and Catherine Flood, 'Introduction,' in Grindon and Flood, *Disobedient Objects*, 18.

68.    Vaughan-Williams, 'The UK Border Security Continuum,' 1077.

69.    Gavin Grindon and Catherine Flood, 'Introduction,' in Grindon and Flood, *Disobedient Objects*, 9.

70.    Bishop, *Artificial Hells*, 91.

71.    Gavin Grindon and Catherine Flood, 'Introduction,' in Grindon and Flood, *Disobedient Objects*; Sara Ahmed, *Willful Subjects* (Durham: Duke University Press, 2014).

72.    Gavin Grindon and Catherine Flood, 'Introduction,' in Grindon and Flood, *Disobedient Objects*, 22.

73.    James Baldwin in Janell Hobson, *Body as Evidence: Mediating Race, Globalizing Gender* (Albany: SUNY Press, 2012).

74.    Sarah Lamble, 'Retelling Racialized Violence, Remaking White Innocence: The Politics of Interlocking Oppressions in Transgender Day of Remembrance,' *Sexuality Research & Social Policy* 5/1 (March 2008), 35.

75.    Marilys Guillemin and Lynn Gillam, 'Ethics, Reflexivity, and "Ethically Important Moments" in Research, Ethics, Reflexivity, and "Ethically Important Moments" in Research,' *Qualitative Inquiry* 10/2 (2004), 261–80.

76.    Cooper, 'Can Projects of Reimagining Complement Critical Research?'

77.    Cooper, 'Can Projects of Reimagining Complement Critical Research?'